STUDY GUIDE

for Stiglitz's Principles of Macroeconomics

Second Edition

STUDY GUIDE

for Stiglitz's

Principles of Macroeconomics

Second Edition

LAWRENCE W. MARTIN
Michigan State University

W · W · NORTON & COMPANY · NEW YORK · LONDON

Printed in the United States of America

ISBN 0-393-96841-3 (pbk.)

W. W. Norton & Company, Inc., 500 Fifth Avenue, New York, N.Y. 10110
http://www.wwnorton.com
W. W. Norton & Company, Ltd., 10 Coptic Street, London WC1A 1PU

1 2 3 4 5 6 7 8 9 0

CONTENTS

PREFACE

This Study Guide is designed to aid in your understanding, assimilation, and use of the material in Joseph Stiglitz's *Principles of Macroeconomics,* Second Edition. The chapters in this volume correspond to those in the main text, and each one is divided into three parts. The first part contains a *Chapter Review,* an *Essential Concepts* section, and a *Behind the Essential Concepts* section. The *Chapter Review* begins with a brief paragraph explaining how each chapter in Stiglitz fits into the overall structure of the text. The *Essential Concepts* section is a summary of the chapter, bringing out the main points covered. *Behind the Essential Concepts* offers suggestions about how to avoid common mistakes and provides some intuitive explanations for difficult concepts. This section also brings out the similarities among related ideas and the common structure of many economic theories and concepts.

The second part of each chapter includes a "Self-Test" with true-or-false, multiple-choice, and completion questions. After reading the chapter in the text and going over the first part of the Study Guide chapter, you should take the self-test. It will help you determine those areas that need further study.

The final part of each chapter is called "Doing Economics: Tools and Practice Problems." This part is designed to teach you the basic skills of economics. The only way to do this is to sharpen up your pencil and try some exercises. If you're willing (or your teacher has assigned this material), I think you'll find the program useful. For each type of problem, there is a Tool Kit box that gives step-by-step instructions about how to use the appropriate tool, a worked problem with a step-by-step solution that follows the procedure outlined in the Tool Kit box, and several practice problems for you to do. Answers are provided at the end of each chapter.

Best of success with your course!

Part One

Introduction

Chapter 1

THE AUTOMOBILE AND ECONOMICS

Chapter Review

The story of the automobile in the United States is a rich one, introducing as it does the principal ideas of economics. The dominant idea is that economics is about the choices made by the three major groups of participants: individuals or households, firms, and the government. These choices control the allocation of resources, another central concern of economics. The automobile story also highlights the three markets on which this book focuses: product, labor, and capital. The chapter closes with a discussion of how economists use models and theories to describe the economy and why they sometimes disagree. This chapter sets the stage for the introduction of the basic economic model in Chapter 2.

ESSENTIAL CONCEPTS

1 The brief history of the automobile given here illustrates the broad and varied subject matter of economics and many of the important themes of this book. We see the importance of investors and entrepreneurs and the risks they face, and the central roles of research, technological advance, and patents. The problem of incentives appears both in the conflicting interests of Henry Ford and his investors and in the effect of high wages on his workers. The upheavals caused by oil price increases in the 1970s and the influx of competition from foreign producers show us how the U.S. economy now functions in the world economy. Finally, a large and growing government presence has mandated environmental and safety regulations, supplied money to bail out a major producer, and provided protection against foreign competition.

2 Economics studies how **choices** are made by individuals, firms, governments, and other organizations and how those choices determine the allocation of resources. **Scarcity,** the fact that there are not enough resources to satisfy all wants, requires that choices must be made by individuals and by the economy as a whole. The fundamental questions that an economy must answer are the following:

a What is produced, and in what quantities?
b How are these goods produced?
c For whom are these goods produced?
d Who makes economic decisions, and by what process?

3 The U.S. economy is a mixed one that relies primarily on private decisions to answer the basic economic questions. **Markets,** which exist wherever and whenever exchanges occur, influence the choices of individuals and firms, but government also plays a prominent role. For

starters, the government sets the legal structure within which market forces operate. It also regulates private activity, collects taxes, produces some goods and services, and provides support for the elderly, poor, and others.

4 Trade takes place between individuals and firms in three major markets: the **product market,** the **labor market,** and the **capital market.** Figure 1.1 sketches the interactions. Notice that in general, individuals buy goods and services from firms; they also supply labor and funds for investment to firms.

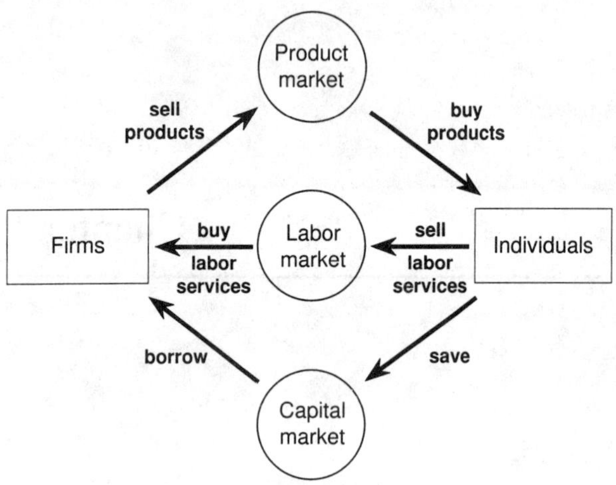

Figure 1.1

5 There are two broad branches in economics. **Microeconomics** studies the product, labor, and capital markets, focusing on the behavior of individuals, households, firms, and other organizations that make up the economy. **Macroeconomics** looks at the performance of the economy as a whole and at such aggregate measures as unemployment, inflation, growth, and the balance of trade.

6 Economics uses models and theories, which are sets of assumptions and conclusions, to understand and predict the behavior of the economy. Economists want to discover and interpret relationships among economic variables and especially to distinguish where there is causation and where there is only correlation.

7 Economists are frequently asked to give advice regarding public policy, and often they disagree, for two major reasons: they disagree about what is the appropriate theoretical model of the economy, and about the effects a policy will have.

BEHIND THE ESSENTIAL CONCEPTS

1 In this book you will learn many economic theories and models. Models and theories are simplified representations of the vast and complex economic world. The way that a model is made simple and workable is through assumptions. We assume that only certain factors are relevant to the problem at hand. Then we derive conclusions from the assumptions and test the model by comparing its predictions with what we know of the world.

You need to do two different things with the models that you will come across in your study of economics. First, you must understand how the model works—specifically, what is assumed and how the conclusions follow. The second task is to evaluate how well the model explains what it is supposed to explain. As you read the many arguments and pieces of evidence, keep in mind how they fit with the model's basic assumptions and conclusions.

2 Economic **variables** are measurable, and they change. The price of potatoes is an economic variable; so is the rate of unemployment. We look for two types of relationships among these variables. First, we are interested in whether certain economic variables move together. For example, during the 1980s, the U.S. government ran up unprecedented peacetime budget deficits and also very high trade deficits. These two deficit variables were **correlated.** But we are also interested in whether a change in one variable **causes** a change in another variable. Specifically, did the high government budget deficits of the 1980s cause the large trade deficits? Before economists make conclusions, they require a sound model that shows how a change in an economic variable was caused and also some evidence that the model's assumptions are appropriate and that its predictions have actually occurred.

3 **Positive economics** focuses on questions about how the economy works. What does it do, and why does it do it? For example, how were the budget and trade deficits of the 1980s related? **Normative economics,** on the other hand, typically asks what should be done. Should we reduce the federal budget deficit? Keep in mind, however, that normative economics cannot prescribe which value to hold; it describes the appropriate policy given the value.

4 Microeconomics and macroeconomics are two ways of looking at the economy. Microeconomics looks from the bottom up; it starts with the behavior of individuals and firms and builds up to an understanding of markets and the economy as a whole. Macroeconomics, on the other hand, is a top-down look, beginning with a description of the performance of aggregate economic variables and then constructing explanations. Micro- and macroeconomics must fit together. The models that explain how individuals, firms, and markets work must be consistent with the models that we use to describe the economy as a whole. An important theme of this book is that the microeconomics in Parts One, Two, and Three provides a firm foundation for the macroeconomics to follow in Parts Four, Five, and Six.

SELF-TEST

True or False

1 Henry Ford patented the internal combustion engine.

2 Henry Ford paid his workers especially high wages because he wanted them to earn enough to buy his cars.

3 By and large, government has kept out of the automobile business.

4 Patents give exclusive rights to market an innovation for a limited period of time.

5 The U.S. government imposed a tariff on Japanese car imports in the early 1980s.

6 Economics studies how individuals, firms, governments, and other organizations make choices and how those choices determine the allocation of the economy's resources.

7 The four basic questions concerning how economies function are what is produced and in what quantities, how are the goods produced, for whom are they produced, and who makes the decisions?

8 Most resource allocation decisions are made by governments in the U.S. economy.

9 In centrally planned economies, most decisions are made by the government.

10 The three major markets are the product, labor, and insurance markets.

11 Microeconomics focuses on the behavior of the economy as a whole.

12 Macroeconomics studies the behavior of firms, households, and individuals.

13 Two economic variables are correlated if there is a systematic relationship between them.

14 When two variables are correlated, it is because changes in one cause changes in the other.

15 Normative economics deals with questions concerning how the economy actually works.

Multiple Choice

1 Henry Ford paid his workers more than the going rate chiefly because

a he feared that the government would set minimum wages if he paid low wages;
b he could thereby obtain a hard-working, productive labor force;
c he did not care about profits, only the well-being of his workers;
d his highly paid workers would buy more of his cars;
e his highly paid workers would pay more taxes.

2 Patents

a give inventors exclusive rights to produce and market their inventions for a limited time;
b allow inventors to charge high prices without fear of competition.
c provide incentives to encourage new inventions;
d are awarded for innovations, not ideas;
e All of the above.

3 In the 1980s, the U.S.government negotiated limitations on exports of Japanese automobiles to the United States. As a result,

a the U.S. automobile industry recaptured its lost market share;
b automobile prices increased;
c Japanese firms set up plants in the United States;
d the Japanese government retaliated with restrictions on exports of U.S. automobiles to Japan;
e b and c.

4 Because resources are scarce,

a questions must be answered;
b choices must be made;
c all except the rich must make choices;
d governments must allocate resources;
e some individuals must be poor.

5 Which of the following is not a fundamental question concerning how economies funtion?

a What is produced, and in what quantities?
b How are the goods produced?
c For whom are they produced?
d Who makes the decisions?
e All of the above are fundamental questions.

6 In market economies, the four basic questions are answered

a by elected representatives;
b in such a way as to ensure that everyone has enough to live well;
c by private individuals and firms, interacting in markets;
d according to the traditional way of doing things;
e by popular vote.

7 In market economies, goods are consumed by

a those who are most deserving;
b those who work the hardest;
c those who are politically well connected;
d those who are willing and able to pay the most;
e those who produce them.

8 Which of the following is not one of the three major markets?

a goods market;
b labor market;
c capital market;
d Common Market;
e all of the above.

9 The detailed study of firms, households, individuals, and the markets where they transact is called

a macroeconomics;
b microeconomics;
c normative economics;
d positive economics;
e aggregate economics.

10 The study of the behavior of the economy as a whole, especially such factors as unemployment and inflation, is called

a macroeconomics.
b microeconomics.
c normative economics.

d positive economics.
e market economics.

11 An economic theory or model is a

a mathematical equation;
b prediction about the future of the economy;
c recommended reform in government policy that pays attention to the laws of economics;
d set of assumptions and conclusions derived from those assumptions;
e small-scale economic community set up to test the effectiveness of a proposed government program.

12 Which of the following is an example of causation?

a Taxes are too high.
b The trade deficits of the 1980s were the direct result of the decade's budget deficits.
c During the 1980s the United States experienced high trade and budget deficits.
d In mixed economies there is a role for government and a role for markets.
e U.S. interest rates fell during the early 1990s.

13 Which of the following is an example of correlation?

a The high budget deficits of the 1980s caused the trade deficits.
b Taxes are too high.
c During recessions, output falls and unemployment increases.
d In mixed economies, there is a role for markets and a role for government.
e Economics studies choices and how choices determine the allocation of resources.

14 Which of the following is an example of normative economics?

a The high budget deficits of the 1980s caused the trade deficits.
b During recessions, output falls and unemployment increases.
c Lower interest rates would encourage investment.
d Interest rates should be reduced to encourage investment.
e Expansionary monetary policy will reduce interest rates.

15 Which of the following is an example of positive economics?

a Taxes are too high.
b U.S. savings rates are too low.
c Lower interest rates would encourage investment.
d Interest rates should be reduced to encourage investment.
e There is too much economic inequality in the United States.

16 In the United States, the question of what is produced and in what quantities is answered

a primarily by private decisions influenced by prices;
b by producing what was produced the previous year;
c primarily by government planning;
d randomly;
e according to majority vote.

17 In which of the following does the government determine what is produced, how, and for whom?

a market economies;
b mixed economies;
c centrally planned economies;
d tradition-bound economies;
e all of the above

18 Choices must be made because

a resources are scarce;
b human beings are choice-making animals;
c government regulations require choices to be made;
d economic variables are correlated;
e without choices, there would be no economics as we know it.

19 Anything that can be measured and that changes is

a a correlation;
b a causation;
c a variable;
d a value;
e an experiment.

20 In the labor market,

a households purchase products from firms;
b firms purchase the labor services of individuals;
c firms raise money to finance new investment;
d households purchase labor services from firms;
e borrowing and lending are coordinated.

Completion

1 Exchanges take place in __________.

2 In a __________ economy, some decisions are made chiefly by government and others by markets.

3 All the institutions involved in borrowing and lending money make up the __________ market.

4 The behavior of the economy as a whole, and especially of certain aggregate measures such as unemployment and inflation, is called __________.

5 The branch of economics that focuses on firms, households, and individuals and studies product, labor, and capital markets is called __________.

6 The statement that crime rates are higher in low-income areas is an example of __________.

7 The statement that poverty leads to crime is an example of __________.

8 Economists use __________, which are sets of assumptions, conclusions, and data, to study the economy and evaluate the consequences of various policies.

9 __________ economics rests on value judgments; __________ economics describes how the economy behaves.

10 The four basic questions that economists ask about the economy are (1) what is produced and in what quantities, (2) __________, (3) for whom are they produced, and (4) who makes the decisions?

Answers to Self-Test

True or False

1	f	6	t	11	f
2	f	7	t	12	f
3	f	8	f	13	t
4	t	9	t	14	f
5	f	10	f	15	f

Multiple Choice

1	b	6	c	11	d	16	a
2	e	7	d	12	b	17	c
3	e	8	d	13	c	18	a
4	b	9	b	14	d	19	c
5	e	10	a	15	c	20	b

Completion

1 markets
2 mixed
3 capital
4 macroeconomics
5 microeconomics
6 correlation
7 causation
8 theories or models
9 Normative, positive
10 how are these goods produced

Chapter 2

BASIC PREMISES

Chapter Review

The concept of scarcity discussed in Chapter 1 implies that choices must be made. This chapter begins to explain how economists think about choice, and how choices are influenced and coordinated by markets. A basic economic assumption is that of rational choice, which simply says that people select the alternative they prefer most from among all those that are available. The alternatives available to any particular firm or individual, of course, depend upon the choices made by other firms and individuals. All of these rational choices must somehow fit together, and markets serve the function of coordinating them. Markets promote voluntary trade. By definition, voluntary trade is mutually beneficial, creating a surplus for both buyer and seller. If it were not, the trade would not take place! An important insight of trade theory is the principle of comparative advantage, which shows how individuals and countries can specialize in production and thereby increase the gains they receive from trade. The next chapter will show how markets help realize some of the potential gains from trade.

ESSENTIAL CONCEPTS

1 The **basic economic model** includes three elements: individuals, firms, and markets. Economic decisions such as what and how much of each type of good to produce, how to produce them, what kind of career to pursue, and how to spend one's earnings are made by **rational, self-interested individuals** and **rational, profit-maximizing firms. Markets** serve the economic role of coordinating these decisions.

2 The basic economic model assumes that markets are **perfectly competitive.** In perfectly competitive markets, there are many consumers and firms, and each is small relative to the size of the overall market. One key feature of perfect competition is that any firm charging more than the going price will lose all of its customers. Without any ability to influence the market price, the firm is a **price taker.**

3 Private **property rights** play an important role in the basic model. They include the right to use resources in certain ways and the right to sell them in markets. These two aspects of property rights provide incentives to use resources efficiently and to transfer resources to their most valuable use.

4 When compensation is tied to performance, people have strong incentives to work hard and be productive, but those who are more fortunate and successful also will earn higher incomes. On the other hand, distributing the output more equally undermines incentives.

This **incentive-equality trade-off** is one of the basic questions facing societies: how should the tax and welfare system be constructed to balance the competing ends of providing strong incentives and promoting equality?

5 **Scarcity** implies that not everyone who desires a good or resource can have it. There is an allocation problem. In market economies, goods are allocated to the highest bidder. Another solution to the allocation problem is to **ration**. Rationing schemes include queues, first-come-first-served, and coupons. Unless supplemented by markets, rationing schemes will likely lead to inefficiencies.

6 The basic economic model assumes that decisions are made rationally, which simply means that individuals and firms balance the benefits and costs of their decisions. Economists see rational decision making as a two-step process. First, find what alternatives are available. This step is the construction of the **opportunity set**. Next, select the best alternative from those within the opportunity set.

7 The chapter presents three types of opportunity sets. The **budget constraint** shows what combinations of goods can be consumed with a limited amount of money. The **time constraint** indicates to what uses limited time can be put. Finally, the **production possibilities curve** depicts the combinations of goods that a firm or an entire economy can produce given its limited resources and the quality of the available technology.

8 The best alternatives in an opportunity set will lie along the outer edge. This is because people prefer more goods to less. Operating on the outer edge also implies that there will be a **trade-off**: more of one option means less of another. For example, on the budget constraint, consuming more of one good means that less money is available to spend on another good. On the time constraint, if an individual devotes more time to one activity, there is less time available for other endeavors. A society that chooses to produce more of one good must settle for less production of other goods.

9 The **opportunity cost** of a good or activity is the option forgone. The opportunity cost of consuming more of one good is consuming less of some alternative good. The opportunity cost of an activity is the other endeavor that would have been, but now cannot be, undertaken. The opportunity cost of producing one good is the necessarily lower production of another.

10 Voluntary trade between rational individuals is **mutually beneficial**; it is good for both buyer and seller. Naturally, the buyer would like a lower price, and the seller prefers a higher price. Both might also benefit from better information. Nevertheless, the fact that the exchange takes place implies that given the information each has at the time of the transaction, both judge that they are better off trading than not trading.

11 Trade between individuals within a country and trade between individuals in different countries take place in markets. The three broad classes of markets are the product, labor, and capital markets. These three markets are all integrated internationally, which has led to a high degree of economic interdependence among nations.

12 Trade is many-sided, or multilateral. A typical person sells labor to an employer and uses the wages she earns both to purchase goods and services from many other firms and to save for future consumption. Similarly, a country may import more from some trading partners and export very little to those countries. With other trading partners, the country may export more than it imports. A country may also buy more goods and services than it sells abroad, and make up the difference by borrowing in capital markets or sending its workers to foreign labor markets.

13 The principle of **comparative advantage** says that individuals and countries will specialize in those goods that they are relatively more efficient in producing. To be relatively efficient means to have a lower opportunity cost. Countries will have a comparative advantage in different goods. Each can import certain goods from abroad for a lower opportunity cost than it would incur producing them at home. Similarly, each can export to foreign countries those goods for which it has a comparative advantage. Comparative advantage can be read off the production possibilities curves by comparing their slopes, called marginal rates of transformation.

BEHIND THE ESSENTIAL CONCEPTS

1 The basic competitive model introduced in this chapter is critical to your understanding of economics. It will be expanded and applied in all the chapters that follow, but you should master the concepts given in this chapter: rational individuals choose the best combinations of goods along their budget constraints, firms maximize profits, and trading takes place in competitive markets, where each individual and firm is a price taker.

2 The opportunity set itself shows all of the alternatives that are available. Because more is generally preferred to less, however, economists focus on the outer boundary of the opportunity set. For example, Figure 2.1 shows an opportunity set for a firm that must divide its resources between the production of canned and frozen vegatables. The entire shaded area shows all of the combinations that are possible. The economist's attention is drawn to the outer edge, the production possibilities curve, because to choose a combination inside (such as point *E*) would be inefficient.

3 The terms "opportunity set," "budget constraint," "trade-off," and "opportunity cost" are related, but they are distinct, and you should take care to understand each one. Figure 2.2 shows the opportunity set for a student who consumes hamburgers and pizzas.

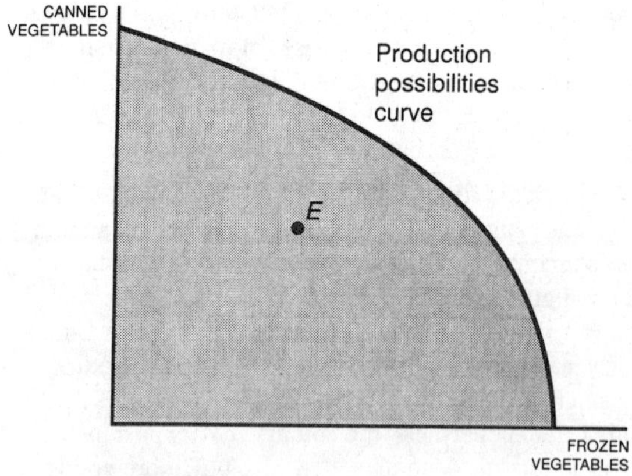

Figure 2.1

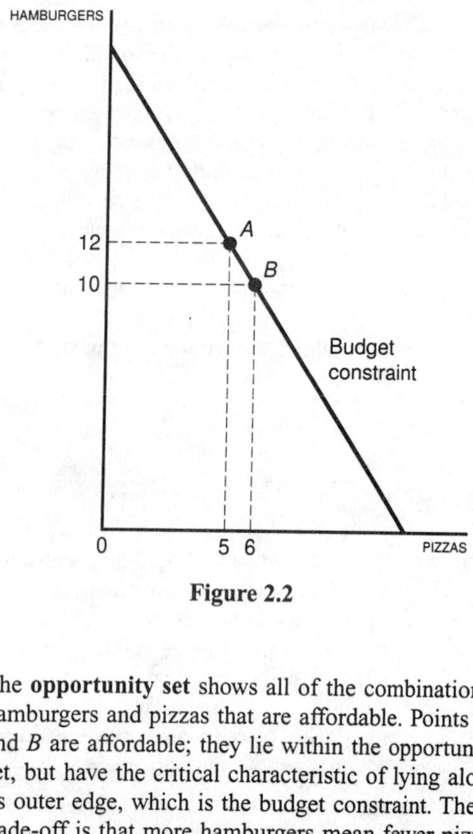

Figure 2.2

The **opportunity set** shows all of the combinations of hamburgers and pizzas that are affordable. Points *A* and *B* are affordable; they lie within the opportunity set, but have the critical characteristic of lying along its outer edge, which is the budget constraint. The trade-off is that more hamburgers mean fewer pizzas. If Joe chooses *B* rather than *A*, he eats another pizza and exactly two fewer hamburgers. The trade-off between any two points measures the opportunity cost. In this case, the opportunity cost of this extra pizza is the two forgone burgers. When the outer edge of the opportunity set is a straight line, the trade-offs will be the same all along the line; when it is a curve, the trade-offs will change.

4 Opportunity costs are forgone alternatives—not money, not time, and not resources. For example, if you spend one hour in class tomorrow, the opportunity cost of attending that class is not the hour itself. That hour will pass whether you go to the class or not. The opportunity cost is what you would have done with that hour. It is the activity you give up. Stricly speaking, the opportunity cost of buying a book for $20 is not the money, but what would have been purchased with the $20 if it had not been spent on the book.

5 **Sunk costs**, outlays that cannot be recovered, are not opportunity costs. Because these expenditures are not affected by the choice of any alternative, they do not represent the opportunity cost of any alternative. For example, suppose that you sign a one-year lease on an apartment and are forbidden to sublet it. When you consider whether to stay in town for the summer or travel abroad, the rent owed your landlord is irrelevant. You cannot do anything about it. Regardless of which alternative you choose, you must pay the rent. The rent is a sunk cost, not an opportunity cost.

6 Be clear about the difference between total costs and marginal costs. Marginal costs are the costs of a little more or a little less of some activity. Before considering going into business, you evaluate the total opportunity costs of the enterprise—all of the costs of setting up the plant, designing and producing the product, and locating the market. When you are considering whether to produce another unit of output, however, it is the marginal opportunity cost that is important. The marginal cost of producing a little bit more is just the added cost incurred when producing more with the plant already set up, the product designed, and the market found. These latter costs are not marginal.

7 An exchange creates and divides a surplus. The surplus is the difference between the value to the seller of what is traded and its value to the buyer. If there is no surplus, the exchange does not take place; the seller simply refuses to trade if he thinks the good is worth more than the buyer is willing to pay. The division of the surplus is another matter. Both the buyer and seller will receive some of the surplus. This is what economists mean when they say that trade is mutually beneficial: each party receives some of the surplus. The buyer pays somewhat less than the maximum she is willing to pay, and the seller receives somewhat more than the minimum she is willing to accept. Of course, whatever the division of the surplus, each would prefer to receive more.

8 When individuals trade, both buyer and seller gain. Each is better off with the trade than he would be if the trade did not take place. Likewise, countries also gain from trade. Trade allows specialization on the basis of comparative advantage, and countries benefit from more goods and services. But although each country as a whole gains from trade, not every individual in each country is better off. Some businesses lose out to foreign competition, and some workers lose jobs. Other businesses gain new markets, and new jobs are created. Thus, international trade creates both gains and losses, but overall, the gains outweigh the losses.

9 To better understand comparative advantage, it helps to distinguish it from **absolute advantage.** A country has an absolute advantage in the production of a good or service if it requires fewer inputs to produce the good than another country. Comparative advantage, on the

other hand, pertains to opportunity costs. As we have seen, the opportunity cost is not the inputs used in production; rather, it is the alternative use of those inputs. Thus, a country (or individual) has the comparative advantage in the production of a good or service if it has the lower opportunity cost.

For instance, assume that only labor is required to produce tomatoes or bookcases. Workers in country A can produce a carload of tomatoes in 40 hours, while workers in country B require 80 hours. Country A has an absolute advantage in producing tomatoes. To determine comparative advantage, however, we must look at how productive those workers are elsewhere in the economy. If the 40 hours of labor in country A produce 2 bookcases, but 80 hours in country B produce only 1, then country B has a comparative advantage in tomatoes. Why? Because a carload of tomatoes has an opportunity cost of 1 fewer bookcase in country B.

SELF-TEST

True or False

1 The basic model of economics seeks to explain why people want what they want.

2 A firm selling in a perfectly competitive market is a price taker because it cannot raise its price without losing all of its customers.

3 Both the right to use a resource in certain ways and the right to transfer that resource are important aspects of private property rights.

4 Rationing by queues wastes the time spent waiting in line.

5 The opportunity set includes only the best available alternative.

6 The budget constraint shows what combinations of goods are affordable, given prices and income.

7 The time constraint shows what activities are possible in the given amount of time.

8 The slope of the budget constraint is the relative price of the two goods.

9 The production possibilities curve shows the boundary of the opportunity set.

10 The principle of diminishing returns says that as more units of any input are added to a production process, total output eventually falls.

11 Sunk expenditures do not represent opportunity costs.

12 Unless the gain from trade is divided equally between buyer and seller, an exchange cannot be mutually beneficial.

13 With multilateral trade, imports from a particular country may not equal exports to that country.

14 The country that can produce a good with the least amount of labor is said to have a comparative advantage in the production of that good.

15 The extent of the division of labor is limited by the size of the market.

Multiple Choice

1 Which of the following is not a building block of the basic economic model?

a assumptions about how firms behave;
b assumptions about how consumers behave;
c assumptions about markets;
d assumptions about the behavior of government;
e All of the above are building blocks of the basic economic model.

2 Individuals and firms in the economy must make choices because of

a diminishing returns;
b rationality;
c scarcity;
d all of the above;
e none of the above.

3 The concept of rationality refers to

a the fact of scarcity;
b the principle of diminishing returns;
c the assumption that individuals have sensible goals;
d the assumption that individuals and firms weigh the costs and benefits of their choices;
e the assumption that individuals and firms are certain of the consequences of their choices.

4 A firm that cannot influence the price it sells its product for is called a

a price maker;
b price taker;.
c rational decision maker;
d none of the above;
e all of the above.

5 In a pure market economy, incentives to work hard and produce efficiently are provided by

a the profit motive;
b government regulations;
c private property rights;
d both the profit motive and private property rights;
e all of the above.

6 Allocating goods by queues and coupons are examples of

a rationing;
b not selling to the highest bidder;
c efficient ways of allocating resources;
d the profit motive;
e a and b.

7 Rationing by queues

a leads to an efficient allocation of resources;
b allocates goods to those willing to pay the most money;
c wastes the time spent waiting in line;
d is an efficient way of allocating scarce goods;
e a and c.

8 When goods are rationed by coupons and the coupons are not tradable,

a the goods do not go to the individuals who value them most;
b a black market may be established;
c individuals will not act rationally;
d a and b;
e none of the above.

9 Choices of individuals and firms are limited by

a time constraints;
b production possibilities;
c budget constraints;
d all of the above;
e none of the above.

10 Fred has $10 to spend on baseball cards and hamburgers. The price of baseball cards is $.50 per pack. Hamburgers sell at a price of $1.00 each. Which of the following possibilities is not in Fred's opportunity set?

a 10 hamburgers and zero packs of baseball cards.
b 5 hamburgers and 10 packs of baseball cards.
c 2 hamburgers and 16 packs of baseball cards.
d 1 hamburger and 18 packs of baseball cards.
e All of the above are in Fred's opportunity set.

11 Renting an apartment, Jorge signs a lease promising to pay $400 each month for one year. He always keeps his word, and therefore he will pay the $400 each month whether he lives in the apartment or not. The $400 each month represents

a an opportunity cost;
b a sunk cost;
c a trade-off;
d a budget constraint;
e diminishing returns.

12 One box of Nature's Crunch Cereal sells for $2.55. Each box comes with a coupon worth $.50 off the purchase price of another box of Nature's Crunch Cereal. The marginal cost of the second box of this product is

a $2.55;
b $3.05;
c $2.05;
d $1.55;
e none of the above.

13 If a firm changes from paying commissions on total sales to paying each member of its sales force a fixed salary, it will likely

a experience lower total sales;
b have greater equality in earnings of its sales representatives;
c see no difference because compensation is a sunk cost;
d a and b;
e none of the above.

14 Voluntary trade between two rational individuals

a benefits the buyer only;
b benefits the seller only;
c benefits the buyer or the seller but not both;
d benefits both the buyer and the seller;
e none of the above.

15 The gains from trade, that is, the difference between the value of a good to the buyer and its value to the seller,

a accrues entirely to the seller;
b accrues entirely to the buyer;
c is always divided equally;
d accrues to the government;
e none of the above.

16 When economists argue that both parties benefit from voluntary trade, they are assuming

a that both parties are well-informed;
b that both parties place the same value on the traded good;
c that both parties desire the same price;
d that the surplus is divided evenly between buyer and seller;
e none of the above.

17 Goods produced in the United States and sold in foreign countries are called

a imports;
b exports;
c either imports or exports;
d capital flows;
e none of the above.

18 For decades, Japan has imported raw materials from Australia, while Australia has purchased heavy equipment from the United States. Furthermore, Japan has exported consumer goods to the United States. This is an example of

a multilateral trade;
b bilateral trade;
c absolute advantage;
d protectionism;
e trade deficit.

19 If the United States has a comparative advantage in the production of a good, then

a fewer resources are required to produce the good in the United States;
b the United States also has an absolute advantage in the production of the good;
c the relative cost of producing the good is lower in the United States;
d the United States will import the good;
e all of the above.

20 The principle of comparative advantage

a applies only to international trade;
b always leads to complete specialization;
c forms the basis for the division of labor;
d is relevant only in the absence of protection;
e all of the above.

Completion

1 A market with large numbers of buyers and sellers, each of whom cannot influence the price, is an example of __________.

2 The right of an owner of a resource to use it in certain ways and to sell it is called a __________.

3 Allocating goods and services by some means other than selling to the highest bidder is called __________.

4 The collection of all available opportunities is called the __________.

5 __________ limit choices.

6 The amount of goods that a business firm is able to produce is called its __________.

7 The idea that as more inputs are used in a production process, each successive input eventually adds less to output is an example of the principle of __________.

8 The fact that more time spent studying means less time available for other activities illustrates a __________.

9 An expenditure that cannot be recovered is a __________ cost.

10 If a country is relatively more efficient at producing a good than its trading partners, then that country is said to have the __________ in the production of that good.

Answers to Self-Test

True or False

1	f	4	t	7	t	10	f	13	t
2	t	5	f	8	t	11	t	14	f
3	t	6	t	9	t	12	f	15	t

Multiple Choice

1	d	6	e	11	b	16	e
2	c	7	c	12	c	17	b
3	d	8	b	13	d	18	a
4	b	9	d	14	d	19	c
5	d	10	e	15	e	20	c

Completion

1 perfect competition
2 property right
3 rationing
4 opportunity set
5 constraints
6 production possibilities
7 diminishing returns
8 trade-off
9 sunk
10 comparative advantage

Doing Economics: Tools and Practice Problems

For the problem sets in this section, we reach into the economist's tool box for four important techniques, each of which will reappear throughout the remainder of the book. Two relate to the opportunity set: budget and time constraints, for which the outer edge of the opportunity set is a straight line; and production possibilities curves, which can be straight lines but more often exhibit diminishing returns and are curved. The remaining two techniques relate to comparative advantage and trade.

STRAIGHT-LINE OPPORTUNITY SETS

The simplest type of opportunity set has an outer boundary that is a straight line. Examples include budget constraints, time constraints, and production possibilities, when there are constant returns. The budget constraint indicates what combinations of goods can be purchased with a limited amount of money. The time constraint indicates what combinations of time-consuming activities can be undertaken with a limited amount of time. The production possibilities curve (in this case it is a straight line) indicates what combinations of goods can be produced. Tool Kit 2.1 shows how to construct these opportunity sets.

Tool Kit 2.1: Plotting the Straight-Line Opportunity Set

Budget constraints, time constraints, and production possibilities are examples of straight-line opportunity sets. To draw the budget constraint you must know the size of the budget and the prices of the goods. The time constraint can be drawn given the total time available and the time requirements for each activity. To plot the production possibilities curve you need to know the resources and the technology. Follow this procedure to plot these straight-line opportunity sets.

Step one: Draw a set of coordinate axes. Label the horizontal axis as the quantity of one good or activity and the vertical axis as the quantity of the other good or activity.

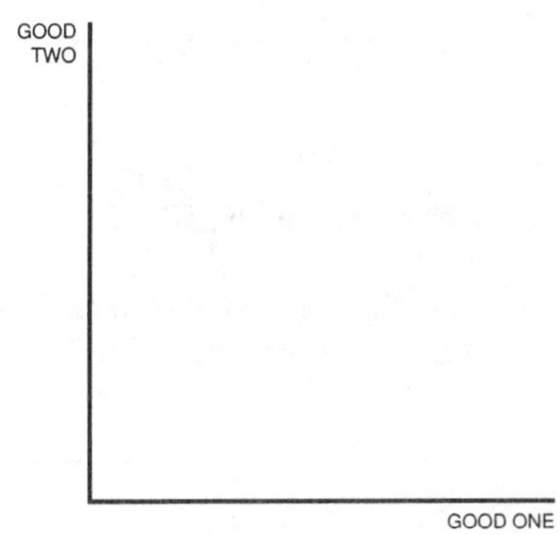

Step two: Calculate the maximum quantity of the good or activity measured on the horizontal axis. Plot this quantity along the horizontal axis.

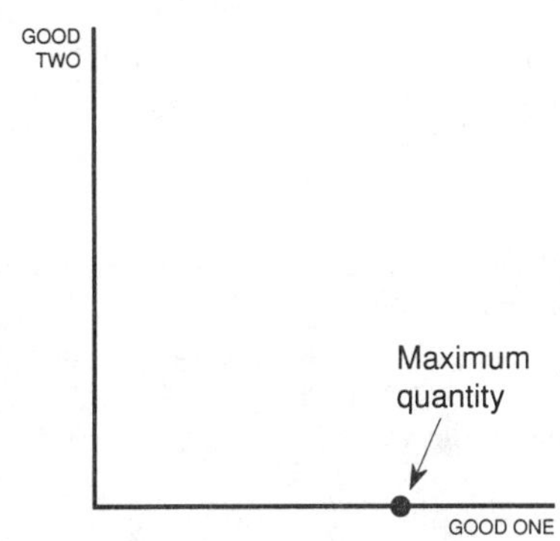

Step three: Calculate the maximum quantity of the good or activity measured on the vertical axis. Plot this quantity along the vertical axis.

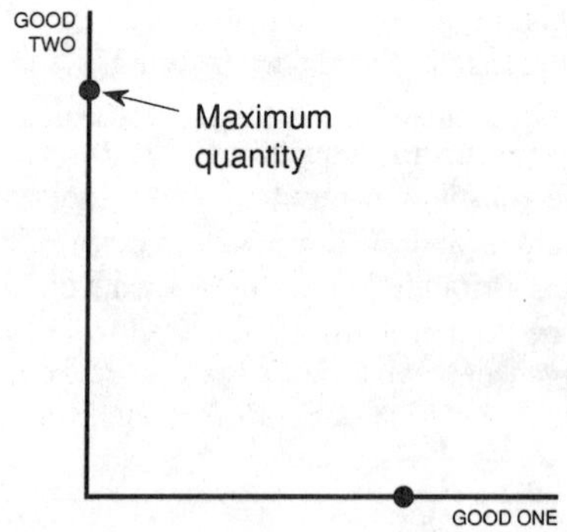

Step four: Draw a line segment connecting the two points. This line segment is the relevant part of the opportunity set.

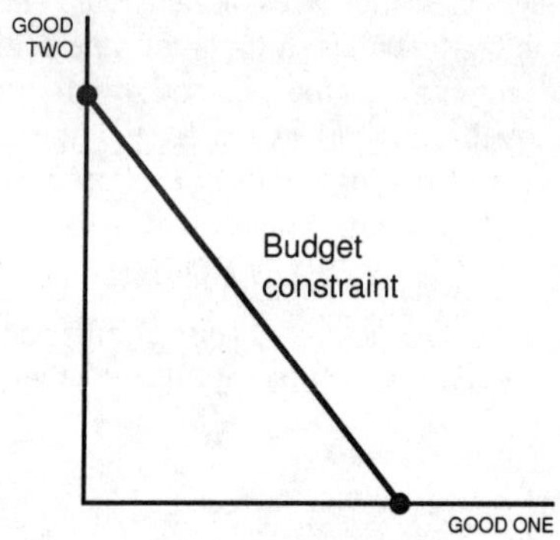

Step five: The slope is the opportunity cost of the good or activity measured on the horizontal axis. In the case of the budget constraint, it is called the relative price, the ratio of the price of the good measured on the horizontal axis divided by the price of the good measured on the vertical axis.

1 (Worked problem: budget constraint) Diana has an entertainment budget of \$200 each month. She enjoys lunches with friends and going to the movies. The price of a typical lunch is \$10. Movie tickets are \$5 each. Construct her opportunity set.

Step-by-step solution

Step one: Draw coordinate axes and label the horizontal one "Lunches" and the vertical one "Movies." (There is no rule as to which good goes where. It would be fine if lunches were measured on the vertical axis and movies on the horizontal.)

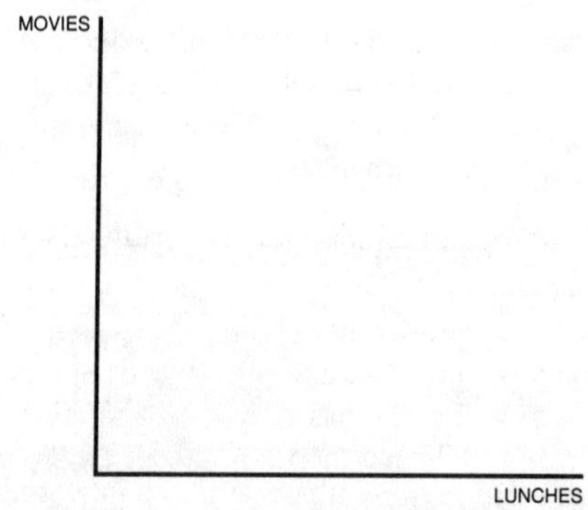

Step two: Calculate the maximum quantity of lunches. This number is \$200/\$10 = 20 lunches. Plot this quantity along the horizontal axis.

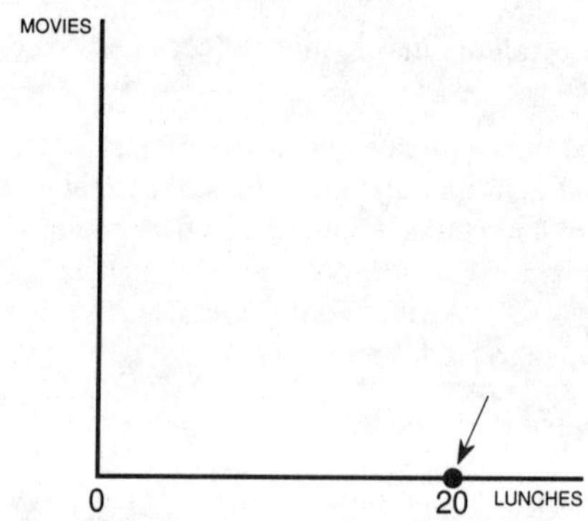

Step three: Calculate the maximum quantity of movies. This number is \$200/\$5 = 40 movie tickets. Plot this quantity along the vertical axis.

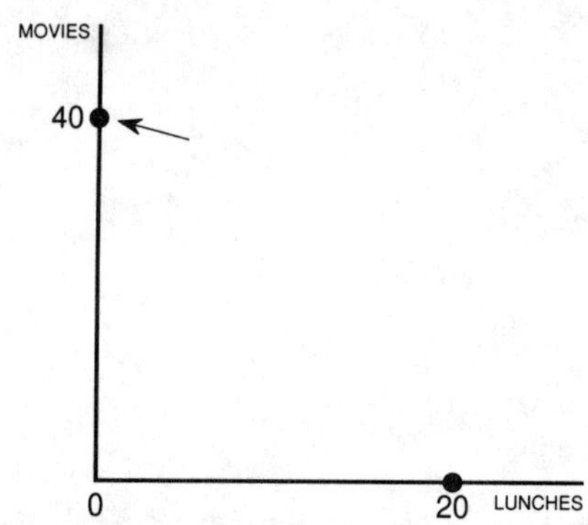

Step four: Draw a line segment connecting these two points. This line segment is the budget constraint.

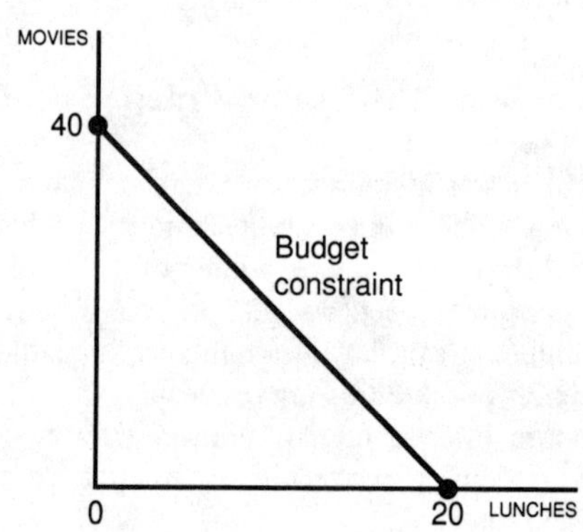

Step five: The slope of the budget constraint is 40/20 = 2. The price ratio is \$10/\$5 = 2. (Strictly speaking, these slopes are negative, but we follow the practice of dropping the negative sign as long as there is no confusion.)

2 (Practice problem: budget constraint) Velma Thomas must pay for both prescription medicine and nursing care for her elderly father. Each bottle of pills costs her \$40, and the price of nursing care is \$100 per day. She has been able to scrape together \$1,000 each month for these expenses. Construct her opportunity set, going through all five steps.

3 (Practice problem: budget constraint) Construct the following opportunity sets.

a Clothing budget per year = \$900; price of suits = \$300; price of shoes = \$90.
b Food budget = \$200 per week; price of restaurant meals = \$20; price of in-home meals = \$5.
c School expense budget = \$1,200 per semester; price of books = \$50; price of courses = \$200.
d Annual state transportation department budget = \$100,000; cost of fixing potholes = \$200; cost of replacing road signs = \$500.

4 (Worked problem: time constraint) Ahmed likes to visit his invalid father across town. Each visit, including transportation and time with Dad, takes 3 hours. Another of Ahmed's favorite activities is his tango lessons. These are given downstairs in his apartment building and take only an hour each. With work and night school, Ahmed has only 15 hours each week to divide between visiting his father and tango lessons. Construct his opportunity set.

Step-by-step solution

Step one: The time constraint works very much like the budget constraint. Plot coordinate axes and label the horizontal one "Visits to Dad" and the vertical one "Tango lessons."

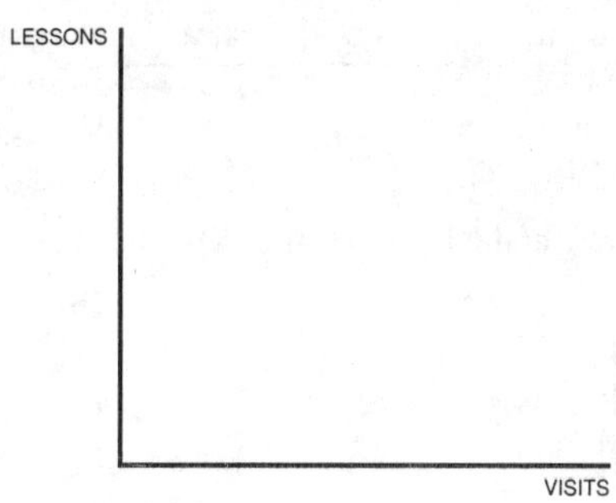

Step two: Calculate the maximum number of visits to his father. This number is 15/3 = 5 visits. Plot this quantity along the horizontal axis.

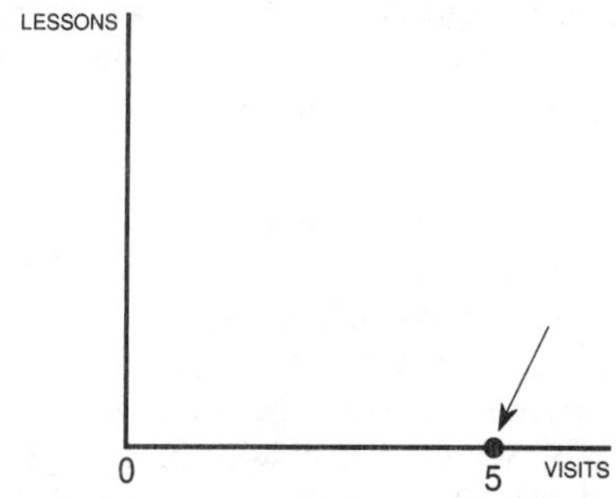

Step three: Calculate the maximum number of tango lessons. This number is 15/1 = 15 lessons. Plot this quantity along the vertical axis.

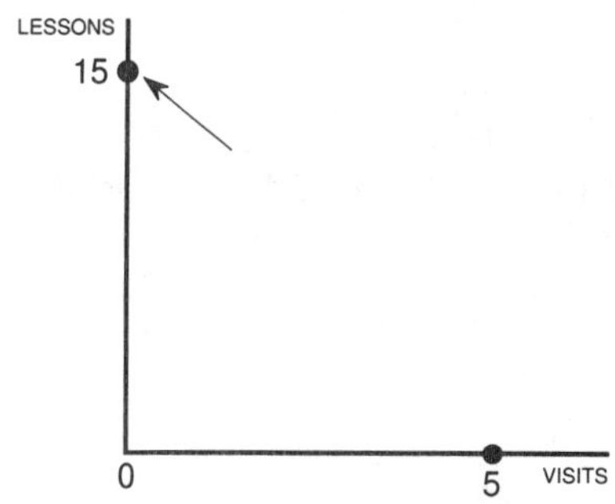

Step four: Draw a line segment connecting these two points. This line segment is the time constraint.

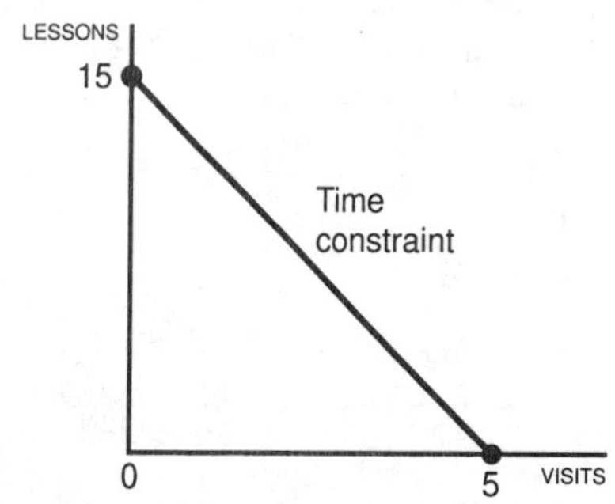

Step five: The slope of the time constraint is 15/5 = 3. The time-requirement ratio is 3/1 = 3.

5 (Practice problem: time constraint) Michael Terranova has two hours to make his house as clean as possible. The place needs vacuuming and dusting. He can dust one piece of furniture in 10 minutes. Each room takes 20 minutes to vacuum. Plot his time constraint.

6 (Practice problem: time constraint) Construct the following opportunity sets.

a Total time available = 6 hours; time required to iron each shirt = 15 minutes; time required to iron each dress = 30 minutes.
b Total time available = 20 days; time required to study each chapter = 1/2 day; time required to write book reports = 2 days.
c Total time available = 40 hours; time required to counsel each disturbed teenager = 2 hours; time required to attend each meeting = 1 hour.

d Total time available = 8 hours; time required to visit each client = 4 hours; time required to telephone each client = 10 minutes.

7 (Worked problem: production possibilities curve) First, assume that there is one resource, which can be used in the production of either of two goods, and that there are no diminishing returns. In this case, the production possibilities curve is a straight line, and we treat it just as we did the budget and time constraints.

There are 25 migrant farm workers employed at San Pueblo vegetable farm. Each worker can pick 4 bushels of cucumbers an hour. Alternatively, each worker can pick 1 bushel of peppers each hour. Each worker can work 8 hours a day. Plot the daily production possibilities curve.

Step-by-step solution

Step one: Plot coordinate axes and label the horizontal one "Cucumbers" (measured in bushels) and the vertical one "Peppers."

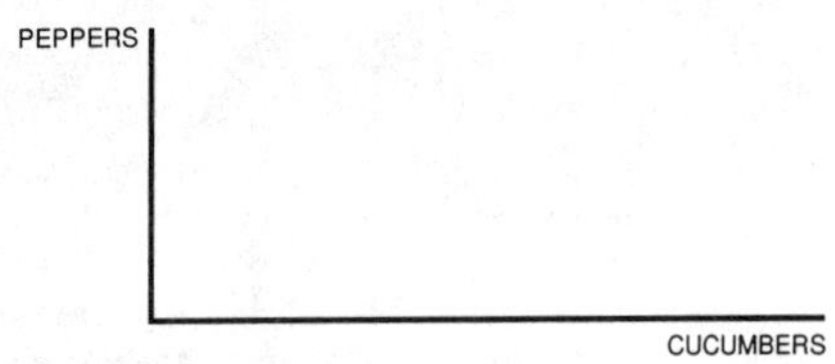

Step two: Calculate the maximum number of cucumbers that can be picked each day. This number is 25 (workers) × 8 (hours) × 4 (bushels an hour) = 800 bushels of cucumbers. Plot this number along the horizontal axis.

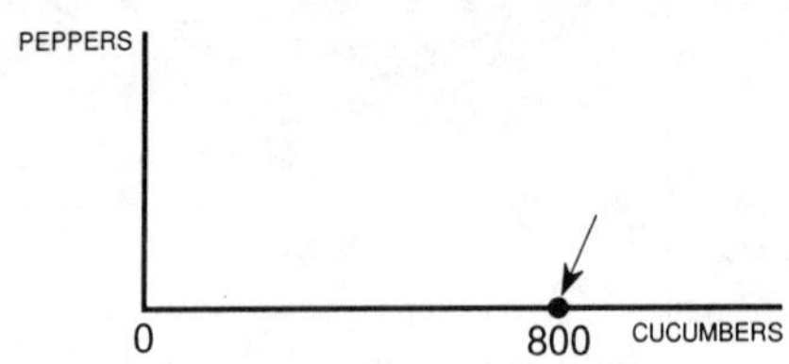

Step three: Calculate the maximum number of peppers that can be picked each day. This number is 25 (workers) × 8 (hours) × 1 (bushel an hour) = 200 bushels of peppers. Plot this number along the vertical axis.

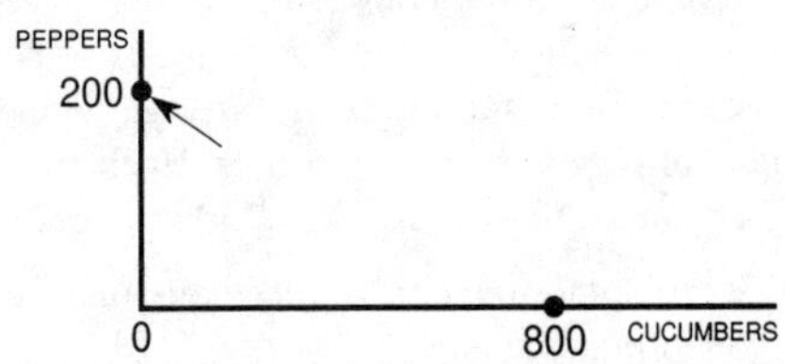

Step four: Draw a line segment connecting these two points. This line segment is the production possibilities curve.

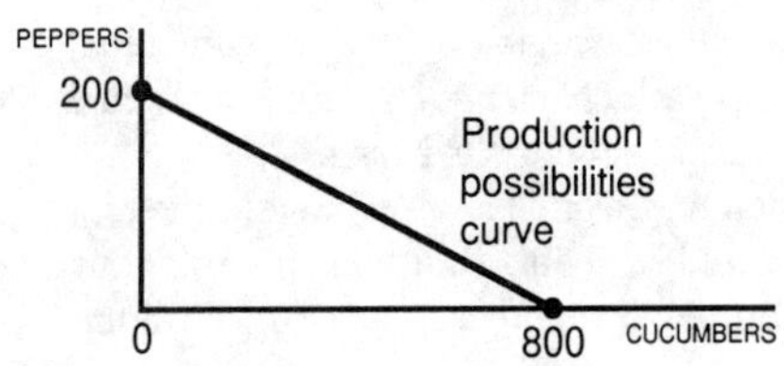

Step five: The slope is 200/800 = 1/4, which means that the opportunity cost of 1 bushel of cucumbers is 1/4 bushel of peppers.

8 (Practice problem: production possibilities curve) Coach Hun has four assistant coaches. They make recruiting visits and also run clinics for local youth. Each can make 32 recruiting visits each week. Alternatively, each can run 8 clinics in a week. Plot the production possibilities curve.

9 (Practice problem: production possibilities curve) Construct the following opportunity sets.

a Total amount of land available = 10 acres of land; output of corn per acre = 2,000 bushels; output of wheat per acre = 1,000 bushels.

b Total amount of labor available = 40 hours; output of donuts per hour = 150; output of sweet rolls per hour = 50.

c Total amount of floor space available = 1,000 square feet; sales of women's sportswear per square foot = \$500; sales of housewares per square foot = \$200.

d Total amount of fuel available = 5,000 gallons; miles per gallon for tank travel = 3; miles per gallon for armored personnel carriers = 9.

PRODUCTION POSSIBILITES WITH DIMINISHING RETURNS

Usually, production is subject to diminishing returns. This means that as more of a resource is used in production, the extra (or marginal) output is less. In other words, although output increases, it does so at a diminishing rate. With diminishing returns the production possibilities curve acquires a convex shape. Tool Kit 2.2 shows how to plot the production possibilities curve when there are diminishing returns.

Tool Kit 2.2: Plotting the Production Possibilities Curve with Diminishing Returns

Diminishing returns mean that as more of some resource is used in production, the extra (or marginal) output declines. Follow this five-step procedure to plot the production possibilities curve with diminishing returns.

Step one: Draw and label a set of coordinate axes.

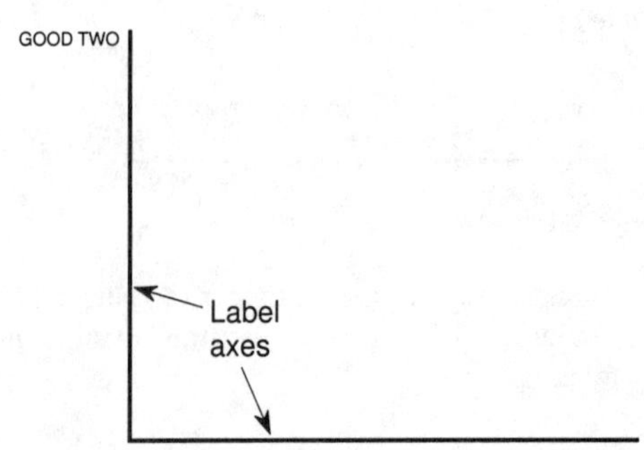

Step two: Calculate the total amount of the good measured on the horizontal axis that can be produced if all of the resource is used. Plot this quantity along the horizontal axis.

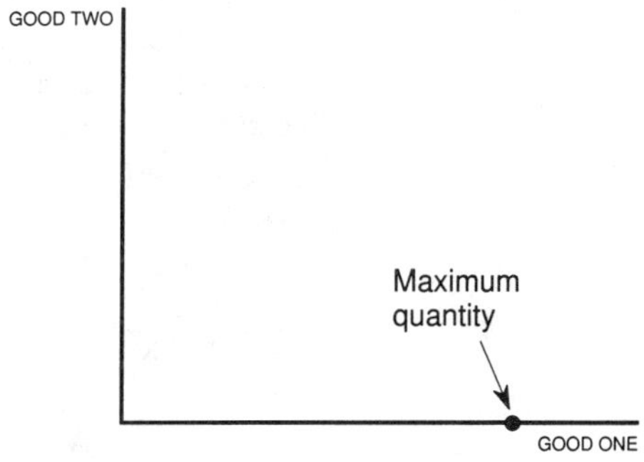

Step three: Calculate the total amount of the good measured on the vertical axis that can be produced if all of the resource is used. Plot this quantity along the vertical axis.

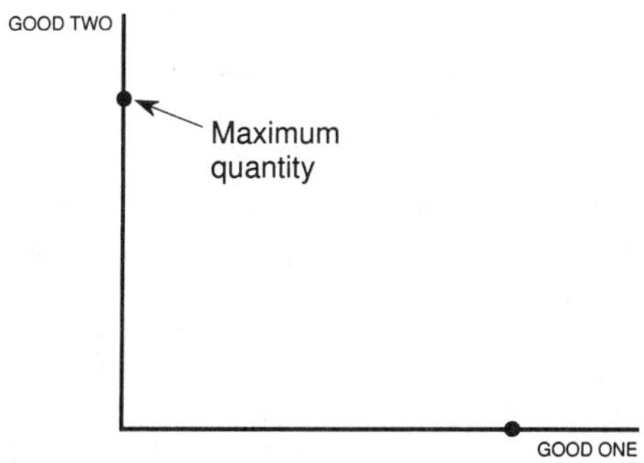

Step four: Calculate and plot several other feasible combinations.

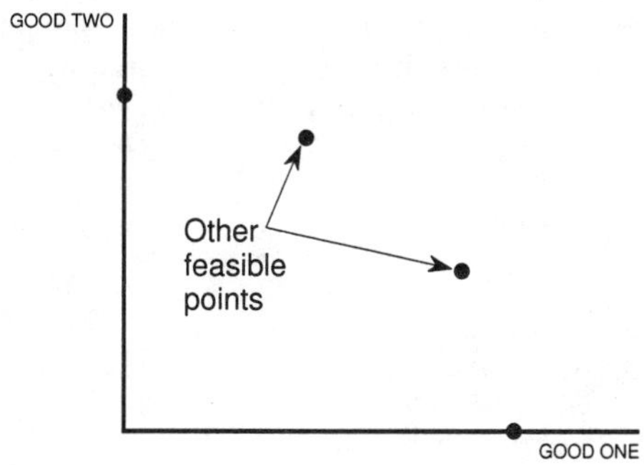

Step five: Draw a smooth curve connecting these points. This curve is the production possibilities curve.

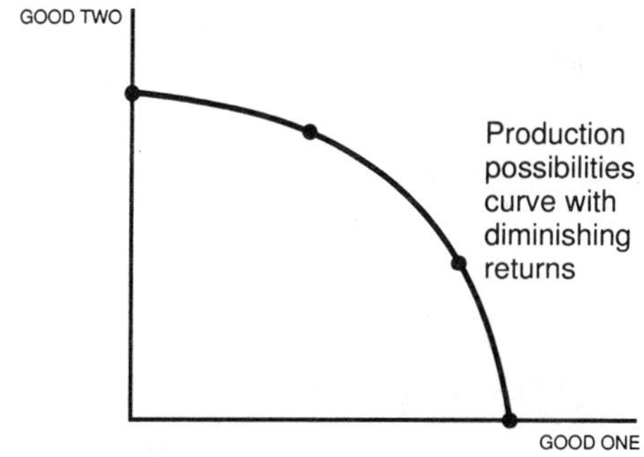

Step six: Verify that the slope is increasing along the curve. Since the slope is the marginal opportunity cost of the horizontal axis good, this reflects diminishing returns.

10 (Worked problem: production possibilities curve with diminishing returns) Iatrogenesis, a medical laboratory, employs 4 lab technicians. Each is equally adept at analyzing throat cultures and distilling vaccines. The table below shows output per day for various numbers of lab technicians.

Technicians doing cultures	Throat cultures	Technicians doing vaccines	Vaccines
1	50	1	20
2	90	2	35
3	120	3	45
4	140	4	50

Plot the production possibilities curve for Iatrogenesis.

Step-by-step solution

Step one: Draw coordinate axes. Label the horizontal one "Throat cultures" and the vertical one "Vaccines."

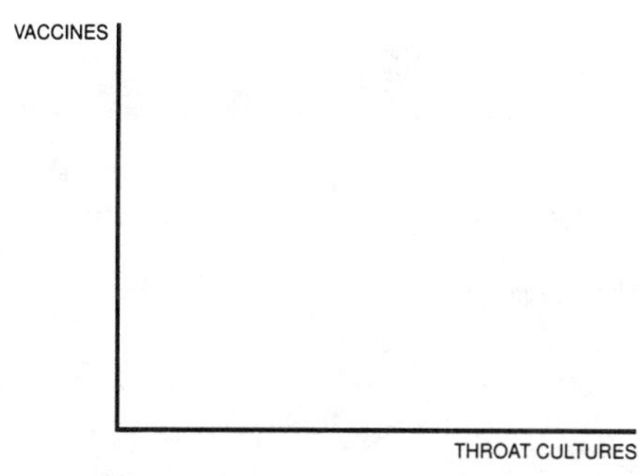

Step two: Calculate the maximum number of throat cultures. If all 4 technicians do throat cultures, the number is 140. Plot this number.

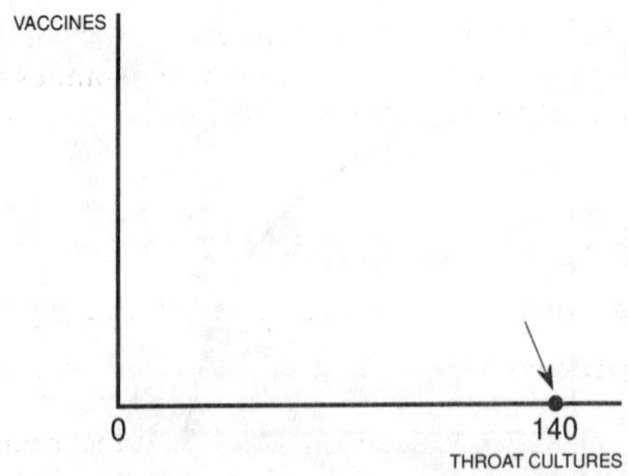

Step three: Calculate the maximum number of vaccines. If all 4 technicians do vaccines, the number is 50. Plot this number.

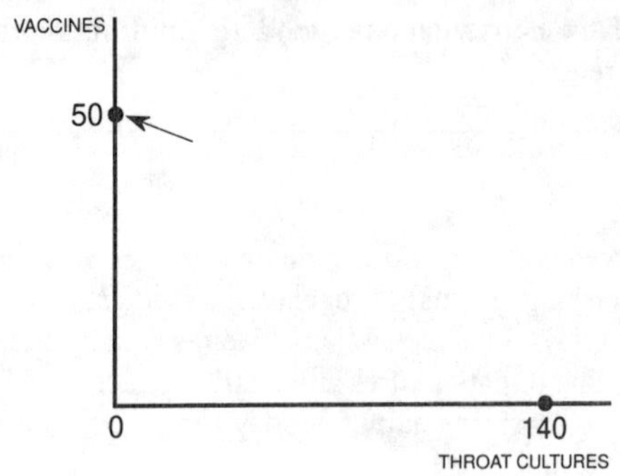

Step four: Calculate several other feasible points. For example, if 1 technician does throat cultures, then 3 can do vaccines. Reading off the table, we see that the combination produced is 50 throat cultures and 45 vaccines. Similarly, if 2 do throat cultures and 2 do vaccines, the outputs are 90 throat cultures and 35 vaccines. Another feasible combination is 120 cultures and 20 vaccines. Plot these points.

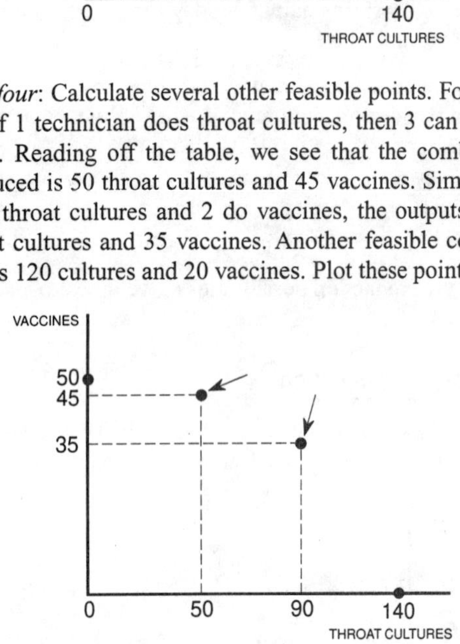

Step five: Draw the production possibilities curve through the points that have been plotted.

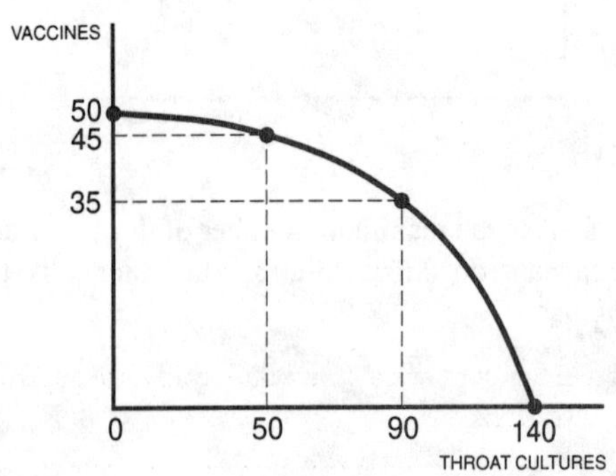

Step six: Observe that, as expected, the slope gets steeper as the number of throat cultures is increased. This indicates diminishing returns.

11 (Practice problem: production possibilities curve with diminishing returns) Enormous State University has a crime problem. Members of the criminal element have stolen many bicycles and a great deal of stereo equipment. To address this crime wave, the campus police have hired 5 new officers. The following table gives the expected number of thefts for various assignments for these new officers.

New police officers assigned to bicycle duty	Reduction in bicycle thefts	New police officers assigned to dorm patrol	Reduction in thefts of stereo equipment
1	25	1	10
2	45	2	18
3	60	3	25
4	70	4	31
5	75	5	36

Plot the production possibilities curve.

12 (Practice problem: production possibilities curve with diminishing returns) Movaway Company has employed 4 maintenance inspectors for their fleet of trucks and forklifts. The following table shows how assigning inspectors leads to fewer breakdowns.

Inspectors assigned to check trucks	Reduced number of truck breakdowns	Inspectors assigned to check forklifts	Reduced number of forklift breakdowns
1	5	1	3
2	9	2	5
3	12	3	6
4	14	4	6

Plot Movaway's production possibilities curve, and verify that it shows diminishing returns.

13 (Practice problem: production possibilities curve with diminishing returns) The Dukakis vegetable farm (located on erstwhile corn-growing land in Iowa) has 800 tons of fertilizer. The following table shows how output of endive and bib lettuce is expected to respond to different amounts of fertilizer.

Fertilizer used on endive crop (tons)	Output of endive (bushels)	Fertilizer used on lettuce crop (tons)	Output of bib lettuce (bushels)
0	1,400	0	2,000
200	2,400	200	3,400
400	3,200	400	4,200
600	3,600	600	4,700
800	4,000	800	5,000

Plot the farm's production possibilities curve, and verify that it exhibits diminishing returns.

COMPARATIVE ADVANTAGE

The most important concept in exchange and production is comparative advantage. Countries have comparative advantage when their opportunity cost is lower. They will export the goods in which they have comparative advantage. Tool Kit 2.3 shows how to use the production possibilities curve to identify comparative advantage and determine the pattern of production and trade.

Tool Kit 2.3: Identifying Comparative Advantage

When a country or individual has a comparative advantage in performing some task or producing some good, that country or individual is relatively more efficient, which means that the country or individual has the lower opportunity cost. The following procedure shows how to identify comparative advantage and predict the pattern of trade. It is written for the case of two-country trade.

Step one: Plot the production possibilities curves for each country. Be sure to be consistent and measure units of the same good along the horizontal axis in each case.

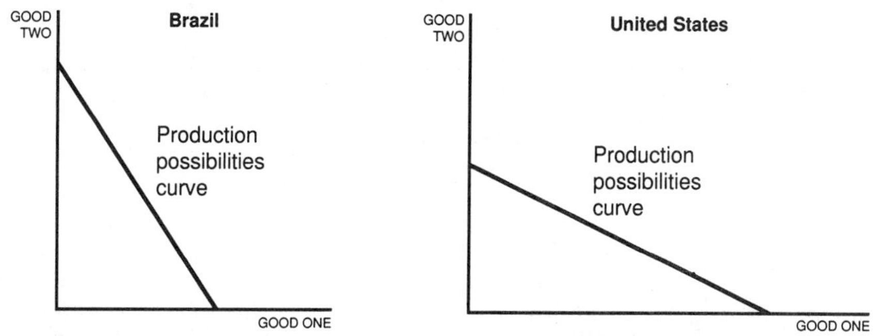

Step two: The slope of the production possibilities curve is the opportunity cost of the good on the horizontal axis, and it indicates the trade-off. The flatter slope implies comparative advantage for producing the good on the horizontal axis.

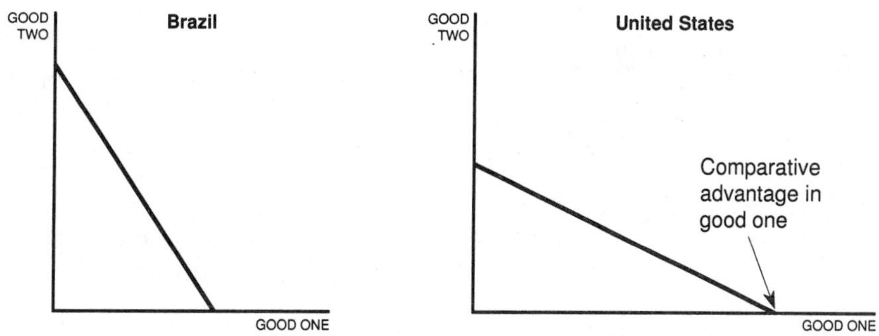

Step three: The steeper slope indicates comparative advantage for the good on the vertical axis.

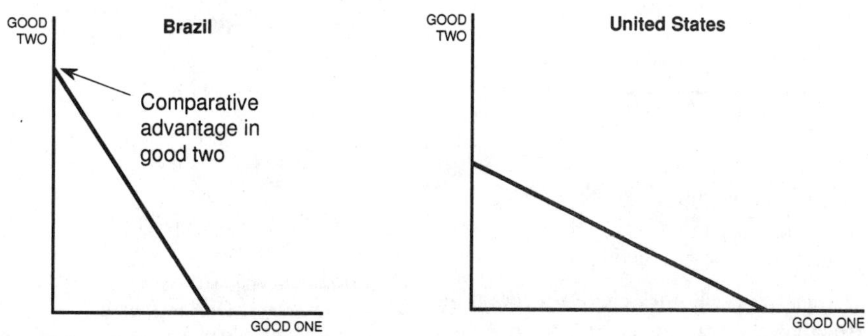

Step four: In a system of free trade, each country will produce more of the good in which it has a comparative advantage, and the relative price will lie somewhere between the opportunity costs of the two countries.

14 (Worked problem: comparative advantage) Workers in the United States and Brazil can produce shoes and computers. The annual productivity of a worker in each country is given in the table below.

Country	Computers	Shoes
United States	5,000	10,000
Brazil	200	5,000

a Which country has a comparative advantage in computers? in shoes?
b Predict the pattern of trade.
c Indicate the range of possible relative prices that would bring about this pattern of trade.

Step-by-step solution

Step one (a): Plot the production possibilities curves. In this problem, the production possibilities curve for one worker in each country will suffice. Measure computers on the horizontal axis.

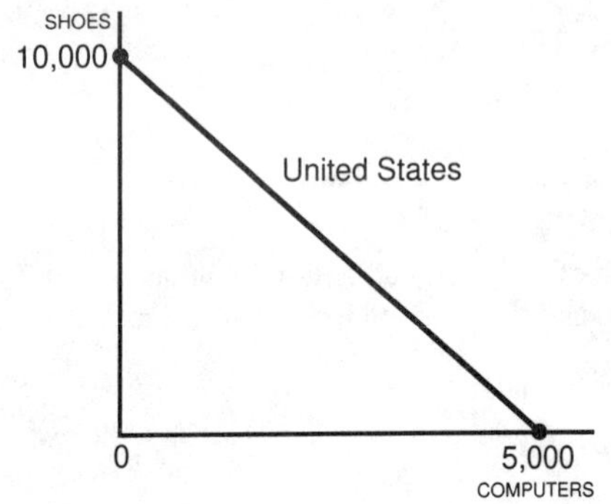

Step two: The production possibilities curve for the United States has the flatter slope; therefore, the U.S. worker has the comparative advantage in the production of computers.

Step three: The production possibilities curve for Brazil is steeper, and the Brazilian worker has the comparative advantage in shoes.

Step four (b and c): Brazil will trade shoes for U.S. computers. The relative price must lie between 2 shoes per computer (the U.S. opportunity cost) and 25 shoes per computer (the Brazilian opportunity cost).

15 (Practice problem: comparative advantage) Workers in Nigeria and neighboring Niger produce textiles and sorghum. The productivities of each are given in the table below.

Country	Textiles (bales)	Sorghum (bushels)
Nigeria	100	500
Niger	50	400

a Which country has a comparative advantage in textiles? in sorghum?
b Predict the pattern of trade.
c Indicate the range of possible relative prices that would bring about this pattern of trade.

16 (Practice problem: comparative advantage) For each of the following, determine which country has the comparative advantage in each good, predict the pattern of trade, and indicate the range of possible relative prices consistent with this pattern of trade.

a

Country	Fish	Wheat (bushels)
Greece	60	80
Poland	35	70

b

Country	Heart bypass operations	Auto parts (containers)
United States	5,000	10,000
Canada	3,000	9,000

c

Country	Scrap steel (tons)	Finished steel (tons)
Thailand	20	20
Laos	10	2

d

Country	Wine (barrels)	Wool (bales)
Portugal	2	2
Great Britain	4	8

GAINS FROM TRADE

When countries trade there is mutual gain, in the sense that their opportunity sets expand beyond their production possibilities curves. To exploit the potential of trade, production and trade must be organized according to comparative advantage. Tool Kit 2.4 shows how both trading partners can gain from trade.

Tool Kit 2.4: Showing the Gains from Trade

When the pattern of trade is based upon comparative advantage, both countries can gain. Specifically, they each can consume a bundle of goods that lies beyond their own production possibilities curve. Follow these five steps.

Step one: Draw the production possibilities curve for each country, identify the country with a comparative advantage in each good, and identify the trade-offs for each country.

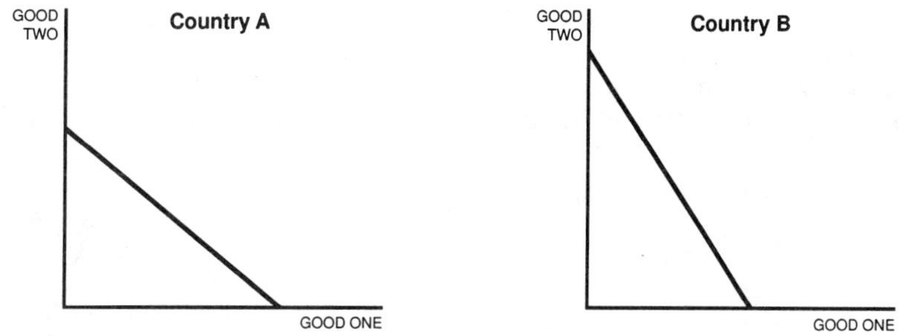

Step two: Choose a relative price between the trade-offs.

Step three: For the country with the comparative advantage in the horizontal-axis good, label the horizontal intercept *A* and draw a line segment from *A* with a slope equal to (–) the relative price. This line segment shows the bundles of goods that the country can consume by trading at the given relative price.

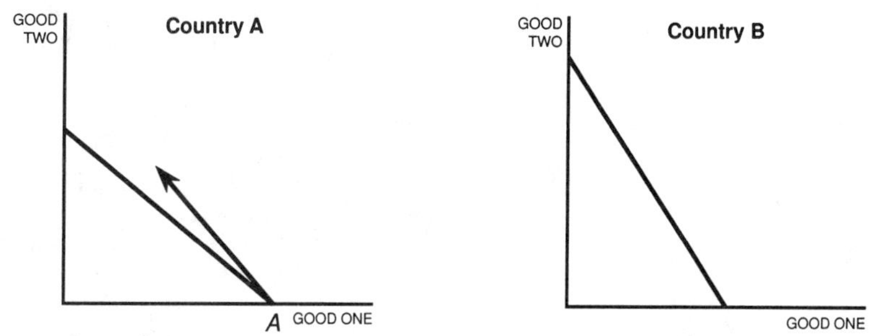

Step four: For the country with the comparative advantage in the vertical-axis good, label the vertical intercept *A* and draw a line segment from *A* with a slope equal to (–) the relative price. This line segment shows the bundles of goods that the country can consume by trading at the given relative price.

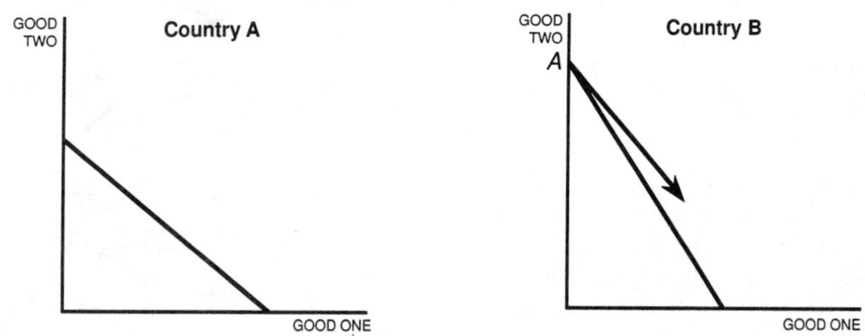

Step five: Pick a pair of consistent points, where A's exports equal B's imports, one on each line segment, and show how each country can benefit from trade.

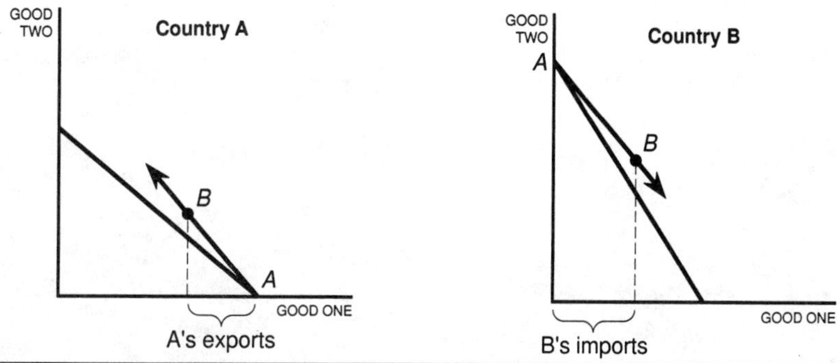

17 (Worked problem: gains from trade) This problem builds upon problem #14. Show that a worker in Brazil and a worker in the United States can benefit by trading on the basis of comparative advantage.

Step-by-step solution

Step one: Identify the country with a comparative advantage in each good and the trade-offs for each country. The U.S. worker has the comparative advantage in computers, and the trade-off is 2 shoes per computer. The Brazilian worker has the comparative advantage in shoes, and the trade-off is 25 shoes per computer.

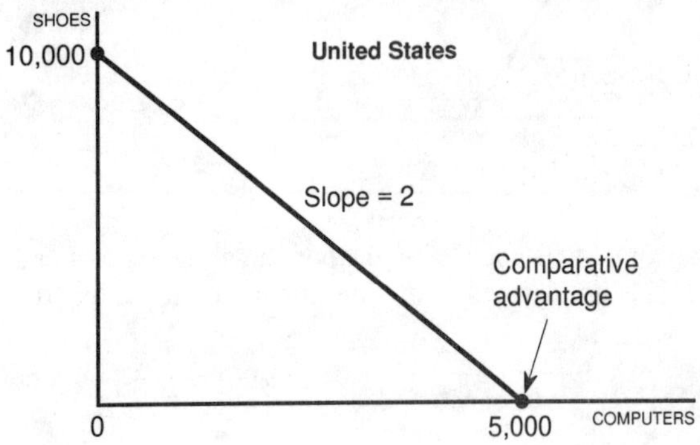

Step two: Choose a relative price between the trade-offs. Let's choose 20 shoes per computer.

Step three: For the country with the comparative advantage in computers, which is the United States, label the horizontal intercept *A* and draw a line segment from *A* with a slope equal to –20. This line segment shows the bundles of goods that the United States can consume by trading at the given relative price.

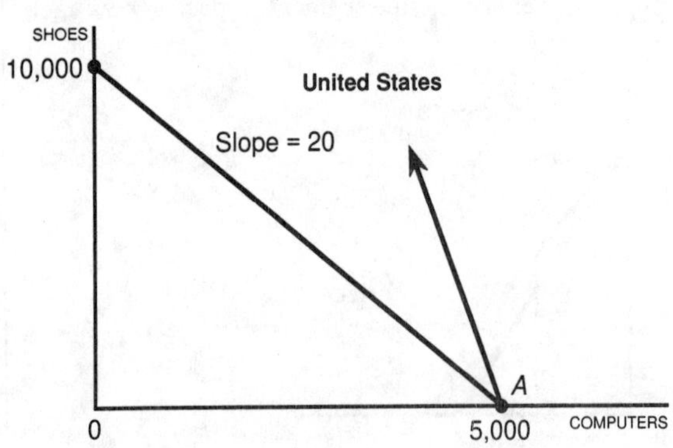

Step four: For the country with the comparative advantage in shoes, label the vertical intercept *A* and draw a line segment from *A* with a slope equal to –20. This line segment shows the bundles of goods that Brazil can consume by trading at the given relative price.

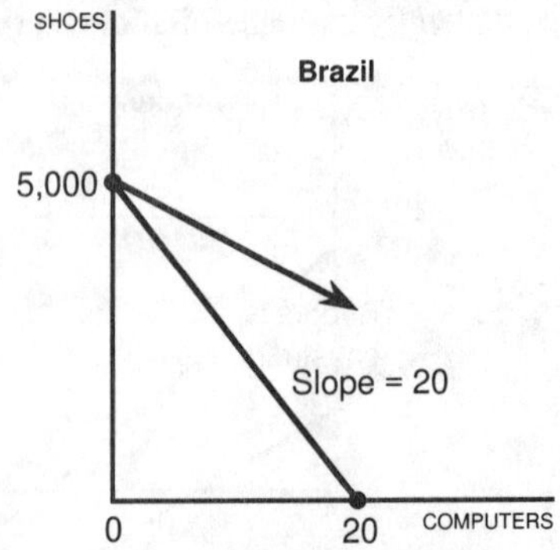

Step five: Pick a pair of consistent points, one on each line segment, and show how each country can benefit from trade. Let the U.S. worker produce 4,800 computers for domestic consumption. This leaves 200 for trade. At a relative price of 20 shoes, the 200 computers trade for 4,000 shoes. Plot the point (4,000, 4,800) and label it *B*. The Brazilian worker must then produce 4,000 shoes for trade. This leaves 1,000 shoes for domestic consumption. The 4,000 shoes trade for 200 computers. Plot the point (200, 1,000) and label it *B*. At this point, the United States exports 200 computers and imports 4,000 shoes, while Brazil imports 200 computers and exports 4,000 shoes. Trade is balanced, and each country consumes beyond its production possibilities curve.

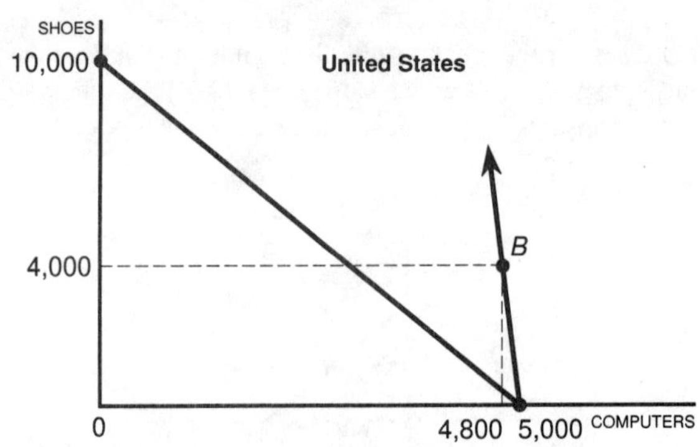

18 (Practice problem: gains from trade) This problem builds upon problem #15. Show that workers in Nigeria and Niger can benefit by trading according to comparative advantage.

Answers to Problems

2

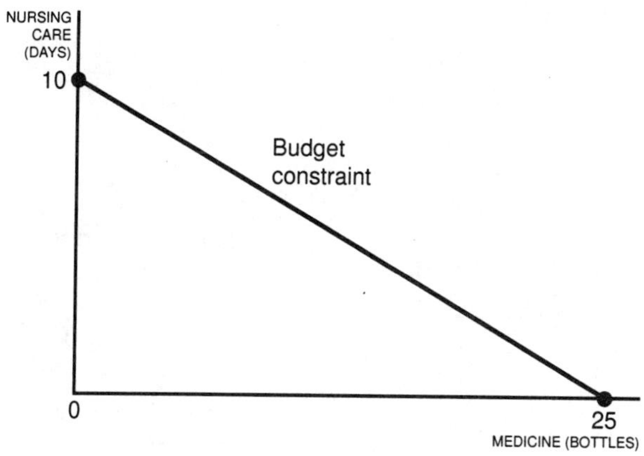

3

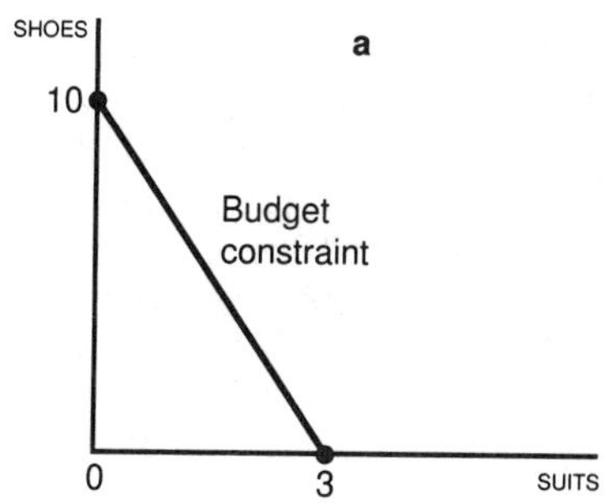

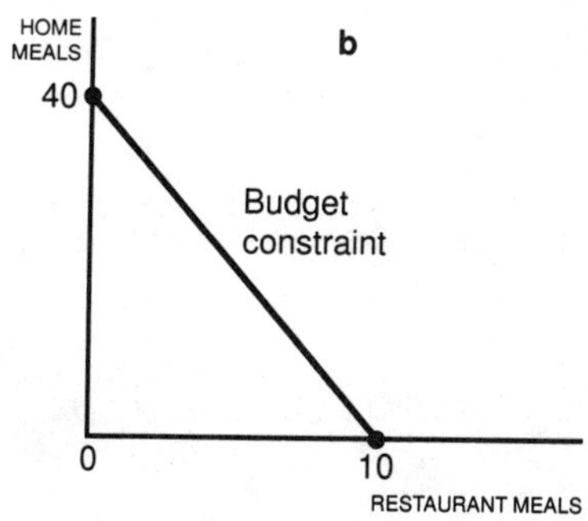

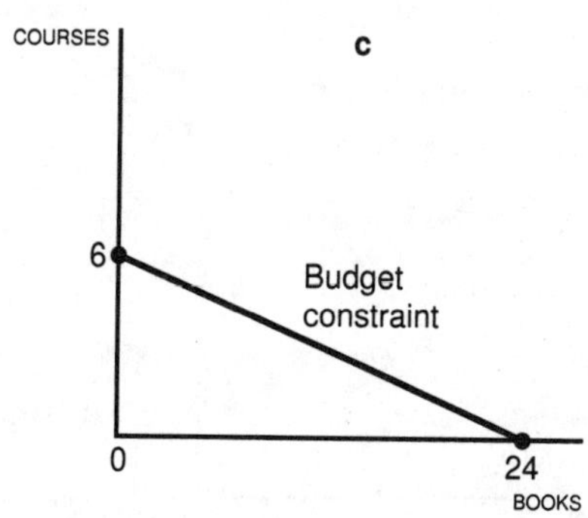

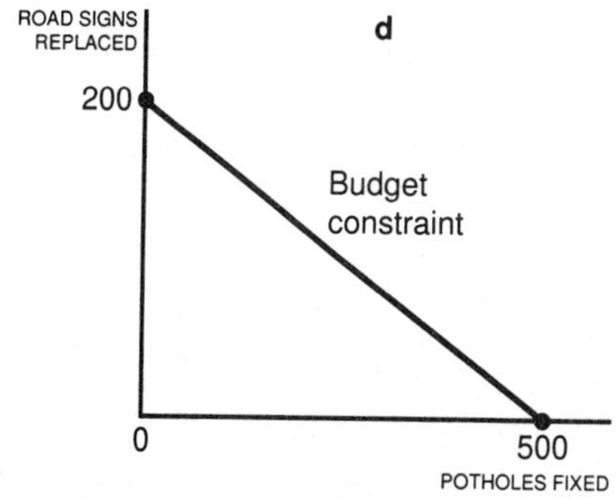

5

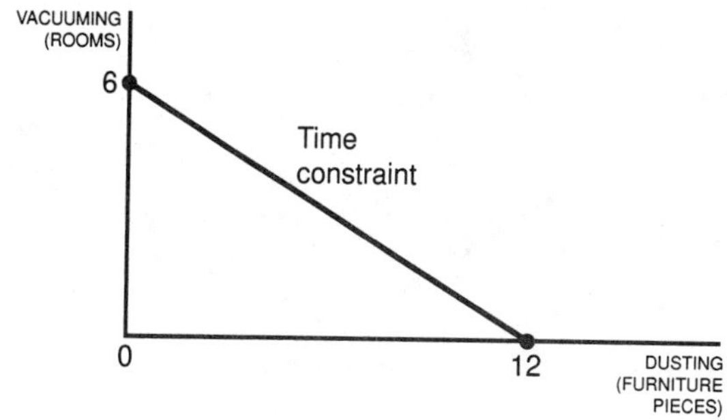

6

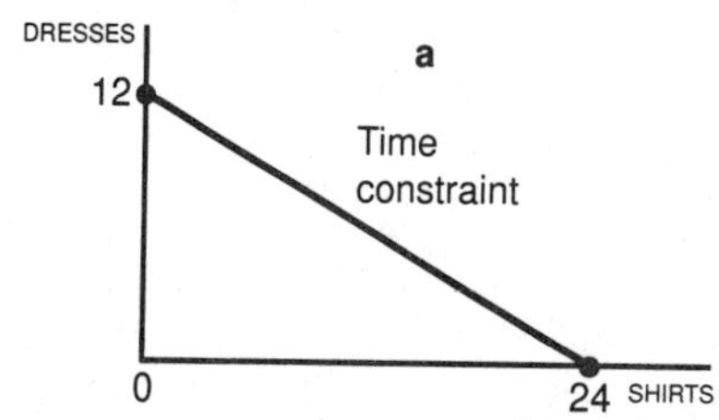

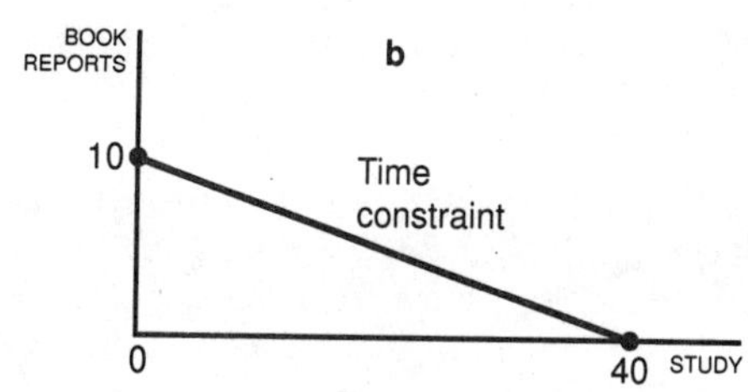

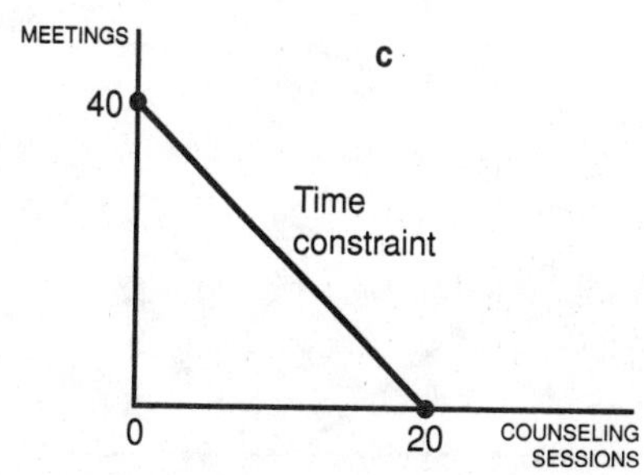

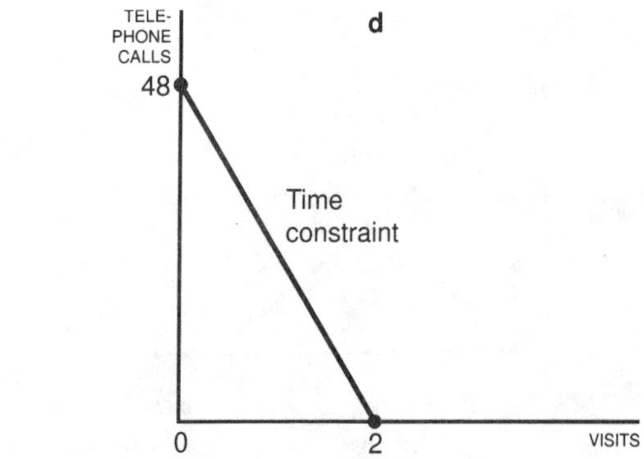

8

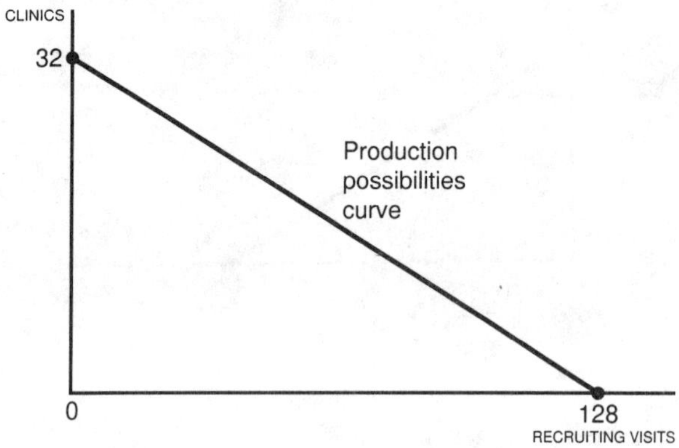

9

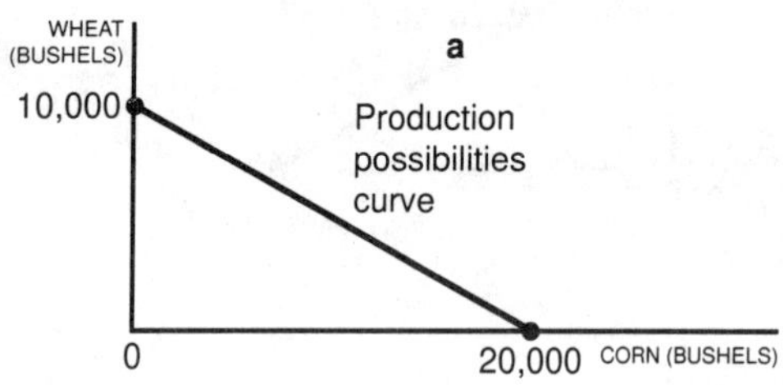

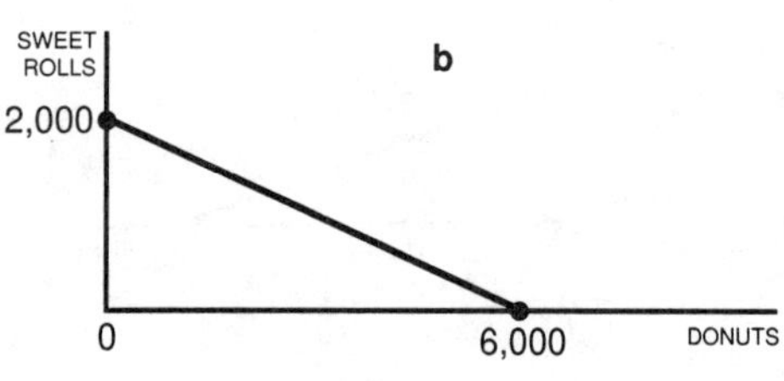

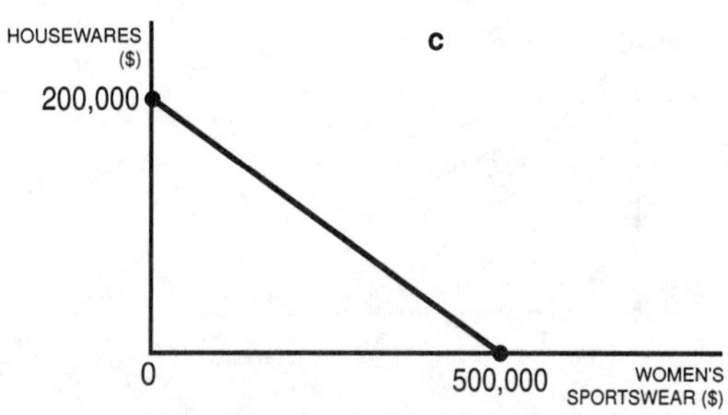

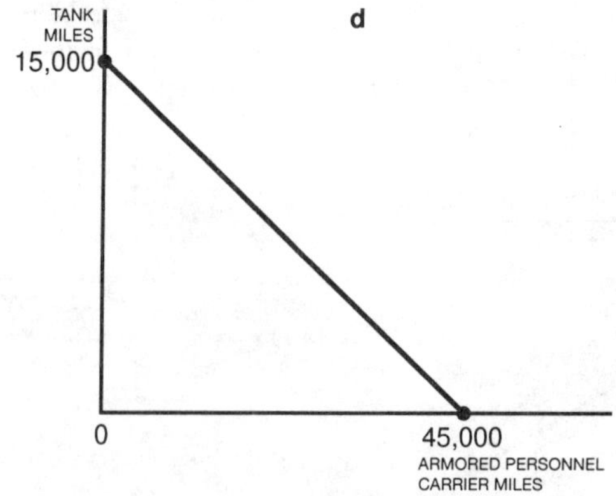

11

Reduction in bicycle thefts	Reduction in thefts of stereo equipment
0	36
25	31
45	25
60	18
70	10
75	0

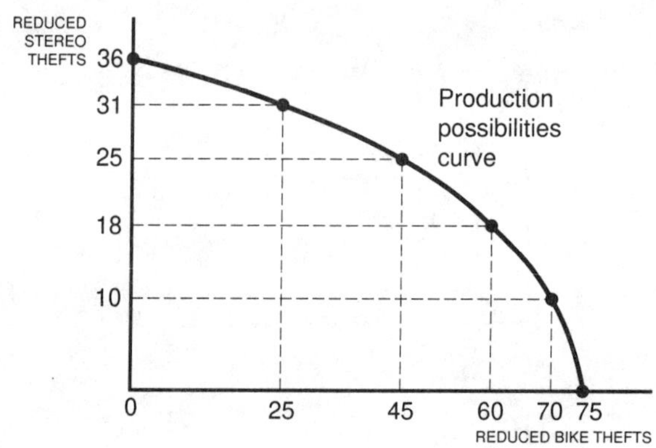

12

Reduced number of truck breakdowns	Reduced number of forklift breakdowns
0	6
5	6
9	5
12	3
14	0

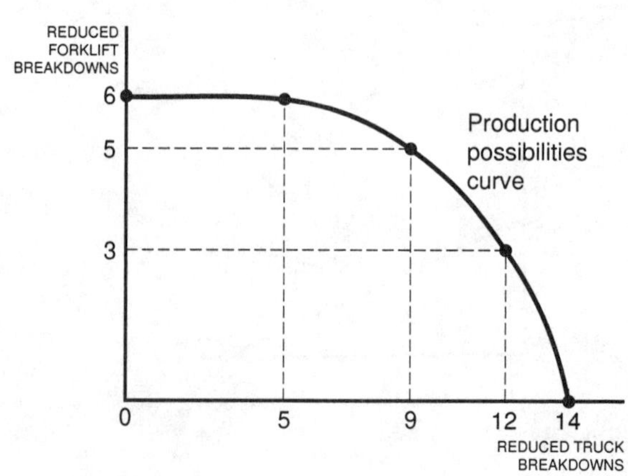

13

Endive (bushels)	Lettuce (bushels)
1,400	5,000
2,400	4,700
3,200	4,200
3,600	3,400
4,000	2,000

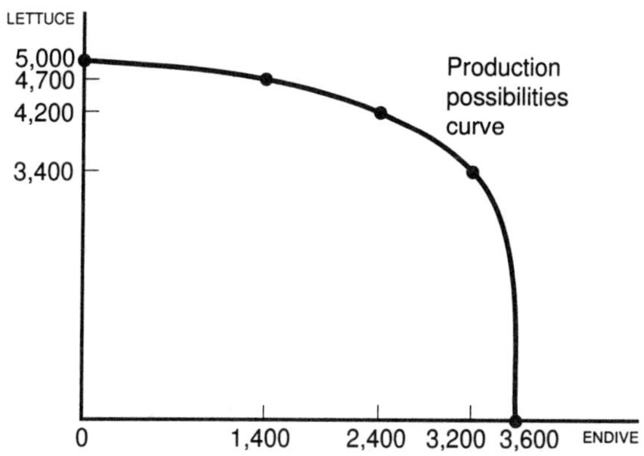

15 *a* Nigeria has a comparative advantage in textiles. Niger has a comparative advantage in sorghum.

b Nigeria will trade its textiles for sorghum from Niger.

c The relative price will lie between 8 bushels of sorghum per bale of textiles and 5 bushels of sorghum per bale of textiles.

16 *a* Greece has a comparative advantage in fish. Poland has a comparative advantage in wheat. Greece will trade its fish for Polish wheat. The relative price will lie between 4/3 bushels of wheat per fish and 2 bushels of wheat per fish.

b The United States has a comparative advantage in heart bypass operations, and Canada in auto parts. The United States will trade heart bypass operations for Canadian auto parts. The relative price will lie between 2 containers of auto parts per operation and 3 containers per operation.

c Thailand has a comparative advantage in finished steel, Laos in scrap steel. Thailand will trade its finished steel for Laotian scrap steel. The relative price will lie between 5 tons of scrap steel per ton of finished steel and 1 ton of scrap steel per ton of finished steel.

d Portugal has a comparative advantage in wine, Great Britain in wool. British wool will be traded for Portuguese wine. The relative price will lie between 1 bale of wool per barrel of wine and 2 bales per barrel of wine.

18 Choose, for example, 6 bushels of sorghum per bale of textiles as the relative price. Nigeria can produce 100 bales of textiles and trade 20 to Niger for 120 bushels of sorghum. The point (80, 120) lies outside its production possibilities curve. Niger can produce 400 bushels of sorghum and trade 120 bushels to Nigeria for 20 bales of textiles. The point (20, 280) lies outside its production possibilities curve.

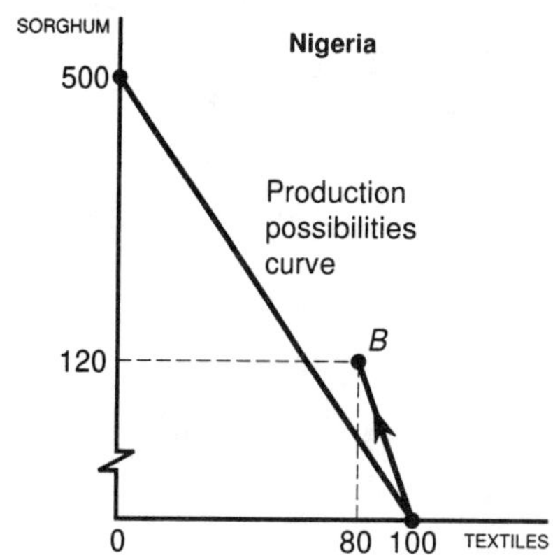

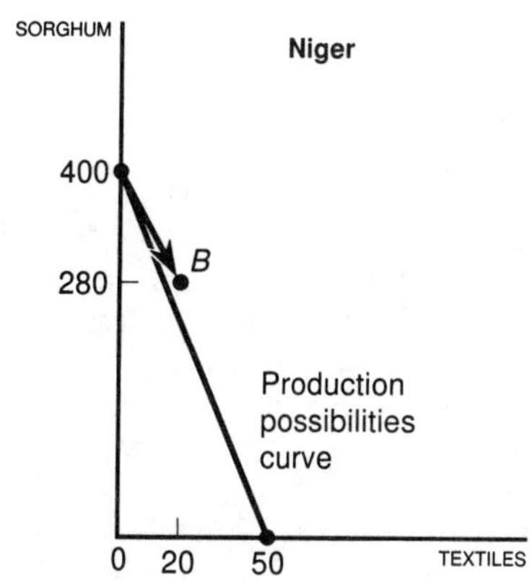

Chapter 3

THE PRICE SYSTEM

Chapter Review

Trade, the markets in which it occurs, and the gains it provides for both buyers and sellers are all important ideas from Chapter 2. Chapter 3 builds the basic model of markets, which is the supply and demand model. The focus is on prices and quantities—how they are determined and how they change when other factors change. It also applies the supply and demand model to major areas of concern to economists: what happens to the quantity demanded or supplied when prices change, and what happens when prices do not adjust, as when the government sets price floors or ceilings.

ESSENTIAL CONCEPTS

1 Households and firms communicate through prices. Prices measure the scarcity of resources and commodities, and high prices give incentives to economize. Prices are determined on markets through the interplay of supply and demand.

2 Consumers **demand** goods and services. They are willing and able to pay, and given a price, they will buy a certain quantity. Several factors influence demand, but the most important is **price.** As the price falls, people buy more of the good or service; as the price rises, they purchase less. The entire relationship between the price and the quantity that a person buys is called the individual **demand curve.**

3 Adding all the individual demand curves gives the **market demand curve.** For every price, ask how much each individual will buy. Add these quantities. The result is the market demand curve, which shows the total amount of the good that will be purchased by all individuals at each price.

4 Many factors affect the demand curve, including changes in income, prices of substitutes and complements, the composition of the population, and people's tastes. This is only a partial list. When one of these factors—or anything else that affects the willingness to pay for the good—changes, the entire demand curve shifts. This shift must be distinguished from the effect of a change in price. When price changes there is a movement along the given demand curve.

5 Firms **supply** goods and services. They are willing and able to produce and sell the good, and at a given price, they will sell a certain quantity. Several factors influence the supply, but the most important is price. As the price rises, producers will supply more; as the price falls, producers will supply less. The entire relationship between the price and the quantity that the producer will sell is called the individual **supply curve.**

6 Adding up all of the individual supply curves gives the **market supply curve.** For every price, ask how much each producer will sell. Add these quantities. The result is the market supply curve, which shows how much of the good will be sold by all producers at each price.

7 Supply is affected by changes in technology and input prices—more generally, anything that causes costs to change. When one of these factors changes, the supply curve shifts. When price changes, on the other hand, there is a movement along the given supply curve.

8 The price at which consumers want to buy exactly the quantity that firms want to sell is the **equilibrium price.** This quantity, which is the same for demand and supply, is the **equilibrium quantity.** It is an equilibrium because there are no forces that would cause it to change. If the price were higher than the equilibrium price, firms would want to sell more than consumers would buy. Unable to sell all of their goods, many firms would compete, by lowering prices, to attract the relatively few consumers. Because this higher price would change, it is not an equilibrium. Similarly, if the price were lower than the equilibrium price, consumers would want to buy more than firms would sell. Seeing the glut of consumers, firms would raise their prices. In sum, if the price is above equilibrium, it falls; if it is below equilibrium, it rises. When price equals the equilibrium price, it does not change.

9 When price falls, quantity demanded increases. If the demand curve is steep, the increase in quantity is smaller than it would be if the curve were flat. Although it might seem natural to measure how the quantity responds to price changes by the slope of the demand curve, economists employ the concept of **elasticity.** They do so because elasticity will produce the same measure no matter what units are used. The **price elasticity of demand** is the percentage change in the quantity demanded brought about by a 1 percent change in price.

10 The price elasticity of demand is greater when there are good, close substitutes available. Usually it is greater when the price is higher, because at higher prices, only those who consider the good essential remain in the market. Both the price elasticity of demand and the **price elasticity of supply** are greater in the long run because individuals and firms have more time to find substitutes and make adjustments. The price elasticity of supply is the percentage change in the quantity supplied brought about by a 1 percent change in price. It is the basic measure of how sensitive the quantity supplied is to changes in price. Typical supply curves are elastic when output is low and excess capacity abounds and inelastic when high output requires full capacity. Elasticity is greater in the long run.

11 **Price ceilings,** when set below the market-clearing price, lead to shortages, which means that the quantity demanded exceeds the quantity supplied. **Price floors,** when set above the market-clearing price, result in surpluses; in this case, the quantity demanded is less than the quantity supplied. In each case, the quantity actually exchanged is less than it is at the market-clearing price. Price is determined by both supply and demand. It is what the market charges consumers for another unit of the good. If supply is abundant, the price may be quite low, even though consumers derive great value from consuming the good. Price equals the marginal value, not the total value, of a good.

BEHIND THE ESSENTIAL CONCEPTS

1 The demand curve is the entire range, or schedule, that indicates how many goods will be purchased at each price. At a given price, this number is called the quantity demanded. In diagrams of demand curves, the quantity demanded is measured along the horizontal axis. To find the quantity demanded, simply read it off the demand curve at the current price. Economists, students, and sometimes professors are sloppy and say "change in demand" without being clear whether they mean a shift in the demand curve or a change in the quantity demanded. The latter is brought about by a change in price, and it involves only a movement along the same demand curve. To guard against confusion in stressful situations (like tests!), say "demand curve" when you refer to the entire schedule of prices and quantities and "quantity demanded" when you want to indicate the number of goods purchased.

2 It is very important to understand why the market demand curve is drawn as it is. When the price rises, the market quantity demanded falls for two reasons. First, each individual buys less. The principle of substitution says that other available goods and services can serve as alternatives, and at higher prices, people switch to consume these substitutes. Second, some individuals find the price to be too high altogether, and they leave the market completely. When the price falls, the opposite happens. People substitute away from other goods and buy more of the one with the lower price. Furthermore, the lower price attracts new consumers to the market.

3 The market supply curve slopes upward. This means that as the price rises, more is offered for sale. Again, there are two reasons. First, firms are willing to sell more at higher prices. Second, higher prices attract new products to the market.

4 Other factors that shift the demand curve include consumer income, tastes, prices of substitutes and complements, and the composition of the population. The supply curve shifts with changes in technology or input prices. While these factors are the most common causes of shifts, they do not comprise a complete list. Anything that affects the willingness and ability to pay for goods shifts the demand curve, and anything that affects costs shifts the supply curve. For example, if it rains in April, the supply of crops may increase, and the demand for umbrellas may also increase.

5 Successful supply and demand analysis proceeds in four steps:

a Start with an equilibrium.

b Figure out which curve shifts.
c Shift the curve and find the new equilibrium.
d Compare the price and quantity at the original and new equilibria.

Be careful to avoid a common pitfall. Suppose you are asked to show the effect of a change in tastes that shifts demand to the right. The failing student's analysis goes like this: "Demand shifts to the right; this increases quantity and price, but the increase in price leads producers to want to supply more, so the supply also shifts to the right." What is wrong with this answer? Stop before the "but." True, the demand shift does raise price and quantity, but that is the end of the story. The increase in price does lead producers to want to supply more. As they supply more, there is a movement along the supply curve, but not a shift. Changes in the price of a good *never shift* the demand curve for that good or the supply curve for that good; rather, changes in the price of a good cause a *movement* along the demand curve or supply curve. There is more discussion on this point and lots of practice problems in the "Doing Economics" section of this chapter.

6 The concept of elasticity appears many times throughout the text, and is worth mastering. Suppose that price falls by 1 percent. We know that quantity will increase as consumers substitute toward the lower price, but by how much? The price elasticity provides the answer. It is the percent change in quantity brought on by a 1 percent change in price.

7 Price ceilings only make a difference if they are set below the market-clearing price (where the supply and demand curves intersect). A price ceiling set above the market-clearing price has no effect. Similarly, a price floor set below the market-clearing price does not do anything.

8 Price floors and ceilings also affect the quantity traded in the market. If there is a price ceiling, then the quantity demanded exceeds the quantity supplied. The supply is the short side of the market, and although consumers would like to buy more of the good, the quantity traded is what producers are willing to sell. This is shown in Figure 3.1A. With price floors, the opposite is true. The demand is the short side of the market, and the quantity traded equals the amount that consumers are willing to buy, as shown in panel B. In each case, we say that the short side of the market determines the actual quantity traded, and the actual quantity traded is less than the market-clearing quantity.

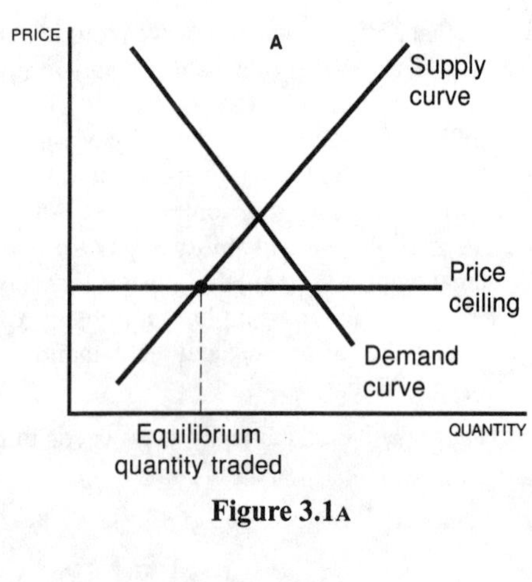

Figure 3.1A

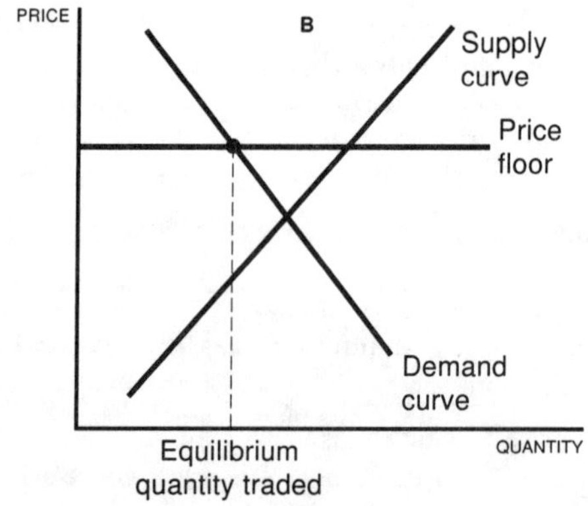

Figure 3.1B

SELF-TEST

True or False

1 Prices provide incentives to help the economy use resources efficiently.

2 As the price falls, the quantity demanded decreases.

3 The market demand curve is the sum of the quantities and prices of each individual demand.

4 The individual demand curve is an example of an equilibrium relationship.

5 One reason why the supply curve slopes upward is that at higher prices, more producers enter the market.

6 In equilibrium, there is neither excess demand nor excess supply.

7 If the price is above the equilibrium price, consumers can buy as much as they are willing.

8 If the price is below the equilibrium price, sellers cannot sell as much as they are willing.

9 The law of supply and demand says that the equilibrium price will be that price at which the quantity demanded equals the quantity supplied.

10 The price elasticity of demand is greater for goods and services that have better close substitutes.

11 The price elasticity of demand is always constant along the demand curve.

12 A price ceiling set above the equilibrium price will have no effect on the market.

13 A price ceiling set below the equilibrium price will have no effect on the market.

14 A price floor set above the equilibrium price in the milk market will lead to a surplus of milk.

15 The price of diamonds is higher than the price of water because diamonds have a higher value in use.

Multiple Choice

1 Market prices

a measure scarcity;
b communicate information;
c provide incentives;
d all of the above;
e a and b.

2 The individual demand curve for a good or service

a gives the quantity of the good or service the individual would purchase at each price;
b gives the equilibrium price in the market;
c shows which other goods or services will be substituted according to the principle of substitution;
d all of the above;
e a and c.

3 If you knew the individual demand curves of each consumer, you could find the market demand curve by

a taking the average quantity demanded at each price;
b adding all of the prices;
c adding up, at each price, the quantities purchased by each individual;
d taking the average of all prices;
e none of the above.

4 As the price rises, the quantity demanded decreases along an individual demand curve because

a individuals substitute other goods and services;
b some individuals exit the market;
c some individuals enter the market;
d the quantity supplied increases;
e a and b

5 As the price rises, the quantity demanded decreases along the market demand curve because

a individuals substitute other goods and services;
b some individuals exit the market;
c some individuals enter the market;
d the quantity supplied increases;
e a and b

6 As the price rises, the quantity supplied increases along an individual supply curve because

a higher prices give firms incentives to sell more;
b the principle of substitution leads firms to substitute other goods and services;
c the market supply curve is the sum of all the quantities produced by individual firms at each price;
d b and c;
e none of the above.

7 If the market price is below equilibrium, then

a there is excess demand;
b there is excess supply;
c consumers will want to raise the price;
d firms will want to lower the price;
e all of the above.

8 If the market price is at equilibrium, then

a the quantity that consumers are willing to buy equals the quantity that producers are willing to sell;
b there is excess demand;
c there is excess supply;
d there are no forces that will change the price;
e a and d.

9 If the market price is above equilibrium, then

a there is excess supply;
b there is excess demand;
c firms will not be able to sell all that they would like;
d consumers will not be able to buy all that they would like;
e a and c.

10 Stationary exercise bicycles and stair-stepper machines are substitutes, according to the aerobically correct. An increase in the price of exercise bicycles will

a shift the demand for stair-stepper machines to the right;
b increase the price of stair-stepper machines;
c increase the quantity of stair-stepper machine sales;
d all of the above;
e none of the above.

11 As people have grown more concerned about saturated fat in their diets, the demand for beef has shifted to the left. The quantity of beef sold has also fallen. This change is a

a movement along the demand curve for beef;
b shift in the supply curve for beef;
c movement along the supply curve for beef;
d a and b;
e none of the above.

12 Which of the following is not a source of shifts in market demand?

a an increase in consumer income;
b a change in tastes;
c an increase in the population;
d a technological advance;
e all are sources of shifts.

13 If the price of an input falls,

a supply shifts to the left;
b demand shifts to the right;
c demand shifts to the left;
d supply shifts to the right;
e none of the above.

14 The quantity demanded is more sensitive to price changes when

a supply is relatively inelastic;
b close substitutes are available;
c consumers are rational;
d consumers are relatively more informed about quality for some goods;
e all of the above.

15 Suppose that price falls by 10 percent and the quantity demanded rises by 20 percent. The price elasticity of demand is

a 2;
b 1;
c 0;
d 1/2;
e none of the above.

16 Suppose that the price elasticity of demand is 1/3. If price rises by 30 percent, how does the quantity demanded change?

a Quantity demanded rises by 10 percent.
b Quantity demanded falls by 10 percent.
c Quantity demanded rises by 90 percent.
d Quantity demanded falls by 90 percent.
e Quantity demanded does not change.

17 The long-run elasticity of supply is greater than the short-run elasticity of supply because

a in the long run, the stock of machines and buildings can adjust;
b in the long run, new firms can enter and existing firms can exit the industry;
c in the long run, customers can discover substitutes;
d a and b;
e all of the above.

18 A price ceiling set below the equilibrium price will

a create a shortage;
b increase the price;
c create a surplus;
d a and b;
e have no effect.

19 A price ceiling set above the equilibrium price will

a create a shortage;
b increase the price;
c create a surplus;
d a and b;
e have no effect.

20 A price ceiling set below the equilibrium price will

a increase the quantity demanded;
b increase the quantity supplied;
c decrease the quantity supplied;
d a and c;
e have no effect.

Completion

1 __________ is defined as what is given in exchange for a good or service.

2 The quantity of the good or service purchased at each price is given by the __________.

3 The quantity of the good or service offered for sale at each price is given by the __________.

4 The law of supply and demand says that at the equilibrium price, the __________ equals the __________.

5 An increase in the price of a good leads to a __________ its demand curve.

6 A change in technology leads to a __________ the supply curve.

7 The percentage change in the quantity demanded as a result of a 1 percent price change is called the __________.

8 If the price elasticity of demand lies between 0 and 1, then we say that demand is relatively __________.

9 A price floor set above the equilibrium price will create a __________.

10 The minimum wage is an example of a __________.

Answers to Self-Test

True or False

1 t	4 f	7 t	10 t	13 f
2 f	5 t	8 f	11 f	14 t
3 f	6 t	9 t	12 t	15 f

Multiple Choice

1 d	6 a	11 c	16 b
2 a	7 a	12 d	17 d
3 c	8 e	13 d	18 a
4 a	9 e	14 b	19 e
5 e	10 d	15 a	20 d

Completion

1 Price
2 demand curve
3 supply curve
4 quantity demanded, quantity supplied
5 movement along
6 shift in
7 price elasticity of demand
8 inelastic
9 surplus
10 price floor

Doing Economics: Tools and Practice Problems

Five techniques receive attention in this section. The first technique shows how to add individual demand and individual supply curves to get market demand and market supply curves. The next technique involves finding the equilibrium price and quantity, where the market clears. Then, some general instructions about supply and demand analysis are given and developed in several problems. We move on to calculate elasticity and finally to analyze the effects of price controls.

MARKET DEMAND AND MARKET SUPPLY

When the price falls, individual demanders want to buy more and individual suppliers want to sell less. These individual demand and supply curves are behavioral relationships. The market demand and market supply curves are found by adding up all of these individual demands and supplies. Tool Kit 3.1 shows how to do this.

Tool Kit 3.1: Calculating Market Demand and Supply

The market demand is the sum of the individual demands. The market supply is the sum of the individual supplies. This tool kit shows how to add the individual demands and supplies.

Step one: Make two columns. Label the left-hand column "Price" and the right-hand column "Quantity."

Price	Quantity

Step two: Choose the highest price at which goods are demanded. Enter this in the first row of the price column.

Price	Quantity
pl	

Step three: Find how many goods each individual will purchase. Add these quantities. Enter the total in the first row of the quantity column.

Price	Quantity
pl	$Q_1 = Q_a + Q_b + Q_c + \cdots$

Step four: Choose the second highest price, and continue the process.

1 (Worked problem: market demand) The individual demands of Jason and Kyle for economics tutoring are given in Table 3.1. Calculate the market demand. (Jason and Kyle are the only two individuals in this market.)

Table 3.1

Jason		*Kyle*	
Price	*Quantity*	*Price*	*Quantity*
$10	6	$10	4
$ 8	8	$ 8	5
$ 6	10	$ 6	6
$ 4	12	$ 4	7

Step-by-step solution

Step one: Make and label two columns.

Price	Quantity

Step two: Choose the highest price. This is $10. Enter this in the first row under price.

Price	Quantity
$10	

Step three: Find the market quantity. Jason would buy 6; Kyle would buy 4. The total is 6 + 4 = 10. Enter 10 in the corresponding quantity column.

Price	Quantity
$10	10

Step four: Repeat the process. The next lower price is $8. Jason would buy 8; Kyle would buy 5. The total is 8 + 5 = 13. Enter $8 and 13 in the appropriate columns.

Price	Quantity
$10	10
$ 8	13

Continue. The entire market demand is given below.

Price	Quantity
$10	10
$ 8	13
$ 6	16
$ 4	19

2 (Practice problem: market demand) Gorman's tomatoes are purchased by pizza sauce makers, by submarine sandwich shops, and by vegetable canners. The demands for each are given in Table 3.2. Find the market demand.

Table 3.2

Pizza sauce		*Submarine shops*		*Vegetable canners*	
Price	*Quantity (bushels)*	*Price*	*Quantity (bushels)*	*Price*	*Quantity (bushels)*
$5	25	$5	5	$5	55
$4	35	$4	6	$4	75
$3	40	$3	7	$3	100
$2	50	$2	7	$2	150
$1	80	$1	7	$1	250

3 (Practice problem: market supply) The technique for finding the market supply curve is the same as for the market demand. Simply sum the quantities supplied at each price. There are three law firms that will draw up partnership contracts in the town of Pullman. Their individual supply curves are given in Table 3.3. Find the market supply curve.

Table 3.3

Jones		*Jones and Jones*		*Jones, Jones, and Jones*	
Price	*Quantity*	*Price*	*Quantity*	*Price*	*Quantity*
$200	0	$200	6	$200	4
$220	0	$220	8	$220	8
$240	0	$240	12	$240	10
$260	8	$260	24	$260	11

EQUILIBRIUM

In equilibrium, markets clear. The market price will settle where the quantity that demanders would like to purchase exactly equals the quantity that suppliers choose to sell. Tool Kit 3.2 shows how to find the equilibrium.

Tool Kit 3.2: Finding the Equilibrium Price and Quantity

The equilibrium price in the demand and supply model is the price at which the buyers want to buy exactly the quantity that sellers want to sell. In other words, the quantity demanded equals the quantity supplied. The equilibrium quantity in the market is just this quantity. Here is how to find the equilibrium in a market.

Step one: Choose a price. Find the quantity demanded at that price and the quantity supplied.

Step two: If the quantity demanded equals the quantity supplied, the price is the equilibrium. Stop.

Step three: If the quantity demanded exceeds the quantity supplied, there is a shortage. Choose a higher price and repeat step one. If the quantity demanded is less than the quantity supplied, there is a surplus. Choose a lower price and repeat step one.

Step four: Continue until the equilibrium price is found.

4 (Worked problem: equilibrium price and quantity) The supply curve and demand curve for cinder blocks are given in Table 3.4. The quantity column indicates the number of blocks sold in one year.

Table 3.4

Demand		*Supply*	
Price	*Quantity*	*Price*	*Quantity*
$2.00	50,000	$2.00	200,000
$1.50	70,000	$1.50	160,000
$1.00	100,000	$1.00	100,000
$0.75	150,000	$0.75	50,000
$0.50	250,000	$0.50	0

a Find the equilibrium price and quantity.
b If the price is $1.50, is the market in equilibrium? Will there be a surplus or a shortage? If so, what is the size of the surplus or shortage? What will happen to the price? Why?
c If the price is $0.75, is the market in equilibrium? Will there be a surplus or a shortage? If so, what is the size of the surplus or shortage? What will happen to the price? Why?

Step-by-step solution

Step one (a): Choose a price. At a price of, say, $2.00, the quantity demanded is 50,000 and the quantity supplied is 200,000.

Step two: The quantities are not equal.

Step three: There is a surplus. The equilibrium price will be lower.

Step four: Continue. Try other prices until the quantity supplied equals the quantity demanded. The equilibrium price is $1.00, where the quantity equals 100,000. We can now see the answers to parts b and c.

Step five (b): If the price is $1.50, the quantity demanded is 70,000, and it is less than the quantity supplied, which is 160,000. There is a surplus of 90,000 (160,000 – 70,000). The price will fall because producers will be unable to sell all that they want.

Step six (c): If the price is $0.75, the quantity demanded is 150,000, and it is greater than the quantity supplied, which is 50,000. There is a shortage of 100,000 (150,000 – 50,000). The price will rise because producers will see that buyers are unable to buy all that they want.

5 (Practice problem: equilibrium price and quantity) The demand curve and supply curve in the market for billboard space along Interstate 6 are given in Table 3.5. The price is the monthly rental price. The quantity column shows numbers of billboards.

Table 3.5

Demand		*Supply*	
Price	*Quantity*	*Price*	*Quantity*
$100	5	$100	25
$ 80	8	$ 80	21
$ 60	11	$ 60	16
$ 40	14	$ 40	14
$ 20	22	$ 20	3

a Find the equilibrium price and quantity.
b If the price is $20, is the market in equilibrium? Will there be a surplus or a shortage? If so, what is the size of the surplus or shortage? What will happen to the price? Why?
c If the price is $80, is the market in equilibrium? Will there be a surplus or a shortage? If so, what is the size of the surplus or shortage? What will happen to the price? Why?

6 (Practice problem: equilibrium price and quantity) Find the equilibrium price and quantity in each of the following markets.

a The supply and demand curves for new soles (shoe repair) are given in Table 3.6.

Table 3.6

Demand		*Supply*	
Price	*Quantity*	*Price*	*Quantity*
$35	17	$35	53
$30	21	$30	37
$25	25	$25	25
$20	30	$20	15
$15	35	$15	0

b The supply and demand curves for seat cushions are given in Table 3.7.

Table 3.7

Demand		*Supply*	
$8	4	$8	32
$7	8	$7	28
$6	12	$6	22
$5	16	$5	19
$4	17	$4	17

SUPPLY AND DEMAND

Supply and demand is probably the most useful technique in microeconomics. Economists use it to study how markets are affected by changes, such as tastes, technology, government programs, and many others. Supply and demand offers a wealth of insights into the workings of the economy. It is very important to master the procedure spelled out in Tool Kit 3.3.

Tool Kit 3.3: Using Supply and Demand

Supply and demand analysis provides excellent answers to questions of the following form: "What is the effect of a change in __________ on the market for __________?" You are well on your way to success as a student of economics if you stick closely to this procedure in answering such questions.

Step one: Begin with an equilibrium in the relevant market. Label the horizontal axis as the quantity of the good or service and the vertical axis as the price. Draw a demand and a supply curve and label them *D* and *S*, respectively.

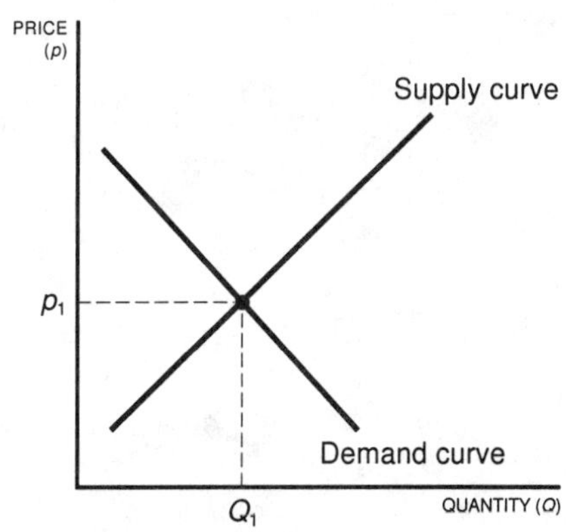

Step two: Figure out whether the change shifts the supply curve, the demand curve, or neither.

Step three: Shift the appropriate curve.

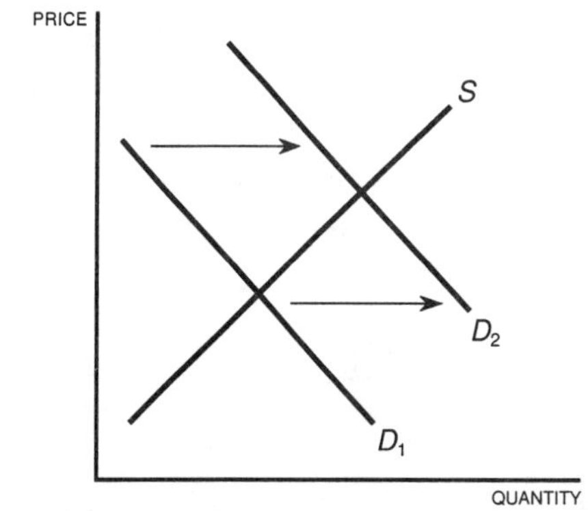

Step four: Find the new equilibrium, and compare it with the original one.

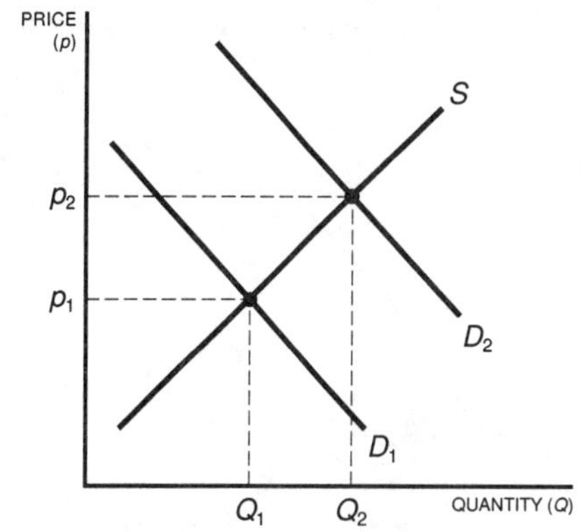

7 (Worked problem: using supply and demand) In response to concern about the fumes emitted by dry cleaning establishments, the Environmental Protection Agency has issued regulations requiring expensive filtering systems. How will this regulation affect the dry cleaning market?

Step-by-step solution

Step one: Start with an equilibrium.

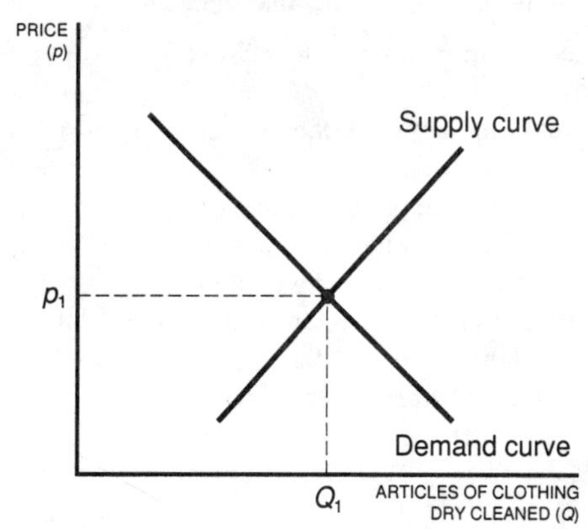

Step two: Figure out which curve shifts. The mandated filtering systems increase the dry cleaning firm's costs, shifting the supply to the left.

Step three: Shift the curve.

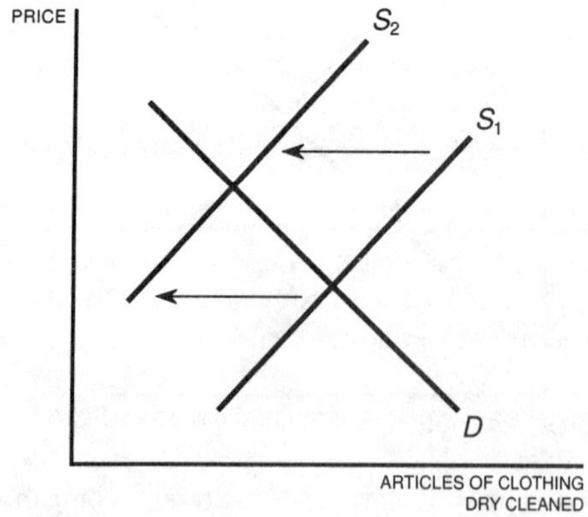

Step four: Find the new equilibrium and compare. The effect of the regulation is to raise the price and lower the quantity of clothes dry cleaned.

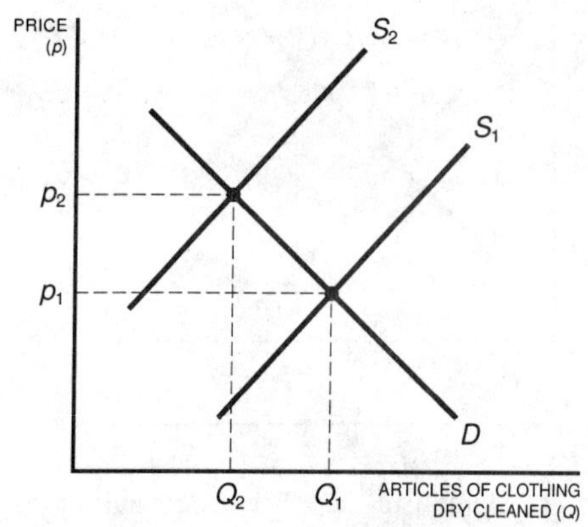

8 (Practice problem: using supply and demand) As the oil market comes to the realization that Kuwait's production will not return to prewar levels, the price of oil has increased by $4 per barrel. Explain the effect of this oil price increase on the market for natural gas.

9 (Practice problem: using supply and demand) For each of the following, show the effects on price and quantity. Draw the diagrams and follow the procedure.

a an increase in income in the market for a normal good
b a decrease in income in the market for a normal good
c an increase in the price of a substitute
d a decrease in the price of a substitute
e an increase in the price of a complement
f a decrease in the price of an complement
g an increase in the price of an input
h a decrease in the price of an input
i an improvement in technology

ELASTICITY

When price changes, how much does quantity change? Economists answer this question with the concept of elasticity. The price elasticity of demand measures how responsive quantity demand is to changes in the price. Similarly, the elasticity of supply measures the responsiveness of quantity supplied to price changes. Tool Kit 3.4 shows how to calculate elasticity. The problems focus on elasticity of demand and illustrate the relationship between elasticity and total revenue.

Tool Kit 3.4: Calculating Elasticity

Elasticity measures how sensitive the quantity is to changes in price. Follow these steps to calculate elasticity.

Step one: To find the elasticity between two points on the demand or supply curve, let p_1 and Q_1 be the price and quantity at the first point and p_2 and Q_2 be the price and quantity at the second point.

Step two: Substitute the prices and quantities into the formula

elasticity = $(Q_1 - Q_2)(p_1 + p_2)/(Q_1 + Q_2)(p_1 - p_2)$.

10 (Worked problem: calculating elasticity) The demand curve for bulletin boards is given below.

Price	Quantity
$35	800
$30	1,000
$25	1,200
$20	1,300

a Calculate total revenue for each price.
b Calculate the price elasticity of demand between $35 and $30, between $30 and $25, and between $25 and $20. Does elasticity change along this demand?
c What is the relationship between elasticity and total revenue?

Step-by-step solution

Step one (a): Total revenue at $35 is 800 × $25 = $28,000. Total revenue at $30 is 1,000 × $30 = $30,000. Continue, and enter the numbers in the table.

Price	Quantity	Total revenue
$35	800	$28,000
$30	1,000	$30,000
$25	1,200	$30,000
$20	1,300	$26,000

Step two (b): Let $35 = p_1, 800 = Q_1, $30 = p_2, and 1,000 = Q_2. Substituting into the formula gives

elasticity = (35 + 30)(1,000 – 800)/(800 + 1,000)(35 – 30)
= 1.44, which is elastic.

Step three: Between $30 and $25,

elasticity = (30 + 25)(1,200 – 1,000)/(1,000 + 1,200)(30 – 25)
= 1, which is unitary elastic.

Step four: Between $25 and $20,

elasticity = (25 + 20)(1,300 – 1,200)/(1,200 + 1,300)(25 – 20)
= 0.36, which is inelastic.

Clearly, the elasticity is not constant. The demand curve is less elastic at lower prices.

Step five (c): Between \$35 and \$30, where the demand is elastic, total revenue rises from \$28,000 to \$30,000 as price falls. Between \$30 and \$25, where the demand is unitary elastic, total revenue is constant at \$30,000 as the price falls. Between \$25 and \$20, where the demand is inelastic, total revenue falls from \$30,000 to \$26,000 as the price falls. These numbers show that when price falls, total revenue increases; when demand is elastic, price stays constant when the elasticity of demand equals 1, and falls when demand is inelastic.

11 (Practice problem: calculating elasticity) The demand curve for bookends is given below.

Price	Quantity
\$10	70
\$ 8	90
\$ 6	120
\$ 4	130

a Calculate total revenue for each price.
b Calculate the price elasticity of demand between each of the adjacent prices. Does elasticity change along this demand?
c What is the relationship between elasticity and total revenue?

12 (Practice problem: calculating elasticity) For each of the following, calculate the total revenue for each price and the price elasticity for each price change, and verify the relationship between elasticity and total revenue.

a

Price	Quantity
\$12	6
\$10	8
\$ 8	10
\$ 6	12

b

Price	Quantity
\$100	80
\$ 80	85
\$ 60	90
\$ 40	95

c

Price	Quantity
\$9	10
\$8	8
\$7	6
\$6	4

PRICE CONTROLS

When the government interferes with the law of supply and demand and sets price controls, the effects can be analyzed with the basic method of supply and demand. To see the effects, start with an equilibrium.

The price control (if it is effective) will change the price without changing either the demand curve or the supply curve. The new equilibrium occurs at the price set by the government, but the quantity demanded is read off the demand curve, and the quantity supplied is read off the supply curve. The actual quantity transacted is always the short side of the market (the smaller of the quantity demanded and the quantity supplied).

The basic results of this analysis are that price ceilings, when set below the market-clearing price, lower the price, cause shortages, and reduce the quantity transacted. Price floors, when set above the market-clearing price, raise the price, cause surpluses, and reduce the quantity transacted. Tool Kit 3.5 shows how to use supply and demand to analyze price controls.

Tool Kit 3.5: Using Supply and Demand for Price Controls

The impact of price controls is made clear through the use of supply and demand. This four step procedure shows how to analyze price controls.

Step one: Start with a market-clearing equilibrium.

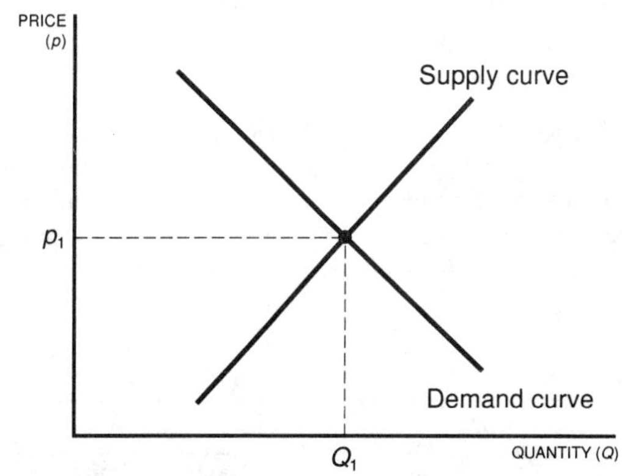

Step two: Identify the controlled price, and decide whether it is a floor or a ceiling.

Step three: Find the new equilibrium price. If it is a price floor set below the market-clearing price or a price ceiling set above the market-clearing price, then the equilibrium is the market-clearing one found in step one. If it is a price floor set above the market-clearing price or a price ceiling set below market clearing, then the controlled price is the equilibrium price.

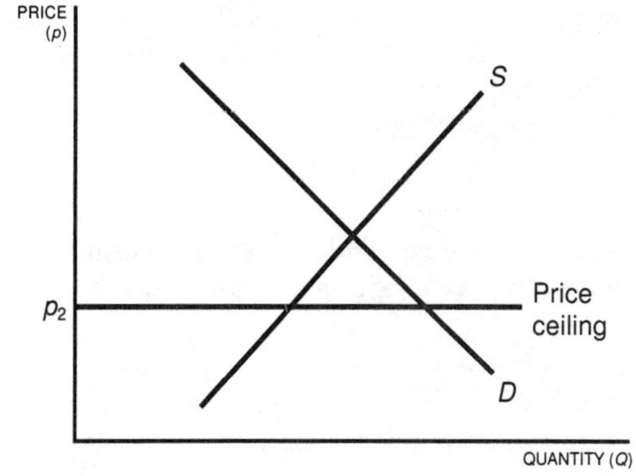

Step four: Determine the shortage or surplus. For a price floor set above the market-clearing price, there is a surplus:

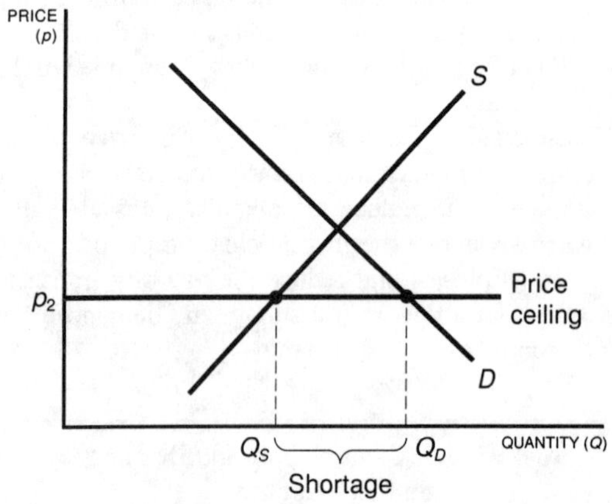

shortage = quantity supplied – quantity demanded.

For a price ceiling set below the market-clearing price, there is a shortage:

surplus = quantity demanded – quantity supplied.

13 (Worked problem: price controls) Dental bills in Yellowville rose again last year. The City Council is considering a bill to place a ceiling on fees that dentists can charge for teeth cleaning. The supply curve and demand curve for teeth cleanings are given in Table 3.8.

Table 3.8

Demand		*Supply*	
Price	*Quantity*	*Price*	*Quantity*
\$65	100	\$65	190
\$60	120	\$60	180
\$55	140	\$55	170
\$50	160	\$50	160
\$45	180	\$45	150
\$40	200	\$40	140

a Find the equilibrium price and quantity for teeth cleanings in Yellowville.

b The City Council passes a price ceiling ordinance, setting the maximum price at \$40 per cleaning. Use supply and demand analysis to determine the effects of the price control.

Step-by-step solution

Step one (a): Find the equilibrium price and quantity. The market clears at a price of \$50 and quantity equal to 160.

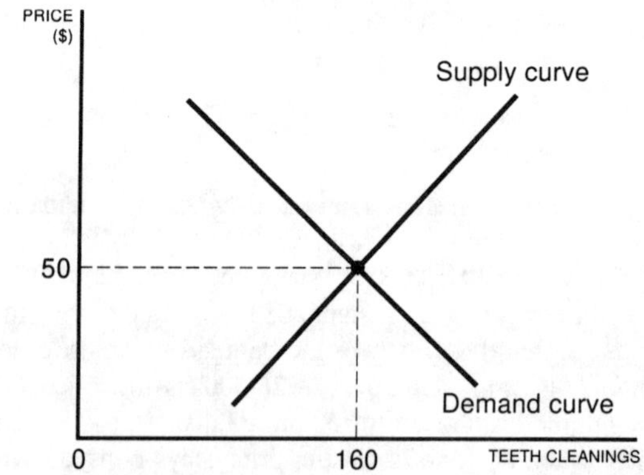

Step two (b): Identify the controlled price and whether it is a floor or a ceiling. The price control is a price ceiling set at \$40.

Step three: Determine the new equilibrium price. The ceiling is below the market-clearing price; therefore, the new price is equal to the ceiling price of \$40.

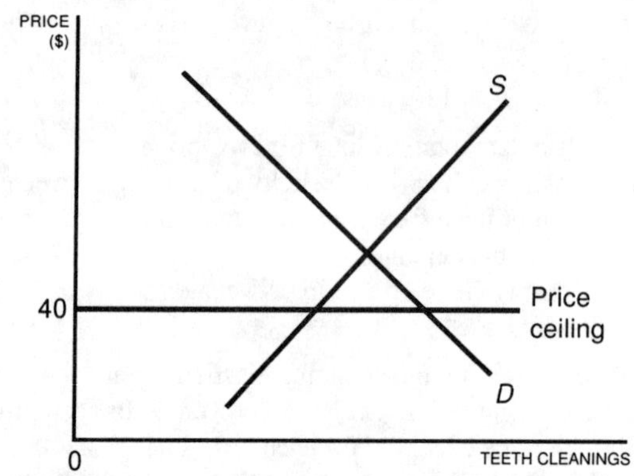

Step four: Determine the shortage or surplus. When the price is \$40, the quantity demanded is 200 and the quantity supplied is 140. Although consumers would like more, there are only 140 cleanings actually performed. This results in a shortage of 200 – 140 = 60 teeth cleanings. The diagram illustrates the solution.

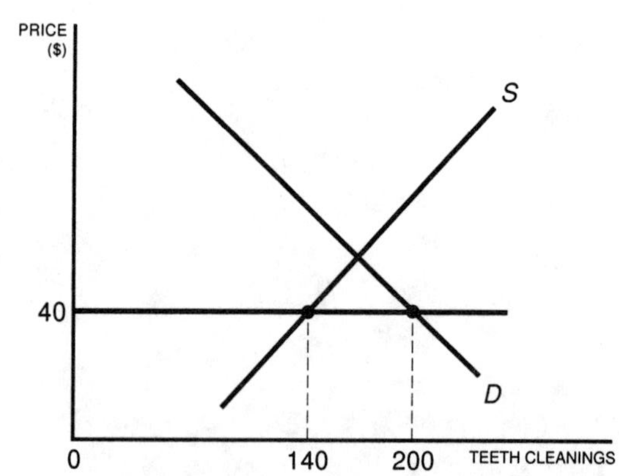

14 (Practice problem: price controls) Many states are considering price ceilings on automobile insurance premiums. In West Dakota, the supply curve and demand curve for automobile insurance policies (\$250 deductible on liability, no collision) are given in Table 3.9.

Table 3.9

Demand		*Supply*	
Price	*Quantity*	*Price*	*Quantity*
$800	1,000	$800	1,800
$750	1,100	$750	1,500
$700	1,200	$700	1,200
$650	1,400	$650	900
$600	1,600	$600	600

a Find the equilibrium price and quantity.
b Suppose that a price ceiling of $650 is imposed. Use supply and demand analysis to determine the effects of the price control.

15 (Practice problem: price controls) Fearful of a restless urban population, Corporal Thug, the new supreme ruler of Costa Guano, attempts to mollify the masses with a wage increase. He mandates that employers must pay at least $8 per day. The supply and demand curves for urban labor are given in Table 3.10.

Table 3.10

Demand		*Supply*	
Wage	*Quantity*	*Wage*	*Quantity*
$8.50	400	$8.50	4,000
$8.00	600	$8.00	3,200
$7.50	700	$7.50	2,600
$7.00	800	$7.00	2,200
$6.50	900	$6.50	1,800
$6.00	1,000	$6.00	1,000

a Find the quantity demanded, the quantity supplied, and the size of the surplus or shortage, if any.
b Democracy comes to Costa Guano! Corporal Thug is overthrown and the minimum wage repealed. Use supply and demand analysis to determine the effects of the price control.

Answers to Problems

2

Price	Quantity (bushels)
$5	85
$4	116
$3	147
$2	207
$1	337

3

Price	Quantity
$200	10
$220	16
$240	22
$260	43

5 *a* Equilibrium price = $40; quantity = 14.
b If the price is $20, there is a shortage of 22 – 3 = 19. The price will be driven up.
c If the price is $80, there is a surplus of 21 – 8 = 13. The price will be driven down.

6 *a* Price = $25; quantity = 25.
b Price = $4; quantity = 17.

8 Oil and natural gas are substitutes, and therefore the demand curve shifts to the right, the price increases, and the quantity increases.

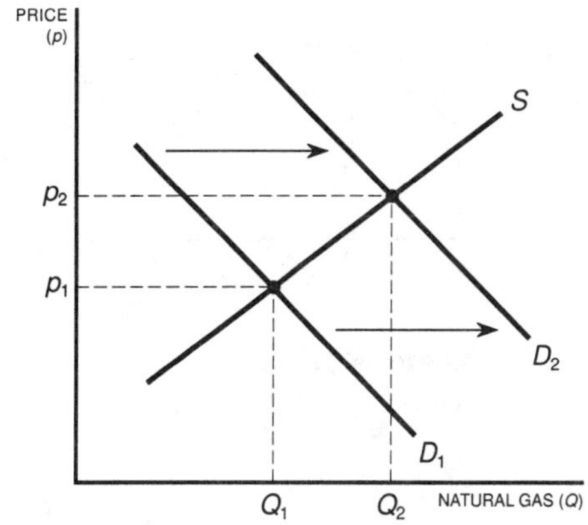

9 *a* Demand shifts to the right, driving the price up and increasing the quantity.

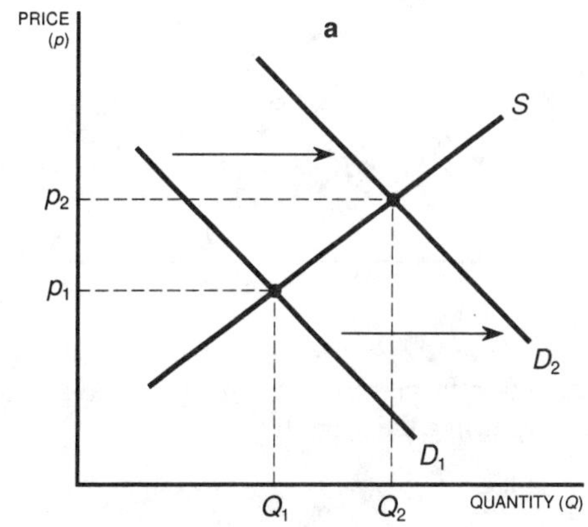

b Demand shifts to the left, driving the price down and decreasing the quantity.

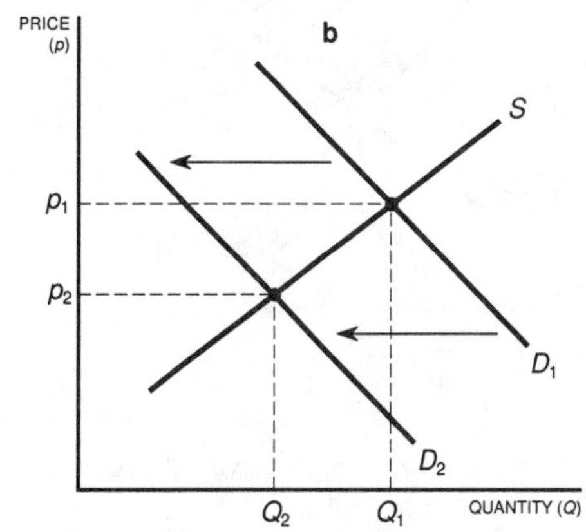

c Demand shifts to the right, driving the price up and increasing the quantity.

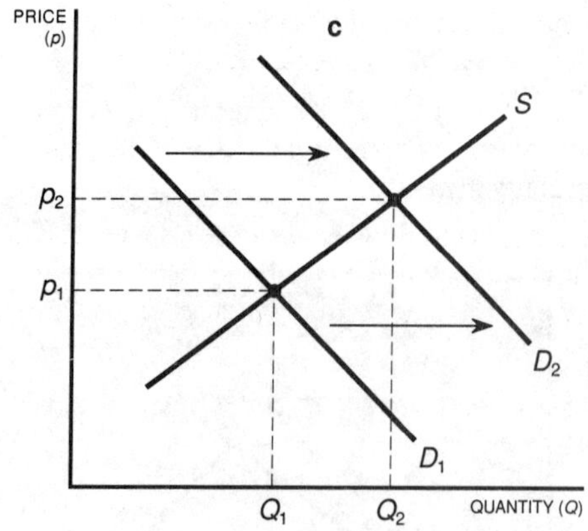

d Demand shifts to the left, driving the price down and decreasing the quantity.

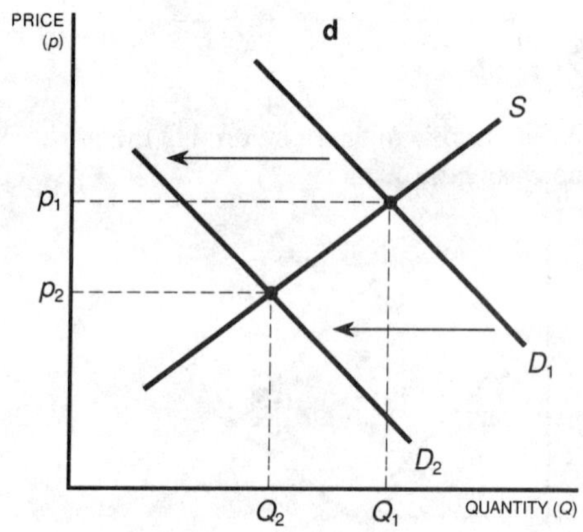

e Demand shifts to the left, driving the price down and decreasing the quantity.

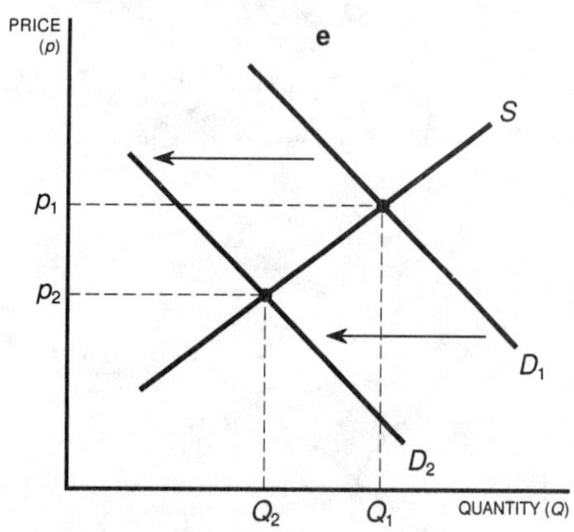

f Demand shifts to the right, driving the price up and increasing the quantity.

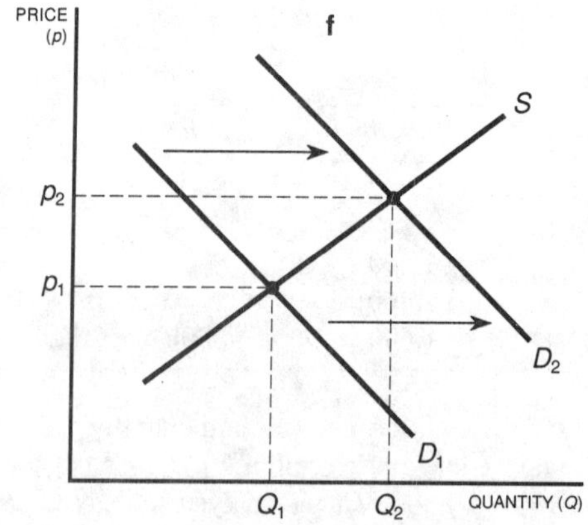

g Supply shifts up (vertically), increasing the price but decreasing the quantity.

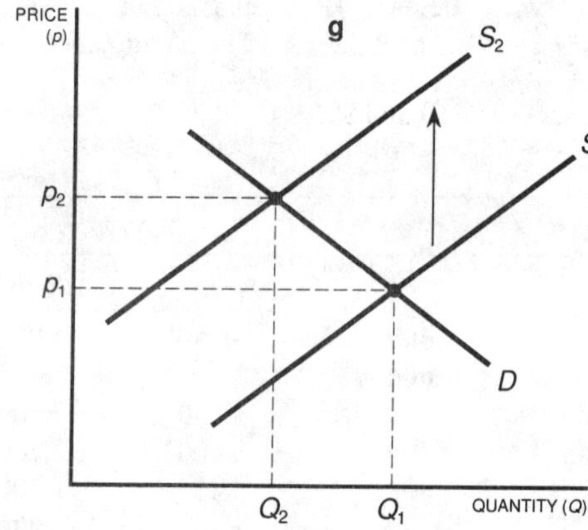

h Supply shifts down (vertically), decreasing the price but increasing the quantity.

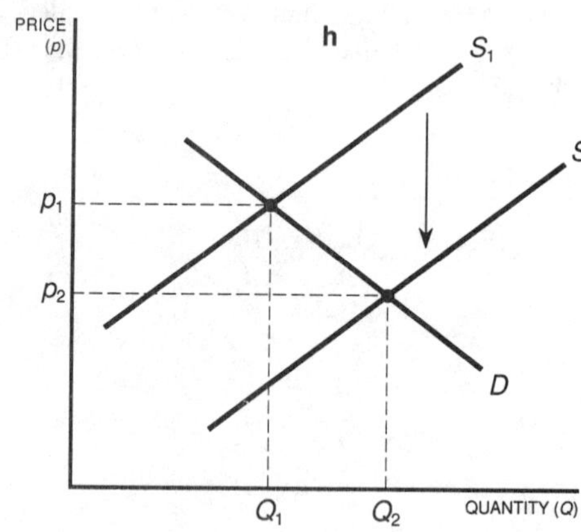

i Supply shifts down (vertically), decreasing the price but increasing the quantity.

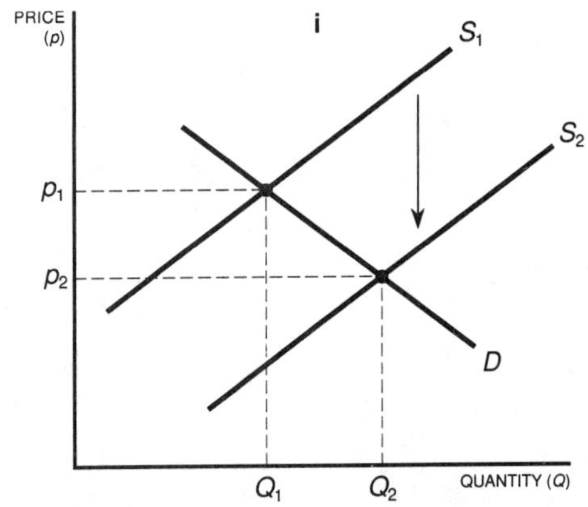

11 *a*

Price	Quantity	Revenue
\$10	70	\$700
\$ 8	90	\$720
\$ 6	120	\$720
\$ 4	130	\$520

b Between \$10 and \$8, elasticity $= (10 + 8)(90 - 70)/(10 - 8)(90 + 70) = 1.125$.
Between \$8 and \$6, elasticity $= (8 + 6)(120 - 90)/(8 - 6)(120 + 90) = 1$.
Between \$6 and \$4, elasticity $= (6 + 4)(130 - 120)/(6 - 4)(130 + 120) = 0.2$.

c When elasticity is 1.125, the demand curve is elastic, and total revenue rises from \$700 to \$720 as price falls. When elasticity is 1, the demand curve is unitary elastic, and total revenue remains constant at \$720 as price falls. Finally, when elasticity is 0.2, the demand curve is inelastic, and total revenue falls from \$720 to \$520 as price falls.

12 In the following tables, the number in the elasticity column corresponding to each price refers to the elasticity over the interval between that price and the next highest price.

a

Price	Quantity	Total revenue	Elasticity
\$12	6	\$72	
\$10	8	\$80	1.57
\$ 8	10	\$80	1.00
\$ 6	12	\$72	0.64

b

Price	Quantity	Total revenue	Elasticity
\$100	80	\$8,000	
\$ 80	85	\$6,800	0.26
\$ 60	90	\$5,400	0.20
\$ 40	95	\$3,800	0.14

c

Price	Quantity	Total revenue	Elasticity
\$9	10	\$ 90	
\$8	14	\$112	2.430
\$7	18	\$126	1.875
\$6	22	\$132	1.300

13 *a* Price = \$700; quantity = 1,200.
b Price = \$650; quantity demanded = 1,400; quantity supplied = 900; shortage = 1,400 – 900 = 500.

14 *a* Wage = \$8.00; quantity demanded = 600; quantity supplied = 3,200; surplus = 3,200 – 600 = 2,600.
b Price = \$600; quantity = 1,000.

Part Two

Full-Employment Macroeconomics

Chapter 4

MACROECONOMIC GOALS AND MEASURES

Chapter Review

Macroeconomics is concerned with the characteristics of the economy as a whole. This chapter of the text introduces three central macroeconomic variables: the unemployment rate, the inflation rate, and gross domestic product, which is the standard measure of the economy's output. We learn how to measure each variable and discover how each is related to the major goals for the performance of the economy: full employment, price stability, and a high rate of economic growth.

ESSENTIAL CONCEPTS

1 Macroeconomics is concerned with the performance of the economy as a whole. The three important indicators—the level of **unemployment**, the **inflation rate**, and the rate of **economic growth**—are related to the three major markets. High unemployment occurs when demand does not equal supply in the labor market. When demand and supply in product markets are not consistent with a stable price level, there is inflation. Low growth results, in part, when the capital market does not allocate enough funds for investments.

2 The **gross domestic product**, or GDP, measures the output of the economy. It is the money value of the goods and services produced within a country in a year. Adjusting the number for inflation gives real GDP. The rate of increase in the real GDP is the primary measure of economic growth. Although the rate averaged around 3 percent per year from 1950 to 1973, it has fallen to about 1 percent per year since.

3 **Potential GDP** measures what the economy could produce if labor and machines were fully employed. The economy fluctuates, producing below potential GDP in the trough of recession and sometimes exceeding it during the peaks of booms. The ups and downs of the economy are sometimes called the **business cycle**, but the actual path of the economy is not regular.

4 GDP can be measured in three equivalent ways. The **final goods approach** computes the market value of goods sold to their ultimate consumers. The **value-added approach** adds up the additional market value created at each step in the process from production to market. The **income approach** adds the total income received by all individuals and profits retained by firms. Another important measure is **net domestic product**, which subtracts depreciation from the GDP.

5 The **labor force** includes those individuals who are either employed or actively seeking employment. The fraction of the labor force that is without work is called the **unemployment rate.** Unemployment is a persistent phenomenon in the United States: from 5.5 to 7.4 percent of the labor force was unemployed in the early 1990s. This represents an enormous waste of resources, and it can be devastating personally for the unemployed and also for communities with high unemployment.

6 Economists distinguish among four types of unemployment. **Seasonal unemployment** occurs when the jobs are available for only part of the year. People who are between jobs make up **frictional unemployment. Structural unemployment**, which is more long-term, arises because the skills of the current labor force do not match the skills required by the available jobs. Finally, **cyclical unemployment** is due to a slowdown in the overall level of economic activity. One of the important tasks of macroeconomics is to understand and reduce cyclical unemployment.

7 The **inflation rate** is the rate of increase in the general level of prices. It is measured using **price indices** such as the consumer price index, or CPI. The annual percentage change in the CPI indicates the increase in the cost of living from one year to the next. Inflation ranged from 3 to 6 percent in the 1980s. Inflation hurts people on fixed incomes because it erodes their purchasing power. When variable, inflation makes borrowing and lending riskier, and it is generally disruptive of the economy.

BEHIND THE ESSENTIAL CONCEPTS

1 If you have a job or are looking for one, then economists count you as a member of the labor force. The unemployment rate is the fraction of the labor force that does not have a job. But the unemployment rate may not measure how hard it is to find work, for several reasons. First, you would be counted as unemployed even if you were only claiming to look for work in order to be eligible for unemployment insurance, or if you were holding out for an unrealistic offer. On the other hand, if, during a recession, you realistically gave up hope of finding a job and stopped looking, you would not be counted as unemployed, but rather as out of the labor force. A **discouraged worker** would be part of the usual decline in the **labor force participation rate** during recessions.

2 Economists use the price index, which is constructed by comparing the cost of a particular basket of goods in different years, to measure inflation. The consumer price index measures your cost of living only if you consume exactly what is in the market basket. It also gives an inexact measure of quality changes and sometimes underestimates the importance of sale items.

3 Similarly, GDP does not quite measure all the output in the economy. It ignores nonmarketed goods, such as the services of unpaid spouses, and it can only be adjusted imperfectly to capture changes in the quality of goods and the value of nonmarketed government services.

SELF-TEST

True or False

1 Productivity refers to output per capita.

2 The gross domestic product measures the money value of goods and services produced within a country during a specific time period.

3 Nominal GDP is real GDP adjusted for inflation.

4 Gross domestic product is the sum of comsumption, investment, government expenditures, and net exports.

5 There are three equally valid ways to compute gross domestic product: final goods, value added, and income.

6 Value added is computed by subtracting a firm's purchases of inputs from its revenues.

7 The unemployment rate measures the percentage of the working-age population that is unemployed.

8 The labor force includes the entire working-age population.

9 Structural unemployment includes those unemployed who have skills that do not match the skills required for currently available jobs.

10 When the economy is on an upswing, cyclical unemployment declines.

11 The price index for the base year equals 100.

12 The wholesale price index is based upon a market basket of goods sold by wholesalers to retailers.

13 The producer price index is based upon a market basket of goods sold by wholesalers to producers.

14 Inflation reduces the purchasing power of people living on fixed incomes.

15 Variable rates of inflation increase the riskiness of borrowing and lending.

Multiple Choice

1 Which of the following is *not* an important macroeconomic goal?

a price stability;
b full employment;
c perfect competition;
d rapid growth;
e All of the above are important macroeconomic goals.

2 The money value of all goods and services produced within a country in a year is the

a gross national product;
b gross domestic product;

c net domestic product;
d depreciation index;
e producer price index.

3 Inflation-adjusted gross domestic product is called

a gross nation product;
b net domestic product;
c nominal gross domestic product;
d real gross domestic product;
e nominal gross national product.

4 If the price level has risen recently, then the real GDP is

a greater than the nominal GDP;
b less than the nominal GDP;
c equal to the nominal GDP;
d greater than the GNP;
e less than the GNP.

5 During recessions, the GDP

a is less than potential GDP;
b is greater than potential GDP;
c is equal to potential GDP;
d bears no predictable relationship to potential GDP;
e rises at a decreasing rate.

6 The final goods approach to GDP

a adds the differences between the revenues and costs of intermediate goods;
b adds all income received by individuals and governments in the economy;
c subtracts the inflation rate from the nominal GDP;
d adds the value of goods, services, and the environment;
e adds the total money value of goods and services purchased by their ultimate users.

7 The value-added approach to GDP

a adds the differences between the revenues and costs of intermediate goods;
b adds all income received by individuals and governments in the economy;
c substracts the inflation rate from the nominal GDP;
d adds the value of goods, services, and the environment;
e adds the total money value of goods and services purchased by their ultimate users.

8 Gross domestic product divided by the number of hours worked equals

a net domestic product;
b real GNP;
c real GDP;
d productivity;
e NDP.

9 The total labor force comprises

a all individuals of working age who are employed;
b all individuals of working age who are unemployed;
c all individuals of working age;
d all heads of households;
e all individuals of working age who are either employed or unemployed.

10 The costs of unemployment include

a underutilization of the economy's resources;
b personal difficulties for unemployed individuals;
c financial troubles for communities with high unemployment;
d exacerbated racial and ethnic divisions;
e all of the above.

11 The unemployment rate is the ratio of the number of unemployed to the

a number of employed;
b total labor force;
c inflation rate;
d gross domestic product;
e adult working-age population.

12 The Department of Labor survey probably

a underestimates the true unemployment rate in that some discouraged workers have given up hope of finding a job;
b overestimates the true unemployment rate in that some discouraged workers have given up hope of finding a job;
c underestimates the true unemployment rate in that some individuals who respond that they are actively seeking work are not;
d overestimates the true unemployment rate in that some individuals who respond that they are actively seeking work are not;
e a and d.

13 Those individuals who are unemployed because they work in seasonal jobs comprise

a seasonal unemployment;
b frictional unemployment;
c structural unemployment;
d cyclical unemployment;
e discouraged-worker unemployment.

14 Those individuals who are temporarily between jobs make up

a seasonal unemployment;
b frictional unemployment;
c structural unemployment;
d cyclical unemployment;
e discouraged-worker unemployment.

15 When the skills required by available jobs are not the same as the skills of the unemployed, there is

a seasonal unemployment;
b frictional unemployment;
c structural unemployment;
d cyclical unemployment;
e discouraged-worker unemployment.

16 In recessions, the level of economic activity declines and there is an increase in

a seasonal unemployment;
b frictional unemployment;

c structural unemployment;
d cyclical unemployment;
e discouraged-worker unemployment.

17 If prices and wages rise at the same rate, the purchasing power of typical workers

a increases;
b decreases;
c remains the same;
d doubles;
e falls to zero.

18 When the inflation rate rises and falls unpredictably,

a lenders gain at the expense of borrowers;
b borrowers gain at the expense of lenders;
c there is no appreciable impact on borrowing and lending;
d borrowing and lending become riskier;
e lending increases, but borrowing falls.

19 The producer price index includes in its market basket a representative bundle of goods

a purchased by consumers;
b sold by wholesalers to retailers;
c sold by producers to wholesalers;
d purchased by government;
e sold by wholesalers to consumers.

20 The price index used to calculate the real gross domestic product is

a the consumer price index;
b the producer price index;
c the weighted average of the producer and consumer price indices;
d the GDP deflator;
e an index of raw material prices.

Completion

1 The money value of all final goods and services produced within the country in a year is called the __________.

2 Dividing nominal GDP by the price level gives __________.

3 The measure of what the economy could produce given normal levels of frictional unemployment and idle productive capacity is called __________.

4 A firm's revenues minus the cost of intermediate goods equal its __________.

5 __________ is calculated by dividing GDP by the number of hours worked.

6 The unemployment rate is the ratio of the number of unemployed to the __________.

7 People who are temporarily between jobs comprise part of __________ unemployment.

8 __________ unemployment is due to a mismatch between the skills of those without jobs and the skills needed to perform the available jobs.

9 __________ unemployment rises in recession and falls in booms.

10 The percentage increase in the price level from one year to the next is called the __________.

Answers to Self-Test

True or False

1	t	6	t	11	t
2	t	7	f	12	t
3	f	8	f	13	f
4	t	9	t	14	t
5	t	10	t	15	t

Multiple Choice

1	c	6	e	11	b	16	d
2	b	7	a	12	e	17	c
3	d	8	d	13	a	18	d
4	b	9	e	14	b	19	b
5	a	10	e	15	c	20	d

Completion

1 gross domestic product
2 real GDP
3 potential GDP
4 value added
5 Productivity
6 labor force
7 frictional
8 Structural
9 Cyclical
10 inflation rate

Doing Economics: Tools and Practice Problems

In this section, we will explore how economists measure economic performance. After learning how to calculate the rate of inflation, we use this technique to construct the price index and to distinguish real and nominal GDP. Finally, we calculate GDP by the final goods, value-added, and income approaches, verifying that the three techniques give equivalent answers. Although the examples are simplified, you should realize that the government agencies responsible for computing inflation and GDP perform their calculations in the same way.

Inflation

Inflation refers to a general increase in the price level. It is calculated by computing the increase in the cost of purchasing a fixed market basket of goods. The United States government has several inflation measures, including the consumer price index, the producer price index, and the GDP deflator. In these problems we focus on the computation of the consumer price index (CPI). Tool Kit 4.1 shows how it is done.

Tool Kit 4.1: Calculating the Inflation Rate

The inflation rate is the percentage increase in the cost of purchasing a predetermined basket of goods. Follow this procedure to calculate the inflation rate.

Step one: Identify the quantities of each good in the market basket:

quantity of good 1 =
quantity of good 2 =
quantity of good 3 =

Step two: Calculate the cost of purchasing the quantities in the market basket at year 1 prices:

(quantity of good 1 × price in year 1)
+ (quantity of good 2 × price in year 1)
+ (quantity of good 3 × price in year 1)
= cost of living at year 1 prices.

Step three: Calculate the cost of purchasing the quantities in the market basket at year 2 prices:

(quantity of good 1 × price in year 2)
+ (quantity of good 2 × price in year 2)
+ (quantity of good 3 × price in year 2)
= cost of living at year 2 prices.

Step Four: Find the percentage change in the two costs of living by using the following formula:

$$\left[\left(\frac{\text{cost of living at year 2 prices}}{\text{cost of living at year 1 prices}}\right) - 1\right] \times 100 = \text{inflation rate.}$$

1 (Worked problem: inflation rate) There are three goods consumed in Euthanasia: fast cars, parachute jumps, and hang gliders. The prices and quantities for each in 1990 and the prices in 1991 are given below.

	1990		1991
Goods	Prices	Quantities	Prices
Fast cars	$20,000	20	$30,000
Parachute jumps	$ 100	2,500	$ 80
Hang gliders	$ 500	400	$ 800

The market basket comprises the 1990 quantities.Calculate the inflation rate.

Step-by-step solution:

Step one: Identify the quantities in the market basket. There are 20 fast cars, 2,500 parachute jumps, and 400 hang gliders.

Step two: Calculate the cost of purchasing the market basket at 1990 prices:

($20,000 × 20) + ($100 × 2,500) + ($500 × 400) = $850,000.

Step three: Calculate the cost of purchasing the market basket at 1991 prices:

($30,000 × 20) × ($80 × 2,500) + ($800 × 400) = $1,120,000.

Step four: Find the percentage change:

($1,120,000/$850,000 – 1) × 100 = 32 percent.

The inflation rate is 32 percent.

2 (Practice problem: inflation rate) In order to determine how to adjust stipends for disabled workers, the Paper Profits Company wants to compute the inflation rate. It has identified a market basket for stipend recipients. This is given below, along with the prices in 1980 (the year of the last adjustment) and in 1990.

Good or service	Quantity	1980 Prices	1990 Prices
Prepared meals	7	$ 5	$ 6
Housecleaning	1	$25	$30
Physical therapy	3	$50	$75
Compact discs	4	$10	$10

Compute the inflation rate.

3 (Practice problem: inflation rate) A recent graduate of Enormous State University, Lamont has dozens of job offers. He has narrowed his search to jobs in two cities: Gotham and Smallville. In order to compare the offers, he must compute the relative cost of living in the two cities. His market basket and prices are given below.

Good or service	Quantity	Gotham price	Smallville price
2-bedroom apartment	1	$1,500	$300
Pickup truck	1	$ 600	$400
Meals	90	$ 10	$ 5

How much more expensive (in percent) is the cost of living in Gotham than in Smallville?

Inflation Adjustment

The distinction between real and nominal values is essential in macroeconomics. Real values are adjusted for inflation; that is, they measure what would have occurred if the dollar maintained its purchasing power. While the technique is appropriate for any dollar value, in these problems we focus on adjusting nominal GDP. Tool Kit 4.2 shows how to adjust for inflation.

Tool Kit 4.2: Adjusting for Inflation

The money value of all goods and services purchased during a year is the nominal GDP. To get a better idea of how actual output changes from year to year, it is important to adjust this number for inflation. Real GDP is nominal GDP adjusted for inflation, and it gives the value of output measured in base year dollars. Follow this procedure to calculate real GDP.

Step one: Calculate this year's price index. Multiply last year's price index by 1 plus the inflation rate:

last year's price index × (1 + inflation rate)
= current year's price index.

Step two: Calculate this year's real GDP. Divide current nominal GDP by the price index and multiply by 100. The result is current real GDP expressed in base year dollars. (To express real GDP in any other year's dollars, simply multiply by the price index in the desired year and divide by 100.)

(nominal GDP/price index) × 100 = real GDP.

4 (Worked problem: adjusting for inflation) The nominal GDP in Monrovia was $2 billion during 1992. The price index for 1991 was 210, and 1992 saw an inflation rate of 30 percent.

a Calculate the price index in 1992.
b Calculate real GDP for 1992. Express it in base year dollars.
c Express real GDP in 1991 dollars.

Step-by-step solution

Step one (a): Calculate the price index for the current year (1992). The price index for 1991 was 210. The inflation rate was 30 percent. The price index for 1992 is

210 × 1.30 = 273.

Step two (b): Calculate this year's real GDP. The current nominal GDP is $2 billion. The 1992 real GDP is

($2 billion/273) × 100 = $732.6 million.

Step three (c): Real GDP in 1991 dollars is

($732.6 × 210)/100 = $1,538 million.

5 (Practice problem: adjusting for inflation) Suppose that the nominal GDP in 1992 is $4 trillion, the 1991 price index is 352, and the 1992 inflation rate is 95 percent.

a Calculate the price index in 1992.
b Calculate real GDP for 1992. Express it in base year dollars.
c Express real GDP in 1991 dollars.

6 (Practice problem: adjusting for inflation) Suppose that sales of new homes total $30 billion in 1992. The 1992 price index is 222. Express the total sales of new homes in base year dollars.

Gross Domestic Product

The market value of all goods and services produced in a year is the gross domestic product. In the macroeconomics section of this book, when we measure the economy's output we will be looking at GDP. It is very important to realize that GDP equals national income; thus it can also be measured by adding all income earned in the economy. Finally, the value added at each step along the production chain gives another equivalent approach to calculating GDP. Tool Kit 4.3 shows how to calculate GDP.

Tool Kit 4.3: Calculating GDP

Gross domestic product is the money value of all goods and services as purchased by their ultimate users. It can be calculated by adding the money value of all final products, by summing the values added by all firms, or by adding the incomes received by all individuals.

Final goods approach

Step one: Determine which goods are purchased by their ultimate users.

Step two: Add the money values (price × quantity) of these goods:

GDP = money value of good 1 +
money value of good 2 + . . .

Value-added approach

Step one: For each firm, compute the value added by subtracting any payments to other firms from its receipts:

value added = receipts – purchases from other firms.

Step two: Sum the values added of each firm:

GDP = value added at firm 1 +
value added at firm 2 + . . .

Income approach

Step one: Find the total wages, total dividends, total interest, and any other form of income for all individuals in the economy.

Step two: Add the totals of each kind of income:

GDP = wages + dividends + interest.

7 (Worked problem: calculating GDP) Suppose that the economy produces three goods: wheat, flour, and bread. All of the wheat is sold to millers. All of the flour is sold to bakers. Consumers buy the bread from the bakers. The income and expenditure accounts for each of the three industries are given in Table 4.1.

Table 4.1

	Expenditures (billions)	*Receipts (billions)*
	Wheat industry	
Wages	$ 40	$ 50
Dividends	$ 0	
Interest	$ 10	
	Flour industry	
Wages	$ 30	$110
Purchases of wheat	$ 50	
Dividends	$ 15	
Interest	$ 15	
	Bread industry	
Wages	$ 60	$200
Purchases of flour	$110	
Dividends	$ 30	
Interest	$ 0	

a Calculate (nominal) GDP using the final goods approach.
b Calculate (nominal) GDP using the value-added approach.
c Calculate (nominal) GDP using the income approach.
d Compare the three answers.

Step-by-step solution

Step one (a): Determine which goods are purchased by their ultimate users. Only bread is a final output.

Step two: Add the money value of these goods. The value of bread is $200. The GDP thus equals $200.

Step three (b): Find the value added for each firm or industry.

Value added in wheat = $50 – $0 = $50;
value added in flour = $110 – $50 = $60;
value added in bread = $200 – $110 = $90.

Step four: Sum the value-added numbers.

GDP = $50 + $60 + $90 = $200.

Step five (c): Find the total wages, dividends, and interest.

Total wages = $40 + $30 + $60 = $130;
total dividends = $0 + $15 + $30 = $45;
total interest = $10 + $15 + $0 = $25.

Step six: Add the totals of each income type.

GDP = $130 + $45 + $25 = $200.

Step seven (d): Compare. Note that the GDP equals $200 billion according to each method.

8 (Practice problem: calculating GDP) The economy of Literaria cuts down trees in order to make paper and uses all its paper for books. The expenditure and income accounts for each of the three industries are given in Table 4.2.

Table 4.2

	Expenditures (billions)	*Receipts (billions)*
	Tree industry	
Wages	$ 80	$100
Dividends	$ 20	
Interest	$ 0	
	Paper industry	
Wages	$100	$250
Purchases of trees	$100	
Dividends	$ 40	
Interest	$ 10	
	Book industry	
Wages	$150	$500
Purchases of paper	$250	
Dividends	$ 50	
Interest	$ 50	

a Calculate (nominal) GDP using the final goods approach.
b Calculate (nominal) GDP using the value-added approach.
c Calculate (nominal) GDP using the income approach.
d Compare the three answers.

9 (Practice problem: calculating GDP) in Computavia, they produce chips, all of which are used in the production of computer hardware. Half of the hardware is purchased by consumers, and half is sold to the software industry. Consumers purchase all of the software. The expenditure and income accounts for each of the three industries are given in Table 4.3.

Table 4.3

	Expenditures (billions)	*Receipts (billions)*
	Chip industry	
Wages	$ 600	$1,000
Dividends	$ 400	
Interest	$ 0	
	Hardware industry	
Wages	$ 600	$2,000
Purchases of chips	$1,000	
Dividends	$ 200	
Interest	$ 200	
	Software industry	
Wages	$ 600	$2,000
Purchases of hardware	$1,000	
Dividends	$ 0	
Interest	$ 400	

a Calculate (nominal) GDP using the final goods approach.
b Calculate (nominal) GDP using the value-added approach.
c Calculate (nominal) GDP using the income approach.
d Compare the three answers.

Answers to Problems

2 [(42 + 30 + 225 + 40)/(35 + 25 + 150 + 40)] – 1] × 100 = 30 percent.

3 [(1,500 + 600 + 900)/(300 + 400 + 450)] – 1] × 100 = 161 percent.

5 *a* 1992 price index = 352 × 1.95 = 686.4.
b 1992 real GDP (base year dollars) = (4/686.4) × 100 = $0.58 trillion.
c 1992 real GDP (1991 dollars) = (0.58 × 352)/100 = $2.042 trillion.

6 (30/222) × 100 = $14 billion.

8 *a* \$500 (books).
b Value added in tree industry = \$100 – 0 = \$100;
value added in paper industry = \$250 – \$100 = \$150;
value added in book industry = \$500 – \$250 = \$250;
total value added = \$100 + \$150 + \$250 = \$500.
c Wages = \$80 + \$100 + \$150 = \$330;
dividends = \$20 + \$40 + \$50 = \$110;
interest = \$0 + \$10 + \$50 = \$60;
total income = \$330 + \$110 + \$60 = \$500.
d Each answer is \$500, which is the GDP.

9 *a* Hardware purchased by consumers = \$2,000/2 = \$1,000;
software purchased by consumers = \$2,000;
total final goods = \$1,000 + \$2,000 = \$3,000.
b Value added in chip industry = \$1,000 – \$0 = \$1,000;
value added in hardware industry = \$2,000 – \$1,000 = \$1,000;
value added in software industry = \$2,000 – \$1,000 = \$1,000;
total value added = \$1,000 + \$1,000 + \$1,000 = \$3,000.
c Wages = \$600 + \$600 + \$600 = \$1,800;
dividends = \$400 + \$200 + \$0 = \$600;
interest = \$0 + \$200 + \$400 = \$600;
total income = \$1,800 + \$600 + \$600 = \$3,000.
d Each answer is \$3,000, which is the GDP.

Chapter 5

MICROFOUNDATIONS

Chapter Review

This chapter uses supply and demand analysis from microeconomics to build the basic competitive model of the entire economy—the general equilibrium. The model is perfect competition, which leads to an efficient allocation of resources without unemployment. Another important point is that markets are interrelated. The chapter closes with a discussion of how real world markets differ in important ways from the basic competitive model. This discussion sets the stage for Chapter 6's macroeconomic look at what determines the economy's aggregate output, price level, and employment.

ESSENTIAL CONCEPTS

1 Households and firms trade in three types of markets: product, capital, and labor. In the **product market,** households are the demanders and firms are the suppliers. In the **labor** and **capital markets,** the situation is reversed; firms demand the labor services and savings that households supply.

2 Households face **budget constraints,** which limit their opportunities to purchase products, save for future consumption, and earn labor income. Given their budget constraints, rational households choose their best alternative.

a The **demand curve** shows how much of a particular product a household will consume at each price. When the price falls, the household chooses a different point along the demand curve and consumes more. When income increases, the household consumes more goods at each price, and the entire demand curve shifts to the right.

b The **supply curve of savings** shows how much the household will save at each interest rate. When the interest rate increases, the household chooses a different point along the supply curve and saves (a little) more. Changes in other factors, such as the price level, shift the entire supply curve. Households also must choose how to invest their savings, balancing the **expected return** with other desirable characteristics of assets, such as risk, liquidity, and tax advantages.

c The **labor supply curve** shows how much the household will choose to work at each real wage rate. When the real wage rate increases, the household chooses a different point along the supply curve and works (a little) more. Changes in other factors, such as household wealth, shift the entire supply curve.

3 In the basic competitive model, firms cannot affect the prices at which they sell their products, the interest rate at which they borrow to invest, or the wage rate at which they hire workers. They must choose the quantities of products, capital, and labor in order to maximize their profits, which equal revenues minus costs.

a The firm's supply curve shows how many goods will be sold at each price. It is found by setting price equal to marginal cost, provided that the market price exceeds average cost. The market supply curve is simply the sum of the supply curves of all individual firms in a particular industry at each price. When the price increases, the firms collectively choose a different point along the supply curve and increase output. When other factors such as real wage rates change, the entire market supply curve shifts.

b The firm's demand for capital shows how much capital the firm chooses to borrow (to finance their investment in capital goods, such as plant and equipment) at each interest rate. When the interest rate falls, the firm chooses a different point along the demand curve and borrows more. When other factors such as the product price or real wage rate change, the entire demand curve shifts.

c The firm's demand for labor shows how much labor the firm chooses to hire at each real wage rate. The economy's demand for labor is the sum of all of the firms' demands. When the wage rate falls, each firm chooses a different point along its labor demand curve and hires more workers. When other factors such as interest rates change, the entire demand curve shifts.

4 Figure 5.1 shows equilibrium in the product, capital, and labor markets. The price in the product market adjusts to the level at which households' demand for output exactly equals the quantity that firms are willing to supply. Also, in the capital market, the interest rate balances households' supply of savings with firms' demand for funds to invest. Finally, the wage rate brings about market clearing in the labor market. When all three markets clear, the economy reaches its **general equilibrium**.

5 The **circular flow** models gives another view of the overall economy. Figure 5.2 shows the simplest view, where households' payments to firms for goods and services are balanced by firms' payments to households of wages, rents, and profits. More complicated versions bring in flows to and from the government, the international economy, and the capital market. The great lesson of this model is that the flows must balance; therefore, any change in one flow, such as reduced taxes, must be balanced by a change in another. Again, we see the interrelatedness of the macroeconomy.

6 Resources are allocated efficiently in the basic competitive model. This means that the economy is on its production possibilities curve, it produces the mix of goods and services that consumers want, and it distributes the goods to the right households in the sense that there are no remaining possibilities for mutually beneficial exchanges. Adam Smith captured this idea with his **"invisible hand"** metaphor, which implies that markets give incentives to individuals and firms for efficient decisions.

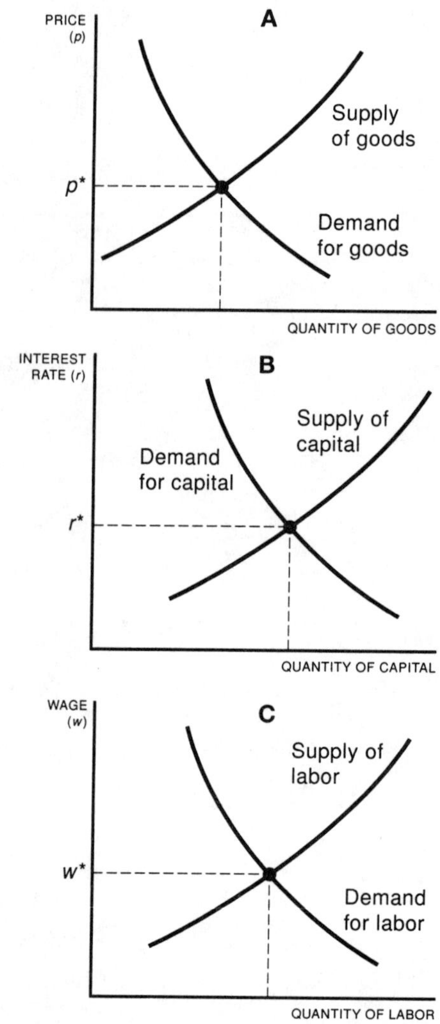

Figure 5.1

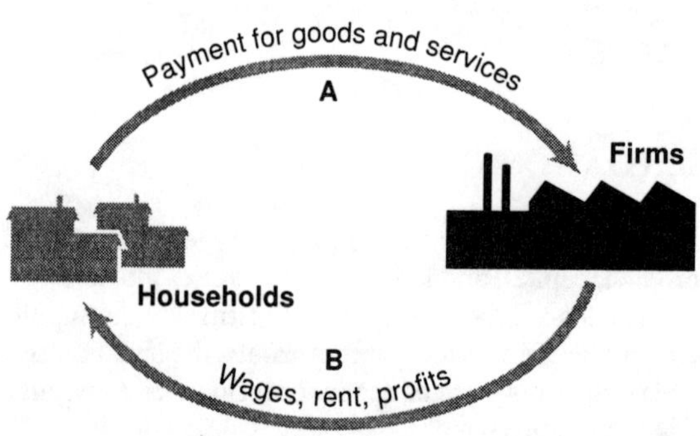

Figure 5.2

7 The real world, unfortunately, is quite different from that envisaged by the basic competitive model. Some market failures lead to inefficiencies, and others cause markets not to clear.

a When firms have market power, they can set price above the competitive level, reduce output, and make additional profits. Examples of **imperfect competition** include monopolies, oligopolies, monopolistic competition among firms with differentiated products, and unions, which can raise wages and reduce employment.

b In the basic competitive model, firms and households have good information about product quality and availability, but in the real world, there is **imperfect information**. If customers are not aware of all prices, firms have a reduced incentive to lower price to competitive levels. Firms that cannot observe their workers' effort or quality may raise wages to improve productivity even if the higher wages lead to unemployment.

c In the basic competitive model, there is a complete set of markets, but in the real world, important markets may be missing. For example, the fact that people who are most likely to have accidents demand more insurance may prevent insurance companies from being able to offer insurance against some types of risk.

d The basic competitive model ignores **technological change** and thus has little to say about productivity and the development of new goods and new ways of producing goods and services. Competition to win patents often results in imperfect competition in the marketing of the patented innovation.

e When households and firms do not face the full benefits and costs of their decisions, there are **externalities,** and the allocation of resources is likely to be inefficient. Important examples include pollution and the risks that management imposes on bondholders.

f In the real world, the economy is not always in equilibrium. It takes time for markets to settle down at the market-clearing prices. Adjustment may be slow because of imperfect information or because of the fact that changes in one market ripple throughout the entire economy.

g Finally, although resources are allocated efficiently in the basic competitive model, there is no way to ensure that the **distribution of income** will be equal. Correcting the market failures that lead to unemployment or recession may help to raise the welfare of lower-income households.

BEHIND THE ESSENTIAL CONCEPTS

1 When product prices, interest rates, or wage rates change, your opportunities change and you will probably make different decisions. Economists distinguish two factors at work in these situations: **substitution** and **income effects**. In the case of the demand for products, both effects work together. On the supply side, where labor or savings are the issue, the effects work against each other.

a If the price of a product like compact discs fell, you would probably buy more. You would buy more because compact discs become relatively less expensive than some other substitute goods, such as cassette tapes or concert tickets, but you would also buy more simply because at lower prices, you are better off and can afford more. The first effect is called the substitution effect, because you substitute toward the good that becomes less expensive. The second effect is the income effect—lower prices make you better off in the same way that higher incomes do. Notice that the two effects work together. Both encourage you to consume more at lower prices.

b If the interest rate rose, on the other hand, you might save more or less. Higher interest rates mean that consuming more in the future is less expensive—you get back more for your savings. This is called the substitution effect and it encourages you to save more, to substitute future consumption for current consumption. Again, however, there is a second effect, because you are better off when the interest rate is higher (if you are a saver!). Because you are better off, you can consume more now and in the future. As you increase your current consumption, you save less. This second effect is the income effect, and it works against the substitution effect.

c If the wage rate rose, again there would be two effects. Higher wage rates mean that leisure is more expensive. You substitute away from the more expensive leisure and work more. At the same time, higher wage rates make you better off and give you the opportunity to consume more of everything, including leisure. For this reason, you are inclined to work less. As in the case of savings, the income and substitution effects work against each other.

2 The three markets are all interrelated. A decrease in the supply of labor, of course, increases the wage rate, but the impact ripples though the economy. Firms substitute capital for labor, and this shifts the demand for capital. Firms supply more products because their costs decrease. Similarly, households may change their savings or product demands. Eventually, it all settles down to a new equilibrium, but the process may take some time.

3 Another example of interrelated markets is the relationship between current and future asset markets. Households and firms can make gains or losses when asset prices change; therefore, they are always on the lookout for hints about future prices. When something causes expectations of future prices to change, asset owners quickly adjust their portfolios. This interrelatedness makes asset markets volatile and leads to some instability. It also points to an essential role for expectations in macroeconomics.

4 It is important to understand the role that the basic competitive model plays in economics. The model shows that if all markets were in perfect working order, the economy would allocate resources efficiently, there would be no unemployment, and there would be no need to study macroeconomics. Of course, the real world is not so perfect. There are inefficiencies, unemployment, and recessions because real-world markets differ from the basic competitive model. In the remaining chapters you will study how imperfect competition leads to the macroeconomic problems that trouble modern economies.

SELF-TEST

True or False

1 In the product market, households are the demanders and firms are the suppliers.

2 In the labor market, households are the demanders and firms are the suppliers.

3 When the wage changes, the household's demand for products shifts.

4 When the wage changes, the household's supply of labor shifts.

5 When the price increases, both the substitution and income effects lead households to demand more of a (normal) good.

6 When the wage increases, both the substitution and income effects lead households to supply more labor.

7 Firms choose the profit-maximizing supply of products by finding the quantity for which price equals marginal cost.

8 Firms do not supply products unless price exceeds average cost.

9 When the wage increases, firms move along their demand curve for labor and hire fewer workers.

10 When the wage increases, firms move along their supply curve and supply more products.

11 In the capital market, the interest rate adjusts to balance households' demand for borrowing with firms' supply of savings.

12 In the basic competitive model, firms are price makers.

13 Shareholders, who are the owners of firms, generally possess good information about the activities of management.

14 When individuals and firms do not face the full benefits and costs of their decisions, there are externalities.

15 In the real world, prices adjust quickly to ensure that all markets clear.

Multiple Choice

1 Which of the following is not one of the three groups of markets used to approach macroeconomic questions?

a product market;
b labor market;
c capital market;
d insurance market;
e none of the above.

2 In the product market,

a households are the demanders and firms are the suppliers;
b households are the suppliers and firms are the demanders;
c both households and firms are suppliers;
d both households and firms are demanders;
e neither households nor firms are demanders or suppliers.

3 In the labor market,

a households are the demanders and firms are the suppliers;
b households are the suppliers and firms are the demanders;
c both households and firms are suppliers;
d both households and firms are demanders;
e neither households nor firms are demanders or suppliers.

4 A decrease in the price of a good

a increases consumption of that good because of the substitution effect;
b increases consumption of that good because of the income effect;
c decreases consumption of that good because of the substitution effect;
d decreases consumption of that good because of the income effect;
e a and b.

5 When the price of a good rises, the substitution effect leads the household to

a reduce demand because they are worse off;
b increase demand because they are worse off;
c increase demand because they are better off;
d decrease demand because the good is more expensive relative to other goods;
e increase demand because the good is more expensive relative to other goods.

6 An increase in the interest rate

a reduces savings because of the substitution effect;
b increases savings because of the income effect;
c decreases savings because of the income effect;
d a and c;
e a and b.

7 An increase in the interest rate leads to

a more savings because the income and substitution effects motivate additional savings;
b less savings because the income and substitution effects motivate less savings;
c slightly more savings because while the substitution effect motivates less savings, it is outweighed by the income effect, which motivates more savings;
d slightly more savings because while the income effect motivates less savings, it is outweighed by the substitution effect, which motivates more savings;
e no change in savings because the substitution and income effects exactly offset each other.

8 The household's supply curve for labor shows the quantity of labor supplied

a at each nominal wage rate;
b at each price level;
c at each real wage rate;
d at each interest rate;
e at each level of household income.

9 When the wage rate rises, the household supplies

a less labor because of the substitution effect;
b more labor because of the substitution effect;
c less labor because of the income effect;
d a and c;
e b and c.

10 In the basic competitive model, firms are

a price takers;
b price makers;
c quantity takers;
d profit takers;
e none of the above.

11 The revenue from the sale of another unit

a is called marginal revenue;
b equals price for a competitive firm;
c equals marginal cost when profits are maximized;
d all of the above;
e none of the above.

12 Typically, the average cost curve is

a flat;
b U-shaped;
c circular;
d downward sloping;
e upward sloping.

13 The firm shuts down when

a price is less than average cost;
b price is less than marginal revenue;
c price is more than marginal revenue;
d price is more than average cost;
e price is more than marginal cost.

14 The situation in which all markets clear is called

a adverse selection;
b credit rationing;
c partial equilibrium;
d general equilibrium;
e circular flow.

15 The balance conditions in the circular flow model are

a behavioral relationships;
b equilibrium relationships;
c identities;
d true only when all markets clear;
e true only in perfect competition.

16 Which of the following is not true in the basic competitive model?

a The economy is on its production possibilities curve.
b The economy produces the mix of goods that consumers want.
c The goods are distributed to the right people in the sense that no additional mutually beneficial exchanges are possible.
d The distribution of income is equitable.
e All of the above are true.

17 With perfect competition, firms face a

a vertical demand curve;
b downward-sloping demand curve;
c horizontal demand curve;
d upward-sloping demand curve;
e horizontal supply curve.

18 Credit rationing refers to

a government programs that provide capital to firms shut out of private capital markets;
b the situation in which a firm cannot afford the going interest rate;
c the situation in which the demand for funds exceeds the supply yet banks are unwilling to increase the interest rate;
d firms' attempts to motivate workers by paying higher wages;
e the fact that those who are most willing to purchase insurance are those most likely to have accidents.

19 In the basic competitive model,

a firms are price takers;
b households and firms have good information about product quality, price, and availability;
c technology is fixed;
d there is a complete set of markets;
e All of the above are true in the basic competitive model.

20 Which of the following is not a limitation of the basic competitive model?

a imperfect competition;
b imperfect information;
c externalities;
d missing markets;
e All of the above are limitations.

Completion

1 The household's __________ shows what products can be purchased at market prices, given its limited income.

2 When the real wage rate falls, the household supplies less labor because of the __________.

3 In the basic competitive model, firms are __________.

4 Firms shut down when price falls below __________.

5 When all markets clear, the economy is said to be in __________.

6 A firm that has no competitors is called a __________.

7 When the quality or location of firms' products is not the same or when firms have different reputations, there is __________.

8 __________ explains why paying higher wages leads to a higher-quality labor force.

9 If households and firms do not face the full costs of their actions, then there are __________.

10 The exclusive right to market and license an invention is called a __________.

Answers to Self-Test

True or False

1	t	6	f	11	f
2	f	7	t	12	f
3	t	8	t	13	f
4	f	9	t	14	t
5	f	10	f	15	f

Multiple Choice

1	d	6	c	11	d	16	d
2	a	7	d	12	b	17	c
3	b	8	c	13	a	18	c
4	e	9	e	14	d	19	e
5	d	10	a	15	c	20	e

Completion

1 demand curve
2 substitution effect
3 price takers
4 average cost
5 general equilibrium
6 monopoly
7 product differentiation
8 Efficiency wage theory
9 externalities
10 patent

Chapter 6

THE FULL-EMPLOYMENT MODEL

Chapter Review

The full-employment model describes the performance of the economy in the long run, after prices and wages have had time to adjust. Equilibrium in the product, labor, and capital markets combines with a balance in international transactions to bring the economy to full-employment production at the level of its productive capacity or potential GDP. This chapter lays out the essentials of the model, and the following one delves into several of its uses.

ESSENTIAL CONCEPTS

1 This chapter's model is the basic competitive model in which households and firms interact in product, labor, and capital markets. Households supply labor to firms for use in producing goods, and they provide savings that finance firms' investments in plant and equipment. Receiving their wages, interest, and dividends, households purchase the goods in the product market. Wages, interest rates, and product prices adjust to equate supply and demand in each market. The markets are interdependent in the sense that what occurs in any one market affects each of the others.

2 The labor market governs job creation and employment. The demand for labor depends on the productivity of workers, and it slopes downward because as the real wage falls, firms hire labor to substitute for capital and to produce additional output. Households determine their supply of labor, which is assumed to be inelastic. As shown in Figure 6.1, the real wage adjusts to the level at which demand and supply are equal. An increase in

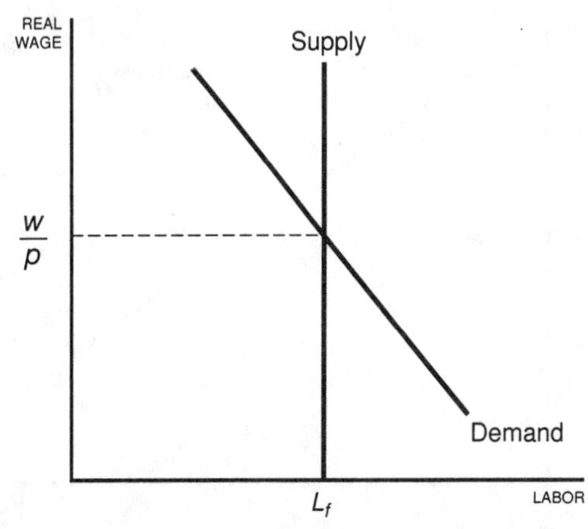

Figure 6.1

labor supply shifts the supply curve to the right, increasing employment and reducing the real wage. An increase in the demand for labor (due to improved technology or additional investment) shifts demand to the right, bidding up wages.

3 The capacity of the economy, also called its **potential gross domestic product** or **full-employment output**, depends upon the available technology, its stock of capital, and the supply of labor. With a given capital stock and technology, the **short-run production function** shows how potential output varies with different quantities of labor. Figure 6.2 illustrates the short-run production function and its property of diminishing returns. It is related to the aggregate supply curve shown in Figure 6.3. Notice that aggregate supply does not depend upon product price. An increase in labor supply represents a movement along the short-run production function and a rightward shift in aggregate supply. An increase in the capital stock or a technological advance also shifts aggregate supply to the right.

4 **Aggregate demand** includes consumption, investment, government expenditures, and net exports. It slopes downward as shown in Figure 6.3, chiefly because as the price level falls, the real value of money and other dollar denominated assets rises and people consume more. In equilibrium the price level adjusts to the intersection of aggregate demand and aggregate supply, and output equals its full-employment level.

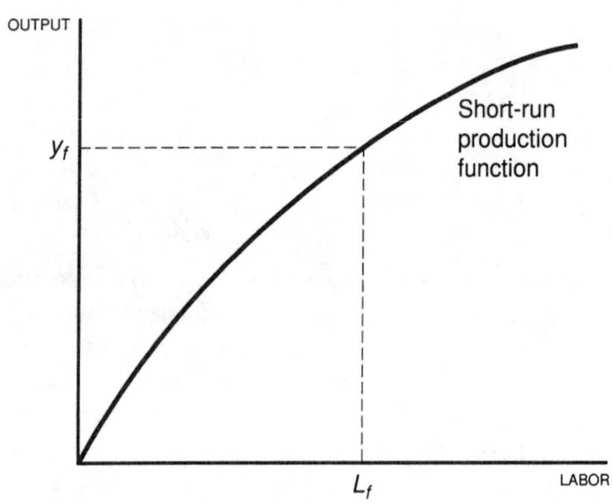

Figure 6.2

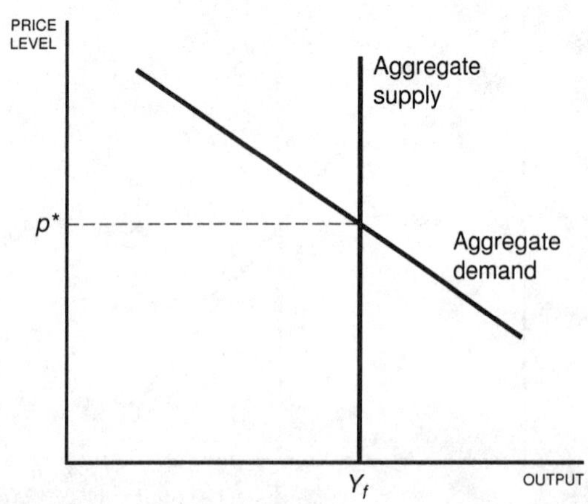

Figure 6.3

5 The savings of households depend upon their disposable income and interest rates. Panel A of Figure 6.4 shows the supply of funds sloping slightly upward; Panel B shows it as vertical. The demand for funds, also called the investment function, results from firms' intentions to invest in plant and capital equipment. It depends upon their expectations of future profitability and the real interest rate. In equilibrium savings equals investment. A rightward shift in investment raises the interest rate. It increases investment only if the supply of funds is elastic (Panel A).

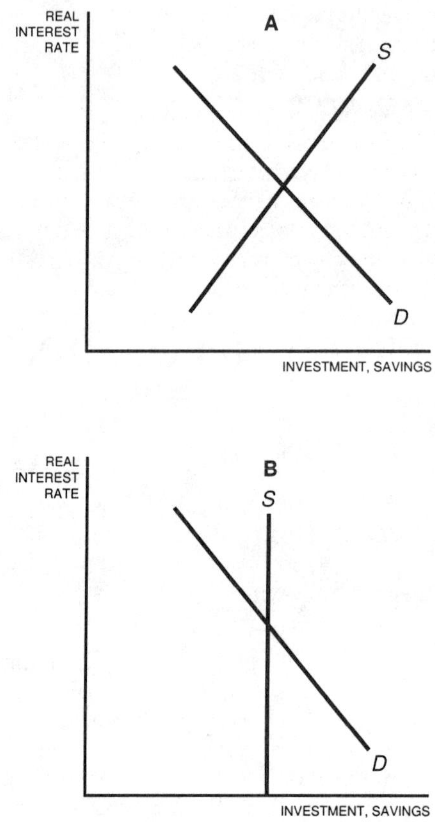

Figure 6.4

6 In the economy's general equilibrium all markets clear. There is full employment because the real wage adjusts to bring the demand for labor equal to the supply. At the equilibrium price level aggregate demand equals aggregate supply in the product market, and the economy produces its potential GDP. Finally, the real interest rate finds its equilibrium level where savings equal investment.

7 The general equilibrium model provides a coherent way to view the effects of various changes as they work their way through the three markets. Here are some examples.

a The introduction of personal computers raises the productivity of workers, shifting demand for labor to the right and increasing real wages. In the product market this new technology manifests itself as a rightward shift in aggregate supply. A look at the capital market shows an increase in savings (because households have more income) and an increase in investment.

b Government expenditures and taxation affect the composition of output. An equal increase in spending and taxes reduces savings and drives up the interest rate. The economy's aggregate supply will not shift, but it will comprise less consumption and investment, offsetting the extra government spending.

c When the economy is at full employment, money is neutral. This means that an increase in the supply of money shifts aggregate demand to the right, increasing the price level, but the real wage, real interest rate, real output, and real investment remain unchanged.

8 Trade affects the goods market because net exports is one of the four components of aggregate demand, and affects the capital market because foreign households provide an additional source of funds. In a **small open economy**, such as Switzerland, the real interest rate is fixed (determined on international capital markets); therefore any change in domestic savings cannot affect investment. The United States is a large open economy, and its size means that changes in U.S. savings affect interest rates and investment. Also, the world capital market is not fully integrated, a fact that makes investment quite sensitive to changes in U.S. savings.

BEHIND THE ESSENTIAL CONCEPTS

1 While the basic competitive model employed in this chapter is the same basic competitive model studied in microeconomics, there is a difference in interpretation. In macroeconomics we study the behavior or aggregates: total output, total employment, the price level, and so on. We proceed as if all firms produced a single good and as if there were only one kind of labor. This simplification directs attention away from the complexity of the economy and allows us to see the major forces involved in the movements of broad measures of economic performance.

2 Remember that the real wage refers to the amount of goods that an hour of work will buy. When you decide to take a part time job, you focus on what your earnings will allow you to purchase, not simply on the dollars. Similarly, in the capital market the real interest rate governs savings and investment decisions. Households put aside funds in order to consume additional goods at some future date. It is the real increase in purchasing power that motivates savings. The price level, on the other hand, is the nominal price level. Aggregate demand affects this price level, but because aggregate supply is vertical, the economy's output is not affected by aggregated demand. Shifts in aggregate demand, whether brought about by changes in the money supply or anything else, affect only the price level, leaving real wages, real interest rates, real investment, and output unchanged. This is an essential feature of the full-employment economy.

3 When the price of pancakes falls, people consume more pancakes. They substitute pancakes for scrambled eggs, cereal, or other breakfast foods. When the price level falls, however, there is no comparable opportunity to substitute. Why then does aggregate demand slope down? The answer has to do with households' wealth. A fall in the price level makes your cash worth more. The same number of dollars now buys more goods. When you experience an increase in wealth, you spend some. The same is true of any asset (such as a government bond) that is not indexed for inflation. A lower price level means greater real wealth and more consumption.

4 When the interest rate rises, you have an incentive to save more. The reason is, of course, that a given amount of savings results in more goods in the future. This idea is called the **substitution effect**: at higher interest rates people save more, in effect substituting future for current consumption. Why is the supply of funds so insensitive to changes in the interest rate? The reason is the other factor, the **income effect**. As the interest rate increases, savers have more lifetime wealth. As we have seen, when people experience an increase in wealth, they increase their consumption. This extra consumption means that savings must fall. This income effect counteracts the substitution effect, leaving the supply of funds almost inelastic.

5 In competitive markets firms are price takers. The usual reason is that they are too small relative to the market to affect the price. Any barley farmer who tried to charge above market prices would find no customers. Charging less simply gives away profits for no gain. It is the same with countries in the international capital market. A small country, such as Belgium, Botswana, or Paraguay, simply does not borrow or lend enough funds to affect world interest rates.

6 Study the structure of the full-employment model with care. The basic division of the economy into the three markets and the channels through which the markets affect each other are constants in macroeconomics. Later in the book, we look at unemployment macroeconomics, where prices are first rigid and then adjust slowly. Although these other models have quite different implications, their basic structures mirror the one studied in this chapter. Furthermore, it is important that you understand them in terms of their difference with the full-employment model. If you think about it, it is "economical" to learn one model well and to use that knowledge as a base for learning the others.

SELF-TEST

True or False

1 In the basic competitive model all markets are interdependent.

2 Macroeconomics focuses on the behavior of aggregate measures such as total employment.

3 An increase in the supply of labor causes the real wage to increase.

4 Like most supply curves, aggregate supply slopes upward.

5 The full-employment level of output is the same as potential GDP.

6 The short-run production function exhibits diminishing returns.

7 When the interest rate rises, the income effect motivates savers to increase their savings.

8 The investment function refers to financial investment.

9 In general equilibrium all markets clear.

10 Computerization in industry will cause the supply of labor to shift to the left.

11 An equal increase in government spending and taxation will reduce private investment and consumption.

12 The neutrality of money in the full-employment economy means that an increase in the supply of money increases the price level but has no real effects on output, employment, or investment.

13 In a small, open economy interest rates are fixed because they are determined on international capital markets.

14 The United States is a small, open economy.

15 Most economists agree that money is neutral when the economy is at full employment.

Multiple Choice

1 In the labor market

a households supply labor;
b the real wage adjusts to clear the market;
c firms use the labor supplied by households to produce output;
d labor supply is assumed to be inelastic;
e all of the above.

2 An increase in the supply of labor causes

a an increase in both the real wage and employment;
b a decrease in both the real wage and employment;
c an increase in the real wage and a decrease in employment;
d a decrease in the real wage and an increase in employment;
e no change in the real wage because supply is assumed to be inelastic.

3 An increase in investment most likely will shift

a the demand for labor to the right;
b the supply of labor to the right;
c the demand for labor to the left;
d the supply of labor to the left;
e both the supply and demand for labor to the right.

4 The real wage

a must be greater than the nominal wage;
b must be equal to the nominal wage when there is full employment;
c must be less than the nominal wage when interest rates are high;
d must be less than the nominal wage if there are payroll taxes;
e none of the above.

5 In this chapter labor supply is assumed to be perfectly inelastic. This means that an increase in the real wage

a increases the quantity of labor supplied;
b decreases the quantity of labor supplied;
c causes no change in the quantity of labor supplied;
d causes the nominal wage to fall;
e causes no change in the nominal wage.

6 The relationship between employment and output, holding the technology and capital stock fixed, is called the

a short-run production function;
b full-employment gross domestic product;
c short-run aggregate supply;
d investment function;
e labor supply curve, which is assumed to be inelastic.

7 The short-run production function exhibits diminishing returns. This means that as more labor is used in production, output

a diminishes due to overcrowding;
b increases at an increasing rate;
c decreases at an increasing rate;
d increases at a decreasing rate;
e decreases at a decreasing rate.

8 Which of the following is not a synonym?

a full-employment level of output;
b potential gross domestic product;
c productive capacity;
d aggregate supply;
e aggregate demand.

9 If the labor force grows,

a aggregate supply shifts to the right;
b aggregate demand shifts to the right;
c both aggregate supply and aggregate demand shift to the right;
d aggregate supply does not shift because it does not depend upon price;
e the real wage rises.

10 Aggregate demand slopes downward because as the price level falls,

a households substitute among goods;
b the real value of money and other dollar denominated assets rises and households increase consumption;
c households fear inflation and stock up on necessities;
d firms reduce their quantity supplied.

e Aggregate demand does not slope down; it is assumed to be inelastic.

11 The income effect of an increase in the real interest rate causes savers to

a reduce savings because they are better off and want to consume more now;
b increase savings because consumption in the future is cheaper;
c reduce savings because they can meet their target level with less savings;
d increase savings because they are better off and want to consume more in the future;
e choose no change in the level of savings.

12 The substitution effect of an increase in the real interest rate causes savers to

a reduce savings because they are better off and want to consume more now;
b increase savings because consumption in the future is cheaper;
c reduce savings because they can meet their target level with less savings;
d increase savings because they are better off and want to consume more in the future;
e choose no change in the level of savings.

13 The supply of funds depends upon

a the interest rate;
b expectations about future profitability;
c disposable income;
d a and c;
e all of the above.

14 The demand for funds depends upon

a the interest rate;
b expectations about future profitability;
c disposable income;
d a and b;
e all of the above.

15 The relationship between the real interest rate and the level of investment is called the

a short-run production function;
b investment function;
c aggregate supply;
d potential GDP;
e aggregate demand.

16 An equal increase in government spending and taxes

a increases investment because the government spending adds to aggregate demand;
b decreases investment because the increased taxes reduce aggregate demand;
c decreases investment because the increased taxes reduce disposable income and households save less;
d increases investment because the real interest rate falls;
e increases investment because the price level rises.

17 An increase in the money supply

a increases the price level;
b increases the real wage;
c increases the real interest rate;
d a and c;
e all of the above.

18 The neutrality of money in the full-employment economy refers to the idea that changes in the supply of money do not change

a investment;
b output;
c the real wage;
d the real interest rate;
e all of the above.

19 In a small open economy

a interest rates are determined on international capital markets;
b interest rates adjust to equate the domestic demand and supply of funds;
c the supply of savings is perfectly inelastic;
d the demand for funds is perfectly inelastic;
e savings does not depend upon the interest rate.

20 In the United States economy

a investment does not depend upon domestic savings;
b interest rates are fixed, determined on international capital markets;
c domestic savings affect interest rates and investment;
d domestic savings affect investment but not interest rates;
e savings are perfectly inelastic.

Completion

1 In the labor market the _________ adjusts to equate the supply and demand for labor.

2 For a given technology and capital stock the relationship between employment and output is called the _________.

3 The aggregate supply curve shows how much output the economy can produce when it is at _________.

4 Aggregate demand is composed of consumption, investment, government expenditures, and _________.

5 When the interest rate rises households are motivated to save less because of the _________ effect.

6 When government spending and taxes rise in the same amount, the interest rate _________, crowding out private investment and consumption.

7 When there is full employment, an increase in the money supply will increase the _________, but will have no effect on output or any other real variable.

8 The _________ of money refers to the idea that at full employment increases in the money supply have no real effects.

9 In a _________ interest rates are fixed, determined on international capital markets.

10 The United States is a _________, open economy.

Answers to Self-Test

True or False

1	t	6	t	11	t
2	t	7	f	12	t
3	f	8	f	13	t
4	f	9	t	14	f
5	t	10	f	15	t

Multiple Choice

1	e	6	a	11	a	16	c
2	d	7	d	12	b	17	a
3	a	8	e	13	d	18	e
4	e	9	a	14	d	19	a
5	c	10	b	15	b	20	c

Completion

1 real wage
2 short-run production function
3 full employment
4 net exports
5 income
6 increases
7 price level
8 neutrality
9 small, open
10 large

Doing Economics: Tools and Practice Problems

The full-employment model occupies a central place in modern economics because in many areas the economy behaves according to its predictions. For example, the long-run performance of the economy corresponds quite closely to the full-employment model. In this chapter we study the full-employment model in four steps. First, we look at the relationship between the short-run production function and the demand for labor. Next, we consider the links between the labor and product markets. Third, we study how the capital and product markets interrelate before we put it all together with some applications. The focus here is on the structure of the full-employment model. Master this subject and unemployment macroeconomics will go smoothly. (The chapter also covers the open economy, but we will defer study of that model until Chapter 7.)

The Short-Run Production Function and the Demand for Labor

The short-run production function shows how much output results from using various amounts of labor, holding the level of capital input and the technology fixed. From this function we can compute the marginal product of labor, which is the extra output resulting from one more unit of the input labor. This curve is the demand for labor. Tool Kit 6.1 shows how to make the derivation.

Tool Kit 6.1: Deriving the Demand for Labor from the Short-Run Production Function

Firms hire workers to produce output. The additional output that one more worker produces is called the marginal product of labor. The marginal product schedule is also the demand for labor, in the sense that firms choose the amount of labor to hire by setting the marginal product equal to the real wage. Follow these steps to derive the demand for labor.

Step one: Identify and plot the short-run production function.

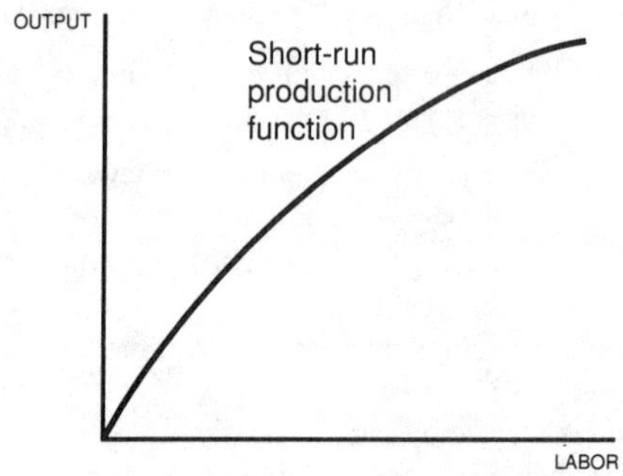

Step two: Compute the marginal product for each level of labor. The marginal product equals the following ratio.

Marginal Product = (Change in Output)/(Change in Labor)

Step three: Plot the marginal product.

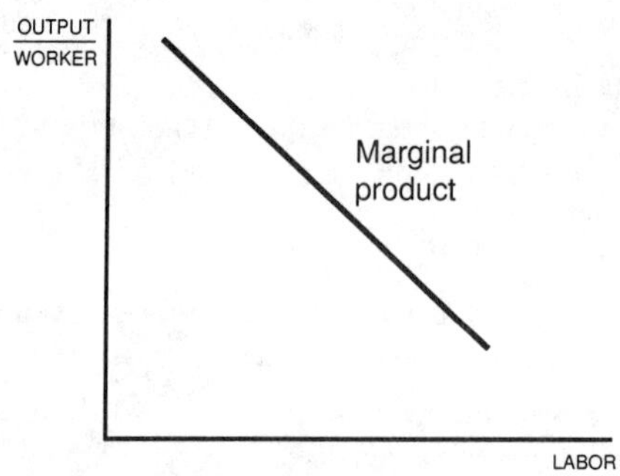

Step four: Identify the real wage. To find the quantity demanded of labor, find the quantity for which the real wage equals the marginal product.

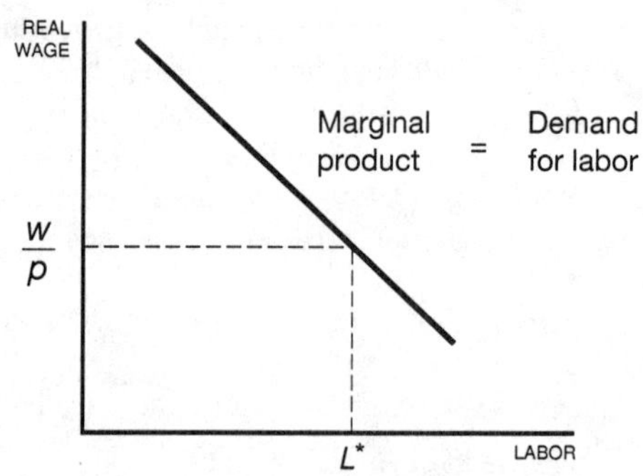

1 (Worked problem: demand for labor) This problem looks at Costa Guano, whose currency is the guano. The short-run production function is given in Table 6.1.

a Find the marginal product schedule.
b Suppose, for example, that the real wage is 300 guanos per year. How much labor is demanded?

Table 6.1

Quantity of labor (million person years)	*Output (millions of guanos)*
0	0
1	600
2	1,100
3	1,500
4	1,800
5	2,000
6	2,100
7	2,150

Step-by-step solution

Step one: Identify and plot the short-run production function. See Table 6.1.

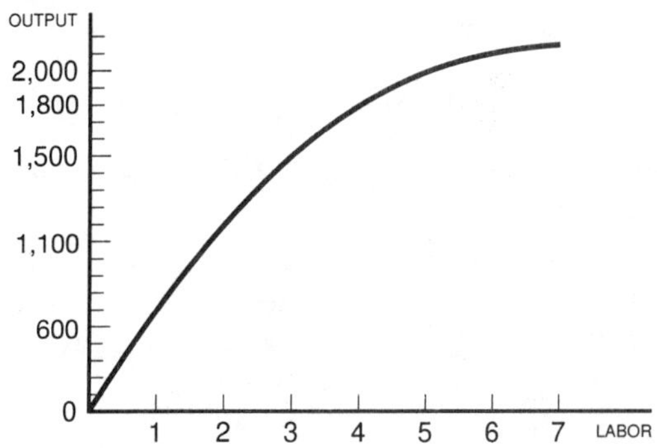

Step two: Compute the marginal product for each level of labor. When the first million workers are used, output rises from 0 to 600 million; therefore the marginal product of this worker is 600. When the second is added, output rises from 600 to 1,100; therefore the second worker's marginal product is 1,100 – 600 = 500. Continuing in the same manner gives the entire marginal product schedule.

Quantity of labor (million person years)	*Marginal product of labor*
1	600
2	500
3	400
4	300
5	200
6	100
7	50

Step three: Plot the marginal product curve.

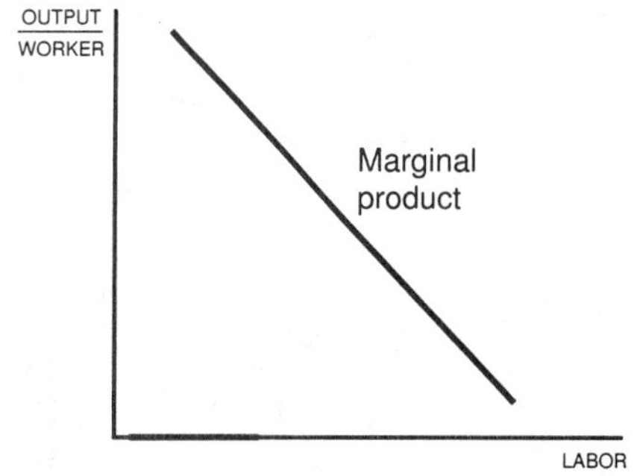

Step four: Find the quantity for which the real wage equals the marginal product. The real wage is 300, which equals marginal product when the quantity of labor is 4.

2 (Practice problem: demand for labor) The short-run production function is given in Table 6.2.

a Find the marginal product schedule.
b Suppose that the real wage is 3 thousand dorals. How much labor is demanded?

Table 6.2

Quantity of labor (million person years)	*Output (billions of dorals)*
0	0
1	25
2	45
3	60
4	70
5	75
6	78
7	80
8	81

3 (Practice problem: demand for labor) In the land of Erehwemos the short-run production function is as given in Table 6.3. The currency is called the wemo.

a Find the marginal product schedule.
b Suppose that the real wage is 3,000 wemos per year. How much labor is demanded?

Table 6.3

Quantity of labor (million person years)	*Output (billions of wemos)*
0	0
1	5
2	9
3	12
4	14
5	15
6	15.5

The Labor Market and the Product Market

The labor market and product market are linked by the short-run production function. The marginal product of labor, derived from the short-run production function, is the demand for labor, which, together with the supply of labor, determines the real wage. We will assume that the supply of labor is perfectly inelastic, an assumption that is not far from the truth. The short-run production function shows how much output will be produced by the supply of labor, and this quantity of output is the aggregate supply in the product market. Note the direction of influence: from the labor market to the product market. The labor market determines the laber supply and, with the production function, it determines the level of output. Changes in the product market have no impact upon the labor market. Tool Kit 6.2 illustrates this linkage.

Tool Kit 6.2: Deriving Aggregate Supply from the Labor Market and Short-Run Production Function

With the supply of labor and the short-run production function, we can find the economy's aggregate supply, which is also called potential GDP, full-employment output, or capacity. The labor market gives the real wage and the production function gives the aggregate supply. Follow these steps.

Step one: Identify the supply of labor and the short-run production function.

Step two: Find the demand for labor. Follow the steps of Tool Kit 6.1.

Step three: Find the equilibrium real wage. This is the real wage that clears the labor market.

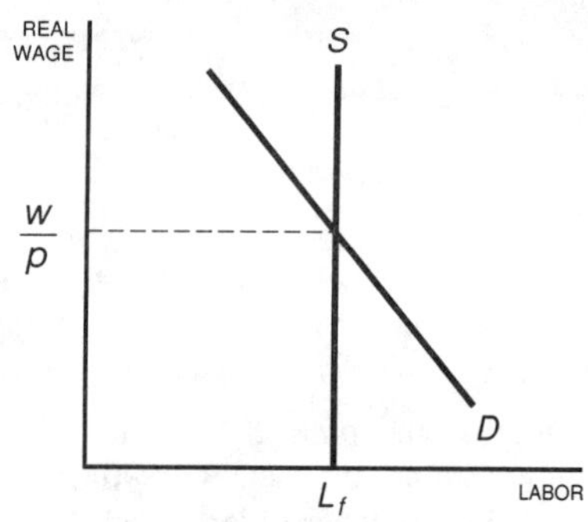

Step four: Find the economy's full employment output. This is the output corresponding to the equilibrium level of labor.

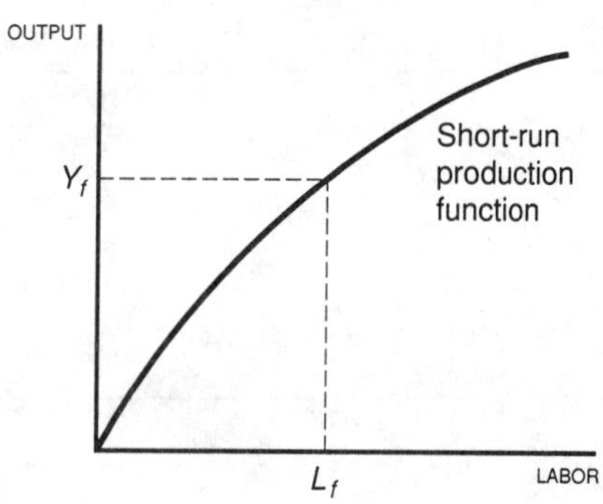

Step five: Plot the aggregate supply curve. This is a vertical line drawn with output equal to its full employment level.

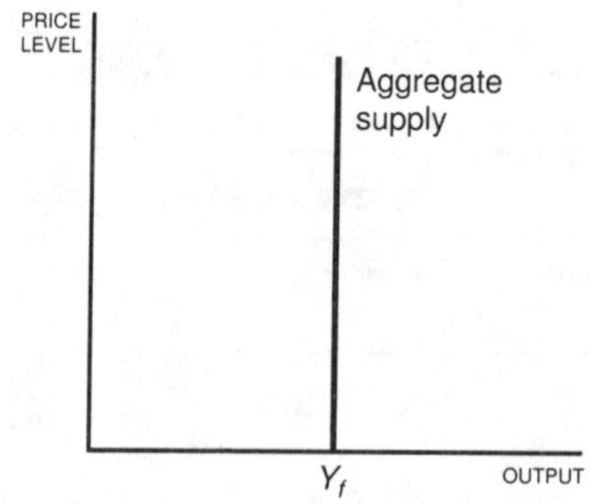

4 (Worked problem: aggregate supply) We continue with Costa Guano, whose production function is given in Table 6.1. The labor supply is inelastic, equal to 5 million.

a Calculate the marginal product schedule.
b Find the equilibrium real wage. Draw a diagram of the labor market.
c Find the economy's potential GDP. Draw the aggregate supply curve.

Step-by-step solution

Step one: Identify the supply of labor and the short-run production function. The production function is given in Table 6.1 and the labor supply equals 5 million.

Step two: Find the demand for labor. The demand for labor is as follows. Notice that it is the same as the marginal product schedule.

Quantity of labor (person years)	Real wage
1	600
2	500
3	400
4	300
5	200
6	100
7	50

Step three: Find the equilibrium real wage. Demand equals supply (5 million) when the wage equals 200.

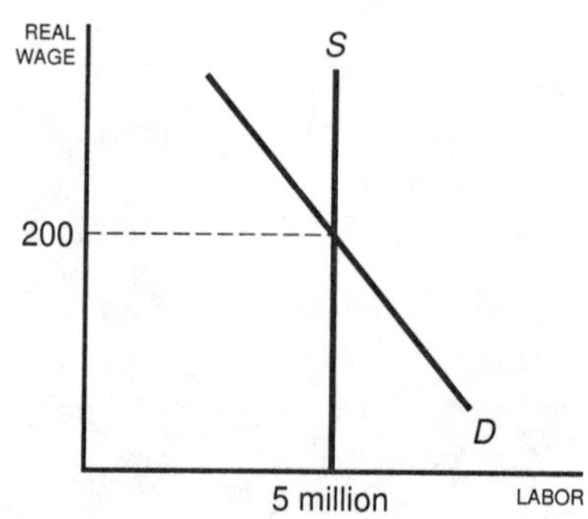

Step four: Find the economy's full-employment output. From the production function, output at 5 million person years equals 2,000 million guanos.

Step five: Plot the aggregate supply curve. Note that output equals 2,000 for each price level.

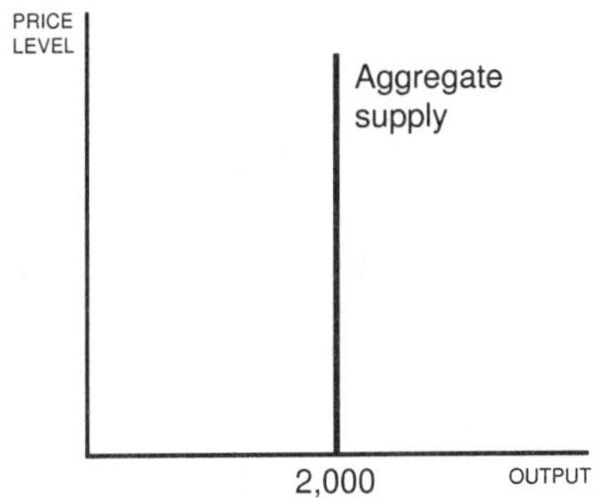

5 (Practice problem: aggregate supply) We continue with the analysis of El Dorado from problem 2. Suppose that the production function is given in Table 6.2 and that the labor supply is inelastic, equal to 3,000 person years.

a Find the demand for labor.

b Find the equilibrium real wage. Draw a diagram of the labor market.

Find the economy's potential GDP. Draw the aggregate supply curve.

6 (Practice problem: aggregate supply) We continue with the country of Erehwemos, where the production function is given in Table 6.3. Suppose that the labor supply is inelastic, equal to 5 million.

a Find the demand for labor.

b Find the equilibrium real wage. Draw a diagram of the labor market.

Find the economy's potential GDP. Draw the aggregate supply curve.

The Product Market and the Capital Market

The capital market determines the quantity of investment. Recall that the real interest rate adjusts to balance the demand and supply of funds. The product market is affected in that investment is one of the four components of aggregate demand. In this case the effects go both ways because the product market affects the capital market through the link between output (which equals income) and savings. For example, an increase in the level of the economy's output will lead households to increase their savings. Tool Kit 6.3 illustrates these linkages.

Tool Kit 6.3: Linking the Product and Capital Markets

The product market determines the economy's output, which equals its income. The capital market is affected because households save a fraction of their income. That fraction is the average propensity to save. The capital market then determines the level of investment, which is one of the components of aggregate demand. Keep straight this two-way influence with the following procedure.

Step one: Identify aggregate supply, aggregate demand (excluding investment), the investment function, and the average propensity to save.

Step two: Find the savings supply (assumed to be inelastic). First, observe that aggregate supply equals output and output equals income. Next, multiply income by the average propensity to save. The product is total savings.

Total savings = income × average propensity to save.

Step three: Find the equilibrum real interest rate and investment level by equating the investment function with total savings.

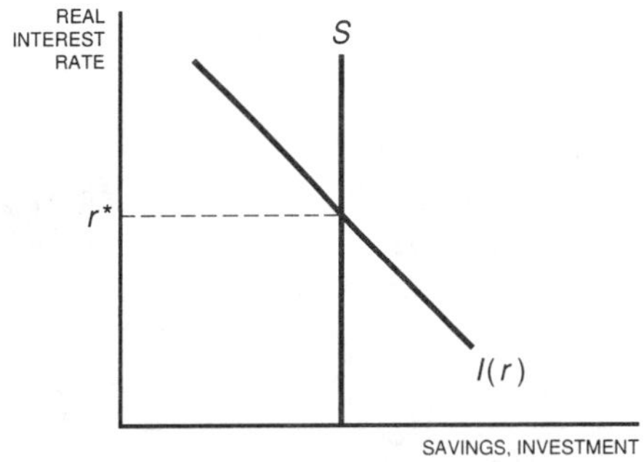

Step four: Find aggregate demand by adding investment to the aggregate demand (excluding investment).

Step five: Find the equilibrium price level by equating aggregate demand and aggregate supply.

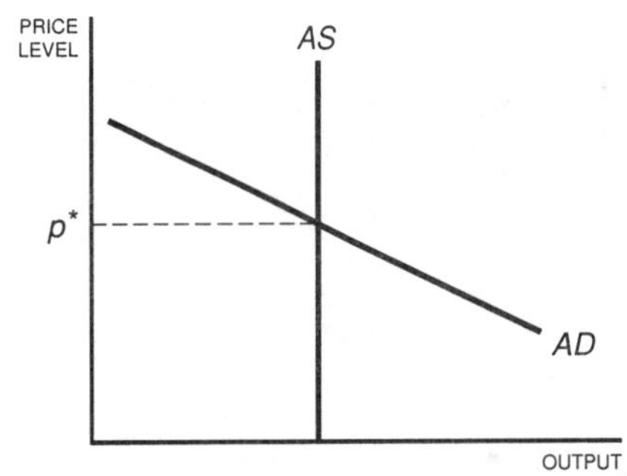

7 (Worked problem: product and capital markets) Continuing the analysis of Costa Guano, recall that the short-run production function is given in Table 6.1 and output equals 2,000 million guanos. Costa Guanoans save 10 percent of their income. The investment func-

tion and aggregate demand (excluding investment) are given in Table 6.4.

a Compute total savings.
b Find the equilibrum real interest rate. Draw a diagram of the capital market.
c Find aggregate demand.
d Find the equilibrium price level. Draw a diagram of the product market.

Table 6.4

Investment function		*Aggregate demand (excluding investment)*	
Investment (millions of guanos)	*Real interest rate*	*Aggregate demand (millions of guanos)*	*Price level*
50	10	1,000	280
75	9	1,200	260
100	8	1,400	240
125	7	1,600	220
150	6	1,800	200
175	5	2,000	180
200	4	2,200	160
225	3	2,400	140

Step one: Identify aggregate supply, aggregate demand (excluding investment), the investment function, and the average propensity to save. See Table 6.4 for the investment function and aggregate demand (excluding investment). Aggregate supply is 2,000 (from problem 4) and the average propensity to save is 0.1.

Step two: Find the savings supply (assumed to be inelastic). Total savings = 2,000 × 0.1 = 200.

Step three: Find the equilibrum real interest rate and investment level by equating the investment function with total savings. The capital market clears when the real interest rate equals 4 percent. Equilibrium investment is then 200.

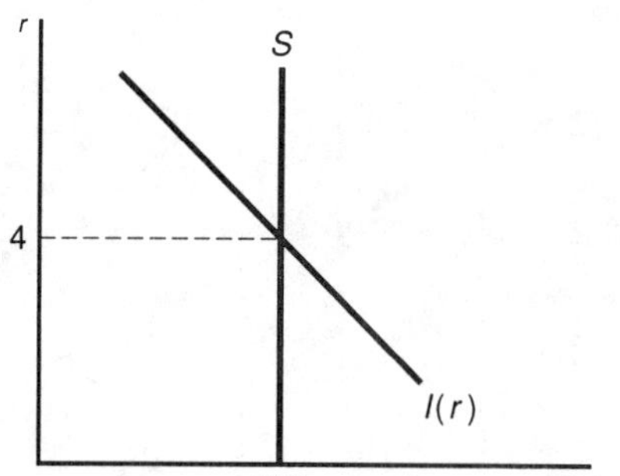

Step four: Find aggregate demand by adding investment to the aggregate demand (excluding investment). Adding investment, which equals 200, to aggregate demand gives the following.

Investment function	Aggregate demand
Aggregate demand (millions of guanos)	Price level
1,200	280
1,400	260
1,600	240
1,800	220
2,000	200
2,200	180
2,400	160
2,600	140

Step five: Find the equilibrium price level by equating aggregate demand and aggregate supply. The product market clears at a price level equal to 200.

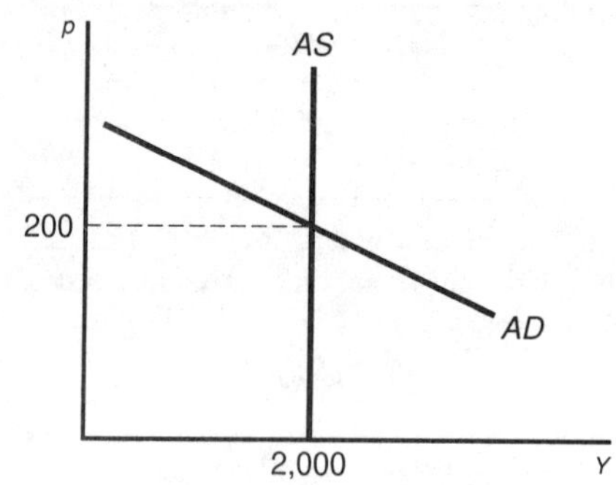

8 (Practice problem: product and capital markets) Continuing the analysis of El Dorado, recall that the short-run production function is given in Table 6.2 and output equals 60 billion dorals. Households save one-sixth of their income in El Dorado. The investment function and the aggregate demand curve (excluding investment) are given in Table 6.5.

a Compute total savings.
b Find the equilibrum real interest rate. Draw a diagram of the capital market.
c Find aggregate demand.
d Find the equilibrium price level. Draw a diagram of the product market.

Table 6.5

Investment function		*Aggregate demand (excluding investment)*	
Investment (billions of dorals)	*Real interest rate*	*Aggregate demand (billions of dorals)*	*Price level*
3	9	45	200
4	8	50	190
5	7	55	180
6	6	60	170
8	5	65	160
10	4	70	150
15	3	75	140
20	2	80	130

9 Continue with the analysis of Erehwemos, the production function of which is given in Table 6.3. Households save one-third of their income. The investment function and the aggregate demand (excluding investment) are given in Table 6.6. National income equals 15 billion.

a Compute total savings.
b Find the equilibrum real interest rate. Draw a diagram of the capital market.
c Find aggregate demand.
d Find the equilibrium price level. Draw a diagram of the product market.

Table 6.6

Investment function		*Aggregate demand (excluding investment)*	
Investment (billions of wemos)	*Real interest rate*	*Aggregate demand (billions of wemos)*	*Price level*
1	10	7	330
2	9	8	320
3	8	9	310
4	7	10	300
5	6	11	290
6	5	12	280
7	4	13	270
8	3	14	260
9	2	15	250

The Labor Market and the Capital Market

The investment function gives the level of investment for each interest rate. It represents firms' judgments about the profitability of potential investments. Since these profits come in the future, the chief determinant of the investment function is business expectations. It also depends upon costs and thus is linked to the labor market through the real wage and to technology. We will not do a separate set of problems here, but keep in mind that the investment function shifts up when technology improves or the real wage falls, and it shifts down in the opposite cases.

The Full-Employment Model

Now we are ready to put the pieces together and use the entire full-employment model to show the effects of various exogenous changes, including shifts in the supply of labor, the short-run production function, the supply of savings, the demand for savings, the money supply, and the size of government. There will be a worked problem and a practice problem for each. As usual, the basic method involves starting with an equilibrium, identifying an exogenous change, shifting curves, finding the new equilibrium, and comparing. This general equilibrium model is complicated because adjustment in one market affects the others, and these effects must be traced through. We will pay special attention to these linkages.

Tool Kit 6.4: Using the Full-Employment Model

The full-employment model is a general equilibrium model. This means that when there is an exogenous change, it starts a process that reverberates through all three markets. To avoid confusion proceed in this step-by-step fashion.

Step one: Start with an equilibrium in the product, labor, and capital markets.

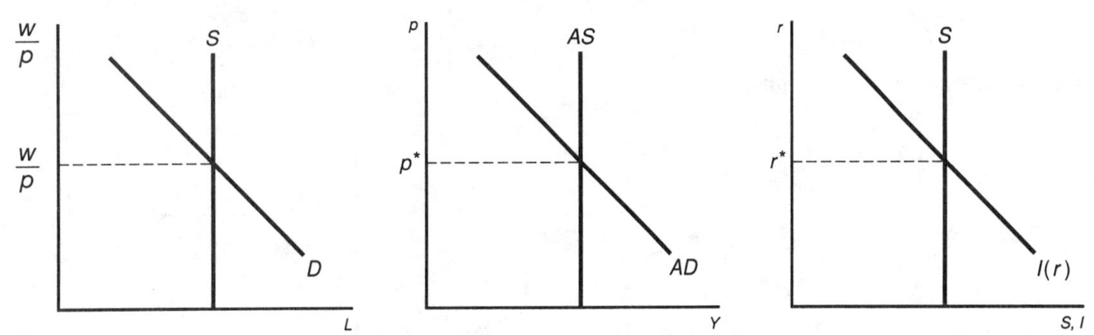

Step two: Identify an exogenous change and determine which curve shifts.

Step three: Shift the curve.

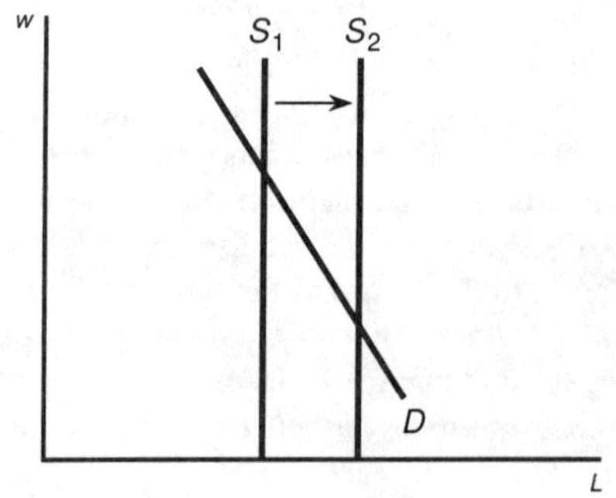

Step four: Find the new (partial) equilibrium in the market where the curve shifted.

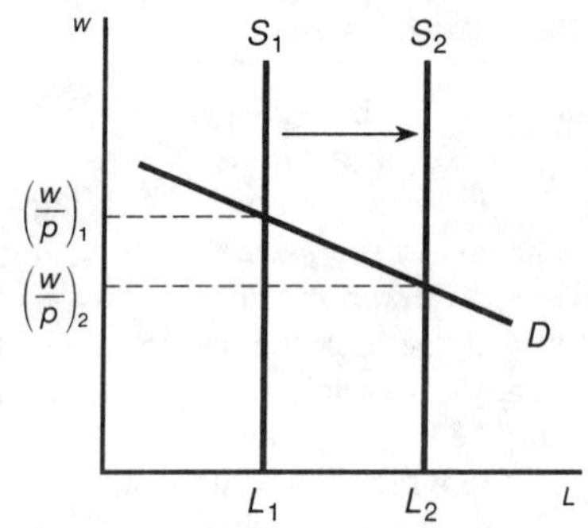

Step five: Trace through the links of the change to the related markets and shift the relevant curves.

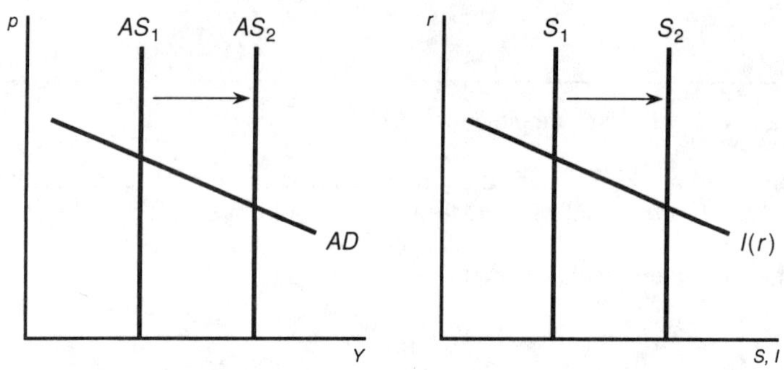

Step six: Find the new general equilibrium and compare.

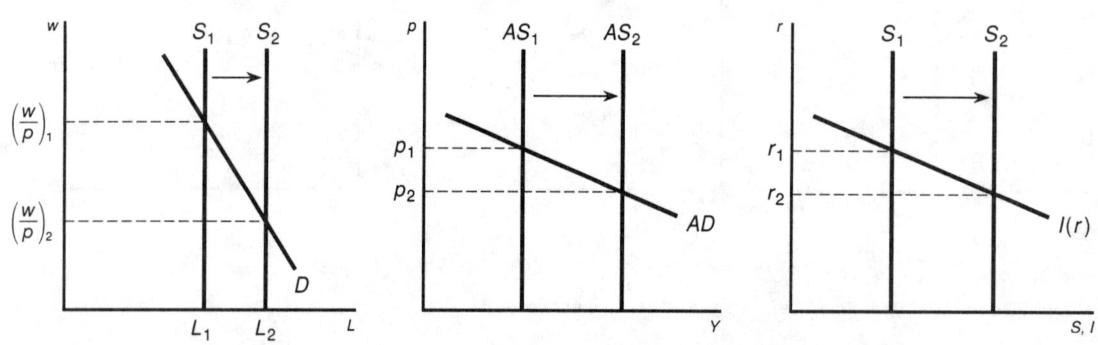

10 (Worked problem: full-employment model) Review problems 1, 4, and 7. This problem continues the analysis of Costa Guano.

a Draw a diagram illustrating the general equilibrium in the Costa Guano economy as solved for in the answers to problems 1, 4, and 7. In the following always begin with this equilibrium.

b Suppose that the money supply increases by 10 percent. Trace through the impact of this change in the economy. Show on the diagrams.

c Now suppose that the demand for investment rises by 50 million guanos at each interest rate. Trace through the impact of this change in the economy. Show on the diagrams.

d Now suppose that savings falls by 25 million. Of course, consumption will also increase by this same amount. Trace through the impact of this change in the economy. Show on the diagrams.

e Government expenditures and taxes increase by 50 million. Trace through the impact of this change in the economy. Show on the diagrams.

f The short-run production function doubles for each level of labor input.

g The supply of labor decreases to 3 million.

Step-by-step solution

Step one (a): Start with equilibrium in the product, labor, and capital markets.

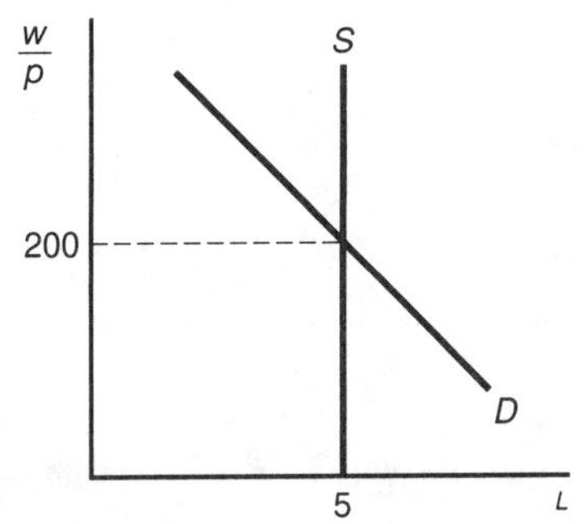

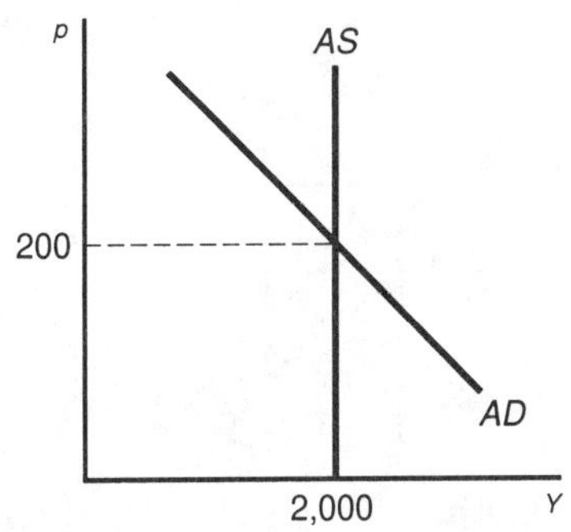

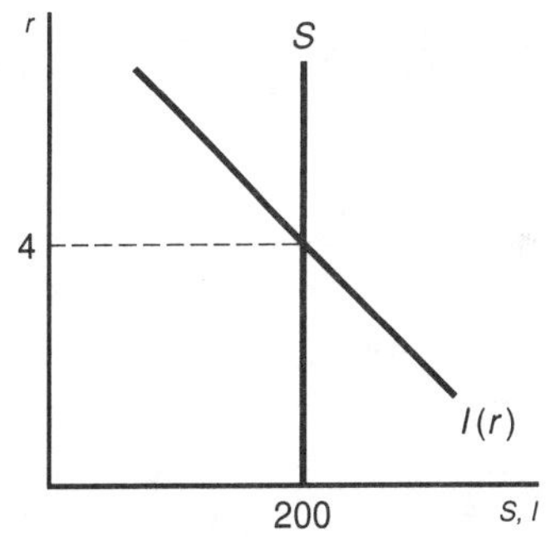

Step two (b): Identify an exogenous change and determine which curve shifts. Aggregate demand shifts up. The new aggregate demand schedule is as follows. Note that the price level has increased 10 percent for each level of output; e.g., 280 + 0.1 (280) = 308.

Aggregate demand (millions of guanos)	Price level
1,200	308
1,400	296
1,600	264
1,800	242
2,000	220
2,200	198
2,400	176
2,600	154

Step three: Shift the curve.

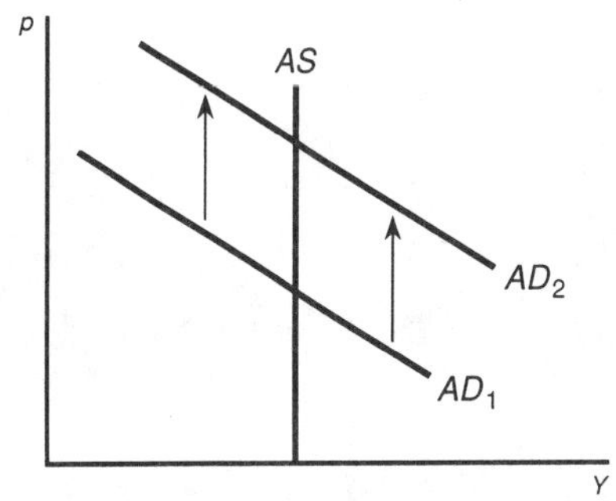

Step four: Find the new (partial) equilibrium in the market where the curve shifted. The new equilibrium price level is 220, which is 10 percent higher.

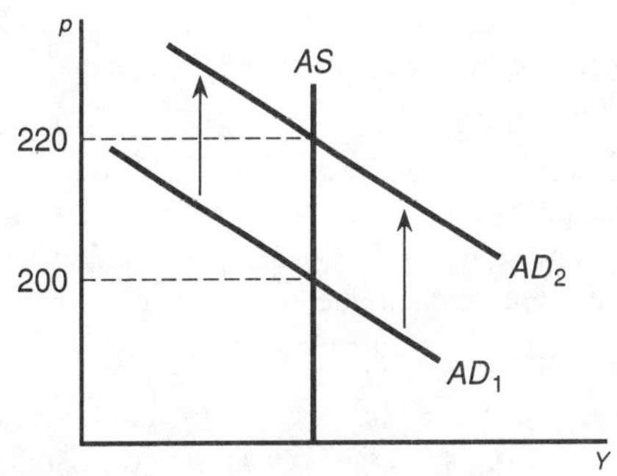

Step five: Trace through the links of the change to the related markets and shift the relevant curves. There are no other effects. Changes in the price level do not affect the capital and labor markets.

Step six: Find the new general equilibrium and compare. The only change is a 10 percent increase in the price level. No real magnitudes change; thus we conclude that the money supply increase is neutral.

Step one (c): Same as above.

Step two: Identify an exogenous change and determine which curve shifts. The investment function shifts up by 50 million at each real interest rate.

Step three: Shift the curve. The new investment function is given below.

Investment function

Investment (millions of guanos)	Real interest rate
100	10
125	9
150	8
175	7
200	6
225	5
250	4
275	3

Step four: Find the new (partial) equilibrium in the market where the curve shifted. The real interest rate rises to 6 percent. Because in this example the supply of savings is inelastic, there is no change in the level of investment.

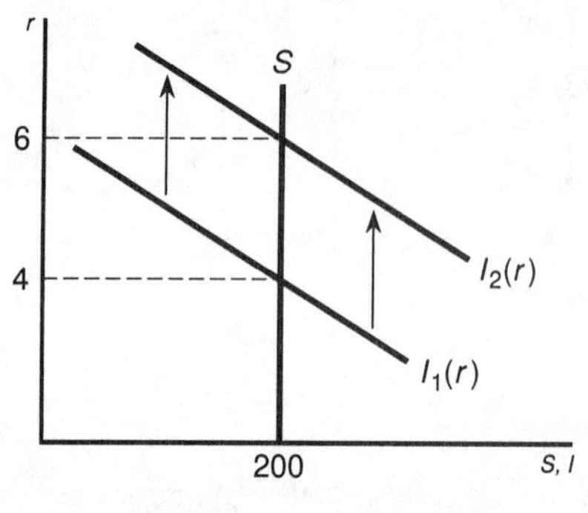

Step five: Trace through the links of the change to the related markets and shift the relevant curves. There are no other real effects. Aggregate demand may shift down because of the interest rate increase, but this would only lead to a fall in the price level.

Step six: Find the new general equilibrium and compare. The only change is the increase in the real interest rate. (If savings supply were upward sloping, there would be an increase in investment at the higher interest rate.)

Step one (d): Same as above.

Step two: Identify an exogenous change and determine which curve shifts. Savings falls to 175 million, and savings supply shifts to the left in the capital market. But the accompanying increase in consumption shifts aggregate demand to the right in the product market.

Step three: Shift the curves. The new aggregate demand is below.

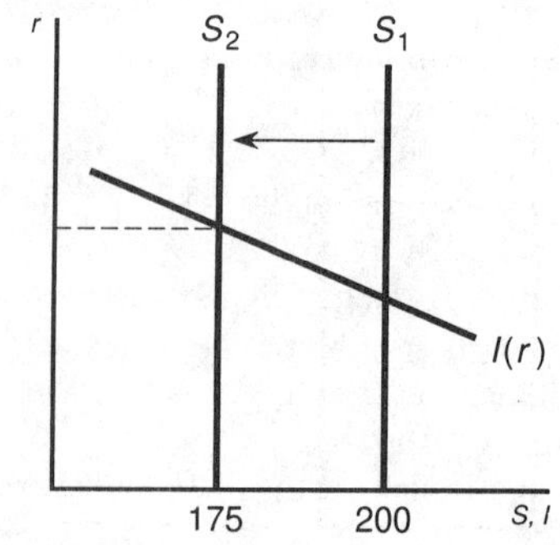

Aggregate demand (millions of guanos)	Price level
1,175	280
1,375	260
1,575	240
1,775	220
1,975	200
2,175	180
2,375	160
2,575	140

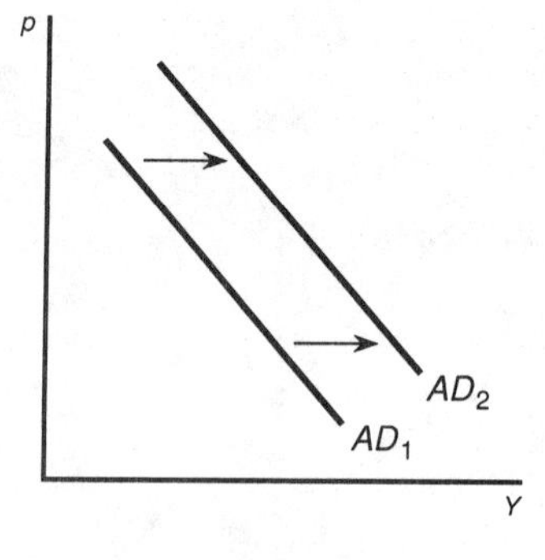

Step four: Find the new (partial) equilibrium in the market where the curve shifted. The real interest rate rises to 5 percent, and investment falls to 175 million. In the product market the price level increases.

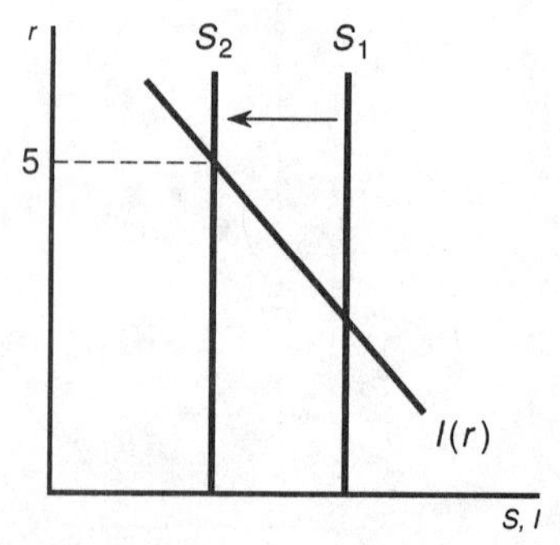

Step five: Trace through the links of the change to the related markets and shift the relevant curves. Aggregate demand must fall by the amount of the decrease in investment. This exactly offsets the increase in consumption; thus the price level returns to its original 200.

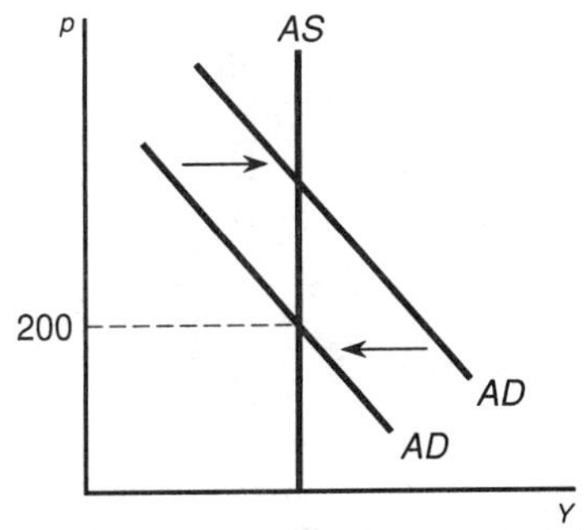

Step six: Find the new general equilibrium and compare. The new equilibrium has the same total output, although its composition is different. There is less investment (now only 175) and more consumption. Note how capital market changes do not affect current output. Of course, as time passes the changes in investment will affect the economy's growth rate.

Step one (e): Same as above.

Step two: Identify an exogenous change and determine which curve shifts. The increase in taxes reduces consumption. This shifts aggregate demand to the left. Because households save 10 percent of their income and consume 90 percent, consumption must fall by 45 million. The increase in government expenditures shifts aggregate demand to the right by 50 million. The net effect is a 5 million increase. In the capital market the supply shifts to the left by 5 million.

Step three: Shift the curves.

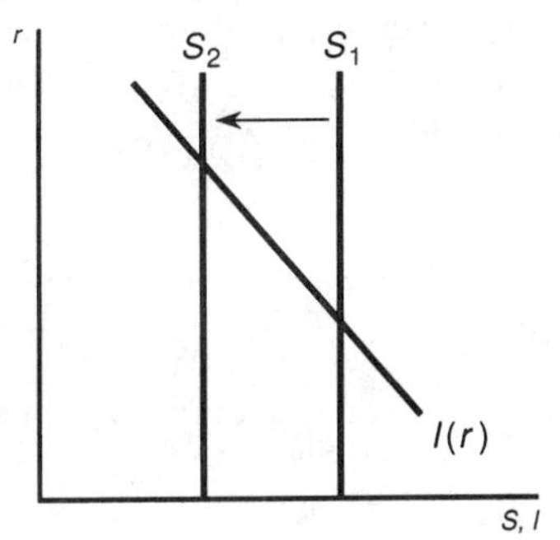

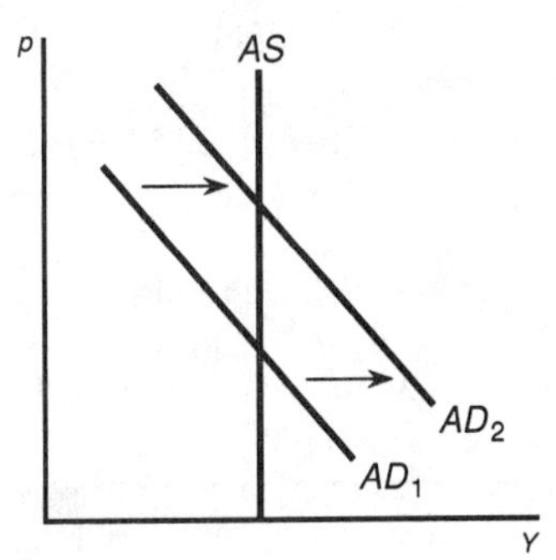

Step four: Find the new (partial) equilibrium in the market where the curve shifted. The real interest rate rises by less than 1 percent, and investment falls by the reduction in savings, which is 5 million. In the product market the price level increases slightly.

Step five: Trace through the links of the change to the related markets and shift the relevant curves. Aggregate demand must fall by the amount of the decrease in investment. This exactly offsets the 5 million increase in step three; thus the price level returns to its original 200.

Step six: Find the new general equilibrium and compare. The new equilibrium has the same total output, although its composition is different. There is less investment (now only 195), less consumption, and more government expenditures.

Step one (f): Same as above.

Step two: Identify an exogenous change and determine which curve shifts. The technological advance shifts the short-run production function up. Usually, this will shift the demands for both capital and labor to the right. In this case, we can calculate the new demand for labor by following the steps sketched in Tool Kit 6.1. Also, because the same amount of labor now produces more output, aggregate supply will shift to the right.

Step three: Shift the curves. The new production function and demand for labor are as follows.

Quantity of labor (million person years)	Output (millions of guanos)	Real wage (same as marginal product)
0	0	
1	1,200	1,200
2	2,200	1,000
3	3,000	800
4	3,600	600
5	4,000	400
6	4,200	200
7	4,300	100

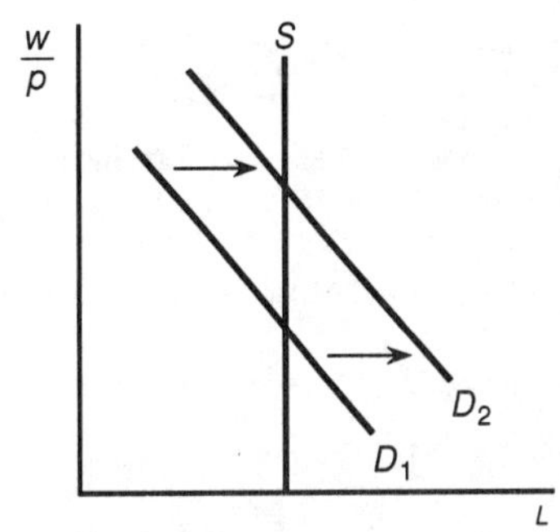

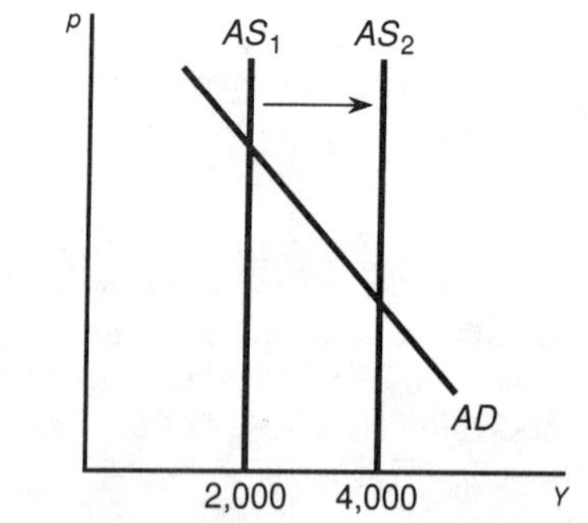

Step four: Find the new (partial) equilibrium in the market where the curve shifted. Labor supply, which equals 5 million, equals labor demand at a real wage of 400. Output increases to 4,000.

Step five: Trace through the links of the change to the related markets and shift the relevant curves. The shift to the right in aggregate supply reduces the price level.

Step six: Find the new general equilibrium and compare. Both output and the real wage double. Also, as firms anticipate higher returns from the better technology, the investment function will shift out, increasing the real interest rate.

Step one (g): Same as above.

Step two: Identify an exogenous change and determine which curve shifts. Labor supply shifts to the left to 3 million.

Step three: Shift the curve.

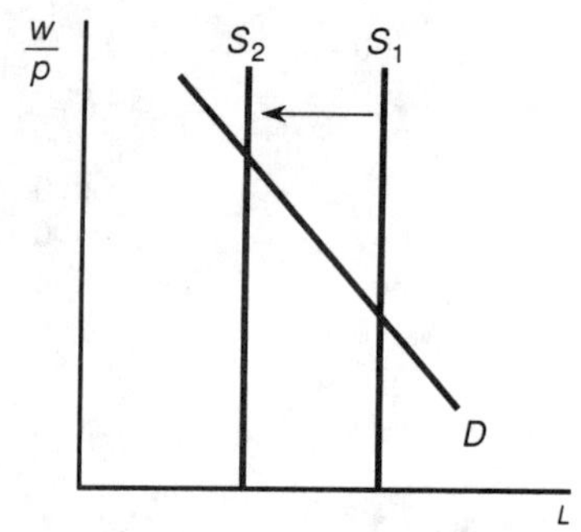

Step four: Find the new (partial) equilibrium in the market where the curve shifted. Note that the real wage increases to 400.

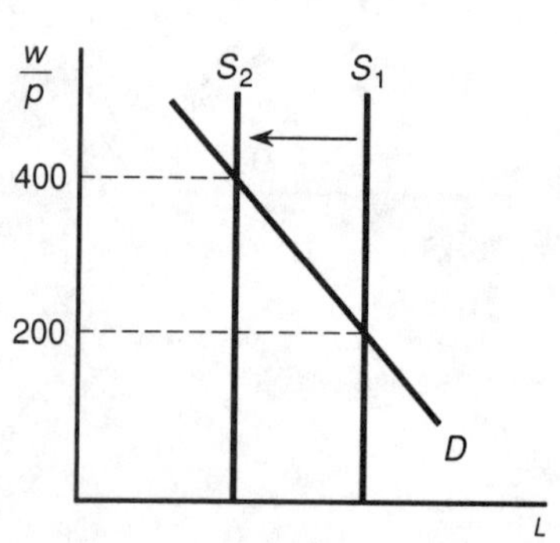

Step five: Trace through the links of the change to the related markets and shift the relevant curves. The reduction in labor reduces output to 1,500 million; thus aggregate supply shifts to the left, increasing the price level. In the capital market, the demand for investment probably falls as firms anticipate higher labor costs.

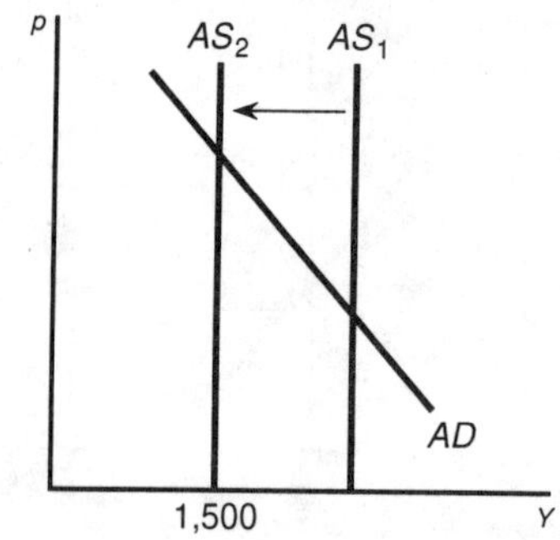

Step six: Find the new general equilibrium and compare.

11 (Practice problem: full-employment model) Review problems 2, 5, and 8. This problem continues the analysis of El Dorado.

a Draw a diagram illustrating the general equilibrium in the El Dorado economy as solved for in the answer to problems 2, 5, and 8. In the following always begin with this equilibrium.

b Suppose that the money supply increases by 20 percent. Trace through the impact of this change in the economy. Show on the diagrams.

c Now suppose that the demand for investment rises by 5 billion dorals at each interest rate. Trace through the impact of this change in the economy. Show on the diagrams.

d Now suppose that savings falls by 5 billion. Of course, consumption will also increase by this same amount. Trace through the impact of this change in the economy. Show on the diagrams.

e Government expenditures and taxes increase by 30 billion. Trace through the impact of this change in the economy. Show on the diagrams.

f The short-run production function doubles for each level of labor input.

g The supply of labor increases to 5 million.

12 (Practice problem: full-employment model) Review problems 3, 6, and 9. This problem continues the analysis of Erewhemos.

a Draw a diagram illustrating the general equilibrium in the Erewhemos economy as solved for in the answer to problems 3, 6, and 9. In the following always begin with this equilibrium.

b Suppose that the money supply increases by 10 percent. Trace through the impact of this change in the economy. Show on the diagrams.

c Now suppose that the demand for investment rises by 3 billion wemos at each interest rate. Trace through the impact of this change in the economy. Show on the diagrams.

d Now suppose that savings falls by 1 billion. Of course, consumption will also increase by this same amount. Trace through the impact of this change in the economy. Show on the diagrams.

e Government expenditure and taxes fall by 3 billion. Trace through the impact of this change in the economy.

f The short-run production function doubles for each level of output.

g The supply of labor decreases to 4 million.

Answers to Problems

2 *a* The marginal product schedule is as follows.

Quantity of labor (million person years)	Marginal product
1	25
2	20
3	15
4	10
5	5
6	3
7	2
8	1

b The quantity of labor demanded is 6 thousand person years of labor.

3 *a* The marginal product schedule is as follows.

Quantity of labor (million person years)	Marginal product
1	5,000
2	4,000
3	3,000
4	2,000
5	1,000
6	500

b The quantity of labor demanded is 3 million person years.

5 *a* The demand for labor is as follows.

Quantity of labor (million person years)	Real wage (dorals per year)
1	25
2	20
3	15
4	10
5	5
6	3
7	2
8	1

b Real wage = 15; output = 60.

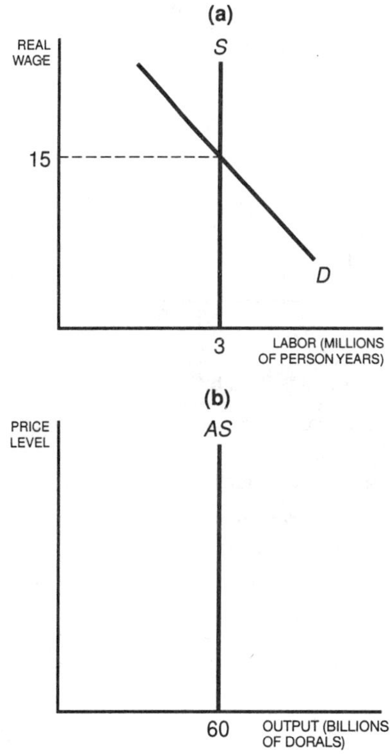

6 *a* The demand for labor is as follows.

Quantity of labor (million person years)	Real wage (wemos per year)
1	5,000
2	4,000
3	3,000
4	2,000
5	1,000
6	500

b Real wage = 1,000 per month; output = 15,000.

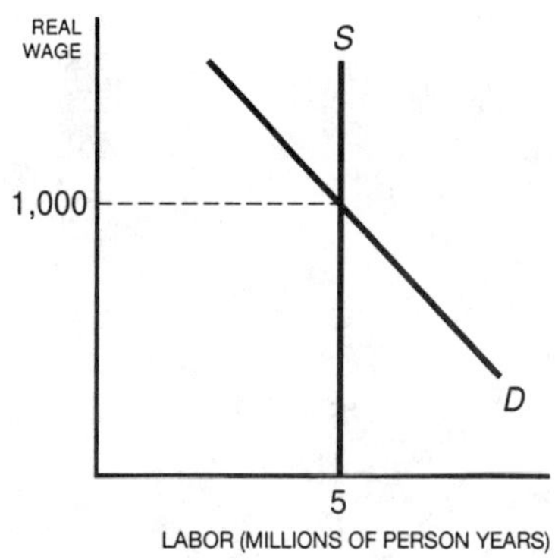

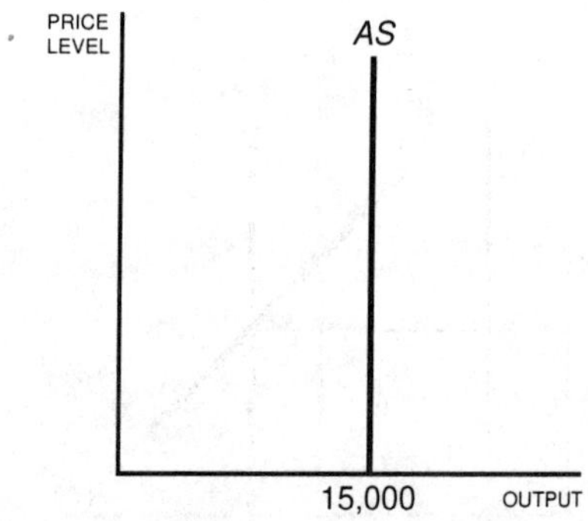

8 *a* Total savings = 10 billion dorals.

b Real interest rate = 4 percent. Investment = 10 billion dorals.

c Aggregate demand is shown below.

Aggregate demand (millions of dorals)	Price level
55	200
60	190
65	180
70	170
75	160
80	150
85	140
90	130

d Equilibrium price level = 190.

9 *a* Total savings = 1/3 × 15 = 5 billion.

b Real interest rate = 6 percent. Investment = 5 billion.

c Aggregate demand is as follows.

Aggregate demand (billion of wemos)	Price level
12	330
13	320
14	310
15	300
16	290
17	280
18	270
19	260
20	250

d Price level = 300.

11 *a* General equilibrium is shown below.

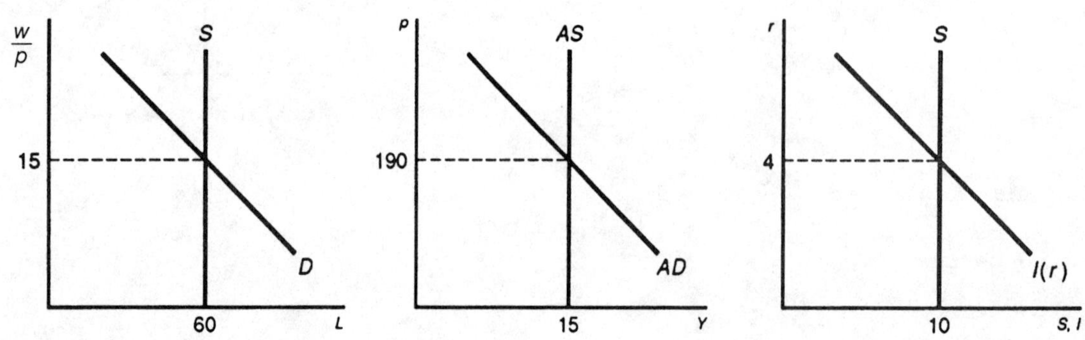

b Aggregate demand shifts up by 20 percent. The new price level equals 228, but there are no other changes. Money is neutral in the full-employment model.

c The real interest rate rises to 7 percent. Because the supply of funds is inelastic, the level of investment remains at 10 billion. There are no other changes. If the supply of funds sloped upward, investment would increase and aggregate demand would shift out, driving up the price level. This would result in less consumption to offset the increase in investment.

d The real interest rate rises to 7 percent. Investment falls to 5 billion. In the product market the increase in consumption shifts aggregate demand to the right by 5 billion, but this is offset by the decrease in investment. The price level remains constant. There are no other changes.

e The increase in taxes reduces disposable income by 30 billion. Since the average propensity to save is one-sixth, savings falls by 5 billion and consumption falls by 25 billion. The supply of savings shifts left and the real interest rate rises to 7 percent. Investment falls by 5 billion. Aggregate demand shifts right by the 30 billion increase in government expenditures, but it shifts left by the 5 billion fall in investment plus the 25 billion fall in consumption. The net effect is no shift in aggregate demand. The price level remains the same and there are no other changes.

f The real wage doubles to 30, and output increases to 120. Aggregate supply shifts right to 120 and the price level falls. Savings increases because national income doubles. Also, the demand for investment would increase.

g The supply of labor shifts to the right, driving the real wage down to 5. Output increases to 75; therefore aggregate supply shifts to the right. The increase in national income increases savings and the supply of funds shifts to the right.

12 *a* General equilibrium is shown below.

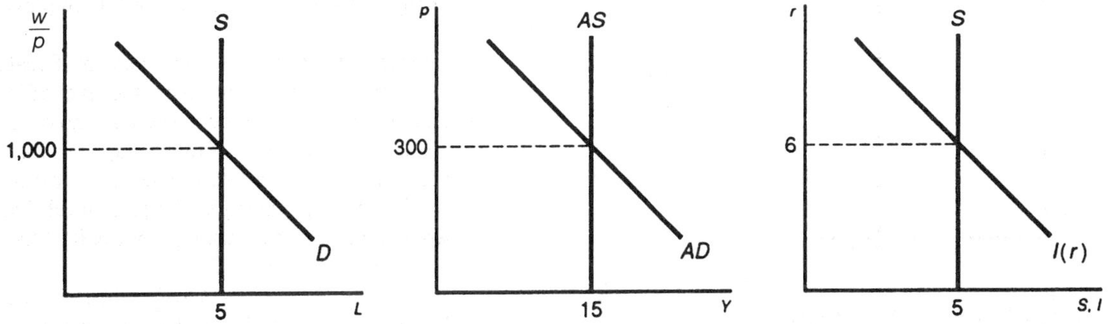

b Aggregate demand shifts up by 10 percent. The new price level equals 330, but there are no other changes. Money is neutral in the full-employment model.

c The real interest rate rises to 9 percent. Because the supply of funds is inelastic, the level of investment remains at 5 billion. There are no other changes. If the supply of funds sloped upward, investment would increase and aggregate demand would shift out, driving up the price level. This would result in less consumption to offset the increase in investment.

d The real interest rate rises to 7 percent. Investment falls by 1 billion. In the product market the increase in consumption shifts aggregate demand to the right by 1 billion, but this is offset by the decrease in investment. The price level remains constant. There are no other changes.

e The decrease in taxes increases disposable income by 3 billion. Since the average propensity to save is one-third, savings rises by 1 billion and consumption rises by 2 billion. The supply of savings shifts right and the real interest rate falls to 5 percent. Investment rises by 1 billion. Aggregate demand shifts left by the 3 billion decrease in government expenditures, but it shifts right by the 1 billion rise in investment plus the 2 billion rise in consumption. The net effect is no shift in aggregate demand. The price level remains the same and there are no other changes.

f The real wage doubles to 2,000, and output increases to 30. Aggregate supply shifts right to 30 and the price level falls. Savings increases because national income doubles. Also, the demand for investment would increase.

g The supply of labor shifts to the left, driving the real wage up to 2,000. Output decreases to 14 billion; therefore aggregate supply shifts to the left. The decrease in national income decreases savings and the supply of funds shifts to the left.

Chapter 7

USING THE FULL-EMPLOYMENT MODEL

Chapter Review

The full-employment model, developed in Chapter 6, is put to use analyzing the budget deficit, the trade deficit, and the causes of economic growth. The center of attention is the capital market and the openness of the economy to international trade and investment. Considerable use is made of two identities: the basic trade identity and the savings-investment identity. With this chapter the discussion of full-employment macroeconomics draws to a close. The next chapter begins the analysis of unemployment macroeconomics.

ESSENTIAL CONCEPTS

1 The **budget deficit** is the difference between what the government receives in taxes and its expenditures. The United States ran especially large deficits during the 1980s. The debt is the total amount owed by the government accumulated over years of deficit and surplus. Although not large based on international comparisons, it rose substantially during the 1980s.

2 National savings is the sum of private savings and government savings. When the government runs a deficit, government savings is a negative number. Thus, an increase in the deficit reduces national savings and shifts the supply of funds in the capital market to the left. In a closed economy this shift must raise interest rates and reduce investment. In a small open economy interest rates are set on international capital markets. Because interest rates are fixed, investment will not change. The reduction in national savings will lead to increased borrowing from abroad.

3 The difference between imports and exports in a given year is the **trade deficit** which, according to the basic trade identity, must equal the inflows of foreign capital. The exchange of currencies for imports, exports, and capital flows is governed by the exchange rate, which is the relative price of two currencies. The **exchange rate** adjusts to bring into balance the demands and supplies of all currencies.

4 In an open economy the **savings-investment identity** says that investment equals total savings, which comprises private savings, government savings (the budget deficit), and foreign inflows of capital. Thus if the budget deficit is increased and private savings and investment remain unchanged, capital flows from abroad (which equals the trade deficit) must also increase. Trade deficits are a problem because the foreign bor-

rowing that finances them accumulates into foreign indebtedness, which reduces the future standard of living. Policies to reduce the trade deficit focus on increasing private savings or reducing the budget deficit. Either would shift the supply of savings to the right.

5 Growth requires a more productive labor force, more and better capital, and technological advances. Investments in human capital, plant and equipment, and research and development enhance economic growth. These investments can be stimulated through the use of investment tax credits or accelerated depreciation. Another approach is to increase savings through individual retirement accounts or tax breaks on investment income. The net effect of these policies must balance the gain in private savings with the increased budget deficit caused by the loss in tax revenue. Finally, reduced government expenditures narrow the budget deficit, but reduced government investment may counteract the increased private investment.

BEHIND THE ESSENTIAL CONCEPTS

1 The connection between budget and trade deficits can be seen by examining two identities: the **basic trade identity** and the **savings-investment identity** for an open economy.

a The basic trade identity is

trade deficit = imports – exports = capital inflows.

This means that if foreign capital flows into the United States (in greater amounts than U.S. capital flows abroad), then the U.S. must run a trade deficit.

b The savings-investment identity for an open economy is

private savings + capital inflows
= investment + federal budget deficit.

This identity says that unless investment falls and savings rise by enough to finance the budget deficit, the deficit results in capital inflows, which the basic trade identity says must equal the trade deficit.

2 **Federal budget deficits** rose dramatically during the 1980s, increasing the nation's debt to record levels even though the 1980s were a time of peace and relative prosperity. The high deficits can be linked to four causes. Taxes were reduced, defense spending increased, Social Security and Medicare payments grew, and the accumulated debt required higher interest payments. At the same time, the U.S. **trade deficit** reached record levels, causing the United States to slip from creditor to debtor nation status.

3 Government borrowing can affect future generations in three ways. First, the burden can be shifted directly to the future generation by increasing taxes after the current generation has retired. Second, borrowing drives up interest rates and crowds out private investment. Finally, since much of the borrowing comes from abroad and foreign investors are attracted by higher U.S. interest rates, current borrowing increases foreign indebtedness. Repayment of foreign debt then requires reduced future living standards.

4 *The federal budget deficit caused the trade deficit* in the following way. Government borrowing to finance the budget deficit drove up interest rates and attracted capital flows from abroad. The increased foreign demand for dollars to lend and invest in the United States led to an appreciation of the dollar. The higher exchange rate made U.S. imports cheaper and U.S. exports more expensive. Foreigners bought fewer of the relatively expensive U.S. exports, while Americans bought more of the relatively cheaper imports, and the trade deficit skyrocketed.

5 The currency market is where different currencies are traded in order to make international transactions. Its price is called the exchange rate, and it is governed by supply and demand in a manner similar to other markets. There is a special language to this market, however. When the price of a country's currency rises, we say that its exchange rate *appreciates*; when it falls, we say that the currency *depreciates*. When the price is high, we say that the currency is strong. A weak currency simply means that the price is low.

SELF-TEST

True or False

1 The federal debt is the difference between what the government receives in taxes and what it spends.

2 Both the budget deficit and the federal debt are much larger for the United States than for most European countries.

3 In a closed economy investment equals private savings.

4 Increased budget deficits reduce national savings.

5 In a small open economy increasing the budget deficit shifts supply to the left, increasing the interest rate and reducing investment.

6 The trade deficit always equals capital inflows from abroad.

7 The exchange rate is the relative price of two currencies.

8 When the price of a country's currency rises, it is said to appreciate.

9 According to the savings-investment identity, investment equals the sum of private savings, government savings, and capital flows from abroad.

10 Although it has run large trade deficits for more than a decade, the United States is still a creditor nation.

11 The trade deficit can be reduced by reducing investment or increasing savings.

12 The main keys to increased growth are improving the

productivity of labor, adding capital, and advancing technology.

13 Human capital is the result of investment in education and training the labor force.

14 The interest elasticity of savings is quite high, indicating that an increase in the after tax rate of return will increase savings substantially.

15 In a large open economy like the United States savings and investment tend to move together.

Multiple Choice

1 During much of the 1980s, the United States ran

a federal budget deficits and trade surpluses;
b federal budget surpluses and trade deficits;
c federal budget and trade surpluses;
d federal budget and trade deficits;
e balanced federal budgets and trade accounts.

2 Which of the following is true of the relative size of United Stated budget deficits and the federal debt?

a Neither the deficits nor the debt are as large as those of many European countries and Canada.
b The deficits are larger than those of European countries and Canada, but the debt has not yet grown as large.
c The deficits are smaller than those of European countries and Canada, but the debt is greater.
d Both the deficits and debt are larger than those of European countries and Canada.
e Neither the deficits nor the debt are as large as those of Japan.

3 The debt/GDP ratio in the United States is about

a 14;
b 20;
c 25;
d 35;
e 50.

4 In a closed economy investment equals

a private savings;
b private savings minus government savings;
c government savings;
d private savings minus government savings minus the budget deficit;
e the trade deficit.

5 In a closed economy an increase in the budget deficit

a reduces the interest rate and investment;
b does not change the interest rate or investment;
c increases the interest rate and investment;
d increases the interest rate but reduces investment;
e decreases the interest rate but increases investment.

6 In a small open economy an increase in the budget deficit

a reduces the interest rate and investment;
b does not change the interest rate or investment;
c increases the interest rate and investment;
d increases the interest rate but reduces investment;
e decreases the interest rate but increases investment.

7 When a German buys a United States government bond, the transaction is an example of

a imports;
b exports;
c capital inflows;
d capital outflows;
e currency exchange.

8 The basic trade identity says that

a imports must equal exports;
b imports must equal capital flows from abroad;
c exports must equal capital flows from abroad;
d the trade deficit must equal capital flows from abroad;
e capital flows from abroad must equal capital flows to overseas economies.

9 If a country invests more overseas than foreign countries invest in it, then

a its trade account must be in balance;
b it must run a trade surplus;
c it must run a trade deficit;
d it must balance its government budget;
e its government deficit must equal the net flow of capital to other countries.

10 The exchange rate is

a the trade deficit between two nations;
b a country's net inflow of capital;
c the relative price of two currencies;
d the rate of appreciation of a country's currency;
e the rate of depreciation of a country's currency.

11 In an open economy, the savings-investment identity says that

a private savings must equal private investment;
b private savings plus capital flows from abroad must equal investment;
c private savings plus capital flows from abroad must equal investment plus the government deficit;
d private savings plus capital flows from abroad must equal the government deficits plus the trade deficit;
e private savings plus capital flows from abroad must equal the government deficit plus the trade deficit plus investment;

12 According to the savings-investment identity for an open economy, investment may be financed from

a private savings;
b government savings;
c capital flows from abroad;
d all of the above;
e a and c.

13 Typically, developing economies

a borrow less than mature economies;

b borrow while mature economies lend;
c lend while mature economies borrow;
d neither borrow nor lend;
e borrow or lend at the same rates as mature economies.

14 In the mid-1980s, the United States
a changed status from a creditor to a debtor nation;
b changed status from a debtor to a creditor nation;
c remained a creditor nation, while running trade deficits;
d remained a debtor nation, increasing foreign indebtedness;
e saw no change in its foreign indebtedness.

15 To reduce the trade deficit, a country can
a shift the investment function to the left or the savings curve to the right;
b shift the investment function to the right or the savings curve to the left;
c shift either the investment function or the savings curve to the right;
d shift either the investment function or the savings curve to the left;
e restrict the importation of foreign goods.

16 To increase investment in a closed economy,
a shift the investment function to the left or the savings curve to the right;
b shift the investment function to the right or the savings curve to the left;
c shift either the investment function or the savings curve to the right;
d shift either the investment function or the savings curve to the left;
e negotiate with foreign counties to reduce world interest rates.

17 Policies to enhance growth include
a investment in human capital;
b investment in plant and equipment;
c investment in research and development;
d public investments;
e all of the above.

18 A 10 percent investment tax credit
a allows firms to deduct 10 percent of the cost of investment from the tax base;
b reduces the firms' tax payments by 10 percent;
c allows firms to subtract 10 percent of the cost of the investment from their tax payment;
d waives taxes on 10 percent of a firm's investments;
e offers the opportunity to borrow funds at a 10 percent discount off the market interest rate.

19 Individual retirement accounts and other tax breaks for savers
a increase savings because households have greater incentive to save;
b decrease savings because smaller tax collection increases the budget deficit;
c may increase or decrease savings depending upon the relative magnitude of increased household savings and increased budget deficits;
d reduce savings because households have greater incentive to save;
e increase savings because smaller tax collection increases the budget deficit.

20 For the United States increased private savings will likely
a increase the budget deficit;
b reduce the budget deficit;
c increase investment;
d leave interest rates and investment unchanged;
e cause the dollar to appreciate.

Completion

1 The __________ is the cumulative amount that the government owes.

2 The difference between government expenditures and revenues is the __________.

3 The basic trade identity says that the trade deficit must equal __________.

4 In an open economy, private savings plus capital flows from abroad must equal investment plus the __________.

5 The relative price of two currencies is called the __________.

6 When the price of a country's currency rises, it is said to __________.

7 The United States is currently a __________ nation.

8 Investments in education and training produce __________.

9 An __________ allows firms to subtract a fraction of the cost of an investment from their taxes.

10 The measure of how much private savings increase when the after tax interest rate falls is called the __________.

Answers to Self-Test

True or False

1	f	6	t	11	t
2	f	7	t	12	t
3	t	8	t	13	t
4	t	9	t	14	f
5	f	10	f	15	t

Multiple Choice

1	d	6	b	11	c	16	c
2	a	7	c	12	d	17	e
3	d	8	d	13	b	18	c
4	a	9	b	14	a	19	c
5	d	10	c	15	a	20	c

Completion

1 federal debt
2 budget deficit
3 capital inflows from abroad
4 budget deficit
5 exchange rate
6 appreciate
7 debtor
8 human capital
9 investment tax credit
10 interest elasticity of savings

Doing Economics: Tools and Practice Problems

The discussion of the three major topics of this chapter—budget deficits, trade deficits, and growth—centers on the capital market. Government finances budget deficits by borrowing funds on the capital market. Trade deficits, through the basic trade identity, result in flows of foreign capital to the capital market. The engine of growth is investment in research, human capital, and capital equipment, and this investment must be financed with capital obtained on the capital market. An essential aspect of the capital market is its openness to international borrowing and savings. We first look at the model of the small open economy and then study the model most appropriate to the United States, the large open economy. Throughout the discussion, the trade and savings investment identities will play an important role.

The Small Open Economy

The international capital market is so huge that a small country's borrowing and lending have no effect on interest rates. Thus, a small open economy can borrow and lend on international markets at a fixed interest rate. Because its investment equals its quantity demanded at that fixed interest rate, domestic savings have no effect on investment. This separation of savings and investment implies that the most important effects of budget deficits concern flows of foreign capital. Another implication identifies trade deficits as a result of domestic savings and investment decisions. Tool Kit 7.1 shows how the small open economy model works.

Took Kit 7.1: Using the Small Open Economy Model

For a small open economy the interest rate is fixed, determined on international capital markets that are large relative to the size of the economy. If the interest rate clears the domestic market, the trade account is balanced. Higher interest rates imply a trade surplus; lower interest rates imply a trade deficit. Follow these steps to analyze the working of the capital market for a small open economy.

Step one: Identify the world interest rate, the demand, and the supply of funds.

Step two: Find the level of investment. This is quantity demanded, and it is read off the demand curve at the world interest rate.

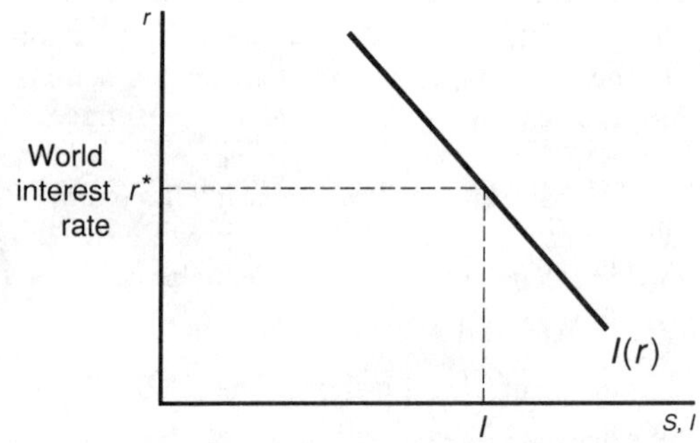

Step three: Find the level of savings. This is the quantity supplied, and it is read off the supply curve at the world interest rate.

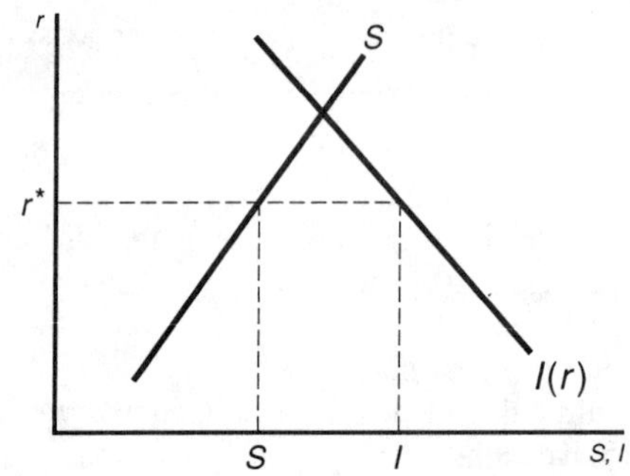

Step four: Find the level of capital inflows or outflows. If the quantity demanded exceeds the quantity supplied, then the country imports capital. Otherwise capital is exported.

Capital inflows from abroad = quantity demanded − quantity supplied (if positive).

Capital outflows to abroad = quantity supplied − quantity demanded (if positive).

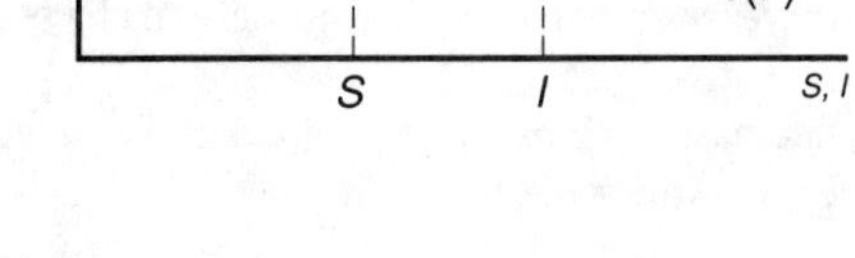

Step five: Find the trade deficit or surplus. If there are capital inflows, the country runs a trade deficit. If there are capital outflows, the country runs a trade surplus.

Trade deficit = inflows of foreign capital.

Trade surplus = outflows of foreign capital.

1 (Worked problem: small open economy) Costa Guano is a small open economy facing a world interest rate equal to 10 percent. Its domestic demand and supply of funds are given in Table 7.1.

a Find the level of investment.
b Find the level of savings.
c Find the level of capital inflows or outflows.
d Does the country run a trade deficit or surplus? How much is it?

Table 7.1

Interest rate (percent)	*Demand for funds (millions of guanos)*	*Supply of funds (millions of guanos)*
15	100	100
14	110	90
13	120	80
12	130	70
11	140	60
10	150	50
9	160	40
8	170	30

Step-by-step solution

Step one: Identify the world interest rate, the demand, and the supply of funds. The world interest rate is 10 percent and the demand and supply of funds are given in Table 7.1.

Step two: Find the level of investment. When the interest rate is 10 percent, the demand for funds (investment) equals 150 million.

Step three: Find the level of savings. At an interest rate equal to 10 percent, savings (supply of funds) equals 50 million.

Step four: Find the level of capital inflows or outflows. The quantity demanded exceeds the quantity supplied, so the country imports capital.

Capital inflows from abroad = quantity demanded – quantity supplied = 150 – 50 = 100 million.

Step five: Find the trade deficit or surplus. If there are capital inflows, the country runs a trade deficit.

Trade deficit = inflows of foreign capital = 100 million.

2 (Practice problem: small open economy) El Dorado is a small open economy facing a world interest rate equal to 9 percent. Its domestic demand and supply of funds are given in Table 7.2.

a Find the level of investment.
b Find the level of savings.
c Find the level of capital inflows or outflows.
d Does the country run a trade deficit or surplus? How much is it?

Table 7.2

Interest rate (percent)	*Demand for funds (millions of dorals)*	*Supply of funds (millions of dorals)*
11	200	400
10	225	350
9	250	300
8	275	250
7	300	200
6	325	150
5	350	100

3 (Practice problem: small open economy) Erehwemos is a small open economy facing a world interest rate equal to 15 percent. Its domestic demand and supply of funds are given in Table 7.3.

a Find the level of investment.
b Find the level of savings.
c Find the level of capital inflows or outflows.
d Does the country run a trade deficit or surplus? How much is it?

Table 7.3

Interest rate (percent)	*Demand for funds (millions of wemos)*	*Supply of funds (millions of wemos)*
20	50	50
19	60	45
18	70	40
17	80	35
16	90	30
15	100	25
14	110	20

Large Open Economy

The United States is a large open economy. This means that domestic savings affects interest rates and the level of investment. Approximately 80 percent of additional savings is invested in the United States. The remaining savings flows abroad. We can analyze large open economies by distinguishing between the domestic and total supply of funds. Tool Kit 7.2 shows how this is done.

Tool Kit 7.2: Using the Large Open Economy Model

Unlike the small open economy model, where foreign savings is perfectly elastic, for the large open economy foreign savings is upward sloping. The interest rate is determined where the total savings supply intersects the domestic demand for funds. Follow these steps.

Step one: Identify the foreign supply of savings, the domestic supply of savings, and the domestic demand for funds (investment function).

Step two: Calculate the total savings supply curve. For each interest rate add the quantity of foreign and domestic savings.

Total savings = foreign savings + domestic savings.

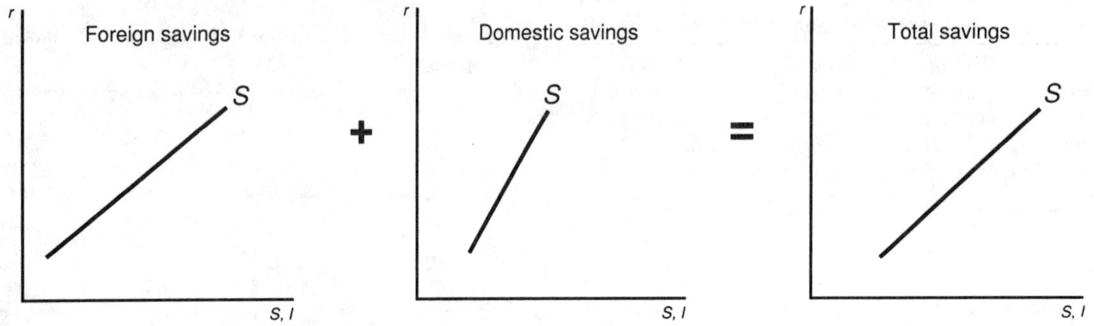

Step three: Find the interest rate that clears the market.

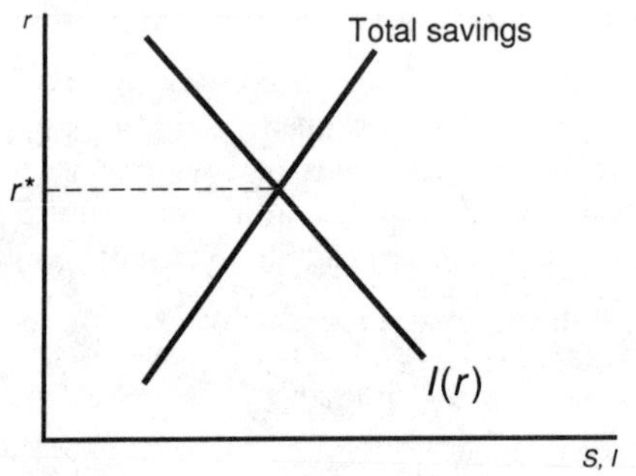

Step four: Find the level of investment. This is the quantity demanded at the equilibrium interest rate.

Step five: Find the level of domestic savings. This is read off the domestic supply of funds at the equilibrium interest rate.

Step six: Calculate the level of capital flows. Recall that this is also the level of the trade deficit.

Capital inflows from abroad = trade deficit = quantity demanded – quantity supplied (if positive).

Capital outflows to abroad = trade surplus = quantity supplied – quantity demanded (if positive).

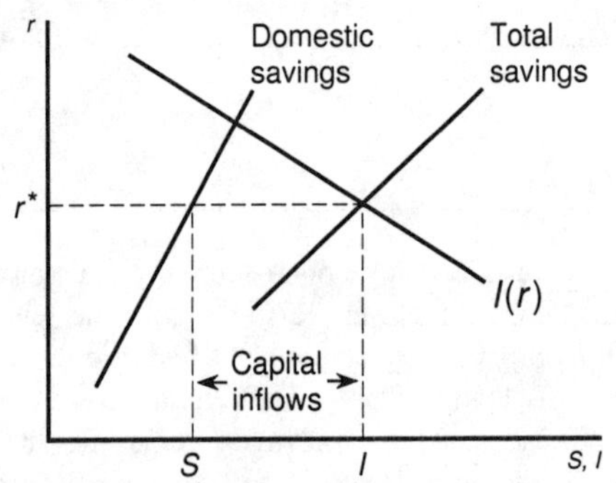

4 (Worked problem: large open economy) Table 7.4 gives the foreign supply of funds, the domestic supply of funds, and the demand for funds (investment function) for a large open economy.

a Calculate the total supply of funds.
b Find the equilibrium interest rate.
c Does this country import or export capital? How much?
d What is the size of the trade deficit or surplus?

Table 7.4

Interest rate (percent)	*Foreign supply (billions of dollars)*	*Domestic supply (billions of dollars)*	*Domestic demand (billions of dollars)*
12	10,000	15,000	13,000
11	9,000	13,000	16,000
10	8,000	11,000	19,000
9	7,000	9,000	22,000
8	6,000	7,000	25,000
7	5,000	5,000	30,000

Step-by-step solution

Step one: Identify the foreign supply of savings, the domestic supply of savings, and the domestic demand for funds. They are given in Table 7.4.

Step two: Calculate the total savings supply curve. For each interest rate add the quantity of foreign and domestic savings.

Total savings = foreign savings + domestic savings.

At 12 percent total savings = 10,000 + 15,000 = 25,000. At 11 percent total savings = 9,000 + 13,000 = 22,000. Continuing, we get the total supply.

Interest rate (percent)	Total supply (billions of dollars)
12	10,000 + 15,000 = 25,000
11	9,000 + 13,000 = 22,000
10	8,000 + 11,000 = 19,000
9	7,000 + 9,000 = 16,000
8	6,000 + 7,000 = 13,000
7	5,000 + 5,000 = 10,000

Step three: Find the interest rate that clears the market. Supply and demand are equal at $19,000 million when the interest rate is 10 percent.

Step four: Find the level of investment. This is the quantity demanded at the equilibrium interest rate, and it equals $19,000 million.

Step five: Find the level of domestic savings. This is read off the domestic supply of funds at the equilibrium interest rate. At 10 percent the domestic supply is $11,000 million.

Step six: Calculate the level of capital flows. Recall that this is also the level of the trade deficit. Since demand exceeds supply, there will be inflows of capital.

Capital inflows from abroad = trade deficit
= quantity demanded – quantity supplied
= 19,000 – 11,000 = $8,000 million.

5 (Practice problem: large open economy) Table 7.5 gives the foreign supply of funds, the domestic supply of funds, and the demand for funds (investment function) for a large open economy.

a Calculate the total supply of funds.
b Find the equilibrium interest rate.
c Does this country import or export capital? How much?
d What is the size of the trade deficit or surplus?

Table 7.5

Interest rate (percent)	*Foreign supply (billions of dollars)*	*Domestic supply (billions of dollars)*	*Domestic demand (billions of dollars)*
15	1,000	500	900
14	800	400	1,200
13	600	300	1,500
12	400	200	1,800
11	200	100	2,100
10	100	50	2,500

6 (Practice problem: large open economy) Table 7.6 gives the foreign supply of funds, the domestic supply of funds, and the demand for funds (investment function) for a large open economy.

a Calculate the total supply of funds.
b Find the equilibrium interest rate.
c Does this country import or export capital? How much?
d What is the size of the trade deficit or surplus?

Table 7.6

Interest rate (percent)	*Foreign supply (billions of dollars)*	*Domestic supply (billions of dollars)*	*Domestic demand (billions of dollars)*
8	200	50	100
7	180	45	110
6	160	40	130
5	140	35	140
4	120	30	150
3	100	25	160
2	80	20	170

Answers to Problems

2 *a* Investment = 250.
b Savings = 300.
c Capital outflows = 50.
d Trade surplus = 50.

3 *a* Investment = 100.
b Savings = 25.

c Capital inflows = 75.

d Trade surplus = 75.

5 *a*

Interest rate (percent)	Total supply (billions of dollars)
15	1,000 + 500 = 1,500
14	800 + 400 = 1,200
13	600 + 300 = 900
12	400 + 200 = 600
11	200 + 100 = 300
10	100 + 50 = 150

b Interest rate = 14 percent.

c Capital inflows = 1,200 – 400 = 800.

d Trade deficit = 800.

6 *a*

Interest rate (percent)	Total supply (billions of dollars)
8	200 + 50 = 250
7	180 + 45 = 225
6	160 + 40 = 200
5	140 + 35 = 175
4	120 + 30 = 150
3	100 + 25 = 125
2	80 + 20 = 100

b Interest rate = 4 percent.

c Capital inflows = 150 – 30 = 120.

d Trade deficit = 120.

Part Three

Unemployment Macroeconomics

Chapter 8

OVERVIEW OF UNEMPLOYMENT MACROECONOMICS

Chapter Review

Beginning the unemployment part of the course, this chapter sketches how the full-employment model is modified to study downturns in the economy when there is excess capacity and unemployment persists at a high rate. The discussion of the consequences of fixed wages and price for the labor, product, and capital markets provides the framework for the remainder of this part. (In Part Four we see how wages and prices adjust slowly, leading to the investigation of dynamics.) The chapter concludes by applying this framework to recent macroeconomic history.

ESSENTIAL CONCEPTS

1 Slow adjustment of wages to changes in the supply and demand for labor is the basic explanation for the high levels of unemployment that periodically trouble the economy. This chapter and the others in Part Three develop the model of the economy under the assumptions that wages and prices are rigid and that there is no net change in the capital stock. While this is a simplification, it does expose the basic structure of the economy and gives results that mirror the behavior of labor and product markets in the short run.

2 The aggregate labor market includes all of the workers and jobs in the economy. If the wages settle at the market-clearing level, the economy would be at full employment. Anyone willing to work at the going wage could find a job. In reality, this is not the case, because wages are somewhat inflexible. When the demand for labor shifts to the left and the wage fails to adjust downward, unemployment exists. The key to understanding unemployment lies in three issues: what causes shifts in the demand for labor; why do wages fail to adjust; and why does the shortage take the form of unemployment rather than a shared reduction in hours among workers. The latter issues are postponed until Part Four; the issue of shifts in labor demand is the focus here.

3 In the product market the vertical aggregate supply intersects with the downward-sloping aggregate demand. If prices settle at the market-clearing level, the economy would produce its potential GDP. Prices are costly to change, however, and in the short run may be rigid. In this case, if demand shifts to the left, for example, the economy's output will fall to the quantity demanded, which is less than aggregate supply. There is excess capacity.

4 Any **demand shock**, such as economic downturns abroad or a loss in business confidence, can bring about a demand shock and production level below the economy's capacity. When there is excess capacity, government may use fiscal policy to shift aggregate demand to the right, restoring full employment without waiting for the slow adjustment of wages and prices. On the other hand, supply shifts have no impact on output when there is excess capacity.

5 The **Federal Reserve Board** uses monetary policy to affect interest rates. This can also shift aggregate demand in that lower interest rates may stimulate investment. The Federal Reserve is also interested in controlling inflation by limiting aggregate demand. It may be too aggressive in raising interest rates, pushing the economy into recession.

6 Examples of the effects of fiscal and monetary policy include the Kennedy tax cut in 1963, a fiscal stimulus that brought the economy out of stagnation into a period of low unemployment, sustained growth, and stable prices, and Federal Reserve chairman Paul Volcker's tight monetary policy, which led to the deep recession of the early 1980s. The most recent recession in 1991 also may have resulted from overaggressive monetary policy, and the reasons for the recovery remain controversial.

BEHIND THE ESSENTIAL CONCEPTS

1 The supply of labor is quite inelastic, but not perfectly so. If the wage rises, more people are willing to work. If the wage that you could currently earn rose high enough, you might get a part-time job, increase the hours at the part-time job you already have, or even drop out of college to get a full-time job. It follows that if the wage falls, individuals voluntarily leave the labor force. Involuntary unemployment, however, differs from voluntary unemployment. If the wage is stuck above the market-clearing level, there is an excess supply of workers, each of whom would like a job at the going wage. Because there is a shortage of jobs, these individuals are involuntarily unemployed.

2 The basic structure of the model developed in this chapter is the same as the full-employment model studied in Chapters 6 and 7. The economy divides into three markets: product, labor, and capital. Further, the various supplies and demands have essentially the same interpretation, and the markets are interdependent. The key difference is that here we assume that price and wages are rigid, whereas in the full-employment version, prices adjust to clear the markets. The reason for the two approaches is that the economy behaves in the long run as the full-employment model predicts. This is natural because prices and wages have time to adjust in the long run. However, in the short run, before there is time for adjustment, the fixed price approach works better.

3 While aggregate demand plays a minor role in full-employment macroeconomics, it takes center stage in unemployment macroeconomics. With fixed prices the short side of the product market determines the output level. When demand exceeds supply, supply is the short side, output is at full employment, but there is upward pressure on prices. When demand falls short of supply, demand is the short side, and output is set at the intersection of demand and the price level. According to this model economic downturns result from insufficient demand.

4 In microeconomics we often look at one market at a time. Macroeconomics, however, is a general equilibrium discipline. We must keep an eye on product, labor, and capital markets. The fundamental lesson from general equilibrium analysis is that markets are linked. The key link between the product and labor market is that shifts in output bring about shifts in the demand for labor. The key link between the capital and product market is that interest rates affect investment and consumption, the two chief components of aggregate demand.

SELF-TEST

<u>True or False</u>

1 The basic explanation for unemployment is that wages do not adjust quickly to their market clearing levels.

2 The focus of this chapter is the short run, when prices and wages are rigid and the net change in the capital stock is small.

3 Involuntary unemployment results when the demand for labor shifts to the right and wages fail to adjust.

4 If reductions in the demand for labor were shared equally among workers, there would not be unemployment, but rather underemployment.

5 The supply curve for labor is quite elastic.

6 If the labor supply curve is upward sloping and wages adjust, then any reduction in the number of jobs represents involuntary unemployment.

7 Most economists agree that the primary causes of disturbance in the labor market are shifts in the demand curve.

8 In the model of the product market prices are assumed to be rigid.

9 A rightward shift in aggregate demand leads to excess capacity and involuntary unemployment.

10 When the economy experiences excess capacity, a rightward shift in aggregate supply increases output.

11 When the economy experiences excess capacity, a rightward shift in aggregate demand increases output.

12 Lower interest rates encourage investment, shifting aggregate demand to the right.

13 The Federal Reserve Board controls monetary policy.

14 The Kennedy tax cut shifted aggregate supply to the right, avoiding a recession.

15 Paul Volcker's restrictive monetary policies shifted aggregate demand to the left, causing the recession of the early 1980s.

Multiple Choice

1 Unemployment macroeconomics deals with the short run, a period of time when

a product prices are rigid;
b nominal wages are rigid;
c real wages are rigid;
d the net change in the capital stock is small;
e all of the above.

2 The basic model of the labor market in this chapter is based on the assumption that

a wages are fixed;
b product prices are fixed;
c interest rates and product prices are fixed;
d wages and product prices are fixed;
e wages, interest rates, and product prices are fixed.

3 In modern economies, the labor supply curve is

a perfectly elastic;
b relatively flat;
c horizontal;
d relatively inelastic;
e downward sloping.

4 Suppose that the demand for labor increases. If the supply of labor is perfectly inelastic, then

a wages increase;
b employment increases;
c both wages and employment increase;
d wages decrease;
e both wages and employment decrease.

5 If the wage is the market-clearing wage, then

a any unemployment is involuntary;
b any unemployment is voluntary;
c unemployment is voluntary at low wages and voluntary at high wages;
d the supply of labor is relatively elastic;
e none of the above.

6 If every worker who wants a job at prevailing wages has one, then there is

a full employment;
b no voluntary unemployment;
c no inflation;
d b and c;
e all of the above.

7 Suppose the demand curve for labor shifts to the left. Then

a there is full employment if wages are flexible;
b if wages are inflexible, there is involuntary unemployment;
c there is unemployment if the supply of labor is relatively inelastic;
d the supply of labor will also shift to the left;
e a and b.

8 Suppose the demand curve for labor shifts to the left. If wages are rigid, then

a most workers work fewer hours;
b wages rise;
c most workers work more hours;
d most workers work the same number of hours, but some individuals will not be able to find employment;
e most workers work more hours, but some job vacancies will not be filled.

9 The aggregate supply curve is

a vertical;
b relatively flat at low levels of output but relatively steep at higher levels of output;
c relatively steep at low levels of output but relatively flat at higher levels of output;
d relatively inelastic;
e horizontal.

10 The aggregate demand and supply model of the product market presented in this chapter is based on the assumption that

a wages are fixed;
b product prices are fixed;
c interest rates and product prices are fixed;
d wages and product prices are fixed;
e wages, interest rates, and product prices are fixed.

11 There is excess capacity when

a aggregate supply is to the left of aggregate demand at the fixed price level;
b aggregate demand is to the left of aggregate supply at the fixed price level;
c the price level is fixed above its market clearing level;
d the demand for labor is elastic;
e interest rates are set on international capital markets.

12 When there is excess capacity

a an increase in aggregate demand has no effect on output;
b an increase in aggregate supply puts upward pressure on prices;
c a decrease in aggregate supply puts upward pressure on prices;
d an increase in aggregate demand increases output with little effect on prices;
e an increase in aggregate supply increases output and reduces the price level.

13 When there is excess demand

a output is below the economy's potential GDP;
b output is above the economy's potential GDP;
c output equals the economy's potential GDP;
d there is downward pressure on prices;
e *a* and *d*.

14 When there is excess demand

a an increase in aggregate demand has no effect on output;

b an increase in aggregate supply puts upward pressure on prices;
c a decrease in aggregate supply puts upward pressure on prices;
d an increase in aggregate demand increases output with little effect on prices;
e none of the above.

15 When the government increases defense spending in order to shift aggregate demand to the right it is engaging in

a monetary policy;
b fiscal policy;
c supply restrictions;
d protectionism;
e monetary stimulus.

16 Monetary policy is controlled by the

a U.S. Treasury Department;
b Congress;
c President;
d Federal Reserve;
e b and c.

17 Monetary policy affects aggregate demand through its effect on

a capacity;
b unemployment;
c interest rates;
d real wages;
e the price level.

18 The Kennedy administration's 1963 tax cut caused

a aggregate demand to shift to the left;
b aggregate supply to shift to the left;
c aggregate demand to shift to the right;
d aggregate supply to shift to the right;
e no change in either aggregate supply or demand.

19 The oil price shocks of the early 1970s caused

a aggregate demand to shift to the left;
b aggregate supply to shift to the left;
c aggregate demand to shift to the right;
d aggregate supply to shift to the right;
e no change in either aggregate supply or demand.

20 The onset of the 1991 recession was due in part to

a overaggressive monetary policy;
b the Gulf War inspired oil price shock;
c a weak banking system in the aftermath of the savings and loan crisis;
d all of the above;
e none of the above.

Completion

1 When employers pay the market-clearing wage, any unemployment is __________.

2 If the demand for labor shifts to the left and there is no adjustment in wages, unemployment __________.

3 If the price level is greater than the level at which aggregate demand equals aggregate supply, then there is an excess __________ of goods.

4 Leftward shifts in aggregate demand that lead to downturns in the economy are called __________.

5 When the government increases its expenditures in order to shift aggregate demand to the right and eliminate excess capacity it is performing __________.

6 The __________ controls monetary policy.

7 During a period of excess capacity, a rightward shift in __________ leaves output unchanged.

8 When there is full employment, a rightward shift in __________ puts upward pressure on prices.

9 The Kennedy tax cut shifted the aggregate __________ curve to the __________.

10 In the early 1980s, the Federal Reserve Board took actions that caused the aggregate __________ curve to shift to the __________, leading to both a recession and a reduction in inflation.

Answers to Self-Test

True or False

1	t	6	f	11	t
2	t	7	t	12	t
3	t	8	t	13	t
4	t	9	f	14	f
5	f	10	f	15	t

Multiple Choice

1	e	6	a	11	b	16	d
2	e	7	e	12	d	17	c
3	d	8	d	13	c	18	c
4	a	9	a	14	a	19	b
5	b	10	d	15	b	20	d

Completion

1 voluntary
2 increases
3 supply
4 demand shocks
5 fiscal policy
6 Federal Reserve
7 aggregate supply
8 aggregate demand
9 demand, right
10 demand, left

Doing Economics: Tools and Practice Problems

In the aggregate labor market, the economy's levels of employment, unemployment, and real wages are determined. Unemployment results from the failure of wages to adjust to the market-clearing level, and several problems explore this relationship between sticky wages and unemployment. The output of the economy is determined in the product market, but with rigid prices it may not be clear. The key to analyzing how low output is affected by changes in the economy is to find out whether the initial equilibrium is at the intersection of aggregate demand and supply or one of excess demand or supply. Several problems study this issue.

Unemployment and Rigid Wages

When real wages remain stuck above market-clearing levels, the number of workers willing to work at the going wage exceeds the number of jobs available. This excess supply of labor is involuntary unemployment and is part of the overall unemployment rate. In this section we calculate the real wage by adjusting the nominal wage for inflation and then determine the level of unemployment. Tool Kit 8.1 shows how to proceed.

Tool Kit 8.1: Determining the Unemployment Rate

Above market-clearing real wages lead to unemployment. The level of unemployment is the amount of excess supply in the labor market. Follow these steps to see this relationship.

Step one: Identify the demand curve, the supply curve, and the nominal wage and price level.

Step two: Find the real wage by adjusting the nominal wage for inflation:

real wage = (nominal wage/price index) × 100.

Step three: Substitute the real wage into the demand curve and find the quantity demanded. This is the number of jobs available.

Step four: Substitute the real wage into the supply curve and find the quantity supplied. This is the number of workers willing to work at the going wage.

Step five: Find the quantity of unemployment by subtracting the quantity demanded from the quantity supplied:

unemployment =
quantity supplied – quantity demanded.

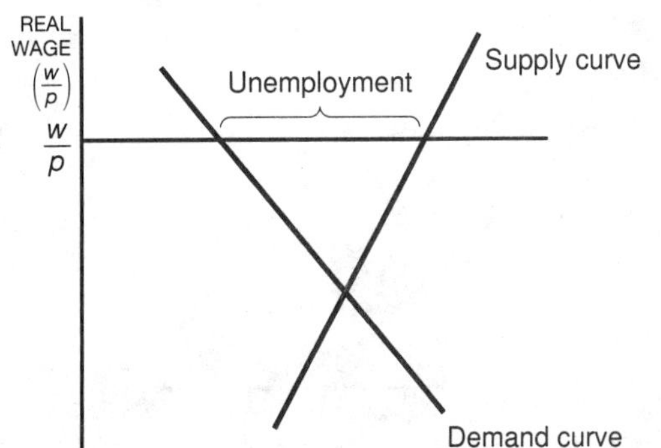

1 (Worked problem: unemployment rate) The nominal wage level equals $2,400 per month, and the price index equals 120. Table 8.1 gives the demand and supply of labor. Find the level of unemployment.

Table 8.1

Real wage	*Demand*	*Supply*
$2,400	6,000	18,000
$2,200	7,000	16,000
$2,000	8,000	14,000
$1,800	9,000	12,000
$1,600	10,000	10,000
$1,400	11,000	8,000
$1,200	12,000	6,000

Step-by-step solution

Step one: Identify the demand curve, the supply curve, and the nominal wage and price level. The demand and supply are given in Table 8.1, the nominal wage is $2,400, and the price index equals 120.

Step two: Find the real wage by adjusting the nominal wage for inflation:

real wage = ($2,400/120) × 100 = $2,000.

Step three: Substitute the real wage into the demand curve, and find the quantity demanded. It is 8,000.

Step four: Substitute the real wage into the supply curve, and find the quantity supplied. It is 14,000.

Step five: Find the quantity of unemployment by subtracting the quantity demanded from the quantity supplied:

unemployment = 14,000 – 8,000 = 6,000.

2 (Practice problem: unemployment rate) Suppose that the nominal wage level remains at $2,400, as in problem 1, and the demand and supply curves remain as in Table 8.1 but the price level increases to 150. Find the new level of unemployment.

3 (Practice problem: unemployment rate) Suppose that the nominal wage is $3,300, the price index is 150, and the demand and supply curves are as given in Table 8.1. Find the level of unemployment.

4 (Practice problem: unemployment rate) For each of the following, find the level of unemployment given the demand and supply of labor shown in Table 8.2.

a Nominal wage = $50,000; price level = 100.
b Nominal wage = $50,000; price level = 125.
c Nominal wage = $50,000; price level = 167.
d Nominal wage = $60,000; price level = 120.

Table 8.2

Real wage	*Demand*	*Supply*
$60,000	8,000	26,000
$55,000	10,000	25,000
$50,000	12,000	24,000
$45,000	14,000	23,000
$40,000	16,000	22,000
$35,000	18,000	21,000
$30,000	20,000	20,000
$25,000	22,000	19,000

The Labor Market with Rigid Wages

When either the demand or supply of labor shifts and wages fail to adjust to the market-clearing level, there is unemployment. In modern economies, wages exhibit downward rigidity, although they do adjust upward when conditions warrant. In the following problems real wages are assumed to be inflexible downward, but flexible upward. Tool Kit 8.2 shows how to analyze labor markets under these conditions.

Tool Kit 8.2: Analyzing the Labor Market with Rigid Real Wages and Unemployment

If the labor market is at its market-clearing equilibrium and demand or supply shifts, it may not move to the new market-clearing equilibrium if the real wage does not adjust. Follow these steps to analyze a labor market in which the real wage is rigid when market conditions call for it to fall.

Step one: Start with a market-clearing equilibrium in the labor market.

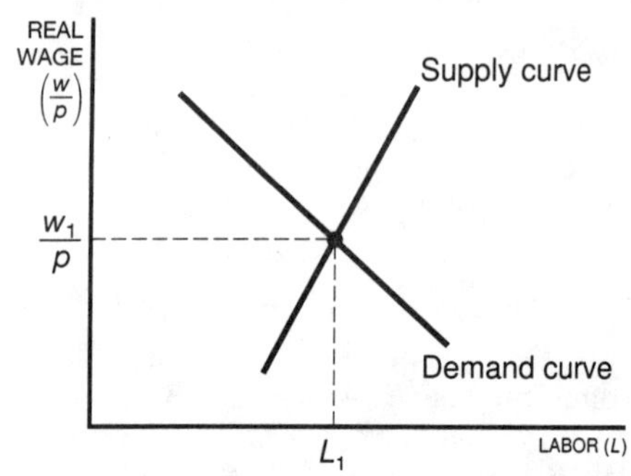

Step two: Identify a cause, and determine which curve shifts.

Step three: Shift the supply or demand curve.

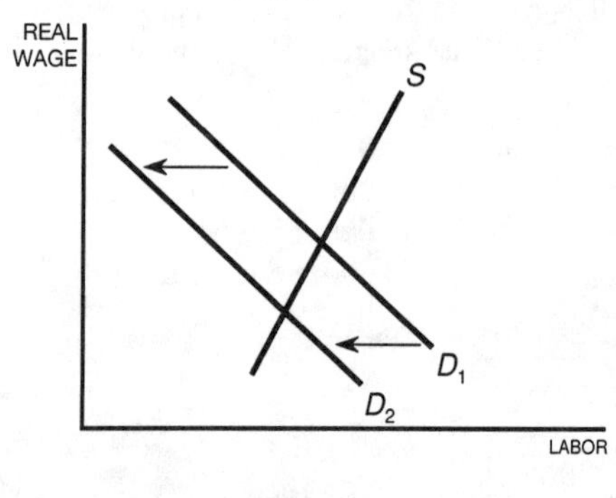

Step four: Find the new equilibrium. If there is excess demand, increase the real wage to the market-clearing level. If there is excess supply, keep the real wage constant.

Step five: Show the level of unemployment as the difference between quantity demanded and quantity supplied.

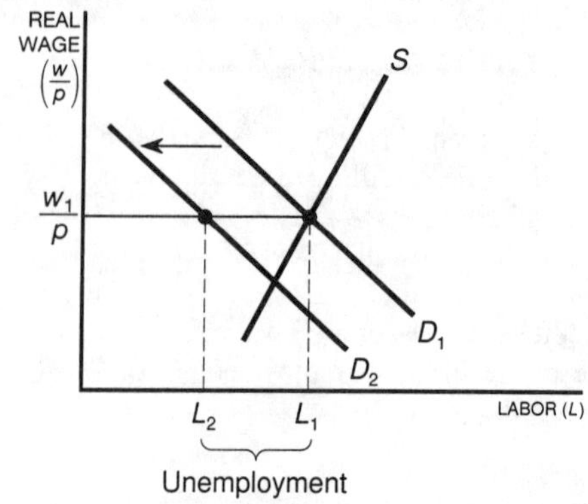

5 (Worked problem: rigid wages) Suppose a deep recession strikes the economy. Show the effect on real wages, unemployment, and the labor market.

Step-by-step solution

Step one: Start with an equilibrium.

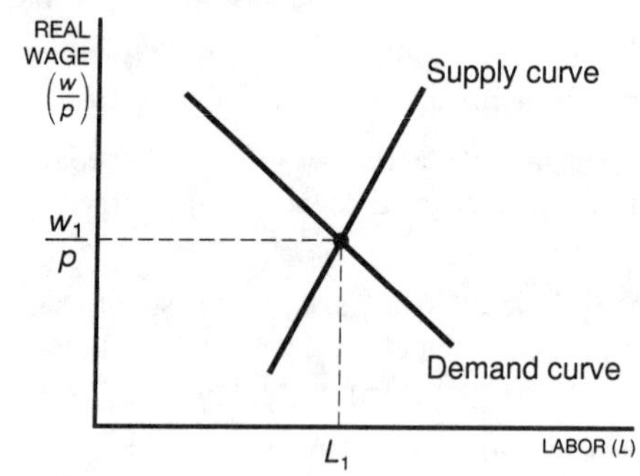

Step two: Identify a cause, and determine which curve shifts. The economy's output falls in a recession, and this reduces the demand for labor.

Step three: Shift the demand curve. It shifts left.

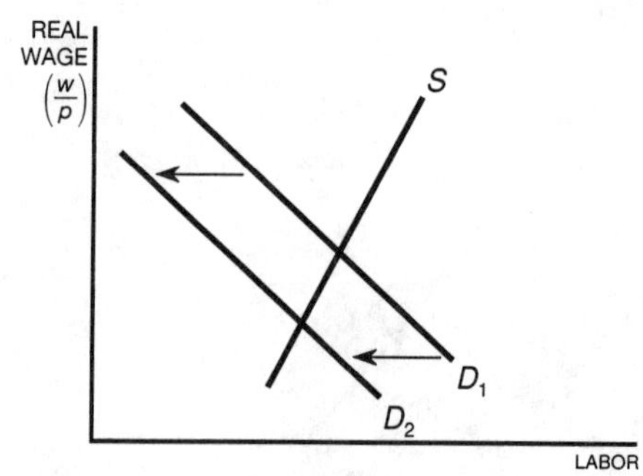

Step four: Find the new equilibrium. Although there is an excess supply of labor, wages do not adjust downward, because they are assumed rigid.

Step five: Show the level of unemployment.

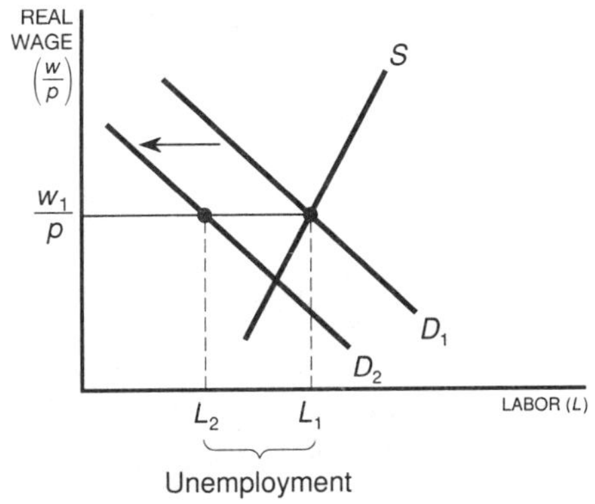

6 (Practice problem: rigid wages) Strife abroad leads to a wave of new immigration. Show the effect on real wages, unemployment, and the labor market.

7 (Practice problem: rigid wages) For each of the following, show the effect on real wages, unemployment, and the labor market.

a The economy booms, and its output increases.
b As barriers fall, millions of women enter the labor market.
c The demand for U.S. exports soars, and the economy's output expands to meet the demand.
d The baby bust generation reaches working age, and the number of new entrants declines.
e Recession overseas reduces the demand for U.S. exports, and the economy falls into a recession.

The Product Market with Rigid Prices

When prices are rigid, the economy may not reach equilibrium at full employment. In this case the short-run equilibrium will occur where the rigid price level meets the short side of the market. If aggregate demand is less than aggregate supply, the economy will have excess capacity. If aggregate demand at this price level exceeds aggregate supply, the economy will produce at capacity, but the price level will remain below the intersection. In these two cases the economy responds differently to shifts in aggregate demand or supply. Tool Kit 8.3 shows how to analyze the product market with rigid prices.

Tool Kit 8.3: Using Aggregate Demand and Supply When Prices are Rigid

When prices are rigid, aggregate demand and supply shift for the same reasons they shift when prices are flexible. Table 8.3 lists some important causes of these shifts. The difference is that output must adjust to the short side of the market. These steps show how to find the short-run equilibrium when prices are rigid.

Table 8.3

Shifts in aggregate demand: changes in consumption, investment, government spending, or net exports.

Shifts in aggregate supply: increases in capacity (aggregate supply shifts right) or changes in import prices (aggregate supply shifts up or down).

Step one: Start with an equilibrium. This may be at the intersection of aggregate supply and demand or not.

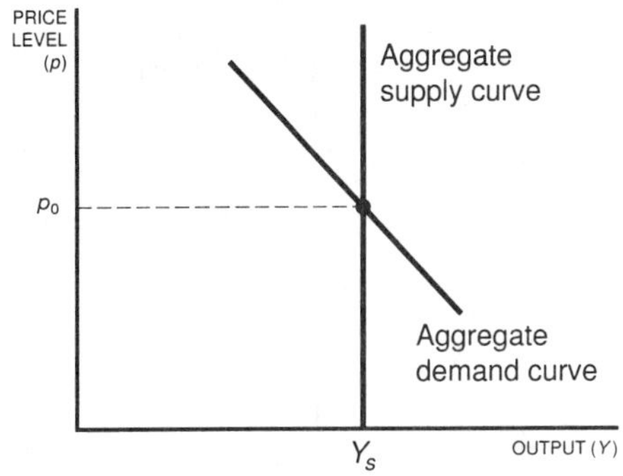

Step two: Identify an exogenous cause and determine which curve shifts and in what direction.

Step three: Shift the curve.

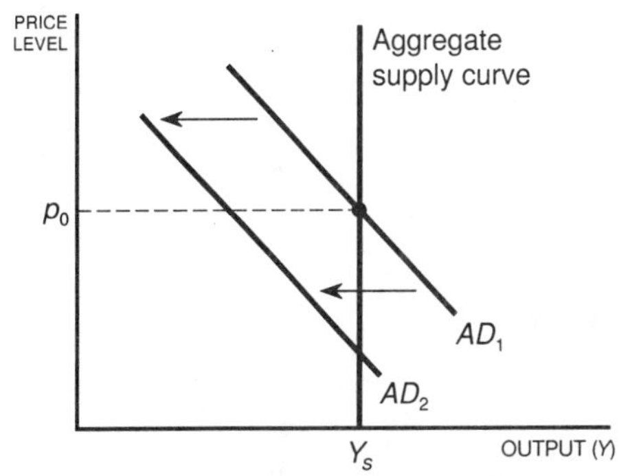

Step four: Find the new equilibrium level of output. This will occur at the intersection of the rigid price level and the short side of the market; that is the lesser of aggregate demand or supply.

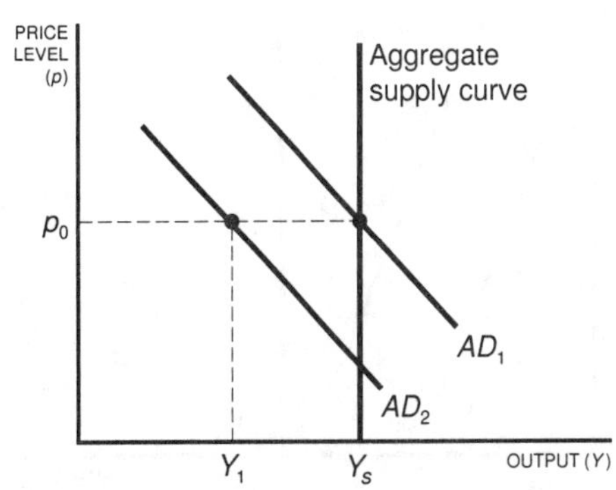

8 (Worked problem: aggregate demand and supply) The economy is in deep recession with high unemployment and a great deal of excess capacity. The government grants an investment tax credit, and firms respond with larger levels of private investment. Show the effect on equilibrium output.

Step-by-step solution

Step one: Start with an equilibrium. Because the economy is in deep recession, this will be on the flat portion of the aggregate supply curve.

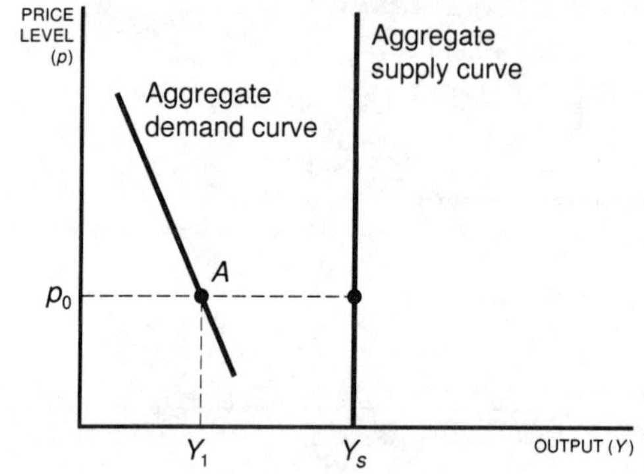

Step two: Identify a cause, and determine which curve shifts and in what direction. The increase in investment shifts aggregate demand to the right.

Step three: Shift the curve.

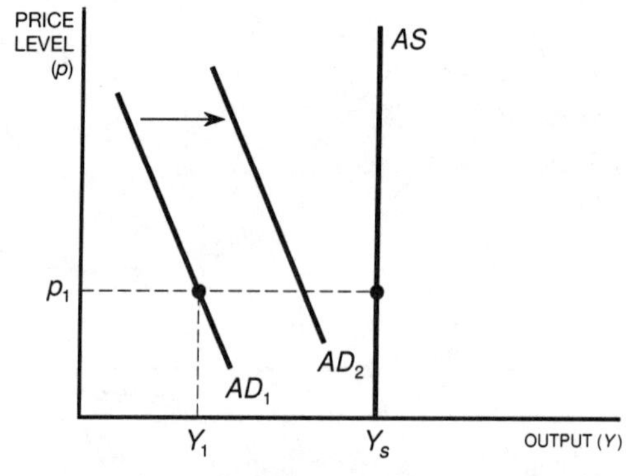

Step four: Find the new equilibrium, and compare the output and price levels. Output increases with little or no change in the price level.

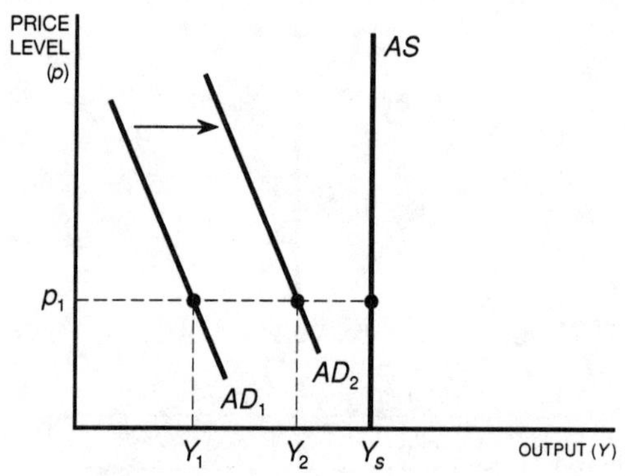

9 (Practice problem: aggregate demand and supply) The economy is brimming with activity. Although unemployment and idle production capacity are at 10-year lows, foreign demand for U.S. exports surges still higher. Show the effect on equilibrium output.

10 (Practice problem: aggregate demand and supply) For each of the following, show the effect on equilibrium output.

a The economy is in equilibrium at the intersection of aggregate demand and aggregate supply. Tight monetary policy raises interest rates, and this causes a dramatic decline in new investment.
b The economy is in deep recession, and the government stimulates private consumption with a tax cut.
c The economy is at maximum capacity, and the government increases its spending.
d The economy is in equilibrium at the intersection of aggregate demand and aggregate supply. The government increases income taxes.
e The economy is in deep recession, and foreign demand for exports falls still further.
f The economy is in equilibrium at the intersection of aggregate demand and aggregate supply. The price of imported oil rises by 50 percent.
g The economy is in deep recession, and the price of imported oil rises by 50 percent.
h The economy is at maximum capacity. There is excess demand. Capacity expands.

Answers to Problems

2 Real wage = ($2,400/150) × 100 = $1,600; unemployment = 10,000 – 10,000 = 0.

3 Real wage = ($3,300/150) × 100 = $2,200; unemployment = 16,000 – 7,000 = 9,000.

4 *a* Real wage = ($50,000/100) × 100 = $50,000; unemployment = 24,000 – 12,000 = 12,000.
b Real wage = ($50,000/125) × 100 = $40,000; unemployment = 22,000 – 16,000 = 6,000.
c Real wage = ($50,000/167) × 100 = $30,000; unemployment = 20,000 – 20,000 = 0.
d Real wage = ($60,000/120) × 100 = $50,000; unemployment = 24,000 – 12,000 = 12,000.

6 The supply curve shifts to the right, and the wage fails to adjust downward; this results in unemployment equal to $L_s - L_1$.

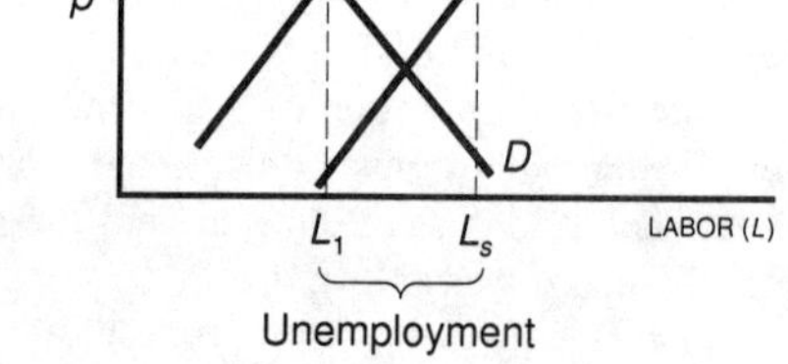

7 *a* The demand curve shifts to the right, and wages adjust upward to clear the market.

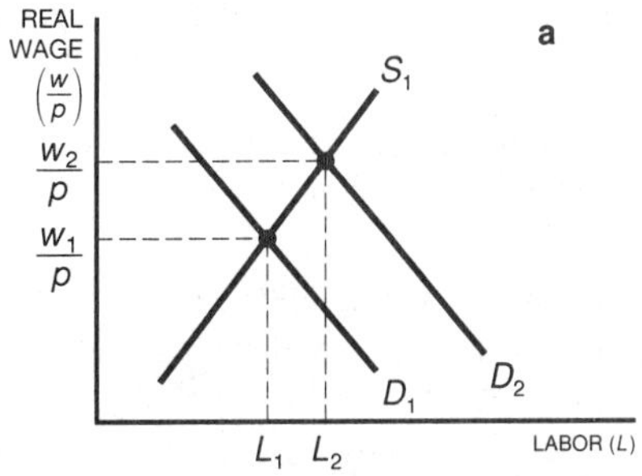

b The supply curve shifts to the right, and the wage fails to adjust downward; this results in unemployment equal to $L_s - L_1$.

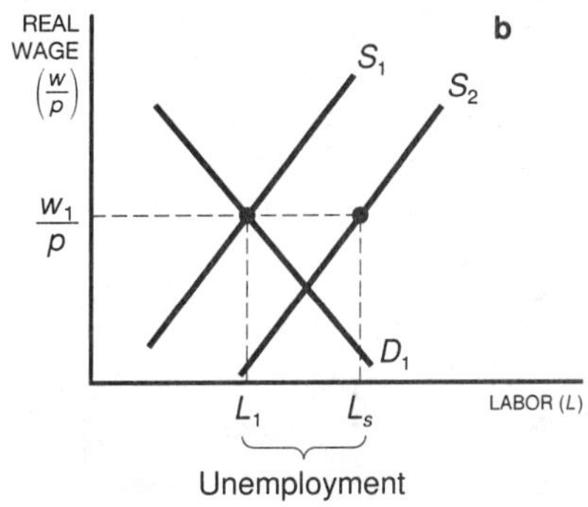

c The demand curve shifts to the right, and wage adjusts upward to clear the market.

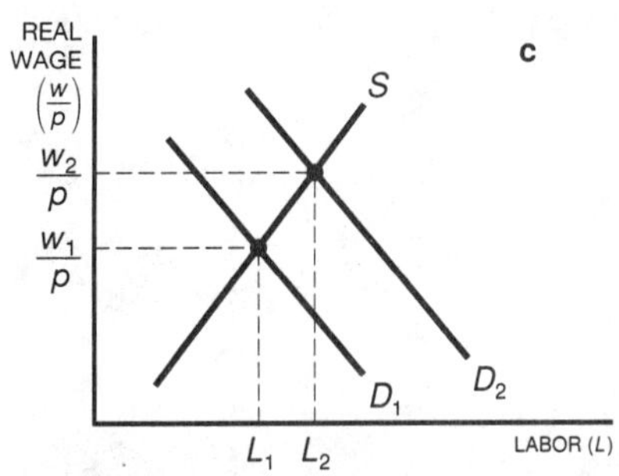

d The supply curve shifts to the left, and the wage adjusts upward to clear the market.

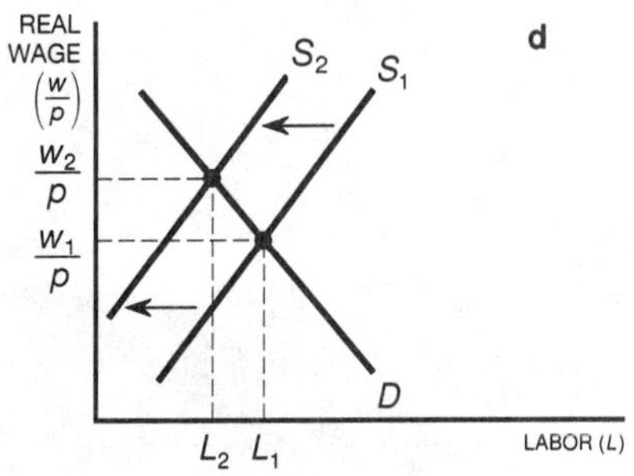

e The demand curve shifts to the left, and the wage fails to adjust downward; this results in unemployment equal to $L1 - L_s$.

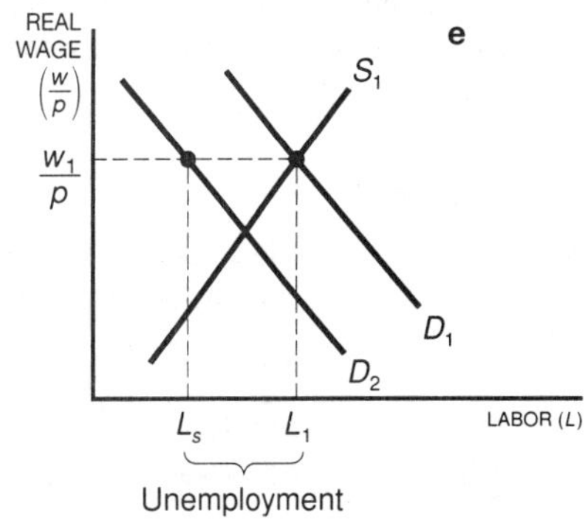

9 Aggregate demand shifts to the right; this leaves output unchanged.

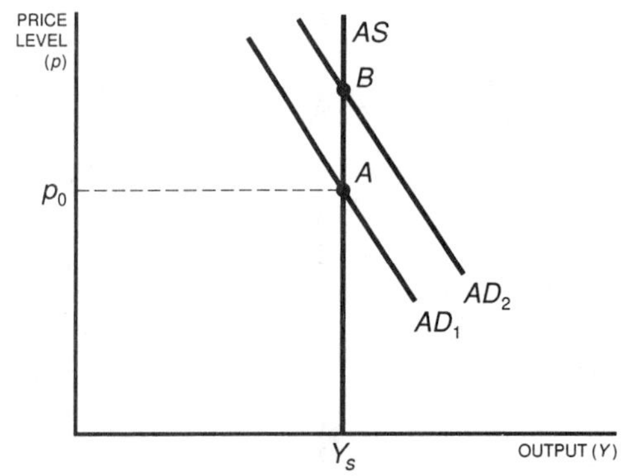

10 *a* Aggregate demand shifts to the left and decreases output.

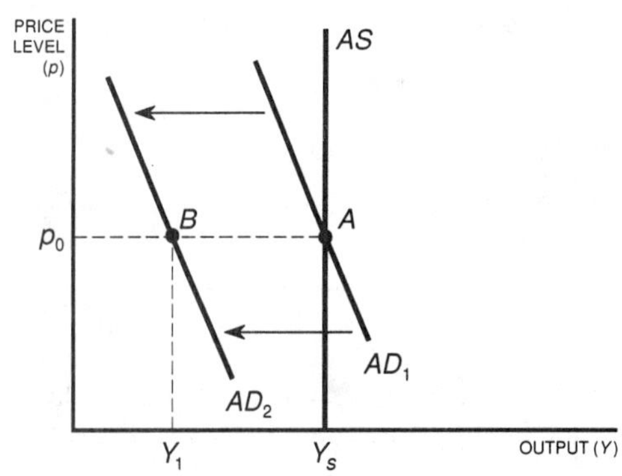

b Aggregate demand shifts to the right; this increases output.

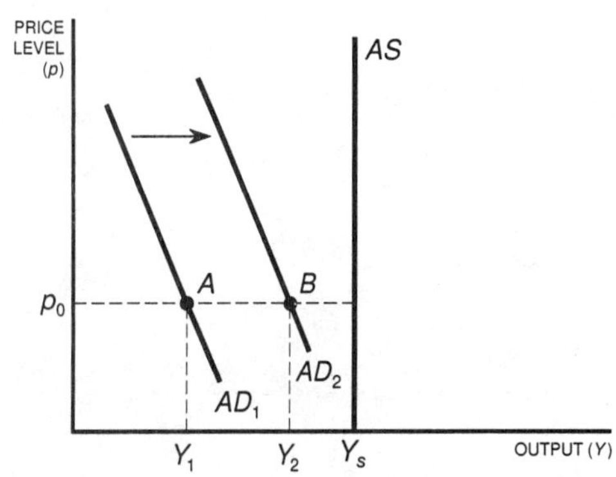

c Aggregate demand shifts to the right; this leaves output unchanged.

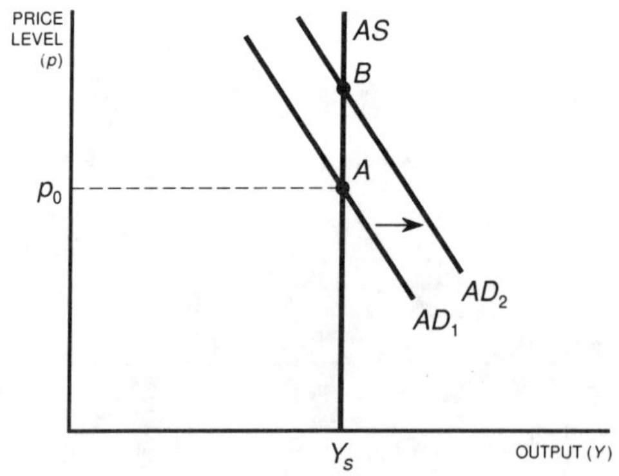

d Aggregate demand shifts to the left and decreases output.

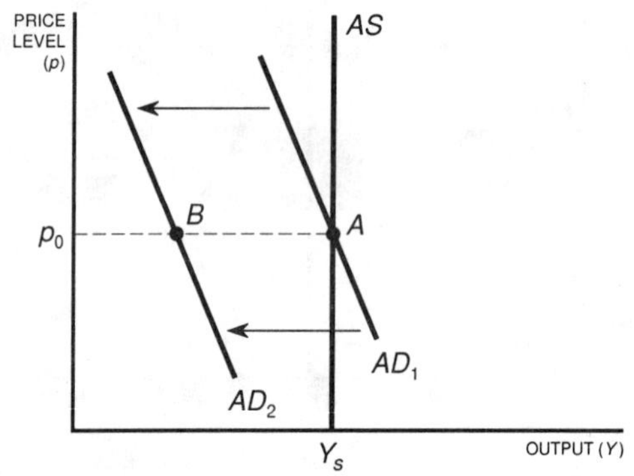

e Aggregate demand shifts to the left; this decreases output.

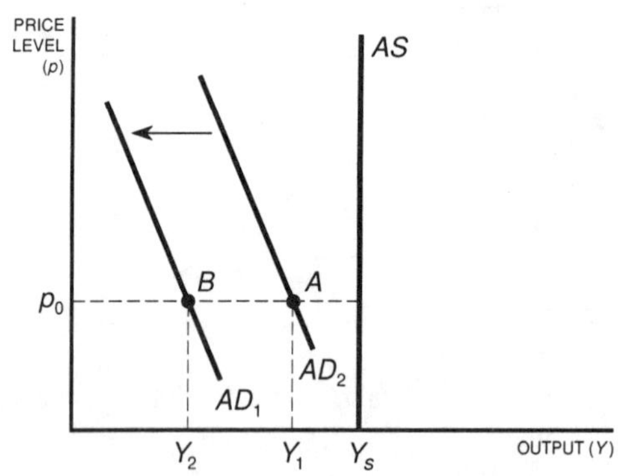

f Aggregate supply shifts to the left; this decreases output.

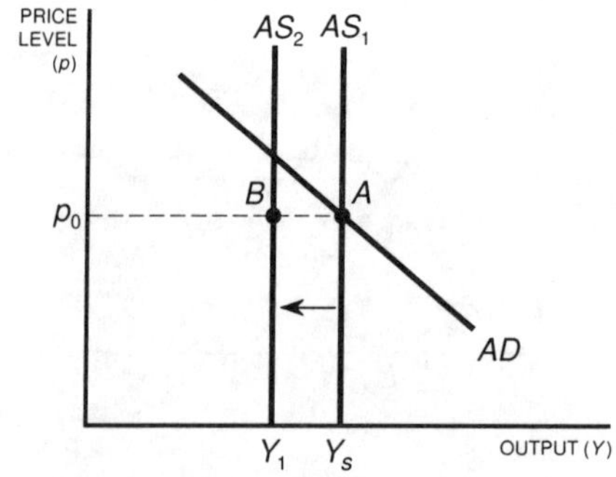

g Aggregate supply shifts to the left; this leaves output unchanged.

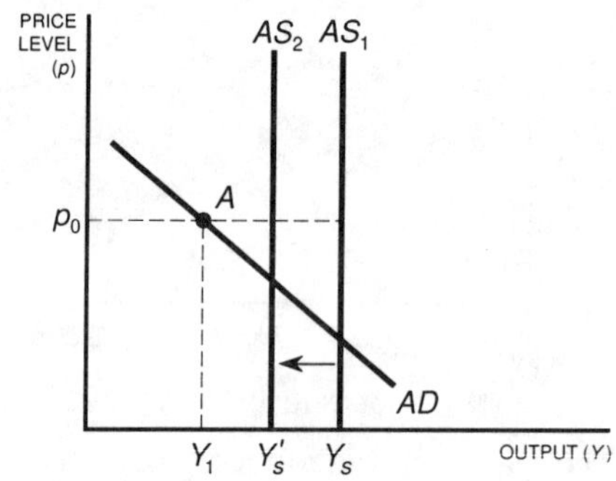

h Aggregate supply shifts to the right; this increases output.

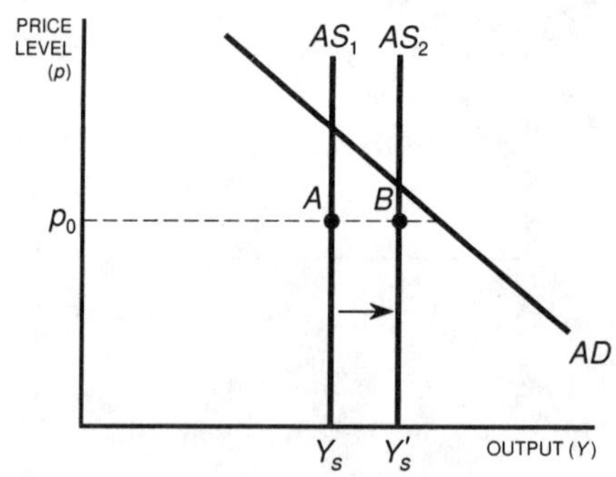

Chapter 9

AGGREGATE DEMAND

Chapter Review

Chapter 8 showed how in the short run the economy's level of output is governed by aggregate demand. This chapter takes a look behind aggregate demand and explains what it is composed of and how it is determined. Income-expenditure analysis is used to show how the economy reaches an equilibrium on the demand side and why the equilibrium changes. The multiplier process, by which changes in spending ripple through the economy, is explained.

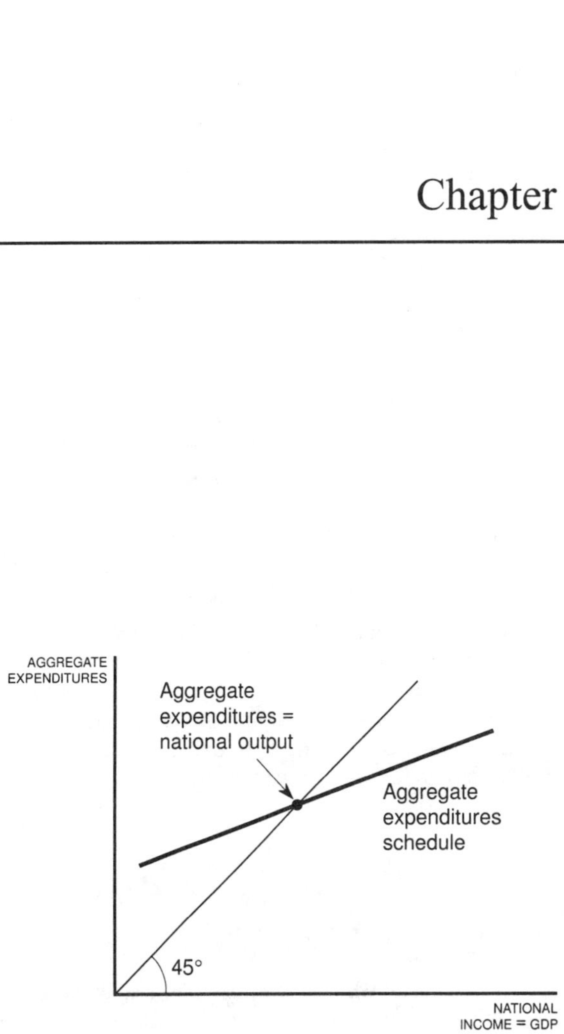

Figure 9.1

ESSENTIAL CONCEPTS

1 **Income-expenditure analysis** starts with the assumption that the price level is fixed. Aggregate expenditures then depend upon national income, and the **aggregate expenditures schedule,** drawn in Figure 9.1, shows how aggregate expenditures increase as national income increases. Because national income equals national output (GDP), the horizontal axis also measures output. Aggregate expenditures equal output where the aggregate expenditures schedule crosses the 45-degree line. This is the equilibrium, and at this point all of the economy's output is purchased.

2 Aggregate expenditures comprise consumption, investment, government purchases, and net exports, as shown by the equation

$$AE = C + I + G + E.$$

Changes in any of the components of expenditure shift the aggregate expenditures schedule up or down and cause equilibrium output to change. In Figure 9.2 *AE* shifts up and output increases.

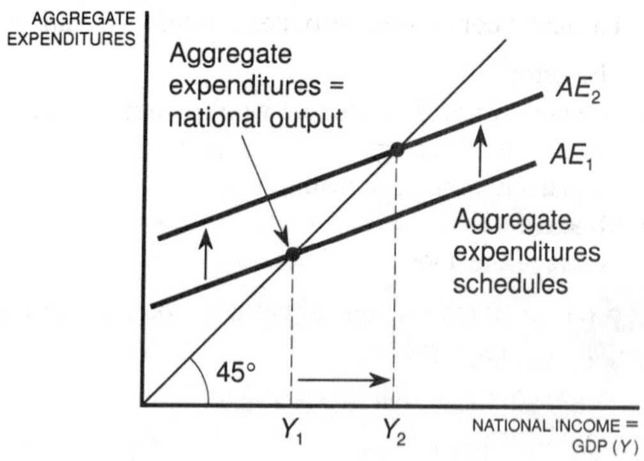

Figure 9.2

3 The **consumption function** describes the relationship between income and consumption. The additional consumption resulting from a one-dollar increase in income is the **marginal propensity to consume** (*MPC*), which is the slope of the consumption function. The **marginal propensity to save** (*MPS*) is the additional amount saved out of a one-dollar increase in income.

4 The **investment multiplier** shows that when aggregate expenditures shift, the change in output is greater than the change in spending. It works as follows. Suppose investment increases. This investment causes incomes to rise and, through the marginal propensity to consume, causes a second round of extra consumption spending. This extra round of consumption further increases incomes and generates a third round of spending. The process continues, and the ultimate increase in output equals the multiplier times the initial change in spending. The formula for the multiplier is $1/(1 - \text{MPC})$.

5 Income taxation makes the consumption function flatter because some of the extra income is taken in taxes, rather than spent. Similarly, in an open economy, some spending leaves the economy for imported goods, further flattening the aggregate expenditures schedule. Both taxes and imports cause the multiplier to be smaller.

BEHIND THE ESSENTIAL CONCEPTS

1 You might wonder why we need an entire chapter on aggregate demand. Although it appears simple (just another downward-sloping demand), the aggregate demand curve masks some complexity. Income-expenditure analysis shows that the amount of aggregate demand at any given price level is an equilibrium, where desired spending is brought into equality with output. Like most equilibria in the economy, this one requires some adjustment time as inventories rise or fall toward their appropriate level and as successive rounds of spending work their way through the economy. For some purposes we may be satisfied with limiting our attention to the aggregate demand curve. Other purposes require the deeper look given by the income-expenditure approach.

2 You might wonder what role prices play in income-expenditure analysis. Prices are determined by supply and demand, but here we are concerned only with the demand side. At this level of analysis, prices are fixed; one way of thinking about this is that the economy is operating on the flat portion of the aggregate supply curve.

3 How does the economy reach equilibrium without price adjustment? **Inventories** play the key role.

a If GDP is below equilibrium, then households and firms want to buy more than the economy produces. Firms notice this when they sell the goods they have on inventory. Firms produce more to restore inventories, and GDP increases.

b If GDP is above equilibrium, the story is reversed. Households and firms buy less than the economy produces, inventories of unsold goods accumulate, and firms cut back on production. GDP falls.

4 A helpful way to understand the multiplier process and why the multiplier is smaller when there are taxes and trade is to think in terms of injections and leakages. Suppose that the economy gets an injection of new spending, say an increase in exports. Some people will receive this money, and they will save some and spend some. We say that the money that is saved "leaks" out of the system. The money that is spent becomes other people's income; they in turn save some and spend some, and the process continues. The total amount of spending generated is a multiple of the initial injection. But any leakage reduces the total amount of spending. Clearly, taxes go to the government. That is a leakage. Money spent on imports goes abroad—another leakage. More leakages means less spending and a smaller multiplier.

SELF-TEST

True or False

1 Aggregate expenditures include what households, firms, and government spend on goods and services produced in the United States.

2 As income increases by one dollar, aggregate expenditures increase by less than one dollar.

3 The statement that national income equals national output is an example of an equilibrium relationship.

4 The statement that aggregate expenditures equal national output is an example of an equilibrium relationship.

5 Unplanned inventories equal zero in equilibrium.

6 The aggregate expenditures schedule gives total desired spending at each price level.

7 Aggregate expenditures equal consumption plus investment plus government purchases plus net exports.

8 Net exports equal imports minus exports.

9 The relationship between a household's income and its consumption is called its consumption function.

10 Disposable income equals national income plus taxes.

11 The marginal propensity to consume equals the marginal propensity to save.

12 The multiplier equals 1 divided by the marginal propensity to consume.

13 An increase in investment causes equilibrium output to increase by more than the change in investment.

14 A higher tax rate on income means that the multiplier is larger.

15 Imports increase as income increases.

Multiple Choice

1 This chapter focuses on the case where

a aggregate demand equals aggregate supply;
b aggregate demand is greater than aggregate supply;
c aggregate demand is less than aggregate supply;
d prices are fully flexible;
e the economy's capacity is fully utilized.

2 The aggregate expendures schedule traces out the relationship between the economy's total expenditures and national income.

a keeping output fixed;
b at a given price level;
c as price changes to clear the product market;
d holding consumption fixed;
e holding net exports fixed.

3 As income increases, aggregate expenditures

a increase;.
b decrease;
c remain the same;
d increase or decrease depending on how product prices change;
e increase or decrease depending on events in the capital market.

4 The marginal propensity to consume gives

a the fraction of extra income that will be consumed;
b the ratio of consumption to income;
c the fraction of extra consumption that comes from wage income;
d the fraction of extra consumption that comes from interest and dividends;
e the ratio of consumption out of wage income to consumption out of interest and dividend income.

5 The aggregate expenditures schedule

a is horizontal;
b is horizontal for low levels of output, upward sloping for intermediate levels of output, and steep at high levels of output;
c is upward sloping;
d is downward sloping;
e is a 45-degree line.

6 If national income were zero, consumption would

a be zero;
b be positive because people would borrow or consume out of savings;
c equal autonomous consumption;
d b and c;
e none of the above.

7 The statement that national income is equal to national output is an example of

a an equilibrium relationship;
b an identity;
c a behavioral relationship;
d a hypothesis;
e an assumption.

8 The statement that aggregate expenditures equal aggregate output is an example of

a an equilibrium relationship;
b an identity;
c a behavioral relationship;
d a hypothesis;
e an assumption.

9 In equilibrium, it is true that

a the output of the economy must be purchased;
b aggregate expenditures equal national output;
c aggregate expenditures equal what households, firms, and government want to spend at the equilibrium level of national income;
d unplanned inventories equal zero;
e all of the above.

10 An upward shift in the aggregate expenditures schedule occurs when

a households, firms, and government decide to spend more at each level of income;
b households, firms, and government decide to spend less at each level of income;
c households, firms, and government decide to spend less at each price level;
d households, firms, and government decide to spend more at each price level;
e the economy is in recession.

11 Which of the following is not a component of aggregate expenditures?

a consumption;
b investment;
c government purchases;
d net exports;
e taxes.

12 The household's consumption function traces out the relationship between its consumption and its

a investment;
b income;
c taxes;
d inflation rate;
e total expenditure.

13 The slope of the aggregate expenditures schedule equals

a zero;
b the average propensity to save;
c the marginal propensity to save;
d the average propensity to consume;
e the marginal propensity to consume.

14 The marginal propensity to save equals

a the marginal propensity to consume;
b 1 plus the marginal propensity to consume;
c 1 minus the marginal propensity to consume;
d the reciprocal of the marginal propensity to consume;
e none of the above.

15 Autonomous consumption is

a the extra consumption out of an additional dollar of income;
b the ratio of consumption to disposable income;
c that part of consumption that does not depend on disposable income;
d the extra savings out of an additional dollar of income;
e the level of consumption when desired inventories equal zero.

16 When investment increases, equilibrium output

a increases by more than the change in investment;
b increases by less than the change in investment;
c increases by the same amount as the change in investment;
d decreases by less than the change in investment;
e decreases by more than the change in investment.

17 In the simple model without taxes, the multiplier equals

a 1 divided by the marginal propensity to save;
b the marginal propensity to save;
c the marginal propensity to consume;
d 1 divided by the marginal propensity to consume;
e zero.

18 Adding taxes to the income-expenditure model causes

a disposable income to be less than national income;
b the aggregate expenditures schedule to be flatter;
c the multiplier to be smaller;
d the aggregate consumption function to be flatter;
e all of the above.

19 The amount of each extra dollar of disposable income spent on imports is the

a marginal propensity to import;
b marginal propensity to consume;
c marginal propensity to save;
d marginal propensity to export;
e marginal propensity to invest.

20 Adding international trade to the income-expenditure model causes

a the multiplier to be larger;
b the aggregate expenditures schedule to be flatter;
c the aggregate expenditures schedule to be steeper;
d the equilibrium level of output to be lower;
e a and c.

Completion

1 The relationship between the economy's total expenditures and national income is summarized by the __________.

2 The __________ traces the relationship between consumption and disposable income.

3 The portion of consumption that does not depend upon income is called __________.

4 The fraction of additional income that is consumed is called the __________.

5 National output increases by more than the amount of a given increase in investment by a factor called the __________.

6 When firms cannot sell all that they produce, they experience an increase in __________.

7 The relationship between national income and imports is summarized by the __________.

8 The additional imports purchased as a result of a one-dollar increase in income is called the __________.

9 An economy actively engaged in international trade and investment is called an __________.

10 The difference between imports and exports equals a __________.

Answers to Self-Test

True or False

1	t	6	f	11	f
2	t	7	t	12	f
3	f	8	f	13	t
4	t	9	t	14	f
5	t	10	f	15	t

Multiple Choice

1	c	6	d	11	e	16	a
2	b	7	b	12	b	17	a
3	a	8	a	13	e	18	e
4	a	9	e	14	c	19	a
5	c	10	a	15	c	20	b

Completion

1 aggregate expenditures schedule
2 consumption function
3 autonomous consumption
4 marginal propensity to consume
5 multiplier
6 unplanned inventories
7 import function
8 marginal propensity to import
9 open economy
10 trade deficit

Doing Economics: Tools and Practice Problems

The topic of this section is income-expenditure analysis. We begin with an explanation of the tools needed and follow with problems involving economies with no taxes or imports. For each, we find the consumption function, calculate the aggregate expenditures schedule, and solve for the economy's equilibrium output. We then study the multiplier process, which shows how a change in spending brings about a larger change in equilibrium output. Finally, we consider progressively more complicated problems with income taxes and imports, where the net export function must be calculated. An important lesson of these latter problems concerns how taxes and imports affect the multiplier and the stability of the economy.

Tool Kit 9.1: Finding the Aggregate Consumption Function

Aggregate expenditures equal the sum of consumption, investment, government spending, and net exports. The first step is to find the aggregate consumption function, which shows the level of consumption that corresponds to each level of national income.

Step one: Identify the marginal propensity to consume (*MPC*), autonomous consumption, and the income tax rate.

Step two: Calculate the aggregate consumption function by substituting various values of national income into the following formula:

aggregate consumption = autonomous consumption + [national income (1 – tax rate)] × MPC.

(Note that the term in brackets is disposable income, which equals national income when the tax rate is zero.)

Tool Kit 9.2: Finding the Net Export Function

In an open economy, net exports must be included in aggregate expenditures. The **net export function** shows the level of net exports that corresponds to each level of national income.

Step one: Identify the marginal propensity to import (*MPI*), the tax rate, and the level of exports.

Step two: Calculate the import function by substituting various levels of national income into the following formula:

imports = [national income (1 – tax rate)] *MPI.*

Step three: Find the net export function by subtracting imports from exports for every level of national income:

net exports = exports – imports.

Tool Kit 9.3: Finding the Aggregate Expenditures Schedule

With the aggregate consumption and net export functions in place, the aggregate expenditures schedule can be calculated. The aggregate expenditures schedule shows the level of aggregate spending corresponding to each level of national income.

Step one: Identify the aggregate consumption function, the level of investment spending, the level of government spending, and the net export function.

Step two: Calculate the aggregate expenditures schedule by summing consumption, investment, government spending, and net exports for each level of national income:

$$AE = C + I + G + X.$$

Tool Kit 9.4: Using Income-Expenditure Analysis to Determine the Equilibrium

We find the equilibrium level of output and national income (which are always equal), where the aggregate expenditures schedule crosses the 45-degree line. At this point, consumers, firms, government, and foreigners spend just enough to purchase the economy's output.

Step one: Identify the aggregate expenditures schedule.

Step two: Choose a level of national income, and find the corresponding level of aggregate expenditures. If they are equal, stop. This is the equilibrium level of output.

Step three: If aggregate expenditures exceed national income, then inventories will fall, firms will increase production, and output will expand. Choose a greater level of national income, and repeat step one. If aggregate expenditures are less than national income, then inventories will rise, firms will cut back production, and output will decrease. Choose a lower level of national income, and repeat step one.

Step four: Continue until the equilibrium is found.

Tool Kit 9.5: Using Multiplier Analysis to Find the Ultimate Change in Output Caused by an Initial Change in Spending

The great lesson of income-expenditure analysis is that an initial change in spending ripples through the economy and ultimately results in a larger change in output. The process by which this happens is the multiplier process, and the multiplier itself shows how much larger than the initial change in spending is the ultimate change in output.

Step one: Identify the marginal propensity to consume, the tax rate, the marginal propensity to import, and the initial change in spending.

Step two: Calculate the multiplier. Use the appropriate formula:

no taxes or imports:	$1/(1 - MPC)$
income taxes:	$1/[1 - MPC\,(1 - \text{tax rate})]$
open economy (no taxes):	$1/[1 - (MPC + MPI)]$
open economy with taxes:	$1/[1 - (MPC - MPI)(1 - \text{tax rate})]$.

Step three: Calculate the ultimate change in output by multiplying the initial change in spending by the multiplier:

change in output = (change in spending) × multiplier.

Step four: Verify the result in step three by adding the change in spending to the original aggregate expenditures schedule and solving for the new equilibrium level of output.

1 (Worked problem: income-expenditure analysis) For years, Costa Guano has remained closed to foreign trade and investment. The government of the isolated nation spends no money and collects none in taxes. Autonomous consumption is 300 million guanos (the currency of Costa Guano), and the marginal propensity to consume equals 0.8. Finally, domestic private investment equals 100 million guanos.

a Find the aggregate consumption function.
b Find the aggregate expenditures schedule.
c Calculate equilibrium output and national income.
d Brimming with confidence, Costa Guano's firms increase their investment spending by 100 million (for a total of 200 million). Calculate the multiplier and the ultimate change in output brought about by this increase in investment.

Step-by-step solution

Step one (a): Find the aggregate consumption function. Identify the *MPC*, autonomous consumption, and the tax rate. The *MPC* is 0.8, autonomous consumption is 300 million, but the tax rate is zero.

Step two: Calculate the aggregate consumption function. When national income equals zero, aggregate consumption equals autonomous consumption (300 million). At 500 million in national income, consumption equals 300 + 0.8 (500) = 700 million. Continuing, we derive Table 9.1.

Table 9.1

National income (millions of guanos)	*Aggregate consumption*
0	300
500	700
1,000	1,100
1,500	1,500
2,000	1,900
2,500	2,300
3,000	2,700

Step one (b): Find the aggregate expenditures schedule. Identify the aggregate consumption function, investment, government spending, and the net export function. The aggregate consumption function is given in Table 9.1, and investment equals 100 million. Government spending and net exports equal zero.

Step two: Calculate the aggregate expenditures schedule adding investment and consumption, as shown in Table 9.2.

Table 9.2

National income	*Aggregate consumption*	*Investment*	*Aggregate expenditures*
0	300	100	400
500	700	100	800
1,000	1,100	100	1,200
1,500	1,500	100	1,600
2,000	1,900	100	2,000
2,500	2,300	100	2,400
3,000	2,700	100	2,800

Step one (c): Calculate equilibrium output and national income. Identify the aggregate expenditures schedule. It appears in Table 9.2.

Step two: Choose a level of national income. When national income is 2,000 million, aggregate expenditures equal 2,000 million. Consumers and firms purchase exactly the economy's output of 2,000 million.

Step one (d): Calculate the multiplier and the ultimate change in output brought about by this increase in investment of 100 million (from 100 to 200). Identify the marginal propensity to consume, the tax rate, the marginal propensity to import, and the initial change in spending. The *MPC* is 0.8, the initial change in spending is 100 million. There are no taxes or imports.

Step two: Calculate the multiplier. Because there are no taxes or imports, the multiplier equals

$1/(1 - MPC) = 1/(1 - 0.8) = 1/0.2 = 5.$

Step three: Calculate the ultimate change in output:

change in output = 100 × 5 = 500 million.

Step four: Verify the result in step three by adding the change in spending to the original aggregate expenditures schedule and solving for the new equilibrium level of output. The new aggregate expenditures schedule is given in Table 9.3.

Table 9.3

National income	*Aggregate consumption*	*Investment*	*Aggregate expenditures*
0	300	200	500
500	700	200	900
1,000	1,100	200	1,300
1,500	1,500	200	1,700
2,000	1,900	200	2,100
2,500	2,300	200	2,500
3,000	2,700	200	2,900

The new equilibrium level of output is 2,500 million, which is 500 million more than originally. It checks!

2 (Practice problem: income-expenditure analysis) El Dorado, an insular economy closed to foreign trade and investment, has no income-based taxes, and its government spends nothing. The marginal propensity to consume is 0.9, autonomous consumption is 5 billion dorals (the currency of El Dorado), and private investment totals 1 billion. (Hint: Choose national income in intervals of 10 billion; that is, 0, 10, 20, etc.)

a Find the aggregate consumption function.
b Find the aggregate expenditures schedule.
c Calculate equilibrium output and national income.
d After a period of stability, investment in El Dorado jumps to 2 billion dorals. Calculate the multiplier and the ultimate change in output brought about by this increase in investment.

3 (Practice problem: income-expenditure analysis) In Erehwemos, there is no taxation and also no government spending. The economy is closed to the outside world. All investment is undertaken by private domestic firms, and the total is 2 billion wemos (the Erehwemosian currency). The marginal propensity to consume is 0.75, and autonomous consumption is 2 billion. (Hint: Choose national income levels in intervals of 4 billion; that is, 0, 4, 8, 12, etc.)

a Find the aggregate consumption function.
b Find the aggregate expenditures schedule.
c Calculate equilibrium output and national income.
d Investment climbs to 4 billion. Calculate the multiplier and the ultimate change in output brought about by this increase in investment.

4 (Worked problem: income-expenditure analysis) This problem builds on problem 1. Recognizing the need for infrastructure investment, the government of Costa Guano institutes an income tax with a flat rate of 25 percent and spends 300 million. Private investment continues at 200 million, the marginal propensity to consume is 0.8, and autonomous consumption equals 300 million. The economy remains closed to foreign trade.

a Find the consumption function.
b Find the aggregate expenditures schedule.
c Find the equilibrium level of output.
d Suppose that the government raises its spending by 200 million (for a total of 500 million). Calculate the multiplier, and solve for the ultimate change in output brought about by the increase in government spending.

Step-by-step solution

Step one (a): Identify the marginal propensity to consume, autonomous consumption, and the income tax rate. The *MPC* is 0.8, autonomous consumption equals 300 million, and the income tax rate is 25 percent.

Step two: Calculate the aggregate consumption function. When national income equals zero, aggregate consumption equals autonomous consumption (300 million). At 500 million in national income, aggregate consumption = 300 + [500 (1 – 0.25)] × 0.8 = 600. Continuing, we derive Table 9.4.

Table 9.4

National income (millions of guanos)	*Aggregate consumption*
0	300
500	600
1,000	900
1,500	1,200
2,000	1,500
2,500	1,800
3,000	2,100

Step one (b): Identify the aggregate consumption function, investment, government spending, and the net export function. The aggregate consumption function is given in Table 9.4, investment equals 200 million, and government spending equals 300 million. Net exports remain zero.

Step two: Calculate the aggregate expenditures schedule by adding consumption, investment, and government spending, as shown in Table 9.5.

Table 9.5

National income	*Aggregate consumption*	*Investment*	*Government spending*	*Aggregate expenditures*
0	300	200	300	800
500	600	200	300	1,100
1,000	900	200	300	1,400
1,500	1,200	200	300	1,700
2,000	1,500	200	300	2,000
2,500	1,800	200	300	2,300
3,000	2,100	200	300	2,600

Step one (c): Identify the aggregate expenditures schedule. It appears in Table 9.5.

Step two: Choose a level of national income. When national income is 2,000 million, aggregate expenditures equal 2,000 million. Consumers and firms purchase exactly the economy's output of 2,000 million.

Step one (d): Identify the marginal propensity to consume, the tax rate, the marginal propensity to import, and the initial change in spending. The *MPC* is 0.8, and the initial change in spending is 200 million. The tax rate is 25 percent, but there are no imports.

Step two: Calculate the multiplier. Because there is an income tax but no imports, the multiplier equals

$$1/[1 - MPC\,(1 - \text{tax rate})] = 1/[1 - 0.8\,(1 - 0.25)] = 1/(1 - 0.6) = 1/0.4 = 2.5.$$

(In problem 1, there was no income tax and the multiplier equalled 5. Here, the income tax reduces the multiplier to 2.5.)

Step three: Calculate the ultimate change in output:

change in output = 200 × 2.5 = 500 million.

Step four: Verify the result in step three by adding the change in spending to the original aggregate expenditures schedule and solving for the new equilibrium level of output. The new aggregate expenditures schedule is given in Table 9.6.

Table 9.6

National income	*Aggregate consumption*	*Investment*	*Government spending*	*Aggregate expenditures*
0	300	200	500	1,000
500	600	200	500	1,300
1,000	900	200	500	1,600
1,500	1,200	200	500	1,900
2,000	1,500	200	500	2,200
2,500	1,800	200	500	2,500
3,000	2,100	200	500	2,800

The new equilibrium level of output is 2,500 million, which is 500 million more than originally. It checks. The economy is more stable with the income tax, for it took a 200-million change in spending to change output by 500 million in problem 1, where there was no tax.

5 (Practice problem: income-expenditure analysis) This problem builds on problem 2. An income tax system is passed by El Dorado's Council of Ministers. The flat tax rate is 1/9 on all income, and the government plans to spend 3 billion. The marginal propensity to consume remains at 0.9, autonomous consumption is 5 billion, and private investment continues at 2 billion.

a Find the consumption function.
b Find the aggregate expenditures schedule.
c Find the equilibrium level of output.
d Suppose that the government raises its spending by 4 billion (for a total of 7 billion). Calculate the multiplier, and solve for the ultimate change in output brought about by the increase in government spending.

6 (Practice problem: income-expenditure analysis) This problem builds on problem 3. Erehwemos institutes an income tax with a flat rate of 1/3. The government spends 2 billion wemos. The marginal propensity to consume remains at 0.75, autonomous consumption equals 2 billion, and private investment equals 4 billion.

a Find the aggregate consumption function.
b Find the aggregate expenditures schedule.
c Calculate equilibrium output and national income.
d Responding to the war threat from neighboring Erehwon, the government doubles spending. The increase in government spending is 2 billion (for a total of 4 billion). Calculate the multiplier and the ultimate change in output brought about by this increase in government spending.

7 (Worked problem: income-expenditure analysis) This problem builds on problems 1 and 4. Costa Guano has opened its economy to foreign trade. It exports 500 million in world markets. Its citizens have developed tastes for foreign goods, however, and their marginal propensity to import is 1/3. Autonomous consumption remains at 300 million, investment equals 200 million, government spending has returned to 300 million, the marginal propensity to consume is 0.8, and the tax rate is 25 percent.

a Find the aggregate consumption function.
b Find the net export function.
c Find the aggregate expenditures schedule.
d Find the equilibrium level of output.
e Suppose that exports increase by 325 million (for a total of 825 million). Calculate the multiplier, and solve for the ultimate change in output brought about by the increase in exports.

Step-by-step solution

Step one (a and b): The aggregate consumption function is the same as in problem 4 and is given in Table 9.4. Identify the marginal propensity to import, the tax rate, and the level of exports. The *MPI* equals 1/3, the tax rate is 25 percent, and the level of exports equals 500 million guanos.

Step two: Calculate the import function. When national income is zero, so are imports. When national income is 500 million, imports = [500 × (1 – 0.25)] × 1/3 = 125 million. Continuing, we derive the import function in Table 9.7.

Table 9.7

National income	*Imports*
0	0
500	125
1,000	250
1,500	375
2,000	500
2,500	625
3,000	750

Step three: Find the net export function. When national income is zero, net exports are 500 – 0 = 500 million. When national income is 500, net exports are 500 – 125 = 375. Continuing, we derive the net export function in Table 9.8.

Table 9.8

National income	*Exports*	*Imports*	*Net exports*
0	500	0	500
500	500	125	375
1,000	500	250	250
1,500	500	375	125
2,000	500	500	0
2,500	500	625	–125
3,000	500	750	–250

Step one (c): Identify the aggregate consumption function, investment, government spending, and the net export function. The aggregate consumption function is given in Table 9.4, investment equals 200 million, government spending is 300 million, and the net export function appears in Table 9.8.

Step two: Calculate the aggregate expenditures schedule by adding consumption, investment, government spending, and net exports. Table 9.9 gives the results.

Table 9.9

National income	*Aggregate consumption*	*Invest-ment*	*Govern-ment spending*	*Net exports*	*Aggregate expenditures*
0	300	200	300	500	1,300
500	600	200	300	375	1,475
1,000	900	200	300	250	1,650
1,500	1,200	200	300	125	1,825
2,000	1,500	200	300	0	2,000
2,500	1,800	200	300	–125	2,175
3,000	2,100	200	300	–250	2,350

Step one (d): Identify the aggregate expenditures schedule. It is given in Table 9.9.

Step two: Choose a level of national income. When national income equals 2,000 million, aggregate expenditures equal 2,000 million, and this is the equilibrium level of output.

Step one (e): Identify the marginal propensity to consume, the tax rate, the marginal propensity to import, and the initial change in spending. The *MPC* is 0.8, the tax rate is 25 percent, the *MPI* equals 1/3, and exports increase by 325 million.

Step two: Calculate the multiplier. The multiplier

$= 1/[1 - (MPC - MPI)(1 - \text{tax rate})]$

$= 1/[1 - (0.8 - 1/3)(1 - 0.25)] = 20/13 = 1.54.$

Note that in the open economy, the multiplier is smaller than in the closed economy of problem 4.

Step three: Calculate the ultimate change in output:

change in output = 325 × 20/13 = 500.

Step four: Verify the result in step three by adding the change in exports to the original aggregate expenditures schedule (Table 9.9) and solving for the new equilibrium level of output. The new aggregate expenditures schedule is given in Table 9.10. (Note that the increase in exports increases net exports by 325 million.)

Table 9.10

National income	*Aggregate consumption*	*Invest-ment*	*Govern-ment spending*	*Net exports*	*Aggregate expenditures*
0	300	200	300	825	1,625
500	600	200	300	700	1,800
1,000	900	200	300	575	1,975
1,500	1,200	200	300	450	2,150
2,000	1,500	200	300	325	2,325
2,500	1,800	200	300	200	2,500
3,000	2,100	200	300	75	2,825

The new equilibrium level of output is 2,500 million, which is 500 million more than originally. It checks. The open economy is yet more stable because it took a 325 million change in spending to change output by 500 million.

8 (Practice problem: income-expenditure analysis) This problem builds on problems 2 and 5. The new economics minister wins the day with a brilliant argument against protectionism, and El Dorado opens its economy. Its exports surge to 14 billion. The marginal propensity to import is 9/40, the marginal propensity to consume remains at 0.9, autonomous consumption is 5 billion, private investment is 2 billion, and the government spends 3 billion.

a Find the consumption function.
b Find the net export function.
c Find the aggregate expenditures schedule.
d Find the equilibrium level of output.
e Suppose that exports increase by 4 billion (for a total of 18 billion). Calculate the multiplier, and solve for the ultimate change in output brought about by the increase in exports.

9 (Practice problem: income-expenditure analysis) This problem builds on problems 3 and 6. With peace at hand, the Erehwemos economy is opened to foreign trade and investment. Exports equal 8/3 (2.67) billion, and the marginal propensity to import is 0.25. Government spending has returned to 2 billion, but private investment remains at 4 billion. Autonomous consumption is also 2 billion, and the marginal propensity to consume remains at 0.75. Finally, the tax rate is 1/3.

a Find the aggregate consumption function.
b Find the net export function.
c Find the aggregate expenditures schedule.
d Calculate the equilibrium output and national income.
e Exports increase to 16/3 (5.33) billion. Calculate the multiplier and the ultimate change in output brought about by this increase in exports.

Answers to Problems

2 Table 9.11 gives

a the aggregate consumption function and
b the aggregate expenditures schedule.

Table 9.11

National income (billions of dorals)	*Aggregate consumption*	*Investment*	*Aggregate expenditures*
0	5	1	6
10	14	1	15
20	23	1	24
30	32	1	33
40	41	1	42
50	50	1	51
60	59	1	60
70	68	1	69
80	77	1	78
90	86	1	87
100	95	1	96

c Equilibrium output is 60 billion.
d The multiplier is 1/(1 – 0.9) = 10. The change in output is 1 × 10 = 10. Table 9.12 shows that when investment increases to 2 billion, equilibrium output grows to 70 billion. It verifies that equilibrium output increases by 10 (from 60 to 70 billion), as indicated above.

Table 9.12

National income	*Aggregate consumption*	*Investment*	*Aggregate expenditures*
0	5	2	7
10	14	2	16
20	23	2	25
30	32	2	34
40	41	2	43
50	50	2	52
60	59	2	61
70	68	2	70
80	77	2	79
90	86	2	88
100	95	2	97

3 Table 9.13 gives

a the aggregate consumption function and
b the aggregate expenditures schedule.

Table 9.13

National income (billions of wemos)	*Aggregate consumption*	*Investment*	*Aggregate expenditures*
0	2	2	4
4	5	2	7
8	8	2	10
12	11	2	13
16	14	2	16
20	17	2	19
24	20	2	22
28	23	2	25

c Equilibrium output is 16 billion.
d The multiplier is 1/(1 – *MPC*) = 1/(1 – 0.75) = 4. The change in output is 2 × 4 = 8. This is verified by Table 9.14, which shows that the new equilibrium output is 24 billion.

Table 9.14

National income	*Aggregate consumption*	*Investment*	*Aggregate expenditures*
0	2	4	6
4	5	4	9
8	8	4	12
12	11	4	15
16	14	4	18
20	17	4	21
24	20	4	24
28	23	4	27

5 Table 9.15 shows

a the aggregate consumption function and
b the aggregate expenditures schedule.

Table 9.15

National income (billions of dorals)	*Aggregate consumption*	*Investment*	*Government spending*	*Aggregate expenditures*
0	5	2	3	10
10	13	2	3	18
20	21	2	3	26
30	29	2	3	34
40	37	2	3	42
50	45	2	3	50
60	53	2	3	58
70	61	2	3	66
80	69	2	3	74
90	77	2	3	82
100	85	2	3	90

c The equilibrium level of output is 50 billion.
d The multiplier is 1/[1 – *MPC* (1 – *t*)] = 1/[1 – 0.9 (1 – 1/9)] = 5. The change in output is 4 × 5 = 20

billion. Table 9.16 shows that when government spending is 7 billion, the new equilibrium output is 70 billion, which represents an increase of 20 billion.

Table 9.16

National income	*Aggregate consumption*	*Investment*	*Government spending*	*Aggregate expenditures*
0	5	2	7	14
10	13	2	7	22
20	21	2	7	30
30	29	2	7	38
40	37	2	7	46
50	45	2	7	54
60	53	2	7	62
70	61	2	7	70
80	69	2	7	78
90	77	2	7	86
100	85	2	7	94

6 Table 9.17 gives

a the aggregate consumption function and
b the aggregate expenditures schedule.

Table 9.17

National income (billions of wemos)	*Aggregate consumption*	*Investment*	*Government spending*	*Aggregate expenditures*
0	2	4	2	8
4	4	4	2	10
8	6	4	2	12
12	8	4	2	14
16	10	4	2	16
20	12	4	2	18
24	14	4	2	20
28	16	4	2	22

c Equilibrium output is 16 billion.
d The multiplier is $1/[1 - MPC(1 - t)] = 1/[1 - 0.75(1 - 1/3)] = 2$. The change in equilibrium output is $2 \times 2 = 4$ billion, as is verified by Table 9.18, which shows that the new equilibrium output is 20 billion.

Table 9.18

National income	*Aggregate consumption*	*Investment*	*Government spending*	*Aggregate expenditures*
0	2	4	4	10
4	4	4	4	12
8	6	4	4	14
12	8	4	4	16
16	10	4	4	18
20	12	4	4	20
24	14	4	4	22
28	16	4	4	24

8 Table 9.19 shows

a the aggregate consumption function,
b the net export function, and
c the aggregate expenditures schedule.

Table 9.19

National income (billions of dorals)	*Aggregate consumption*	*Investment*	*Government spending*	*Net exports*	*Aggregate expenditures*
0	5	2	3	14	24
10	13	2	3	12	30
20	21	2	3	10	26
30	29	2	3	8	42
40	37	2	3	6	48
50	45	2	3	4	54
60	53	2	3	2	60
70	61	2	3	0	66
80	69	2	3	–2	72
90	77	2	3	–4	78
100	85	2	3	–6	84

d Equilibrium output is 60 billion.
e The multiplier is $1/[1 - (MPC - MPI)(1 - t)] = 1/[1 - (0.9 - 9/40)(1 - 1/9)] = 2.5$. The change in output is $4 \times 2.5 = 10$. Table 9.20 shows that the new equilibrium output is 70 billion, which indicates an increase of 10 billion.

Table 9.20

National income	*Aggregate consumption*	*Investment*	*Government spending*	*Net exports*	*Aggregate expenditures*
0	5	2	3	18	28
10	13	2	3	16	34
20	21	2	3	14	40
30	29	2	3	12	46
40	37	2	3	10	52
50	45	2	3	8	58
60	53	2	3	6	64
70	61	2	3	4	70
80	69	2	3	2	76
90	77	2	3	0	82
100	85	2	3	–6	84

9 Table 9.21 shows

a the aggregate consumption function,
b the net export function, and
c the aggregate expenditures schedule.

Table 9.21

National income (billions of dorals)	*Aggregate consumption*	*Invest-ment*	*Govern-ment spending*	*Net exports*	*Aggregate expenditures*
0	2	4	2	2⅔	10⅔
4	4	4	2	2	12
8	6	4	2	1⅓	13⅓
12	8	4	2	⅔	14⅔
16	10	4	2	0	16
20	12	4	2	–⅔	17⅓
24	14	4	2	–1⅓	18⅔
28	16	4	2	–2	20

Table 9.22

National income (billions of dorals)	*Aggregate consumption*	*Invest-ment*	*Govern-ment spending*	*Net exports*	*Aggregate expenditures*
0	2	4	2	5⅓	13⅓
4	4	4	2	4⅔	14⅔
8	6	4	2	4	16
12	8	4	2	3⅓	17⅓
16	10	4	2	2⅔	18⅔
20	12	4	2	2	20
24	14	4	2	1⅓	21⅓
28	16	4	2	⅔	22⅔

d Equilibrium output equals 16 billion.

e The multiplier is $1/[1-(MPC-MPI)(1-t)] = 1/[1-(0.75-0.25)(1-⅓)] = 1.5$. The change in output is $(8/3) \times 1.5 = 4$ billion. Table 9.22 shows that the new equilibrium output equals 20 billion, which is an increase of 4 billion.

Chapter 10

CONSUMPTION AND INVESTMENT

Chapter Review

This chapter moves behind aggregate expenditures and gives a deeper look at two of its components—consumption and investment. The important issues involve how consumption and investment are determined and the causes of shifts in the consumption and investment functions. This chapter concludes the discussion of income-expenditure analysis. The next three chapters move on to the topics of money and monetary policy.

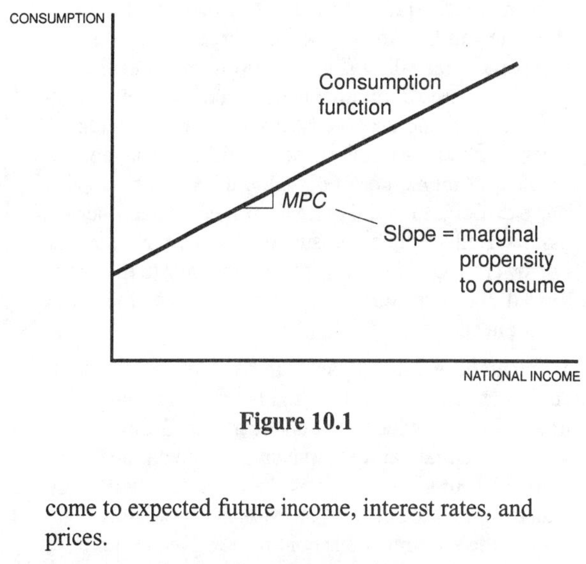

Figure 10.1

ESSENTIAL CONCEPTS

1 What determines **consumption** expenditures? The basic building block is the **Keynesian consumption function,** which gives the relationship between consumption and current income. Figure 10.1 shows that as current income increases by one dollar, consumption increases by the marginal propensity to consume. Other, more future-oriented theories of consumption are the **life-cycle hypothesis** and the **permanent income hypothesis.** These hypotheses shift the focus away from current income to expected future income, interest rates, and prices.

2 The life-cycle hypothesis asserts that individuals plan their consumption over their entire lifetime. Thus, people save during their working years when income is high in order to provide for consumption during retirement. Because savings play such an important role, cur-

rent and expected future interest rates as well as expected future income have significant effects on the level of consumption. The life-cycle hypothesis is a future-oriented explanation. It implies that the relationship between consumption and current income would be quite flat, as shown in Figure 10.2.

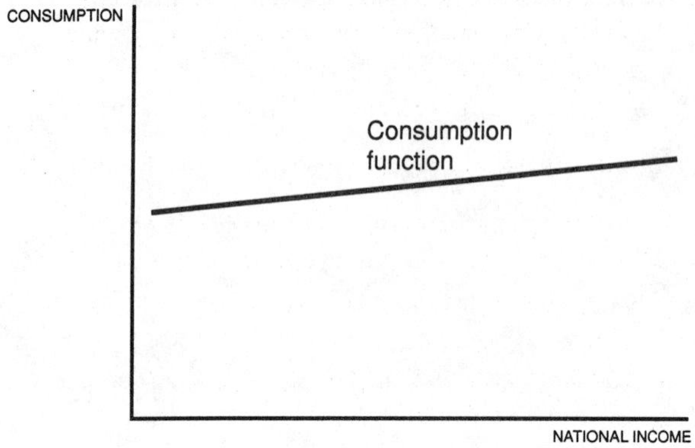

Figure 10.2

3 The permanent income hypothesis also argues that people rationally plan their present and future consumption, saving in good years to provide extra consumption in bad years. Again, the focus is on both current and future income, interest rates, and prices. The permanent income hypothesis reconciles the discrepancy between the aggregate and the individual: over time, aggregate consumption increases in the same proportion as income, while for individuals consumption increases by a smaller proportion than income.

4 In reality, the relationship between current income and consumption is not as flat as the future-oriented theories suggest. Two explanations of why consumption seems to be more dependent on current income involve **durable goods consumption** and **credit rationing.** When incomes fall during recessions, individuals postpone purchases of durable goods. Because they are uncertain when and if good times will return, they take the safer alternative of making do with old durable goods. Further, when incomes fall, individuals find borrowing more difficult than the permanent income hypothesis asserts. Banks also are unsure of the future incomes of borrowers and are reluctant to lend money to the unemployed. It is safer for banks to lend money to those who do not need it!

5 **Investment** includes firms' purchases of new plant and equipment and inventories, and households' purchases of new houses, which are durable goods. Business investment in plant and equipment is based on the expectation that future profits from the investment will more than outweigh the current investment expenditure. Of course, the firm must discount future revenues and costs; therefore, the interest rate is important. The investment schedule gives the total value of investment at each rate of interest. Lower interest rates increase the present value of profits and lead to more investment.

6 Firms face technological risks and market risks and they demand compensation, the size of which depends upon the size of the risks, their ability to share the risks, and their willingness to bear the risks themselves. The other important factor is the availability of funds. During recessions the investment schedule shifts to the left because expectations of profits decrease, risks appear larger, risk-sharing opportunities diminish, firms grow less willing to bear risks, and available funds dry up.

7 Firms hold inventories of inputs in order to **facilitate production;** a firm can be sure that the inputs will be there when needed. Firms may hold inventories of output in order to **smooth production;** that is, the firm can produce at a steady rate and always have enough to meet a highly variable consumer demand. Nonetheless, inventories are much more variable than output and contribute to the instability of the economy. During downturns, for example, it is less risky for firms to cut production and sell off inventories than to continue to produce in the hope that good times will return.

BEHIND THE ESSENTIAL CONCEPTS

1 The marginal propensity to consume out of current income is quite high, and thus the consumption function slopes up rather steeply. Why, then, do we study the future-oriented theories of consumption, which stress the future and predict a flat consumption function? The answer is that the life-cycle and permanent income hypotheses provide a deeper understanding of consumption, especially of what factors might cause the Keynesian consumption function to shift and the stability of the relationship. For example, in recessions, people become pessimistic about future incomes and postpone durable goods purchases, shifting the consumption function and aggregate expenditures down. Remember that the central questions in macroeconomics involve the fluctuations in the economy; therefore, it is vital to understand the causes of the changes.

2 The life-cycle and permanent income hypotheses involve borrowing and savings; thus, they teach us the importance of capital markets. If you were always able to obtain credit, your consumption would not vary much. You could borrow in low-income years (such as during college), live well, and repay during high-income years. But capital markets are not perfect; credit rationing suggests that banks are reluctant to let you borrow against future earnings. When your income is less during recessions and you need money, the best available option is to postpone major purchases. Imperfect capital markets make consumption more variable, and thus they are at the center of the discussion about economic ups and downs.

3 To see why business investment is volatile and why it fluctuates over the business cycle, put yourself in the shoes of a business owner. The economy is in recession, and customers are not buying your products. Profits are

down, and you have little retained earnings to spend on investment. The bank will not lend to you because it perceives your precarious financial position. Even if you could obtain funds, a recession is not the time to take risks. During good times, a failed investment may only mean lower profits; during bad times, it may mean bankruptcy. The safest option is to postpone purchases of new plant and equipment, cut production, and sell off inventories.

4 While modern macroeconomists of every school think that a firm microeconomic foundation for their theories is essential, the differences between microeconomics and macroeconomics are interesting. Microeconomics focuses largely on prices. In the basic competitive model, prices always adjust and clear the market. Even when imperfect competition is the subject, economists focus on the failure of prices to capture all costs and benefits or to find the right level. In macroeconomics, especially the new Keynesian approach, prices do not do their job, and markets do not always clear. Consumption is driven by income, not so much by prices. There is still an equilibrium, but it is one in which income, not price, adjusts until desired aggregate spending equals output.

SELF-TEST

True or False

1 The Keynesian consumption function describes the relationship between consumption and permanent disposable income.

2 According to the life-cycle hypothesis, people save during working years to provide for consumption during retirement.

3 According to the permanent income hypothesis, people save during good years to offset low income during bad years.

4 The future-oriented theories of consumption imply that the consumption function is relatively flat.

5 The future-oriented theories of consumption imply that the multiplier is large.

6 Future-oriented theories of consumption imply that current income is relatively less important than wealth.

7 Spending on durable goods is less variable than spending on nondurable goods.

8 A borrower is credit rationed if she cannot afford the interest rate at which banks are willing to lend.

9 Consumption depends more on current disposable income than the future-oriented theories of consumption imply.

10 The investment spending relevant for aggregate expenditures includes purchases of capital equipment by firms and purchases of shares by individuals.

11 Almost all of the volatility in investment is explained by variations in real interest rates.

12 Firms finance most investment out of retained earnings.

13 Firms usually perceive that investment is riskier during recessions.

14 Opportunities to share risk increase during recessions.

15 In the United States economy, inventories fluctuate less than output because firms try to smooth production and produce at a steady rate.

Multiple Choice

1 The view that current disposable income determines current consumption is consistent with the

a Keynesian consumption function;
b life-cycle hypothesis;
c permanent income hypothesis;
d all of the above;
e b and c.

2 The idea that individuals save during working years in order to provide for consumption during retirement is called the

a Keynesian consumption function;
b life-cycle hypothesis;
c permanent income hypothesis;
d all of the above;
e b and c.

3 The theory that people save in good years to provide for extra consumption in bad years is called the

a Keynesian consumption function;
b life-cycle hypothesis;
c permanent income hypothesis;
d b and c;
e all of the above.

4 Which of the following emphasize(s) that expected future income affects current consumption?

a Keynesian consumption function;
b life-cycle hypothesis;
c permanent income hypothesis;
d all of the above;
e b and c.

5 Which of the following imply(ies) that a temporary tax cut will significantly increase current consumption?

a Keynesian consumption function;
b life-cycle hypothesis;
c permanent income hypothesis;
d all of the above;
e b and c.

6 According to the future-oriented consumption theories, the multiplier is

a quite small;
b zero;
c large;
d small in recessions but large in booms;
e large in recessions but small in booms.

7 If the price of an asset that an individual owns rises, then that individual is said to receive

a human capital;
b capital gains;
c retained earnings;
d temporary income;
e disposable income.

8 Which of the following are reasons why consumption depends more on current income than the future-oriented theories might suggest?

a Individuals can postpone purchases of durable goods when current income falls.
b Banks are reluctant to lend money to people whose current income is low.
c Individuals can see through the corporate veil, reducing their consumption when profits fall.
d Government tax and spending policies do not affect individual consumption.
e a and b.

9 An individual is credit rationed if

a he cannot afford the interest charged on a loan;
b banks charge a higher rate of interest to reflect their perception of the risk that he will not repay on schedule;
c he is unable to borrow even though he is willing to pay the interest, and the interest rate reflects the risk of lending to him;
d he has no savings;
e he has no current income.

10 The component of aggregate expenditures that is most variable is probably

a investment;
b consumption;
c government expenditures;
d net exports;
e They are equally variable.

11 For aggregate expenditure calculation, which of the following is not included in investment spending?

a purchases of new capital goods;
b inventories accumulated in anticipation of sales;
c purchases of used capital goods;
d purchases of new homes;
e none of the above.

12 Before investing, businesses must

a predict future revenues;
b predict future costs;
c adjust future revenues and costs for inflation;
d compute the present value of profits using the real interest rate;
e all of the above.

13 The investment function describes the total value of investment at each

a price level;
b level of disposable income;
c level of national income;
d level of GDP;
e rate of interest.

14 Real interest rates

a are quite volatile, reflecting instability in the capital market;
b vary enough to provide a good explanation of short-term variations in investment;
c vary little;
d are irrelevant to the investment decision;
e change very little but lead to large changes in the level of investment because investment demand is quite elastic.

15 The compensation that firms require to justify the risk of investment depends upon

a their ability to share the risks;
b their willingness to bear the risks;
c the magnitude of the risks;
d all of the above;
e none of the above.

16 Most investment is financed

a out of retained earnings;
b by borrowing at the real interest rate;
c by issuing new shares;
d by selling bonds;
e by raising product prices.

17 Firms invest less during recessions because

a retained earnings fall as revenues decline faster than expenses;
b as individual firms cut back on investment and inventories, national output falls owing to the multiplier effect, further reducing the profitability of investment;
c banks are less willing to lend because they foresee a greater risk that the loans will not be repaid;
d firms' forecasts of the profitability of investment become more pessimistic;
e all of the above.

18 The theory that investment is more volatile than output because firms try to keep a constant ratio of their capital stock to output is called

a the investment accelerator;
b Tobin's q;
c the investment multiplier;
d the production-facilitating theory;
e the production-smoothing theory.

19 Which of the following correctly states the correlation between inventories and output according to the two theories of inventory investment?

a Both production smoothing and production facilitating imply that output and inventories are negatively correlated.
b Both production smoothing and production facilitating imply that output and inventories are positively correlated.
c Production smoothing implies that output and in-

ventories are negatively correlated, but production facilitating implies that they are positively correlated.

d Production smoothing implies that output and inventories are negatively correlated, but production facilitating implies that they are positively correlated.

e Neither theory implies anything about the correlation.

20 Ways of stimulating investment include

a increasing business confidence by maintaining high output and full employment;

b tax breaks for investment, such as the investment tax credit;

c increasing the availability of credit through monetary policy;

d direct government lending programs;

e all of the above.

Completion

1 The present discounted value of expected future wages is called __________.

2 According to the __________ hypothesis, people save during their working years in order to increase consumption after retirement.

3 The __________ hypothesis argues that people save during good earning years to provide extra consumption during bad years.

4 The Keynesian consumption function stresses the relationship between consumption and __________.

5 Future-oriented theories of consumption, such as the permanent income and life-cycle hypotheses, imply that the aggregate expenditures schedule is __________.

6 The ability to postpone purchases of durable goods and the fact that it is difficult to borrow against future earnings make consumption __________ dependent on current income.

7 Changes in the level of __________ are the principal reason for the economy's instability.

8 Most firms finance most of their investment through __________.

9 Inventories generally __________ during recessions.

10 The __________ theory explains why inventories would decrease during recessions.

Answers to Self-Test

True or False

1	f	6	t	11	f
2	t	7	f	12	t
3	t	8	f	13	t
4	t	9	t	14	f
5	f	10	f	15	f

Multiple Choice

1	a	6	a	11	c	16	a
2	b	7	b	12	e	17	e
3	c	8	e	13	e	18	a
4	e	9	c	14	c	19	c
5	a	10	a	15	d	20	e

Completion

1 human capital
2 life-cycle
3 permanent income
4 current income
5 relatively flat
6 more
7 investment
8 retained earnings
9 increase
10 production facilitating

Doing Economics: Tools and Practice Problems

Using income-expenditure analysis is the first subject in this section. We see how factors that cause changes in consumption and investment bring about shifts in the aggregate expenditures schedule and new equilibrium levels of output. Next, we look carefully at the notion of Ricardian equivalence and study how government fiscal policies might be offset by private savings and borrowing, leaving consumption unchanged. In the real world, consumption is affected by government tax and spending policies. One important explanation involves the cost and availability of credit. Several problems show how imperfect capital markets lead to the failure of Ricardian equivalence.

INCOME-EXPENDITURE ANALYSIS

Income-expenditure analysis can be used to answer such questions as "What is the effect on output of a change in interest rates?" In general, when some economic event causes a change in consumption or investment, the aggregate expenditures schedule will shift and bring about a change in the equilibrium level of output. Table 10.1 lists some important factors that change consumption and investment.

Tool Kit 10.1: Using Income-Expenditure Analysis

Changes in consumption or investment will shift the aggregate expenditures curve and bring about a change in output. The change in output will be a multiple of the initial change in spending. Follow these steps.

Table 10.1

Shifts in Aggregate Expenditures

Changes in consumption, which are related to changes in wealth, real interest rates, credit availability, or estimates of future earnings.

Changes in investment, which are related to changes in real interest rates, stock prices, credit availability, retained earnings, expectations of profitability, perceptions of risk, or willingness to bear risk.

Step one: Start with an equilibrium.

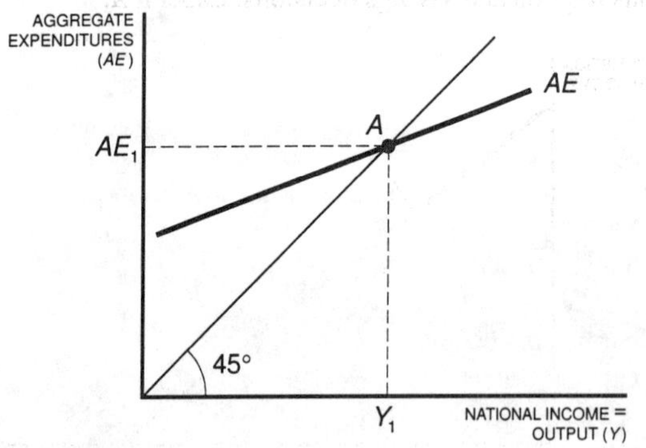

Step two: Identify a cause, and determine its effect on consumption, investment, or both.

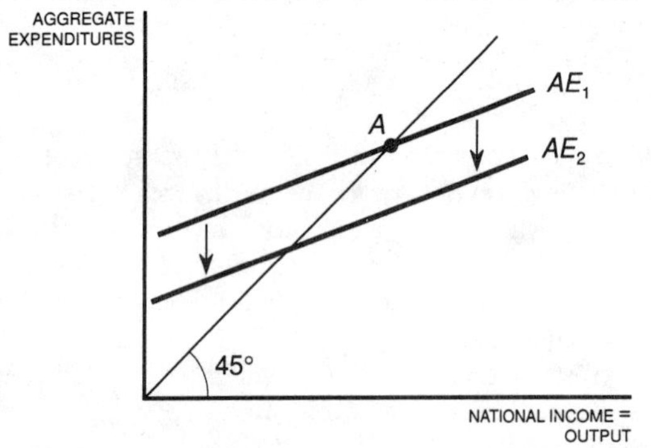

Step three: If consumption or investment increases, shift the aggregate expenditures schedule up; if either decreases, shift the schedule down.

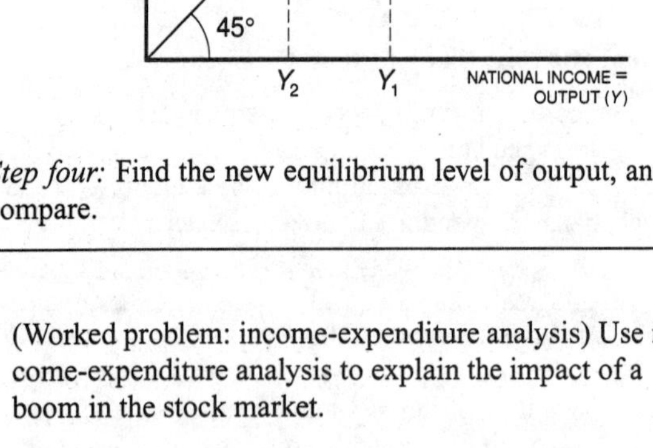

Step four: Find the new equilibrium level of output, and compare.

1 (Worked problem: income-expenditure analysis) Use income-expenditure analysis to explain the impact of a boom in the stock market.

Step-by-step solution

Step one: Start with an equilibrium.

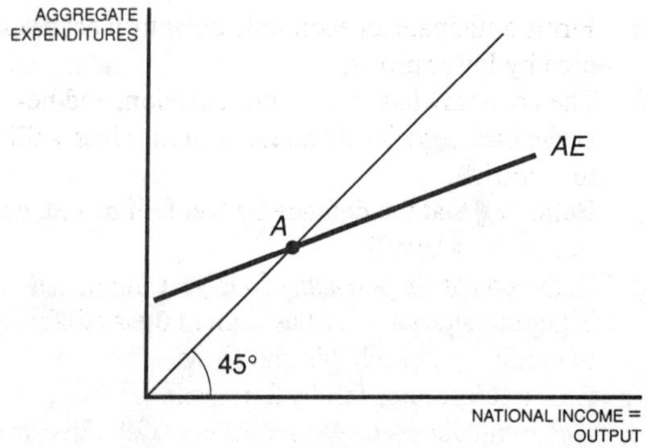

Step two: Identify a cause, and determine its effect on consumption, investment, or both. The increase in stock prices makes individuals wealthier, inducing them to increase consumption. Firms can finance more investment by issuing new shares; thus, investment increases.

Step three: Shift the aggregate expenditures schedule. Because both consumption and investment increase, it shifts up.

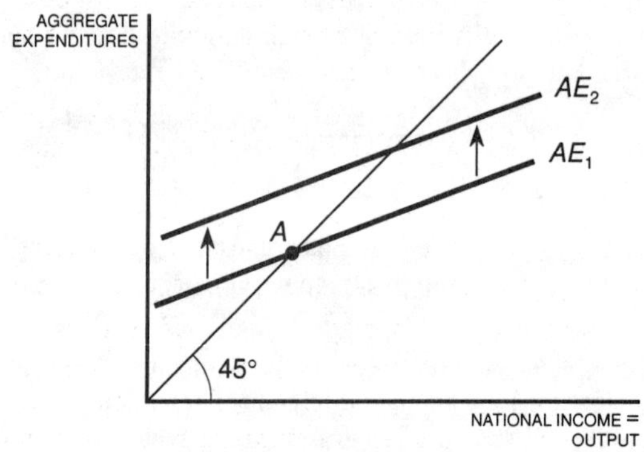

Step four: Find the new equilibrium, and compare. In the new equilibrium, output is greater. The increase in stock prices has brought about an increase in the economy's output.

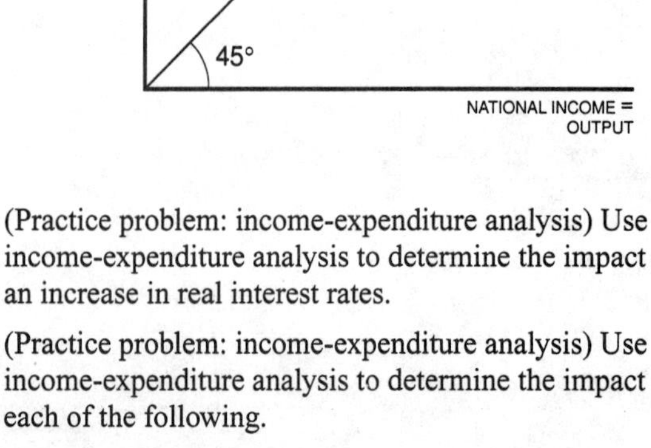

2 (Practice problem: income-expenditure analysis) Use income-expenditure analysis to determine the impact of an increase in real interest rates.

3 (Practice problem: income-expenditure analysis) Use income-expenditure analysis to determine the impact of each of the following.

a Firms anticipate an economic downturn accompanied by lower profits.
b The economy has fallen into recession, and because bankruptcies threaten, firms are less willing to bear risk.
c Believing that the defence budget will be cut, consumers fear layoffs.
d Retained earnings reach a four-year high.
e Tight monetary policy has limited the availability of credit for households and firms.
f Real interest rates fall by 2 percent.
g Uncertain about the consequences of the free-trade agreement with Mexico, firms perceive a risky future.
h Loose monetary policy increases the availability of credit.

THE BARRO-RICARDO ARGUMENT

When the government increases spending without a tax increase, it finances its deficit by selling bonds. Today's bonds must be repaid, however. This means that future taxpayers are liable for the debts incurred to finance current spending. The notion of Barro and Ricardo says that households will save now in order to be able to pay the future tax liability, and these savings will completely offset the effects of government deficit finance. In this section, we see how this might be true if capital markets were perfect, and several reasons why private savings do not offset government deficits in the real world: credit constraints and different interest rates for borrowing and lending. The lesson is that imperfect capital markets are an important reason why fiscal policy can be effective.

Tool Kit 10.2: Exploring the Barro-Ricardo Argument

The household's budget constraint shows what combinations of current and future consumption are possible given expectations of current and future income and interest rates. We can use it to analyze the Barro-Ricardo argument that private savings offset budget deficits and thus fiscal policy is ineffective. Follow this procedure.

Step one: Draw the two-period budget constraint for the typical household. (Follow the procedure outlined in Chapter 2.)

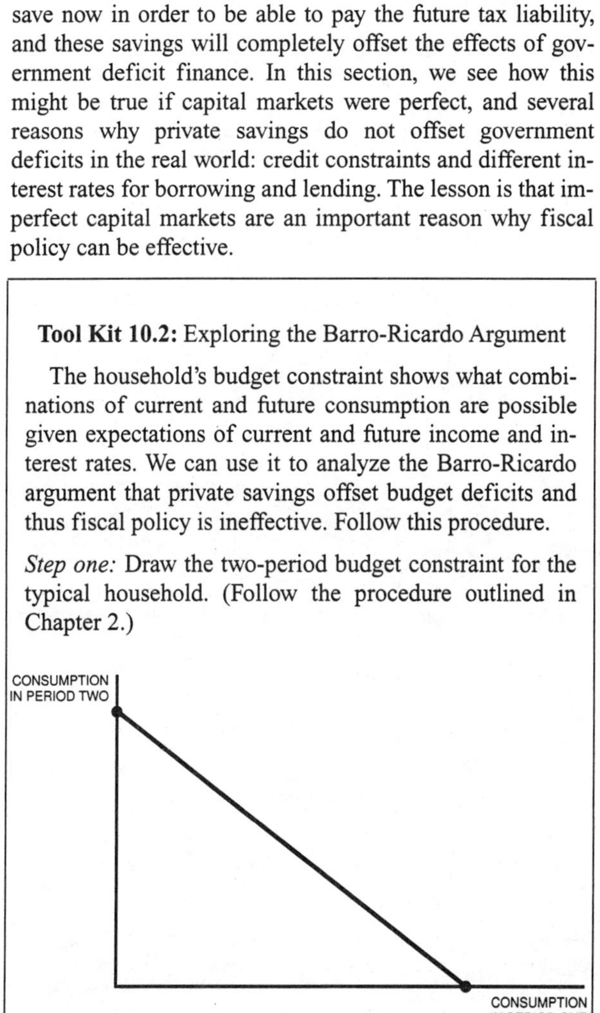

Step two: Choose a point that reflects the household's consumption and savings decisions. Label it *A*.

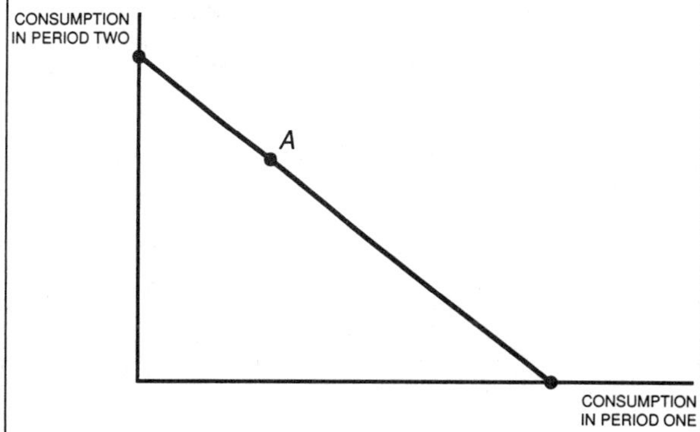

Step three: Show the effect of government borrowing by adding the extra spending to current consumption (the horizontal coordinate of *A*) and subtracting the future tax liability from future consumption (the vertical coordinate of *A*). Label the new point *B*.

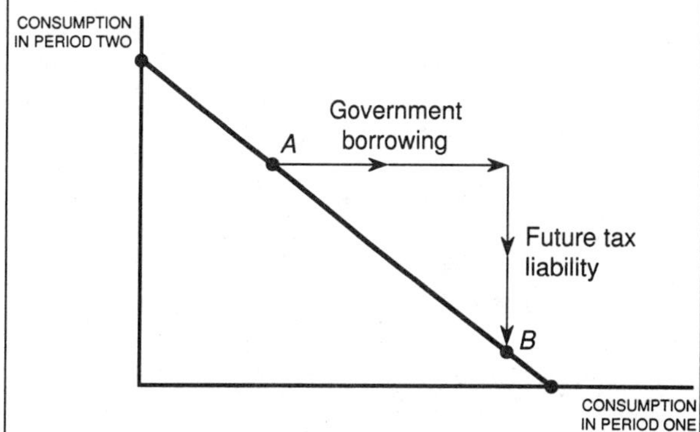

Step four: Determine if point *B* lies on or above the original budget constraint.

Step five: If *B* is on the original budget constraint, then Ricardian equivalence holds, and the household will save to return to point *A* because *A* indicates their preferred decision. If *B* is above the original budget constraint, Ricardian equivalence is not true, and the household may choose to consume more today.

4 (Worked problem: Barro-Ricardo) Doctor Campbell and her husband make $210,000 per year and expect that their real earnings will continue for at least 10 years. Although they expect a 50 percent real interest rate over the 10-year period, they neither borrow nor save. The government passes a college subsidy program that will give the Campbells an extra $10,000 this year. It finances this program by issuing 10-year bonds that pay a 50 percent real rate of return over the period. The Campbells expect that they will pay their share of the tax liability when the bonds come due in 10 years. Analyze how the program will affect the Campbells' savings decision and whether Ricardian equivalence would hold.

Step-by-step solution

Step one: Draw the two-period budget constraint. The present discounted value of their income equals \$210,000 + [\$210,000 × (1/1 + .50)] = \$350,000, which is the horizontal intercept. The future equivalent is [\$210,000 × (1 + .50)] + \$210,000 = \$525,000, which is the vertical intercept. The slope is 525,000/350,000 = 1.50, which is 1 plus the interest rate.

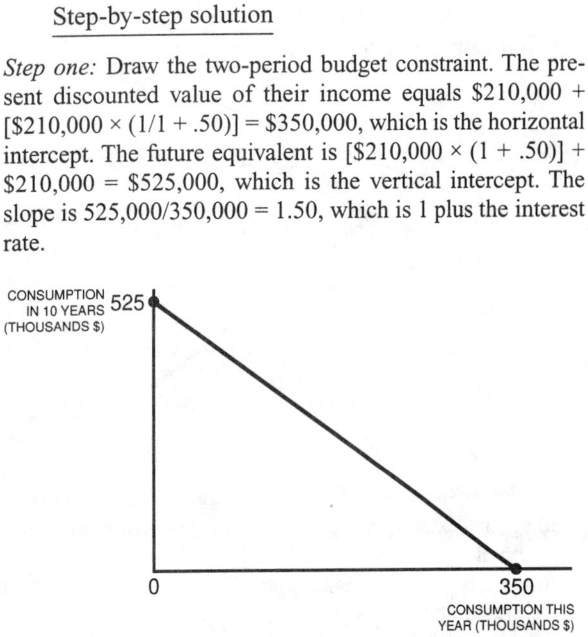

Step two: Choose a point that reflects the household's consumption and savings decisions. The Campbells neither save nor borrow, so they choose to consume \$210,000 in each year.

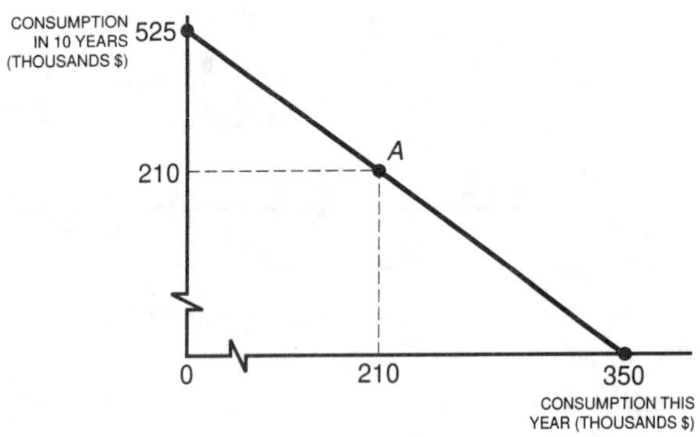

Step three: Show the effect of the program. It gives the Campbells \$10,000 now, but it takes away \$10,000 × (1 + .50) = \$15,000 in 10 years. This moves their chosen point from *A* to *B*.

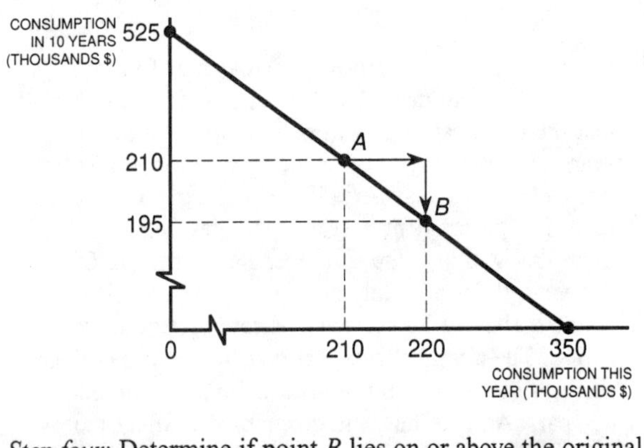

Step four: Determine if point *B* lies on or above the original budget constraint. Clearly, *B* is on the same budget constraint.

Step five: If B is on the original budget constraint, then Ricardian equivalence holds, and the household will save to return to point *A* because *A* indicates their preferred decision. The Campbells merely increase their savings to \$10,000. The principal and interest will be just enough to pay the tax increase that they expect in 10 years. The government borrowing is exactly offset by private savings.

5 (Practice problem: Barro-Ricardo) The typical person in Ricardania earns 20,000 ricks (the local currency) annually. The real interest rate is 5 percent per year, and the typical person borrows 2,000 ricks. The government decides to stimulate the economy by giving each person 5,000 ricks. To finance this grant, the government sells one-year bonds that also pay 5 percent. Taxes will be increased next year to pay off the bonds. Analyze how the grant will affect the typical person's borrowing and savings decisions and also whether Ricardian equivalence would hold in Ricardania.

6 (Worked problem: Barro-Ricardo) Return to the Campbells of problem 4. All information is the same except the real interest rate for borrowing, which is now 100 percent over the 10-year period. Analyze how the program will affect the Campbells' savings decision and whether Ricardian equivalence would hold.

Step-by-step solution

Step one: Draw the two-period budget constraint. The vertical intercept remains as in problem 4, but the horizontal intercept now equals the present value of income discounted at 100 percent = \$210,000 + [\$210,000 × 1/(1 + 1.00)] = \$315,000.

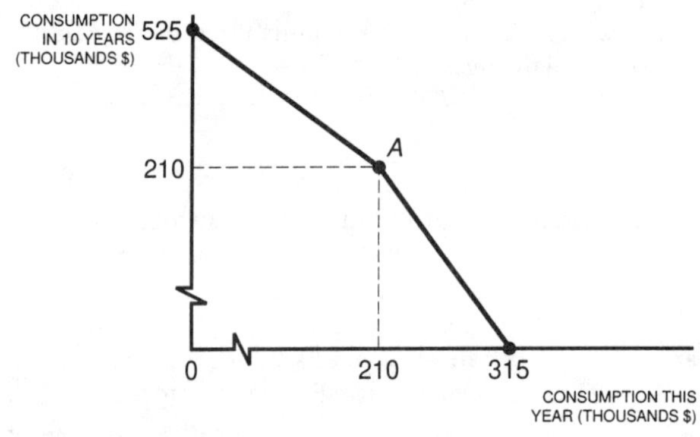

Step two: Choose a point that reflects the household's consumption and savings decisions. The Campbells continue to choose to consume \$210,000 in each period.

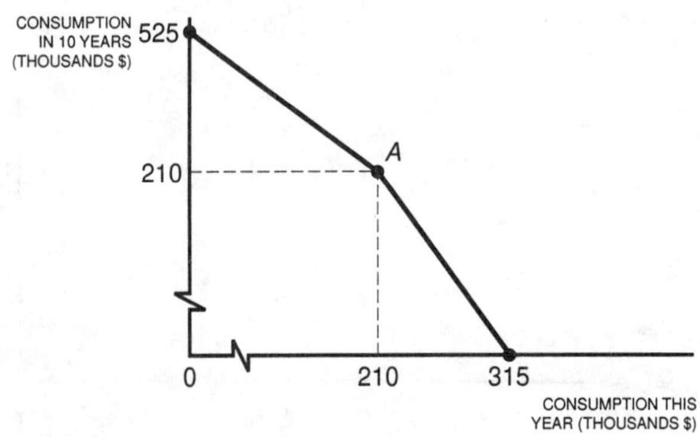

Step three: Show the effect of the government program. As in problem 4, it increases current consumption by \$10,000 and reduces future consumption by \$15,000, as shown by point *B*.

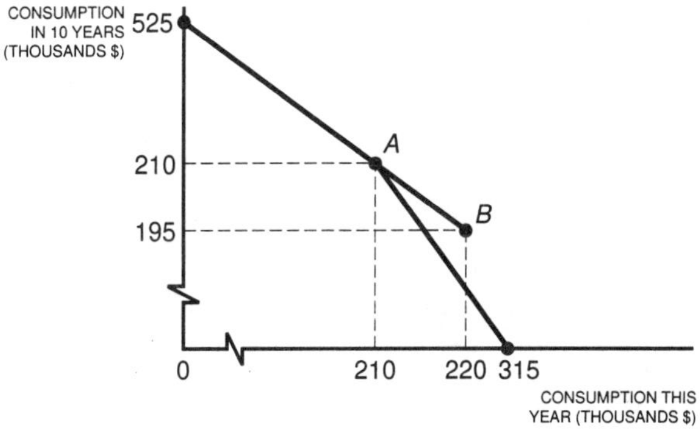

Step four: Determine if point *B* lies on or above the original budget constraint. It is now above.

Step five: If *B* is above the original constraint, Ricardian equivalence is not true, and the household may choose to consume more today. The deficit finance allows the Campbells to consume more today than it would if they had to borrow the money from a bank. They may choose any point on the line segment between *B* and *A,* and their choice will indicate more consumption. In this case, the government deficit increases consumption.

7 (Practice problem: Ricardian equivalence) Return to problem 5, and suppose that all information is the same except that the borrowing interest rate is 20 percent. Analyze how the grant will affect the typical person's borrowing and savings decisions and also whether Ricardian equivalence would hold in Ricardania.

8 (Practice problem: Ricardian equivalence) Although the Johnsons earn \$50,000 per year after taxes and expect to continue to earn the same in real terms for the next 5 years, they have a bad credit history and cannot borrow. They could earn 25 percent on their savings, but they do not have any. Analyze the effect on the Johnsons' budget constraint of a current tax cut of \$10,000 financed by a five-year bond paying 25 percent over the period. The bond will be repaid with tax increases, and the Johnsons expect that their share of the tax increase will pay off the bonds issued to finance their share of the current tax cut.

Answers to Problems

2 The increase in real interest rates reduces consumption (durable goods purchases fall) and investment, shifts aggregate expenditures down, and reduces output.

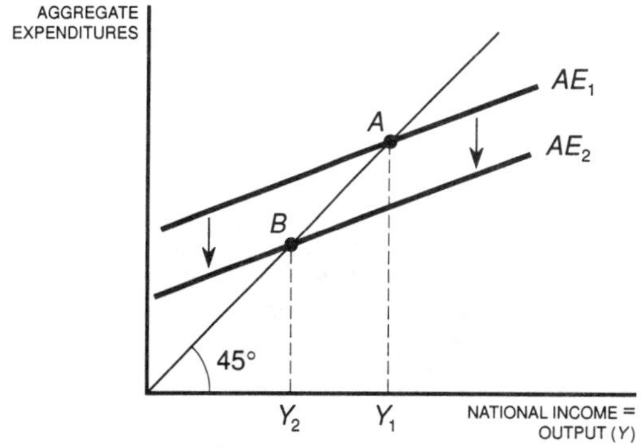

3 *a* Investment falls, shifting aggregate expenditures down and reducing output.

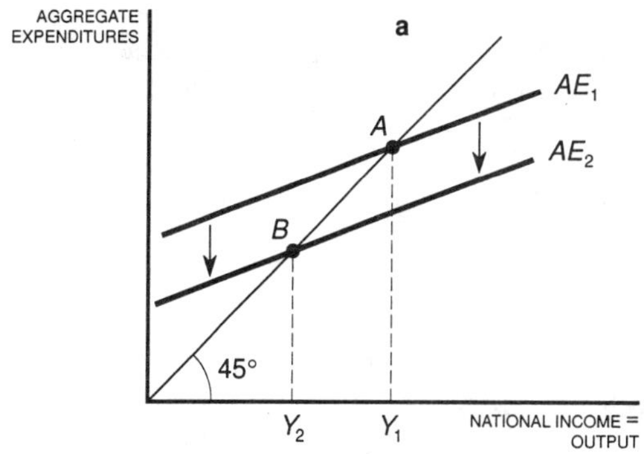

b Investment falls, shifting aggregate expenditures down and reducing output.

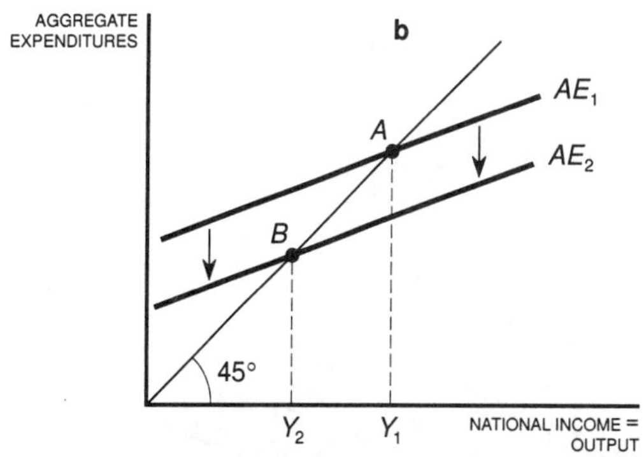

c Consumption falls, shifting aggregate expenditures down and reducing output.

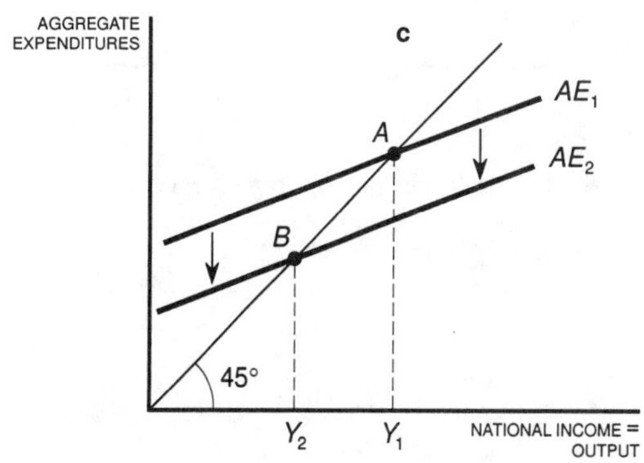

d Investment increases, shifting aggregate expenditures up and increasing output.

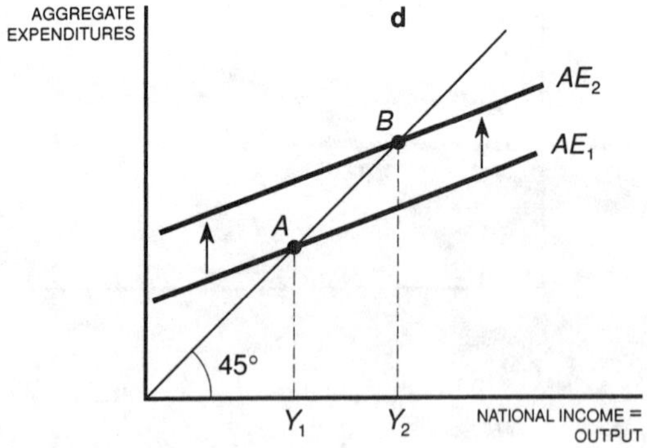

e Investment and purchases of durable goods fall, shifting aggregate expenditures down and reducing output.

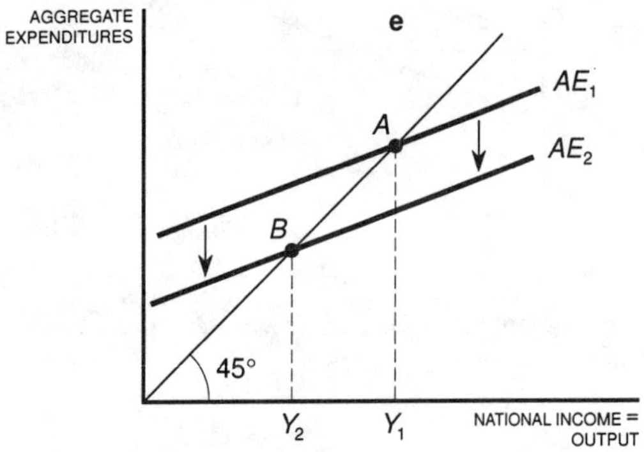

f Investment and purchases of durable goods rise, shifting aggregate expenditures up and increasing output.

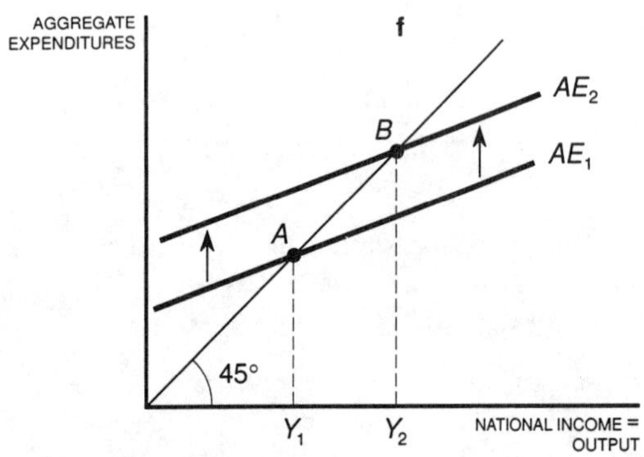

g Investment falls, shifting aggregate expenditures down and reducing output.

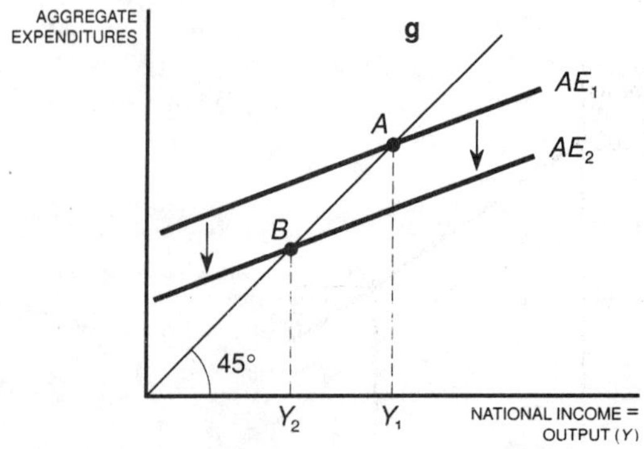

h Investment increases, shifting aggregate expenditures up and increasing output.

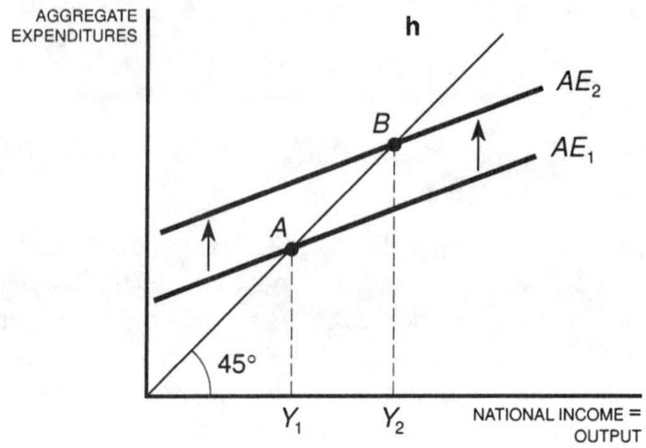

5

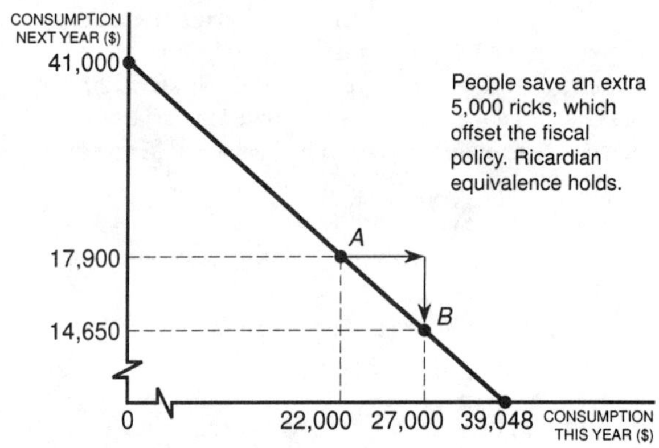

7

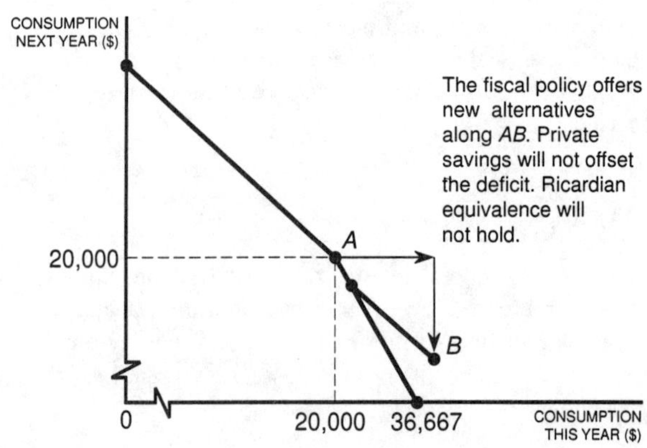

8

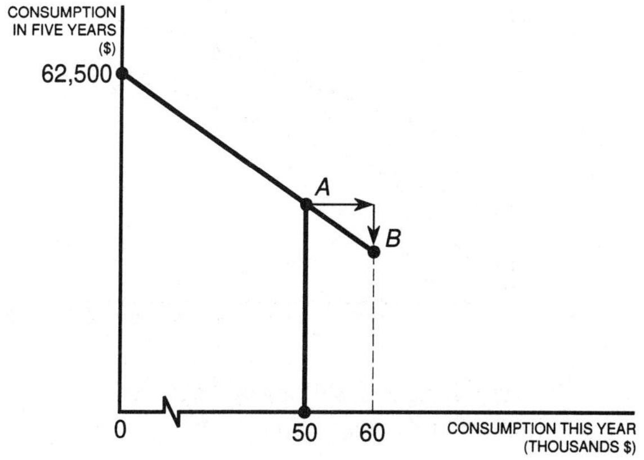
CONSUMPTION IN FIVE YEARS ($)
62,500
A
B
0
50
60
CONSUMPTION THIS YEAR (THOUSANDS $)

Chapter 11

MONEY, BANKING, AND CREDIT

Chapter Review

This chapter begins the study of money. What money is and the purposes it serves in the economy are the first two topics. The discussion then introduces the concept of the money supply and explains how the banking system creates money. The chapter also discusses the Federal Reserve, the institution of government responsible for regulating the money supply, ensuring the availability of credit, and promoting the stability of the banking system. This material on money, banking, and credit is complemented by the next chapter's study of how money affects the real economy in the short run. This part concludes with Chapter 13, the analysis of monetary and fiscal policy.

ESSENTIAL CONCEPTS

1 Economists define **money** by what it does. Money serves three functions. It is a **medium of exchange,** facilitating trades between firms and households. It is a **store of value,** permitting individuals to buy and sell at different times. Finally, it is a **unit of account,** helping people measure the relative value of different goods.

2 Since there are many financial assets that perform money's three functions to some degree, the **money supply** is measured in several ways. The most important measure is **M1,** which includes currency, traveler's checks, and demand deposits (checking accounts). Other measures, such as **M2** and **M3,** include progressively less liquid assets. The liquidity of an asset refers to how easy it is to convert into M1. The now rather common practice of buying on credit using credit cards or home equity loans makes specifying the size of the money supply more difficult.

3 The **financial system** includes all the institutions that help savers and borrowers transact. **Financial intermediaries,** such as banks and savings and loan associations, are the firms that stand between savers and borrowers. The **Federal Reserve** is the central bank of the United States. It regulates banks to ensure their financial health and also controls the money supply and availability of credit to promote and stabilize overall economic activity.

4 While the Federal Reserve (or Fed) controls the money supply, money itself is created by the banking system. Banks operate on the **fractional reserve system,** which means that they keep only a fraction of deposits on hand as reserves. Thus, an intitial deposit (or other increase in

reserves) results in additional loans, which ultimately return to the banking system as more deposits. The process of deposit expansion continues until total deposits have grown by a multiple of the initial deposit. The **money multiplier** is the relationship between the initial deposit and the ultimate change in total deposits.

5 The Federal Reserve has three instruments for controlling the money supply. Most important, it buys and sells government bonds. This activity is called **open market operations.** The Fed also specifies the level of **required reserves** that banks must keep on hand or on deposit at the Fed. Finally, the Fed Sets the **discount rate,** which is the interest rate charged to banks when borrowing from the Fed.

6 Ensuring the stability of the United States banking system and reducing the threat of bank runs are important responsibilities of the Federal Reserve and other government agencies. The Fed acts as a lender of last resort, providing liquidity to troubled banks, and it sets reserve requirements. Government-mandated capital requirements add to the incentives that bank owners have to manage risks carefully. The Federal Deposit Insurance Corporation insures depositors against bank failure.

BEHIND THE ESSENTIAL CONCEPTS

1 How do the Fed's instruments affect the money supply? Each works by increasing or decreasing banks' reserves, affecting the money available for loans.

a When the Fed engages in open market operations, it buys and sells bonds. If it buys a bond, for example, the money that it pays is deposited in a bank. The bank's reserves increase, and it in turn can grant new loans.

b When the Fed decreases reserve requirements, banks can reduce their reserves and again make new loans.

c When the Fed increases the discount rate, banks know that borrowing from the Fed will be more expensive. They guard against having to borrow by keeping more reserves and making fewer loans.

2 Figure 11.1 will help you keep straight how open market operations affect the money supply. On the left is the Fed's vault, where it keeps stacks of bonds and currency. The currency in the vault is not money, because it is not in the economy. On the right is the economy. If the Fed buys bonds, currency flows from the vault into the economy and increases the money supply. If the Fed sells bonds, the money it receives leaves the economy and goes into the vault, where it is no longer money.

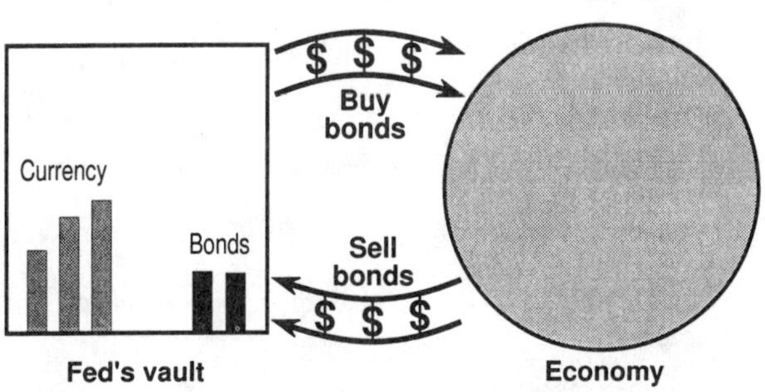

Figure 11.1

3 Both the Federal Reserve and the U.S. Treasury sell government bonds. You can keep the two straight if you remember why the bonds are sold. The Treasury sells bonds to borrow money to finance government spending. When the Treasury sells bonds, the money is spent, and it stays in the economy. The Fed sells bonds to reduce the money supply. When the Fed sells bonds, the money it receives goes into the Fed's vault and leaves the economy.

4 You should not confuse the money multiplier in this chapter with the fiscal multiplier introduced in Chapter 9. They are two different concepts. The fiscal multiplier shows that an increase in aggregate expenditures—for example, in investment—brings about a larger increase in output. The money multiplier shows that an increase in reserves leads to a larger increase in total deposits.

5 The *workings* of the fiscal and money multipliers, however, are similar. With the fiscal multiplier, an initial increase in spending creates additional income, which leads to a second round of spending when some of the income is consumed. The sequence is spending—income—additional spending, etc. Each successive round of spending is smaller, and the process ultimately settles down.

With the money multiplier, an initial increase in deposits leads to new loans, which ultimately are deposited back in the banking system. The sequence here is deposits—loans—deposits—additional loans, etc. Each successive round of deposits is smaller, and again the process ultimately settles down.

6 The *formulas* for the multipliers are also similar. The fiscal multiplier equals 1 divided by the marginal propensity to save. You can think of savings as a leakage, which makes the next round of spending smaller than the last one. The formula for the money multiplier is 1 divided by the reserve ratio. Again, in that they are not loaned out, reserves are like a leakage, and making the next round of deposits smaller than the previous round.

7 One of the fundamental trade-offs in economic life is risk and incentives. We have seen this notion many times, and it appears again in this chapter on the subject of deposit insurance. The Federal Deposit Insurance Corporation (FDIC) protects your money against loss in case of bank failure. Because you know that your money is safe, you seek the highest rate of interest and have little incentive to worry about the financial health of the bank. Banks know how you think and are motivated to grant risky loans, seeking high average returns so that they can afford to pay high rates of interest. Thus, deposit insurance reduces the risk for depositors, but it creates incentives that lead to reckless lending. This problem led to the savings and loan crisis in the 1980s,

and it is the motivation for regulations such as capital requirements that promote bank safety.

SELF-TEST

True or False

1 The term "money" refers only to currency and coins in circulation.

2 The store of value function of money refers to its use as a measure of the relative value of goods.

3 The money supply is an example of a flow variable.

4 M1 includes currency, traveler's checks, and demand deposits.

5 An asset is liquid if it is easily converted into money (M1).

6 Financial intermediaries are firms that provide a link between savers and borrowers.

7 The Federal Reserve is the central bank of the United States.

8 The Federal Reserve is an independent agency funded out of the profits of its operations.

9 A bank's net worth equals its liabilities minus its assets.

10 Banks operate on the fractional reserve system, which means that they hold only a fraction of the amount of deposits in reserve.

11 The money multiplier implies that total deposits increase by a multiple of an initial deposit.

12 The Federal Reserve controls the money supply by mandating maximum interest rates that banks can charge their best customers.

13 The discount rate is the interest rate that the Fed charges on loans to banks.

14 Open market operations refer to the buying and selling of government bonds by the Federal Reserve.

15 Federal deposit insurance lessens the risk faced by depositors but also reduces their incentives to monitor the performance of banks.

Multiple Choice

1 Trade without the use of money is called

a double coincidence of wants;
b medium of exchange;
c barter;
d unit of account;
e multiple deposit.

2 Double coincidence of wants refers to

a the fact that in order for two individuals to barter, each must have what the other wants and want what the other has;
b the fact that money must be both a store of value and a medium of exchange;
c the unlikely possibility that two individuals will have exactly the same tastes;
d the fact that dividends are taxed twice;
e the fact that the Federal Reserve engages in open market operations and sets the discount rate.

3 The use of money to facilitate exchange is its

a medium of exchange function;
b store of value function;
c unit of account function;
d double coincidence of wants function;
e fractional reserve function.

4 The use of money to measure the relative value of goods and services is its

a medium of exchange function;
b store of value function;
c unit of account function;
d double coincidence of wants function;
e fractional reserve function.

5 The use of money as a means of preserving purchasing power for a time period is its

a medium of exchange function;
b store of value function;
c unit of account function;
d double coincidence of wants function;
e fractional reserve function.

6 The economic definition of money is

a currency, traveler's checks, and demand deposits;
b M1;
c anything that acts as a medium of exchange, store of value, and unit of account;
d anything that avoids the double coincidence of wants problem;
e a and b.

7 Which of the following is not included in M1?

a currency;
b demand deposits (checking accounts);
c traveler's checks;
d certificates of deposit.
e All of the above are included.

8 Which of the following is not included in M2?

a M1;
b certificates of deposit;
c Eurodollar accounts;
d savings accounts up to $100,000;
e All of the above are included.

9 Which of the following is not included in M3?

a M1;
b M2;
c savings accounts over $100,000;
d institutional money-market mutual funds;
e corporate retained earnings.

10 An agreement by a bank to lend up to some specified amount is a

a money market mutal fund;
b certificate of deposit;

c line of credit;
d unit of account;
e savings account.

11 Which of the following are not financial intermediaries?

a banks;
b savings and loans;
c mutual funds;
d life insurance companies;
e All of the above are financial intermediaries.

12 The objectives of government involvement in the financial system include

a protecting consumers;
b stabilizing the level of economic activity;
c protecting banks from unfair competition;
d creating jobs in the financial sector;
e a and b.

13 The central bank of the United States is

a the Bank of America;
b Chase Manhattan Bank;
c the Federal Reserve;
d the U.S. Treasury;
e the Comptroller of the Currency.

14 The Federal Reserve is

a an agency of the executive branch, subject to presidential control;
b an agency funded by Congress and subject to congressional oversight;
c an independent agency funded out of the profits of its operations;
d an agency funded and overseen by the major U.S. banks;
e an agency funded and overseen by the major Wall Street brokerage houses.

15 The fractional reserve system in banking means that banks

a lend a fraction of their money to consumers and a fraction to businesses;
b hold a fraction of the amount on deposit in reserves;
c hold a fraction of the amount on loan in reserves;
d lend a fraction of their money to foreign businesses and a fraction to domestic businesses;
e may or may not belong to the Federal Reserve system.

16 The discount rate is

a the interest rate charged by the Fed on loans to banks;
b the interest rate paid by the Fed on deposits;
c the difference between the interest rate charged by the Fed and that charged in the market;
d the maximum allowable difference between interest charged on loans to consumers and loans to banks;
e the interest rate ceiling on credit card balances.

17 Which of the following is not a way in which the Federal Reserve can increase the money supply?

a Lower the discount rate.
b Reduce the reserve requirement.
c Buy Treasury bills.
d Sell Treasury bills.
e All of the above are ways to increase the money supply.

18 The money multiplier shows that

a the rich get richer;
b an increase in aggregate expenditures brings about a larger increase in national income;
c an increase in reserves leads to a larger increase in total deposits;
d a multiple of deposits must be held as reserves;
e deregulation leads to instability in the banking system.

19 Open market operations, the most important means by which the Fed controls the money supply, involve

a changing the discount rate;
b setting interest rates;
c changing the reserve requirement;
d buying and selling government bonds;
e placing varying restrictions on foreign borrowing and lending.

20 The Federal Deposit Insurance Corporation

a acts as the central bank of United States;
b ensures that banks will not fail;
c insures deposits (of up to $100,000) in case of bank collapse;
d protects banks against unfair foreign competition;
e sets the reserve requirement for bank deposits.

Completion

1 For a trade to take place in a barter economy, each individual must have what the other wants and want what the other has; that is, there must be a __________.

2 Money facilitates exchange; it is performing its __________ function.

3 Money holds on to its purchasing power; it is performing its __________ function.

4 People use money as a measuring rod, taking advantage of the __________ function of money.

5 Currency, traveler's checks, and checking accounts are included in the __________ measure of money.

6 Firms that act as go-betweens for savers and borrowers are called __________.

7 The central bank in United States is called the __________.

8 When the Federal Reserve buys and sells bonds, it is engaging in __________.

9 The minimum level of reserves that banks must keep on hand is its __________.

10 The interest rate charged to banks by the Federal Reserve is called the __________.

Answers to Self-Test

True or False

1	f	6	t	11	t
2	f	7	t	12	f
3	f	8	t	13	t
4	t	9	f	14	t
5	t	10	t	15	t

Multiple Choice

1	c	6	c	11	e	16	a
2	a	7	d	12	e	17	d
3	a	8	e	13	c	18	c
4	c	9	e	14	c	19	d
5	b	10	c	15	b	20	c

Completion

1 double coincidence of wants
2 medium of exchange
3 store of value
4 unit of account
5 M1
6 financial intermediaries
7 Federal Reserve
8 open market operations
9 required reserves
10 discount rate

Doing Economics: Tools and Practice Problems

In this section, we learn about the balance sheet of banks, where assets, liabilities, and net worth are recorded, and use this tool to see how open market operations lead to changes in deposits, to trace through the deposit expansion process, and to compute the money multiplier.

THE BALANCE SHEET

Before we can understand how banks create money, we must master the balance sheet. This keeps track of assets and liabilities as they change when money is deposited and loaned. Tool Kit 11.1 shows how to construct the bank's balance sheet and to compute its net worth.

Tool Kit 11.1: Constructing the Balance Sheet

The balance sheet is a "T-account," with assets listed on the left and liabilities and net worth on the right. When anything changes, net worth must adjust to keep the right and left sides in balance. To create a balance sheet, follow this procedure.

Step one: Make a T-account. Label the left column "Assets" and the right column "Liabilities and net worth."

Assets	Liabilities and net worth

Step two: Enter each of the assets (outstanding loans, bond holdings, reserves) in the left column, and sum the assets.

Assets	Liabilities and net worth
Loans	
Bonds	
Deposits	
Total assets	

Step three: Enter each of the liabilities (deposits) in the right column, and sum the liabilities.

Assets	Liabilities and net worth
Loans	Deposits
Bonds	
Deposits	
Total assets	

Step four: Compute net worth by subtracting liabilities from assets:

net worth = assets – liabilities.

Enter net worth in the right column.

Assets	Liabilities and net worth
Loans	Deposits
Bonds	
Deposits	Net worth
Total assets	

Step five: Sum the right and left columns, and check that the balance sheet is in balance.

Assets	Liabilities and net worth
Loans	Deposits
Bonds	
Deposits	

Total assets = total liabilities + net worth.

1 (Worked problem: balance sheet) President Bank has $18 million in outstanding loans, $3 million in government bonds, reserves of $4 million, and deposits equal to $20 million. Compute its net worth, and construct the balance sheet.

Step-by-step solution

Step one: Make a T-account.

President Bank's Balance Sheet

Assets	Liabilities and net worth

Step two: Enter each of the assets (outstanding loans, bond holdings, reserves) in the left column, and sum the assets.

President Bank's Balance Sheet

Assets	Liabilities and net worth
Loans outstanding = $18 million Government bonds = $3 million Reserves = $4 million Total assets = $25 million	

Step three: Enter each of the liabilities (deposits) in the right-hand column, and sum the liabilities.

President Bank's Balance Sheet

Assets	Liabilities and net worth
Loans outstanding = $18 million Government bonds = $3 million Reserves = $4 million Total assets = $25 million	Deposits = $20 million

Step four: Compute net worth:

net worth = 18 + 3 + 4 – 20 = $5 million.

Enter net worth in the right-hand column.

President Bank's Balance Sheet

Assets	Liabilities and net worth
Loans outstanding = $18 million Government bonds = $3 million Reserves = $4 million Total assets = $25 million	Deposits = $20 million Net worth = $5 million

Step five: Sum the right and left columns, and check that the balance sheet is in balance.

President Bank's Balance Sheet

Assets	Liabilities and net worth
Loans outstanding = $18 million Government bonds = $3 million Reserves = $4 million Total assets = $25 million	Deposits = $20 million Net worth = $5 million Total liabilities plus net worth = $25 million

2 (Practice problem: balance sheet) First Bank has $220 million in outstanding loans, $10 million in government bonds, $25 million in reserves, and $240 million in deposits. Compute its net worth, and construct its balance sheet.

3 (Practice problem: balance sheet) Second Bank has $400 million in outstanding loans, $25 million in government bonds, $50 million in reserves, and $450 million in deposits. Compute its net worth, and construct its balance sheet.

MONEY CREATION

Using the fractional reserve system, banks create money. When banks receive a new deposit, they keep only a fraction on hand in reserve and loan out the remainder. But the loans find their way back into the banking system, increasing deposits further and setting off a new round of loans. When the process settles down, total deposits in the banking system have increased by a multiple of the initial deposit.

Tool Kit 11.2: Understanding Deposit Expansion and the Money Multiplier

Banks create money. Through the fractional reserve system deposits result in additional loans and further deposits. Follow these steps to see how the money creation process works through the banking system.

Step one: Construct a combined balance sheet for the banking system.

Step two: Identify the initial deposit, and add it to the banking system's deposits.

Step three: Identify the reserve ratio. Calculate the required increase in reserves made necessary by the initial deposit, and add it to the banking system's reserves:

new required reserves = reserve ratio × initial deposit.

Step four: Calculate the new loans that the deposit allows, and add the amount to the banking system's loans:

new loans = initial deposit – new required reserves.

This completes round one of the deposit expansion process. (Remember to recompute the total assets and liabilities and net worth.)

Step five: Trace through a few more rounds by repeating steps two through four. The initial deposit for round two is the amount of new loans from round one.

Step six: Compute the final expansion in deposits. This will be the increase in the money supply:

final deposit expansion = initial deposit/reserve ratio.

Because there are no other leakages in this example, the money multiplier equals 1/reserve ratio.

4 (Worked problem: deposit expansion and money multiplier) The banking system in Costa Guano has $4 billion in outstanding loans, $1 billion in government bonds, $1 billion in reserves, and deposits of $5 billion. Its reserve ratio is 0.20. (Monetary magnitudes are converted to U.S. dollar equivalents.)

a Construct the combined balance sheet.

b A new deposit of $1 billion arrives from abroad. Trace through three rounds of the deposit expansion process, and compute the final deposit expansion.

Step-by-step solution

Step one (a): Construct a combined balance sheet for the banking system.

Costa Guano's Combined Balance Sheet

Assets	Liabilities and net worth
Loans outstanding = $4 billion Government bonds = $1 billion Reserves = $1 billion Total assets = $6 billion	Deposits = $5 billion Net worth = $1 billion Total liabilities plus net worth = $6 billion

Step two (b): Identify the initial deposit, and add it to the banking system's deposits. The deposit is \$1 billion.

Step three: Identify the reserve ratio. Calculate the required increase in reserves made necessary by the initial deposit, and add it to the banking system's reserves:

new required reserves = 0.20 × 1 = \$0.2 billion.

Step four: Calculate the new loans that the deposit allows, and add the amount to the banking system's loans:

new loans = 1 – 0.2 = \$0.8 billion.

Costa Guano's Combined Balance Sheet (round one)

Assets	Liabilities and net worth
Loans outstanding = \$4.8 billion	Deposits = \$6 billion
Government bonds = \$1 billion	
Reserves = \$1.2 billion	Net worth = \$1 billion
Total assets = \$7 billion	Total liabilities plus net worth = \$7 billion

This completes round one of the deposit expansion process. (Note the new totals.)

Step five: Trace through a few more rounds by repeating steps two through four. The initial deposit for round two is the amount of new loans from round one.

Costa Guano's Combined Balance Sheet (round two)

Assets	Liabilities and net worth
Loans outstanding = \$5.44 billion	Deposits = \$6.8 billion
Government bonds = \$1 billion	
Reserves = \$1.36 billion	Net worth = \$1 billion
Total assets = \$7.8 billion	Total liabilities plus net worth = \$7.8 billion

Costa Guano's Combined Balance Sheet (round three)

Assets	Liabilities and net worth
Loans outstanding = \$5.95 billion	Deposits = \$7.44 billion
Government bonds = \$1 billion	
Reserves = \$1.49 billion	Net worth = \$1 billion
Total assets = \$8.44 billion	Total liabilities plus net worth = \$8.44 billion

Step six: Compute the final expansion in deposits. This will be the increase in the money supply:

final deposit expansion = 1/(0.2) = \$5 billion.

5 (Practice problem: deposit expansion and money multiplier) In El Dorado, the banking system has outstanding loans of \$200 million, government bonds of \$10 million, reserves of \$30 million, and deposits of \$210 million. Its reserve ratio is 1/7. (Monetary magnitudes are converted to dollar equivalents.)

a Construct the combined balance sheet.
b A new deposit of \$49 million arrives from abroad. Trace through two rounds of the deposit expansion process, and compute the final deposit expansion.

6 (Practice problem: deposit expansion and money multiplier) The Erehwemos banking system has outstanding loans of \$45 billion, government bonds of \$2 billion, reserves of \$5 billion, and deposits of \$50 billion. Its reserve ratio is 0.10. (Monetary magnitudes are converted to U.S. dollar equivalents.)

a Construct the combined balance sheet.
b A new deposit of \$5 billion arrives from abroad. Trace through three rounds of the deposit expansion process, and compute the final deposit expansion.

Answers to Problems

2

First Bank's Balance Sheet

Assets	Liabilities and net worth
Loans outstanding = \$220 million	Deposits = \$240 million
Government bonds = \$10 million	
Reserves = \$25 million	Net worth = \$15 million
Total assets = \$255 million	Total liabilities plus net worth = \$255 million

3

Second Bank's Balance Sheet

Assets	Liabilities and net worth
Loans outstanding = \$400 million	Deposits = \$450 million
Government bonds = \$25 million	
Reserves = \$50 million	Net worth = \$25 million
Total assets = \$475 million	Total liabilities plus net worth = \$475 million

5 *a*

El Dorado's Combined Balance Sheet

Assets	Liabilities and net worth
Loans outstanding = \$200 million	Deposits = \$210 million
Government bonds = \$10 million	
Reserves = \$30 million	Net worth = \$30 million
Total assets = \$240 million	Total liabilities plus net worth = \$240 million

b

El Dorado's Combined Balance Sheet (round one)

Assets	Liabilities and net worth
Loans outstanding = \$242 million	Deposits = \$259 million
Government bonds = \$10 million	
Reserves = \$37 million	Net worth = \$30 million
Total assets = \$289 million	Total liabilities plus net worth = \$289 million

El Dorado's Combined Balance Sheet (round two)

Assets	Liabilities and net worth
Loans outstanding = $278 million	Deposits = $301 million
Government bonds = $10 million	
Reserves = $43 million	Net worth = $30 million
Total assets = $331 million	Total liabilities plus net worth = $331 million

Final deposit expansion = 49/(1/7) = $343 million.

6 *a*

Erehwemos's Combined Balance Sheet (round one)

Assets	Liabilities and net worth
Loans outstanding = $45 billion	Deposits = $50 billion
Government bonds = $2 billion	
Reserves = $5 billion	Net worth = $2 billion
Total assets = $52 billion	Total liabilities plus net worth = $52 billion

b

Erehwemos's Combined Balance Sheet (round two)

Assets	Liabilities and net worth
Loans outstanding = $49.5 billion	Deposits = $55 billion
Government bonds = $2 billion	
Reserves = $5.5 billion	Net worth = $2 billion
Total assets = $57 billion	Total liabilities plus net worth = $57 billion

Erehwemos's Combined Balance Sheet (round three)

Assets	Liabilities and net worth
Loans outstanding = $53.55 billion	Deposits = $59.5 billion
Government bonds = $2 billion	
Reserves = $5.95 billion	Net worth = $2 billion
Total assets = $61.5 billion	Total liabilities plus net worth = $61.5 billion

Final deposit expansion = 5/(0.1) = $50 billion.

Chapter 12

MONETARY THEORY

Chapter Review

Chapter 11 showed how the Federal Reserve can use its instruments to bring about changes in the money supply and the availability of credit. This chapter discusses how these changes affect the economy. The most important issues involve changes in the money supply that affect output, prices, or both, and the channels through which these changes operate. There is some disagreement among economists concerning the latter issue, and the chapter outlines the sources of contention and the consequences for monetary policy. The concluding section explains how monetary policy works in the international monetary system of the world's interdependent economies.

ESSENTIAL CONCEPTS

1 With fixed prices, if the money supply is increased, people may either hold onto the money or spend it. If they hold it, aggregate demand will remain unchanged. If they spend it, aggregate demand will shift to the right, and output will increase. This can be seen from the definition of **velocity:**

$$V = pQ/M,$$

where p is the fixed price index, Q is output, and M is the money supply. An increase in M must result in a decrease in V or an increase in Q. The big question in this chapter is how a change in M can affect output.

2 **Traditional monetary theory** starts with the demand for money to facilitate transactions. The opportunity cost of holding money is the **nominal interest rate,** which is determined by the intersection of supply and demand for money. An increase in the money supply lowers interest rates, stimulates investment, and shifts aggregate demand. The resulting increases in output and income shift the demand for money to the right, mitigating the fall in the interest rate.

3 The effectiveness of monetary policy depends upon three factors. First, there is the elasticity of money demand, which indicates how much the interest rate will fall for a given increase in money supply. The next issue is how much additional investment will result from the fall in the interest rate—i.e., sensitivity of investment to the interest rate. Finally there is the size of the multiplier, which measures how much output will increase for a given change in investment. In deep recessions each of these factors is likely to be small, and most economists agree that at these times monetary policy is unlikely to provide much stimulus.

4 Another view, held by monetarists, rearranges the definition of velocity as $M = pQ/V$ and interprets this equation as the demand for money. They assume that velocity is constant and that output is at its full employment level; therefore, an increase in money supply must increase Q by shifting aggregate demand to the right. The assumption about velocity implies that money demand does not depend on the interest rate.

5 Criticism of traditional monetary theory centers around two relationships. First, there is the relationship between money and income. Even if the supply of money affects the volume of transactions, most transactions involve exchanges of financial assets, which have no direct bearing on output. Also, the rise of credit card use and money market checking make traditional forms of money unnecessary. Second, the assumed relationship between interest rates and the demand for money may be undermined by interest-bearing checking accounts. If the checking account pays market interest rates, then the opportunity cost of holding money is zero. At any rate, the fact that real interest rates vary little casts doubt on the traditional view.

6 Monetary policy does work, however. Some recent theories stress alternative mechanisms. A likely channel through which money can affect output is through credit availability. Tight monetary policy may reduce the supply of loans. In addition, there may be portfolio effects whereby, for example, changes in nominal interest rates alter the value of bonds and stocks, affecting the incentives to raise new capital.

7 In the open economy monetary policy also works through exchange rates. For example, lower interest rates reduce the demand for dollars and lower the U.S. exchange rate. This depreciation makes exports attractive to foreign buyers and the resulting increase in net exports shifts aggregate demand. The open economy does limit the ability of the Fed to restrict credit, however, because U.S. borrowers can go elsewhere for funds.

BEHIND THE ESSENTIAL CONCEPTS

1 There are areas of disagreement about monetary theory and policy, but there is also a good deal of common ground. Concerning monetary theory, most economists recognize that the Federal Reserve controls the money supply through the use of its three instruments: open market operations, reserve requirements, and the discount rate. Most economists also agree that the demand for money depends upon income. In the area of monetary policy, economists believe that in deep recessions increases in the money supply will likely be ineffective, in mild recessions increases will shift aggregate demand and help the economy recover, and when the economy is operating at capacity, they will result only in higher prices. Severely restricting the money supply and credit availability, on the other hand, will cause a recession. Also, most economists agree that in the long run, money affects only the price level.

2 There is no consensus about how credit availability and the money supply work their way through the economy, but there are four possibilities.

a A larger money supply lowers interest rates and increases investment.

b A larger money supply directly shifts aggregate demand because velocity is constant.

c A larger money supply brings about higher stock and bond prices, which lead to more consumption and investment.

d Looser credit motivates more lending.

3 The logic of credit rationing is as follows. Banks ration credit because they fear that raising the interest rate would attract low-quality (risky) borrowers, many of whom would default. Because the interest rate remains below market clearing, there is an excess demand for loans.

SELF-TEST

True or False

1 The velocity of money is the ratio of nominal GDP to the price level.

2 The demand for money arising from its use as a unit of account is called the transactions demand for money.

3 The transactions demand for money increases as nominal income increases.

4 The opportunity cost of holding money is the nominal interest rate.

5 According to traditional monetary theory, the nominal interest rate is determined by the intersection of the supply and demand for money.

6 According to traditional monetary theory, an increase in the money supply will lower interest rates and increase investment except during deep recessions.

7 Monetary policy is more effective when the multiplier is large.

8 The theory that the velocity is constant and thus increases in the money supply bring about equal proportional increases in income is called the quantity theory of money.

9 Monetarists believe that money is important and that the government should use active monetary policy to influence the fluctuations in the economy.

10 Until recently, the velocity of money has increased steadily, although the upward trend slowed during recessions.

11 Federal Reserve policies may affect the ability of banks to make loans, but they cannot force banks to lend.

12 Because of credit rationing, interest rates may not rise even though there is an excess demand for money.

13 If the interest rate falls and banks are willing to lend, investment will increase unless firms have an elastic demand for loans.

14 In an open economy an increase in the money supply appreciates the currency and increases net exports.

15 In an open economy the Fed's attempt to restrict the availability of credit may be undermined if borrowers look abroad for funds.

Multiple Choice

1 When the Federal Reserve increases the supply of money,

a individuals may hold the additional money, decreasing velocity;
b individuals may spend the money, leading to more output;
c individuals may spend the money, shifting aggregate demand to the left;
d all of the above.
e a and b.

2 Which definition of money is used in this chapter?

a M1;
b M2;
c M3;
d Eurodollars, money market mutual funds, and deposits in excess of $100,000;
e all of the above.

3 Velocity is defined as the ratio of

a GDP to the price level;
b the price level to GDP;
c GDP to the money supply;
d the money supply to GDP;
e M2 to M1.

4 According to traditional monetary theory, changes in the money supply affect the economy through

a the interest rates;
b the velocity;
c the foreign exchange market;
d the quantity theory of money;
e credit availability.

5 The transactions demand for money refers to money held

a as a medium of exchange;
b as a store of value;
c as a unit of account;
d as a precaution against unexpected need such as illness or job loss;
e as a hedge against deflation.

6 Which of the following will cause an increase in the demand for money?

a an increase in real income;
b an increase in nominal income;
c an increase in velocity;
d an increase in the nominal interest rate;
e an increase in the real interest rate.

7 The opportunity cost of holding money is

a the exchange rate;
b the velocity;
c the real interest rate;
d the nominal interest rate;
e none of the above.

8 Which of the following is not a principle of traditional monetary theory?

a The nominal interest rate is the opportunity cost of holding money.
b The demand for money decreases as the interest rate rises.
c The interest rate is determined by the intersection of money demand and money supply.
d The velocity of money is stable.
e All of the above are principles of traditional monetary theory.

9 Which of the following is a tenet of the traditional theory of monetary policy?

a Monetary policy is ineffective because it cannot affect the interest rate.
b Monetary policy is especially effective in deep recessions when money is scarce.
c Monetary policy is ineffective in deep recessions.
d Monetary policy is ineffective because investment is not affected by changes in interest rates.
e Monetary policy is effective but is too dangerous to use.

10 Monetary policy is more effective when

a the elasticity of money demand is low;
b investment is sensitive to changes in the interest rate;
c the multiplier is low;
d prices are flexible;
e the economy is in deep recession.

11 According to traditional monetary theory, monetary policy affects output by

a altering the availability of credit;
b changing the exchange rate and thus net exports;
c affecting stock prices and thus firms' incentives to raise funds for investment on the stock market;
d changing interest rates and investment;
e changing the size of the government deficit.

12 One criticism of traditional monetary theory is

a real interest rates are too variable to explain the variation in investment;
b most transactions involve the exchange of assets, not the purchase of goods;
c most checking accounts pay no interest;
d the velocity is surely not a constant;
e there are many definitions of money.

13 Monetarists believe that

a the velocity of money is stable over time;
b the velocity of money is unpredictable;
c the quantity theory of money is no longer a sensible way to look at the economy;
d money serves no function as a store of value;

e the velocity of money increases as the money supply grows.

14 According to credit availability theories, an increase in the money supply will stimulate the economy when

a interest rates fall;
b stock prices rise;
c bond prices rise;
d interest rates rise;
e banks make more loans on easier terms.

15 According to credit availability theories, Federal Reserve policies

a affect the ability of banks to lend, but cannot force them to lend;
b affect the willingness of banks to lend, but cannot affect the ability of banks to lend;
c affect the ability and willingness of banks to lend by lowering interest rates;
d may not stimulate the economy if banks buy fewer Treasury bills;
e c and d.

16 Banks may be reluctant to lend even though the return on Treasury bills is lower if

a default rates are high;
b their net worth is low;
c other banks have gone bankrupt;
d all of the above;
e Banks will always seek the higher returns, and if Treasury bill returns are relatively low, banks will not be reluctant to lend.

17 Even though there is an excess demand for credit, banks may not increase the interest rate if

a Treasury bill interest rates are high;
b increased interest rates have an adverse selection effect by attracting riskier borrowers;
c Treasury bill interest rates are low;
d credit rationing is illegal;
e borrowers cannot afford higher interest rates.

18 Portfolio theories of how monetary policy affects the economy focus on the role of money

a as a medium of exchange;
b as a store of value;
c as a unit of account;
d as a precaution against unexpected need such as illness or job loss;
e as a hedge against deflation.

19 According to portfolio theories, the Federal Reserve can increase the money supply, lower interest rates, and shift aggregate demand because

a when interest rates fall, stock prices rise and firms invest more when stock prices are high;
b when interest rates fall, stock prices rise and people increase consumption because they are wealthier;
c open market operations increase banks' reserves, and their response leads to higher stock prices;
d all of the above;
e none of the above.

20 In the open economy an increase in the money supply

a depreciates the exchange rate;
b increases exports;
c reduces imports;
d increases net exports;
e all of the above.

Completion

1 Gross domestic product divided by the money supply equals the __________.

2 Money held for use as a medium of exchange forms the __________.

3 The opportunity cost of holding money is the __________.

4 The view that money affects the economy through changes in interest rates and investment is the __________ monetary theory.

5 According to __________, velocity is constant and increases in the money supply bring about proportionate increases in national income.

6 __________ believe that there is a stable and predictable relationship between the money supply and national income.

7 __________ occurs when there is an excess demand for credit but banks do not raise interest rates for fear of attracting less credit-worthy borrowers.

8 According to __________ theories, changes in the money supply may lead to different levels of investment without changing interest rates.

9 A decrease in the supply of money leads to an __________ of the exchange rate.

10 The open economy __________ the ability of the Fed to limit credit.

Answers to Self-Test

True or False

1	f	6	t	11	t
2	f	7	t	12	t
3	t	8	t	13	f
4	t	9	f	14	f
5	t	10	t	15	t

Multiple Choice

1	e	6	b	11	d	16	d
2	a	7	d	12	b	17	b
3	c	8	d	13	a	18	b
4	a	9	c	14	e	19	d
5	a	10	b	15	a	20	e

Completion

1 velocity
2 money supply
3 nominal interest rate
4 traditional
5 monetarism
6 Monetarists
7 Credit rationing
8 portfolio

9 appreciation
10 reduces

Doing Economics: Tools and Practice Problems

The traditional theory of how changes in the money supply affect the economy argues that money supply determines interest rates in the money market. Although there are problems associated with this theory, it represents the best starting point for the study of monetary policy. In this section, we work problems that trace the channels through which money moves to shift aggregate demand and alter the equilibrium output of the economy. Tool Kit 12.1 explores traditional monetary theory.

Tool Kit 12.1: Using Traditional Monetary Theory

According to this view of money and the economy, the nominal interest rate, which is the opportunity cost of holding money, is determined by the intersection of the supply and demand curves for money. An increase in the supply of money shifts the supply curve to the right and lowers the interest rate. Finally, lower interest rates induce more investment and shift aggregate demand to the right.

Step one: Identify the demand curve for money, the supply curve for money, and the investment function.

Step two: Start with an equilibrium in which the supply and demand curves for money intersect at the nominal interest rate. The level of investment is read off the investment function at this interest rate.

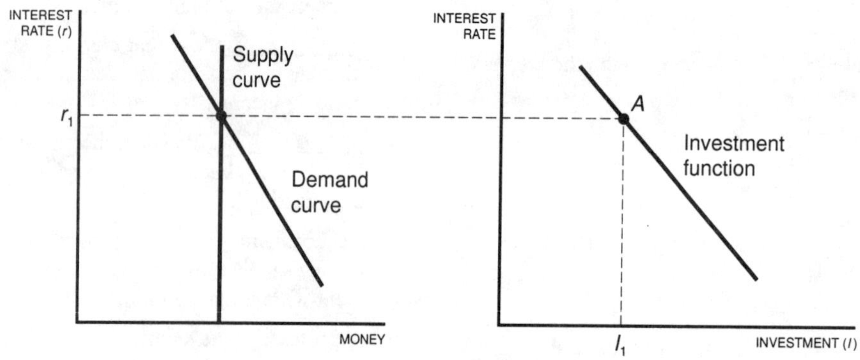

Step three: Shift the money supply curve to reflect the change in the money supply.

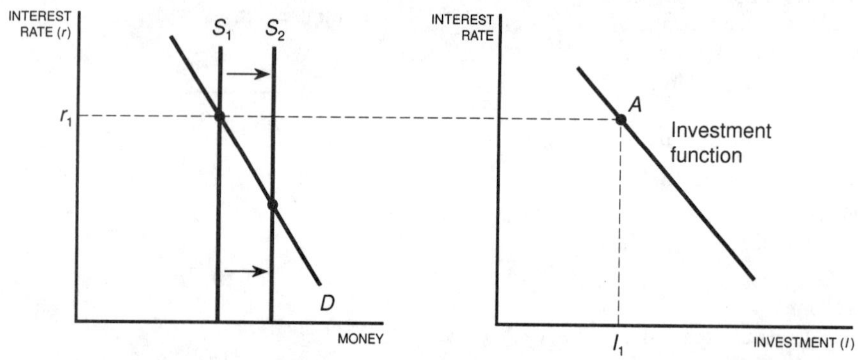

Step four: Find the new equilibrium interest rate.

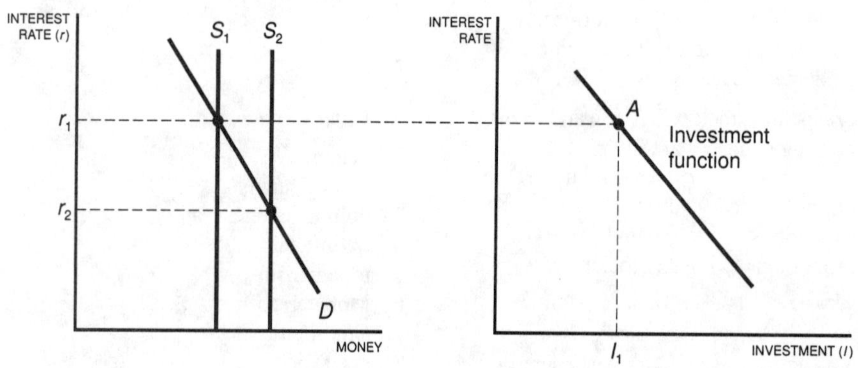

Step five: Determine the change in investment by reading the new level of investment off the investment function.

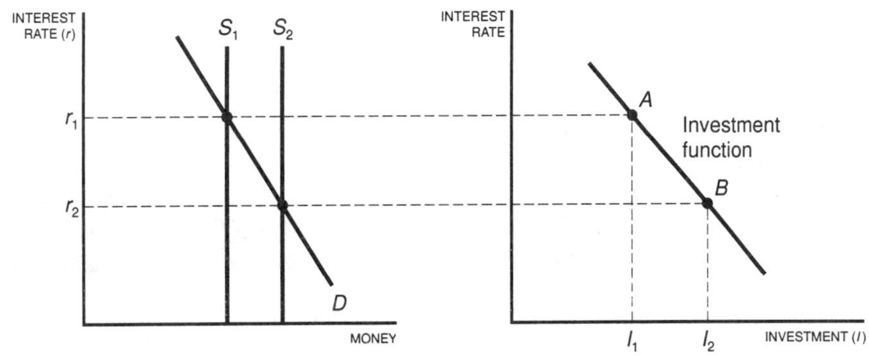

1 (Worked problem: traditional monetary theory) The money demand and investment function are given in Table 12.1. The initial money supply is $1.8 billion.

Table 12.1

Money demand		*Investment function*	
Nominal interest rate	*Money demand (billions $)*	*Real interest rate*	*Investment ($100 million)*
10%	1.0	10%	2
9%	1.2	9%	3
8%	1.4	8%	4
7%	1.6	7%	5
6%	1.8	6%	6
5%	2.0	5%	7
4%	2.2	4%	8

a Find the equilibrium interest rate and level of investment.
b Suppose the Federal Reserve lowers required reserves, and the money supply increases to $2 billion. Determine the new interest rate and level of investment.
c How does aggregate demand shift?

Step-by-step solution

Step one (a): Identify the demand curve for money, the money supply, and the investment function. See Table 12.1 for the money demand and the investment function. The money supply is $1.8 billion.

Step two: Start with an equilibrium in which the supply and demand curves for money intersect at the nominal interest rate. The level of investment is read off the investment function at this interest rate. The initial equilibrium interest rate is 6 percent, which induces firms to invest $600 million.

Step three (b): Shift the money supply curve to reflect the change in the money supply.

Step four: Find the new equilibrium interest rate. It is 5 percent.

Step five: Determine the change in investment by reading the new level of investment off the investment function. Firms increase their investment levels to $700 million, which represents an increase of $100 million.

Step six (c): Aggregate demand shifts to the right.

2 (Practice problem: traditional monetary theory) The money demand and investment function are given in Table 12.2. The initial money supply is $4.2 billion.

Table 12.2

Money demand		*Investment function*	
Nominal interest rate	*Money demand (billions $)*	*Real interest rate*	*Investment ($100 million)*
10%	2.5	10%	2.0
9%	3.0	9%	4.0
8%	3.3	8%	5.0
7%	3.6	7%	6.0
6%	3.9	6%	7.0
5%	4.2	5%	7.5
4%	4.5	4%	8.0

a Find the equilibrium interest rate and level of investment.
b Suppose the Federal Reserve sells bonds, causing the money supply to decrease to $3.6 billion. Determine the new interest rate and level of investment.
c How does aggregate demand shift?

3 (Practice problem: traditional monetary theory) The money demand and investment function are given in Table 12.3. The initial money supply is $5.5 billion.

Table 12.3

Money demand		*Investment function*	
Nominal interest rate	*Money demand (billions $)*	*Real interest rate*	*Investment ($100 million)*
10%	4.5	10%	12.0
9%	5.0	9%	14.0
8%	5.5	8%	15.0
7%	6.0	7%	16.0
6%	6.5	6%	17.0
5%	7.0	5%	17.5
4%	7.5	4%	18.0

a Find the equilibrium interest rate and level of investment.

b Suppose the Federal Reserve buys bonds, causing the money supply to increase to $7 billion. Determine the new interest rate and level of investment.

c How does aggregate demand shift?

Answers to Problems

2 *a* Interest rate = 5 percent; investment = $750 million.
b Interest rate = 7 percent; investment = $600 million.
c Aggregate demand shifts to the left.

3 *a* Interest rate = 8 percent; investment = $1,500 million.
b Interest rate = 5 percent; investment = $1,750 million.
c Aggregate demand shifts to the right.

Chapter 13

FISCAL AND MONETARY POLICY

Chapter Review

The basic model of unemployment macroeconomics is completed in this chapter, which pulls together the material on the real economy from Chapters 9 and 10 with that on the monetary system in Chapters 11 and 12. The chapter compares the effects of fiscal and monetary policy and analyzes some issues concerning their use in the current economy. The next chapter begins the section on dynamics.

ESSENTIAL CONCEPTS

1 **Fiscal policy** is the use of government tax and expenditure policies to improve the performance of the economy. When there is excess capacity an increase in government expenditures or a tax cut shifts aggregate demand to the right, moving the economy toward full employment. Whether the gain in current output is worth the increased indebtedness depends upon how much private investment is crowded out, whether government spending is for consumption or investment, and how much of the deficit is financed by borrowing from abroad.

2 The government can still use fiscal policy even if it is constrained to keep a balanced budget. Although the required tax increase offsets somewhat the effect of higher government expenditures, some stimulus remains. The **balanced budget multiplier** equals one, which means that aggregate demand shifts to the right by exactly the amount of the extra government spending.

3 Monetary policy can also be used. A larger money supply lowers interest rates and makes credit available, increasing private investment. Also, the exchange rate falls, stimulating a rise in net exports. Both combine to shift aggregate demand to the right. Monetary policy is also important as it interacts with fiscal policy. In response to a fiscal stimulus the Fed may pursue an **accommodative monetary policy**. This stance keeps interest rates from rising, which would limit the fiscal stimulus.

4 Monetary and fiscal policy differ in how they affect the composition of output. Monetary policy's lower interest rates bring about more investment. The impact of fiscal policy depends upon the mix of additional expenditures and tax cuts and also upon how government expenditures are divided between consumption and investment.

5 Monetary policy is certainly ineffective in deep recessions. Fiscal policy's power may be limited if consumers anticipate future tax increases to pay off the deficit, if government borrowing increases interest rates (crowding out investment), or if changes in the exchange rate reduce net exports. None of these is likely in deep recessions, however.

6 Monetary policy's impact is delayed by the time it takes lower interest rates to stimulate investment. Government spending in principle can work immediately. It does take time for government to pass laws and administer the spending. Certain programs, such as unemployment insurance and progressive income taxes, act as **automatic stabilizers**, quickly causing greater spending and reduced taxes during recessions.

7 A **balanced budget amendment** requiring the government to avoid deficit would probably destabilize the economy because it would prevent the automatic stabilizers from doing their job. In this case all of the responsibility for stabilization would rest with monetary policy. One compromise would keep the **full-employment deficit** at zero. This is what the deficit would be if the economy were operating at full employment, and it is a measure of fiscal responsibility.

BEHIND THE ESSENTIAL CONCEPTS

1 Government can use fiscal policy in two ways. First, it can stimulate the economy during recessions. Here government takes an active role, making up for the shortfall in private spending. Another approach works automatically. Taxes, such as personal or corporate income taxes, which decrease as income decreases, and programs such as welfare and unemployment insurance act as automatic stabilizers. These programs provide additional spending during downturns without explicit government action.

2 The instruments of government policy include fiscal policy measures such as tax rates and levels of expenditures, and monetary instruments such as open market operations, reserve requirements, and the discount rate. In different circumstances some form of each policy may be appropriate. They differ in their effectiveness, how they change the mix of output, and the speed of implementation.

3 The actual budget deficit computes the difference between government expenditures and tax revenues. When the economy falls into recession, however, tax collections diminish. Households earn less income and pay less income tax. Business profits fall and so do corporate tax collections. Spending increases on unemployment insurance and welfare programs. All of these combine to bring about a deficit without any change in policy. The full-employment deficit measures what the deficit would be at full employment. Tax and expenditure policies that result in no full-employment deficit will nevertheless lead to actual budget deficits when the economy is operating below capacity.

SELF-TEST

True or False

1 Fiscal policy aims to improve macroeconomic performance by promoting fiscal responsibility among banks and other financial intermediaries.

2 When the government increases expenditures or cuts taxes to provide a fiscal stimulus, there is an increase in the federal debt.

3 Government borrowing to finance the deficit may crowd out private investment.

4 If government spending and taxes increase by the same amount, then aggregate demand will not change.

5 The balanced budget multiplier equals one.

6 In a closed economy monetary policy works by changing interest rates and investment.

7 In an open economy monetary policy changes exchange rates and net exports.

8 If the Fed pursues accommodative monetary policy, it will cut the money supply when government spending increases.

9 While monetary policy stimulates investment, fiscal policy may crowd it out.

10 Most economists agree that fiscal policy is ineffective in deep recessions.

11 One problem with fiscal policy is the time it takes for government to take action.

12 The impact of monetary policy is delayed while firms take time to respond to lower interest rates with new investment.

13 Unemployment insurance helps stabilize the economy by increasing government expenditures during recessions.

14 Amending the Constitution to require a balanced budget would place all of the responsibility for stabilizing the economy on the Federal Reserve.

15 The full-employment deficit is what the actual budget deficit would be if the economy were operating at full employment.

Multiple Choice

1 Fiscal policy includes

a maintaining a stable money supply;
b using consumer product safety regulation to promote consumer confidence;
c regulating the banking and securities industries to encourage sound investment;
d using government expenditures and taxation to improve macroeconomic performance;
e funding oversight agencies, such as the General Accounting Office, to ensure that government carries out its fiduciary responsibilities.

2 Providing fiscal stimulus with a current budget deficit affects future generations by

a accumulating a federal debt for which they are responsible;
b reducing current private investment by driving up current interest rates;
c incurring foreign indebtedness by financing the deficit with bonds sold abroad;
d a and b;
e all of the above.

3 An increase in government spending holding the level of taxes constant will

a shift the aggregate expenditures schedule up;
b leave the aggregate expenditures schedule unchanged;
c shift the aggregate expenditures schedule down;
d rotate the aggregate expenditures schedule to the left;
e rotate the aggregate expenditures schedule to the right.

4 An increase in taxes holding the level of government spending constant will

a shift the aggregate expenditures schedule up;
b leave the aggregate expenditures schedule unchanged;
c shift the aggregate expenditures schedule down;
d rotate the aggregate expenditures schedule to the left;
e rotate the aggregate expenditures schedule to the right.

5 An increase in both government spending and taxes, keeping the overall budget balanced, will

a shift the aggregate expenditures schedule up;
b leave the aggregate expenditures schedule unchanged;
c shift the aggregate expenditures schedule down;
d rotate the aggregate expenditures schedule to the left;
e rotate the aggregate expenditures schedule to the right.

6 Deficit spending is financed by

a taxes;
b spending cuts;
c borrowing throught the sale of Treasury bills and bonds to investors;
d printing money;
e the multiplier.

7 Increased government expenditures

a reduce total investment;
b reduce private investment but may increase total investment if the additional government expenditures include public investment, such as roads or research and development;
c increase private investment;
d reduce foreign indebtedness;
e may reduce total investment if the Federal Reserve pursues accommodative monetary policy.

8 The balanced budget multiplier equals

a one;
b zero, because the stimulus provided by increased government spending is offset by the fiscal drag of the tax increase;
c one divided by the marginal propensity to consume;
d one divided by the reserve ratio;
e two.

9 When there is excess capacity, an increase in the money supply leads to

a lower interest rates;
b increased investment;
c greater credit availability;
d exchange rate depreciation;
e all of the above.

10 Accommodative monetary policy refers to

a keeping a strong currency to accommodate importers;
b driving down the exchange rate to promote exports;
c complementing the objectives of fiscal policy by adjusting the money supply to keep interest rates from rising;
d maintaining a stable money supply;
e letting the money supply grow at a rate equal to the growth in output.

11 Crowding out refers to

a the possibility that taxes reduce private investment;
b the effect of inflation on the real value of the accumulated government debt;
c the possibility that government borrowing may reduce private investment;
d the effect of protectionism on the trade balance;
e the effect of imports on the market share of domestic firms.

12 Which of the following illustrates problems with the effectiveness of a policy instrument?

a Even though the Federal Reserve undertakes policies that increase bank reserves, it may not be able to motivate banks to make new loans.
b Looser monetary policy, even though it was designed to increase investment, might instead cause the dollar to depreciate and increase net exports.
c Monetary policy often concentrates its effects on particular sectors, such as export-competing industries or consumer durables.
d There are lags in the government's ability to recognize and implement fiscal programs.
e Individuals may treat tax cuts as temporary and increase consumption.

13 Which of the following illustrates a concern with the effect of a policy instrument on the composition of output?

a Even though the Federal Reserve undertakes policies that increase bank reserves, it may not be able to motivate banks to make new loans.
b Looser monetary policy, even though it was de-

signed to increase investment, might instead cause the dollar to depreciate and increase net exports.

c Monetary policy often concentrates its effects on particular sectors, such as export-competing industries or consumer durables.

d There are lags in the government's ability to recognize and implement fiscal programs.

e Individuals may treat tax cuts as temporary and increase consumption.

14 Mechanisms that increase the government deficit during recessions and decrease it during economic booms are called

a balanced budget multipliers;
b full-employment deficits;
c automatic stabilizers;
d political business cycles;
e none of the above.

15 Automatic stabilizers are

a programs, such as unemployment insurance or progressive taxation, that increase spending during recessions and reduce it during economic booms;
b policy rules that restrain the use of discretionary fiscal and monetary policy;
c the adjustments that individuals with rational expectations make to offset fiscal and monetary policies;
d market responses, such as increased interest rates, that limit the ability of government to stimulate the economy;
e a and c.

16 Which of the following is not an automatic stabilizer?

a income taxes;
b unemployment insurance;
c food stamps;
d Social Security benefits;
e All of the above are automatic stabilizers.

17 Which of the following relates to the issue of lags in monetary and fiscal policy?

a Monetary policy's effectiveness is delayed while businesses wait to undertake new investments.
b Governments take time to make decisions about tax and expenditure changes.
c Exchange rates adjust slowly.
d a and b.
e All of the above.

18 State and local government spending tends to

a increase in booms and decrease in recessions, thus reducing the volatility of the economy;
b increase in booms and decrease in recessions, thus increasing the volatility of the economy;
c decrease in booms and increase in recessions, thus reducing the volatility of the economy;
d decrease in booms and increase in recessions, thus increasing the volatility of the economy;
e be stable over the business cycle and neither increase nor reduce the volatility.

19 A Balanced Budget Amendment to the U.S. Constitution would

a eliminate the ability of the government to provide fiscal stimulus;
b place most of the burden of stabilization on monetary policy;
c probably destabilize the economy by limiting the impact of automatic stabilizers;
d b and c;
e all of the above.

20 The deficit that would occur if the economy were at full employment under current spending and tax policies is called the

a balanced budget multiplier;
b full-employment deficit;
c trade deficit;
d total accumulated government debt;
e real budget deficit.

Completion

1 __________ involves the use of taxation and government spending to improve macroeconomic performance.

2 The balanced budget multiplier equals __________.

3 If the government spends more than it raises in taxes, the deficit is financed by __________.

4 __________ includes infrastructure and spending for education and research.

5 __________ monetary policy furthers the goals of fiscal policy by adjusting the money supply to keep interest rates from rising and crowding out private investment.

6 __________ refers to the possibility that government borrowing may reduce private investment.

7 Mechanisms that reduce government spending or raise taxes in recessions are called __________.

8 State and local government expenditures vary __________ than GDP.

9 The __________ would preclude the use of deficit financed fiscal policy.

10 The __________ equals the deficit that would have occurred if government revenues and spending were at their full-employment levels.

Answers to Self-Test

True or False

1	f	6	t	11	t
2	t	7	t	12	t
3	t	8	f	13	t
4	f	9	t	14	t
5	t	10	f	15	t

Multiple Choice

1	d	6	c	11	c	16	c
2	e	7	b	12	a	17	d
3	a	8	a	13	b	18	b
4	c	9	e	14	c	19	d
5	a	10	c	15	a	20	b

Completion

1 Fiscal policy
2 one
3 borrowing
4 Government investment
5 Accommodative
6 Crowding out
7 automatic stabilizers
8 more
9 balanced budget amendment
10 full-employment deficit

Doing Economics: Tools and Practice Problems

Fiscal policy involves the use of government expenditures and taxation to influence the macroeconomic performance of the economy. It works by shifting aggregate demand: up in the cases of tax cuts or expenditure increases; down when taxes are raised or expenditures decreased. The multiplier plays a crucial role, determining the magnitude of the change in aggregate demand that results from an initial fiscal policy measure. In this section we use income-expenditure analysis to study balanced budget changes in fiscal policy. Tool Kit 13.1 shows how to analyze the impact of changes in government spending accompanied by tax changes of equal size.

Tool Kit 13.1: Analyzing Government Spending with Tax Changes

When there are equal changes in government spending and taxes, output will change by an equivalent amount. Economists say that the balanced budget multiplier is one. Follow these steps.

Step one: Identify the marginal propensity to consume, the initial tax rate, investment, and the level of government spending.

Step two: Compute the consumption function.

Step three: Compute the aggregate expenditures schedule and find the equilibrium level of output.

Step four: Identify the new tax rate and use this information to calculate the new aggregate consumption function.

Step five: Identify the new level of government spending and compute the new aggregate expenditures schedule.

Step six: Find the new equilibrium level of output.

Step seven: Verify that the change in tax revenue equals the change in government spending:

Change in tax revenues = new tax rate × new output – original tax rate × original output.

Step eight: Verify that the balanced budget multiplier equals one:

Multiplier = (Change in output)/(change in government spending).

1 (Worked problem: balanced budget fiscal policy) In Isle de Guano (a neighbor of Costa Guano) the marginal propensity to consume is 0.75 and the tax rate is a rather high 50 percent. Autonomous consumption is 10 million, investment is zero, and government spending is 40 million guanos.

a Compute the aggregate consumption function.
b Compute the aggregate expenditures schedule.
c Find the equilibrium level of output.
d Is the budget balanced?

Suppose that government spending is increased to 60 million and the tax rate is increased to 60 percent.

d Compute the new aggregate consumption function.
e Compute the new aggregate expenditures schedule.
f Find the new equilibrium level of output.
g Compute the change in tax revenues. Is this a balanced budget change in fiscal policy?
h Verify that the change in output equals the change in government spending, i.e., that the multiplier equals one.

Step-by-step solution

Step one: Identify the marginal propensity to consume, the initial tax rate, autonomous consumption, investment, and the level of government spending. The marginal propensity to consume is 0.75 and the tax rate is 50 percent. Autonomous consumption is 10 million, investment is zero, and government spending is 40 million.

Step two: Compute the consumption function. When national income is zero, consumption is 10 million. When national income is 20 million, consumption equals 0.75 × (1 – 0.5) × 20 + 10 = 17.5. Continuing, we derive the consumption function.

National income	Consumption
0	10
20	17.5
40	25
60	32.5
80	40
100	47.5
120	55

Step three: Compute the aggregate expenditures schedule and find the equilibrium level of output. Since investment equals zero and there is no trade, aggregate expenditures equal consumption plus government.

National income	Consumption	Government expenditures	Aggregate expenditures
0	10	40	50
20	17.5	40	57.5
40	25	40	65
60	32.5	40	72.5
80	40	40	80
100	47.5	40	87.5
120	55	40	95

Equilibrium output is 80. The budget is balanced; taxes = 0.5 × 80 = 40 = government expenditures.

Step four: Identify the new tax rate and use this information to calculate the new aggregate consumption function. The new tax rate is 60 percent. When national income is 20 million, consumption equals 0.75 × (1 – 0.6) × 20 + 10 = 16. Continuing, we derive the consumption function.

National income	Consumption
0	10
20	16
40	22
60	28
80	34
100	40
120	46

Step five: Identify the new level of government spending and compute the new aggregate expenditures schedule. Government now spends 60 million. The new aggregate expenditures schedule is as follows.

National income	Consumption	Government expenditures	Aggregate expenditures
0	10	60	70
20	16	60	76
40	22	60	82
60	28	60	88
80	34	60	94
100	40	60	100
120	46	60	106

Step six: Find the new equilibrium level of output. It equals 100.

Step seven: Verify that the change in tax revenue equals the change in government spending.

Change in tax revenues = new tax rate × new output
– original tax rate × original output;
= 0.60 × 100 – 0.50 × 80 = 20 million.

Step eight: Verify that the balanced budget multiplier equals one.

Multiplier = (change in output)/
(change in government spending);
= (100 – 80)/(60 – 40) = 1.

2 (Practice problem: balanced budget fiscal policy) In Silverado (a neighbor of El Dorado) the marginal propensity to consume is 0.8 and the tax rate is one-third. Both autonomous consumption and investment are 100 billion, and government spending is 500 billion dorals.

a Compute the aggregate consumption function.
b Compute the aggregate expenditures schedule.
c Find the equilibrium level of output.
d Is the budget balanced?

Suppose that government spending is decreased to 200 million and the tax rate is decreased to one-sixth.

e Compute the new aggregate consumption function.
f Compute the new aggregate expenditures schedule.
g Find the new equilibrium level of output.
h Compute the change in tax revenues. Is this a balanced budget change in fiscal policy?
i Verify that the change in output equals the change in government spending, i.e., that the multiplier equals one.

3 (Practice problem: balanced budget fiscal policy) In Wohon (a neighbor of Erehwemos) the marginal propensity to consume is 0.9 and the tax rate is one-sixth. Autonomous consumption equals 5 billion and investment is 15 billion, and government spending is 40 billion hons.

a Compute the aggregate consumption function.
b Compute the aggregate expenditures schedule.
c Find the equilibrium level of output.
d Is its budget balanced?

Suppose that government spending is increased to 120 million and the tax rate is increased to three-eighths (0.375).

e Compute the new aggregate consumption function.
f Compute the new aggregate expenditures schedule.
g Find the new equilibrium level of output.
h Compute the change in tax revenues. Is this a balanced budget change in fiscal policy?
i Verify that the change in output equals the change in government spending, i.e., that the multiplier equals one.

Answers to Problems

2 *a* and *b*

National income	Consumption	Investment	Government expenditures	Aggregate expenditures
0	100	100	500	700
300	260	100	500	860
600	420	100	500	1,020
900	580	100	500	1,180
1,200	740	100	500	1,340
1,500	900	100	500	1,500
1,800	1060	100	500	1,660

c Equilibrium output is 1,500.
d Tax revenues = 1/3 × 1,500 = 500 = government expenditures.

e and *f*

National income	Consumption	Invest-ment	Government expenditures	Aggregate expenditures
0	100	100	200	400
300	300	100	200	600
600	500	100	200	800
900	700	100	200	1,000
1,200	900	100	200	1,200
1,500	1,200	100	200	1,400
1,800	1,500	100	200	1,600

g Equilibrium output is 1,200.
h Tax revenues = 1/6 × 1,200 = 200 = government revenues. The budget is still balanced.
i Multiplier = (1,500 – 1,200)/(500 – 200) = 1.

3 *a* and *b*

National income	Consumption	Invest-ment	Government expenditures	Aggregate expenditures
0	5	15	40	60
40	35	15	40	90
80	65	15	40	120
120	95	15	40	150
160	125	15	40	180
200	155	15	40	210
240	185	15	40	240
280	215	15	40	270
320	245	15	40	300

c Equilibrium output is 240.
d Tax revenues = 1/6 × 240 = 40 = government expenditures.
e and *f*

National income	Consumption	Invest-ment	Government expenditures	Aggregate expenditures
0	5	15	120	140
40	27.5	15	120	162.5
80	50	15	120	185
120	72.5	15	120	207.5
160	95	15	120	230
200	117.5	15	120	252.5
240	140	15	120	275
280	162.5	15	120	297.5
320	185	15	120	320

g Equilibrium output is 320.
h Tax revenues = 0.375 × 320 = 120 = government revenues. The budget is still balanced.
i Multiplier = (320 – 240)/(120 – 40) = 1.

Part Four

Dynamics and Macro Policy

Chapter 14

INFLATION: WAGE AND PRICE DYNAMICS

Chapter Review

This chapter begins the study of dynamics, i.e., how things change. The focus is on inflation, its costs, and, in particular, its relationship with unemployment. The Phillips curve summarizes this relationship, and the chapter explains how the Phillips curve relates to the aggregate demand and supply framework. The role of monetary policy receives attention both in its closed and open economy varieties. A more microeconomic discussion of price rigidities closes the chapter.

ESSENTIAL CONCEPTS

1 **Inflation** is a general rise in the price level over time. If anticipated, it causes little disruption because households and firms can plan for and offset any troublesome effects. Inflation hurts lenders because they are repaid with cheaper dollars. It hurts investors because they are taxed on returns from their investments that barely compensate for the higher price level. Holders of currency see inflation erode its purchasing power. Inflation causes further trouble because it distorts relative prices and, when variable, contributes to the riskiness of borrowing and lending. The costs of inflation can be softened somewhat by **indexing,** which means linking future payments to some measure of inflation.

2 When at the current price level aggregate demand exceeds aggregate supply, there is full employment but upward pressure on prices. The opposite is the case when aggregate demand is less than aggregate supply and unemployment is high. The **Phillips curve,** shown in Figure 14.1, illustrates the trade-off between unemployment and inflation. Decreases in inflation increase un-

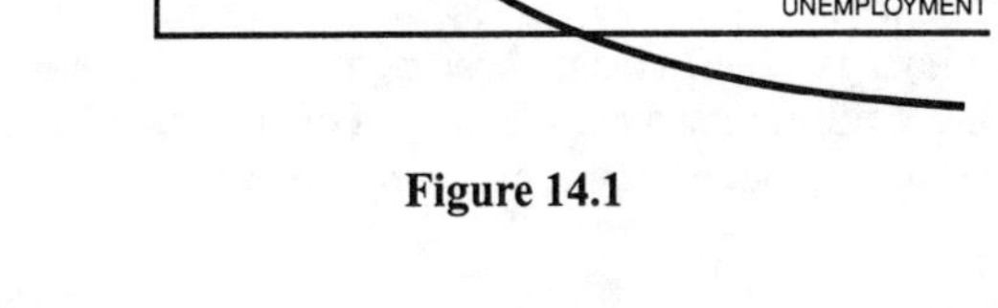

Figure 14.1

employment (at least in the short run) until unemployment reaches its so-called **natural rate,** when the price level is constant.

3 When workers and firms expect inflation, the Phillips curve shifts up. This higher curve is called the **expectations-augmented Phillips curve.** When inflation equals the expected rate, the economy is at its natural rate. If government tries to keep unemployment below this level, inflation will continue to rise, even accelerate. Thus, the natural rate equals the **NAIRU** (non-accelerating inflation rate of unemployment), and it is the unemployment rate consistent with constant inflation. The NAIRU itself varies over time with factors such as the entry of women in the labor force. Currently, it is probably around 5.5 percent in the United States.

4 In the long run firms and workers use all available current and past information and adjust their expectations of inflation. Economists say that they have **rational expectations.** The unemployment rate returns to the NAIRU, which implies that the **long-run Phillips curve** is vertical. This fact means that a country experiencing high inflation may be able to put in place a credible program that convinces firms and workers of its resolve to lower inflation. As they expect lower inflation, the Phillips curve would shift down rapidly, allowing inflation to fall without a rise in unemployment. In other circumstances a long recession may be required.

5 In the long run, when prices and wages have time to adjust, the long-run aggregate supply curve is vertical. The **short-run aggregate supply curve** shows the levels of output at different price levels, holding wages fixed. It is horizontal at low levels of output, then upward sloping and nearly vertical at high price levels. Because machines and workers temporarily can be worked overtime, the vertical portion of the short-run aggregate supply curve lies to the right of the long-run aggregate supply. Finally, equilibrium in the short run depends upon the price level. If the price level is above the intersection of short-run aggregate supply and demand, then output is determined by aggregate demand, the short side of the market. A price level below the intersection implies that output equals short-run aggregate supply.

6 Increases in aggregate demand do not increase the price level when there is excess capacity; otherwise, they put upward pressure on prices. Similarly, when short-run aggregate supply shifts to the left, inflationary pressures form. The former is called **demand-pull inflation**; the latter, **cost-push inflation.** Once underway, **inflation inertia** sets in as expectations of price increases lead workers to demand wage increases.

7 In the long-run full-employment economy more money simply means higher prices. In the short run, when prices are fixed, the money supply affects only output. Monetary policy can set off demand-pull inflation by shifting aggregate demand to the right when the economy is at full employment. Regardless of the reason for the start of inflation, monetary policy has a role in its continuation. Restrictive monetary policy dampens inflation, but accommodative monetary policy may accelerate it if the money supply is allowed to grow faster than the sum of the real growth rate and the existing inflation rate.

8 Relatively high inflation depreciates a country's currency because investors realize that if they hold assets in that currency, inflation will erode its value. Thus, monetary policy affects exchange rates. Investors, of course, form expectations about future monetary policy and inflation rates, and these expectations get built into exchange rates in much the same way that expectations of inflation affect the price level. Investors' expectations can reinforce or counteract the intentions of the monetary authorities.

9 Firms may be reluctant to change prices for three reasons. First, changing prices is expensive. Economists refer to this reason as **menu costs,** analogous to the expense restaurants incur when printing new menus. Second, the uncertainties associated with changing prices may be greater than those associated with changing output. Customers may revise their expectations about prices and postpone purchases if they see prices falling. Finally, in oligopolies, firms may face *kinked demand curves*. Firms can facilitate cooperation by offering to match price cuts. This strategy puts a kink in each firm's demand curve at the current price. Cutting prices gains few extra customers, and firms may prefer to postpone price decreases.

BEHIND THE ESSENTIAL CONCEPTS

1 When inflation is anticipated, its effects are limited. To understand this better, imagine that you are borrowing \$10,000 from your uncle for this year's tuition. To compensate him for living without his money for a year, he wants a 3 percent real rate of return. If there is no inflation, you simply agree to pay him 3 percent interest. If inflation is expected to be 7 percent, you pay him 10 percent interest, which gives him 7 percent to make up for the increase in prices and leaves a 3 percent real return. All contracts can be indexed in this way; therefore a mild, steady rate of inflation does not impose serious costs on the economy.

2 An unpredictable rate of inflation is very costly. Suppose that inflation is uncertain, that it might be 14 percent or 0 percent with equal probability. The average inflation rate is still 7 percent, but now when you borrow from your uncle, there is risk. If you pay the same 10 percent and inflation is zero, your uncle earns a 10 percent real return—a bonanza! On the other hand, if inflation turns out to be 14 percent, he nets negative 4 percent, and receives back less in real terms than he lent. You can see how a variable and unpredictable rate of inflation imposes risks on capital markets.

3 Another of the important costs of inflation involves the tax code. Most economists favor indexing. The tax code

is indexed to some extent; for example, income tax brackets are adjusted each year for inflation. Investment earnings, however, are not indexed. If you start a business for $100,000 and sell it for $150,000 in 5 years and if the inflation rate is 50 percent over those years, then your real return is zero. Nevertheless, you would be liable for taxes on your nominal gains of $50,000. A sensible reform would exempt nominal gains from taxes.

4 When the price is stuck at somewhere other than its market-clearing level, the quantity of output is determined by the short side of the market. If the price is too high to clear the market, then demand is the short side. Although suppliers would like to produce more, there is not enough demand, and thus the output equals the quantity demanded. On the other hand, when the price is too low to clear the market, supply is the short side. Demanders would like to purchase more goods, but only what suppliers can profitably produce is made available. In this case, the output equals the quantity supplied.

5 Inflation in the long run is a simple issue: money growth determines inflation. In the time before relative prices have adjusted to their market clearing levels, however, inflation is a complex issue, involving shocks to aggregate demand and supply, accommodating or restrictive monetary policy, the credibility of the monetary authorities, and expectations. Inflation can arise for nonmonetary reasons and if it is expected to continue, it can persist for a period. Eventually, it will adjust to a rate determined by the growth in the money supply, but the time of adjustment depends upon what investors think the monetary authorities will do. Expectation formation is not an exact science.

SELF-TEST

True or False

1 The U.S. tax system is fully indexed for inflation.

2 Inflation makes it expensive to hold money, because as the price level rises, money becomes less valuable.

3 The Phillips curve shows the relationship between unemployment and inflation.

4 The natural rate of unemployment is the rate that would occur if inflation were zero.

5 When workers and firms expect inflation to increase, the expectations-augmented Phillips curve shifts up.

6 If the government tries to keep the unemployment rate below the NAIRU, the result will be increased inflation.

7 The long-run Phillips curve is downward sloping.

8 The short-run aggregate supply curve can never lie to the right of the long-run aggregate supply.

9 When the price is stuck above the level at which aggregate demand and aggregate supply intersect, output equals aggregate supply.

10 When the price is stuck below the level at which aggregate demand and aggregate supply intersect, output equals aggregate supply.

11 Because inflation is always a monetary phenomenon, demand-pull inflation must start with an increase in the money supply.

12 If international investors expect a restrictive monetary policy, the currency will appreciate.

13 Menu costs refer to the expense of changing prices.

14 Firms perceive greater risk during economic downturns and may choose the safer path of reducing output rather than reducing price.

15 Firms facing a kinked demand curve are unlikely to change price when their costs decrease.

Multiple Choice

1 Cost-of-living adjustments, or COLAs, are a type of

a wage and price control;
b indexation;
c monetary target;
d discretionary monetary policy;
e inflation tax.

2 If not anticipated, an increase in inflation will

a hurt both borrowers and lenders;
b help both borrowers and lenders;
c hurt borrowers but help lenders;
d hurt lenders but help borrowers;
e have no effect on either borrowers or lenders.

3 Inflation

a does not affect taxpayers, because the tax system is fully indexed;
b does not affect taxpayers, because only real income is taxed;
c does not affect taxpayers, because only nominal income is taxed;
d frequently injures investors, who are taxed on high nominal incomes, even though inflation makes their real income small or even negative;
e hurts wage earners but not investors.

4 The inflation tax refers to

a the fact that inflation makes it expensive to hold money;
b the fact that the earnings of investors are not adjusted for inflation;
c the fact that wages are not adjusted for inflation;
d the injury suffered by borrowers in inflationary times;
e the injury suffered by lenders in inflationary times.

5 Inflation often distorts

a nominal prices;
b relative prices;

c absolute prices;
d average prices;
e none of the above.

6 The trade-off between inflation and unemployment is illustrated by the

a aggregate demand curve;
b aggregate supply curve;
c Phillips curve;
d aggregate expenditures schedule;
e money demand curve.

7 The natural rate of unemployment is the rate that prevails

a when there is no inflation;
b during hyperinflation;
c when inflation equals its natural rate;
d when there are no wage and price controls;
e in inflationary spirals.

8 If people expect inflation to be higher, then the

a Phillips curve is vertical in the short run;
b Phillips curve shifts to the right;
c Phillips curve shifts to the left;
d Phillips curve does not shift, because it assumes that expectations are always rational;
e Phillips curve is horizontal in the long run.

9 If the government tries to keep unemployment below the NAIRU,

a inflation will decrease;
b there will be no effect on inflation;
c inflation will increase;
d there will be stagflation;
e the Phillips curve will shift to the left.

10 In the long run the Phillips curve is

a downward sloping;
b upward sloping;
c horizontal;
d vertical;
e increasing at a decreasing rate.

11 When people form expectations based on the structure of the economy, their expectations are said to be

a irrational;
b rational;
c adaptive;
d unrealistic;
e myopic.

12 If the price level is stuck above the level at which aggregate demand and aggregate supply intersect, then

a output is less than firms are willing to supply;
b output is more than firms are willing to supply;
c output is less than the economy is willing to purchase;
d output is more than the economy is willing to purchase;
e a and d.

13 When the price level is stuck above the intersection of aggregate demand and long-run aggregate supply,

a output equals the level at which aggregate demand and long-run aggregate supply intersect;
b output equals aggregate demand at the current price level;
c output equals short-run aggregate supply at the current price level;
d output is greater than it is at the intersection of aggregate demand and aggregate supply;
e c and d.

14 When the price level is stuck below the intersection of aggregate demand and short-run aggregate supply,

a output equals the level at which aggregate demand and aggregate supply intersect;
b output equals short-run aggregate supply at the current price level;
c output equals aggregate demand at the current price level;
d output is less than it is at the intersection of aggregate demand and short-run aggregate supply;
e b and d.

15 Which of the following can cause inflation to begin?

a demand shocks;
b supply shocks;
c monetary shocks;
d wage and price controls;
e a, b, and c.

16 If investors expect restrictive monetary policy,

a the exchange rate will appreciate;
b the exchange rate will depreciate;
c there will be no change in the exchange rate;
d the exchange rate may move up or down depending upon whether these expectations are rational;
e the exchange rate will rise if there is excess capacity but fall if the economy is operating at full employment.

17 The costs of changing prices are called

a variable costs;
b sunk costs;
c fixed costs;
d pricing costs;
e menu costs.

18 During recessions, firms perceive that

a cutting prices is riskier than cutting production;
b increasing prices is riskier than increasing production;
c cutting production is riskier than cutting prices;
d increasing prices is riskier than increasing production;
e none of the above.

19 Which of the following is not true of the beliefs of firms facing a kinked demand curve?

a Their customers will quickly learn of price increases, and they will lose business.

b Other firms' customers will be slow to learn of any price cuts, gaining the firm little new business.
c Rivals may match price cuts.
d Rivals will not match price increases.
e All of the above are true.

20 For a firm facing a kinked demand curve, when its marginal cost increases slightly,
a the price will rise;
b the price will stay the same;
c the price will fall;
d output will increase;
e output will decrease.

Completion

1 Formally linking any payment, such as wages or taxes, to inflation is called __________.

2 The trade-off between unemployment and inflation is represented by the __________.

3 The rate of unemployment that would result if there were no inflation is the __________.

4 If the government tries to maintain the unemployment rate below the __________, inflation will increase.

5 Inflation perpetuated by increases in government or investment spending is __________ inflation.

6 Inflation perpetuated by wage increases is an example of __________ inflation.

7 When both the unemployment rate and inflation rate are high there is __________.

8 If investors expect increased inflation, the exchange rate will __________.

9 The costs of changing prices are called __________.

10 Firms that believe that rivals will match price cuts but not price increases face a __________ demand curve.

Answers to Self-Test

True or False

1	f	6	t	11	f
2	t	7	f	12	t
3	t	8	f	13	t
4	t	9	f	14	t
5	t	10	t	15	t

Multiple Choice

1	b	6	c	11	b	16	a
2	d	7	a	12	e	17	e
3	d	8	b	13	c	18	a
4	a	9	c	14	e	19	e
5	b	10	d	15	e	20	b

Completion

1 indexing
2 Phillips curve
3 natural rate
4 NAIRU
5 demand-pull
6 cost-push
7 stagflation
8 depreciate
9 menu costs
10 kinked

Doing Economics: Tools and Practice Problems

In Chapter 4, we learned how to measure inflation and construct the price index. In this chapter, we use those tools to study cost-of-living provisions in contracts and to make comparisons between prices at different times. The goals are to understand how the economy deals with steady and predictable inflation and to develop a feel for the difference between real and nominal values.

Tool Kit 14.1: Using Cost-of-Living Provisions to Adjust Wages and Prices

Wage agreements between employer and employees, contracts between firms and their suppliers, government entitlement programs, and even the income tax system are indexed for inflation with cost-of-living provisions. These provisions specify that wages, prices, or other important economic variables must be adjusted to reflect inflation. The problems in this section show how to do this using the consumer price index. Table 14.1 gives the consumer price index for every year since 1954. (You can look up these numbers and a wealth of other economic data in the *Economic Report of the President.*)

Step one: Identify the dollar amount to be adjusted, that year's price index, and the current price index.

Step two: Convert the amount to current dollars:

current dollar equivalent = amount
× (current price index/past price index).

1 (Worked problem: cost-of-living provisions) Dan's Steel Company offered a wage of $15 per hour in 1980. A cost-of-living provision in the contrast guaranteed that the nominal wage would be increased to compensate for inflation. Use the consumer price index given in Table 14.1 to calculate the wage in each year since 1980.

Step-by-step solution

Step one: The wage in 1980 was $15. To find the inflation-adjusted wage in 1981, we need the price index in 1980, which is 82.4, and in 1981, which is 90.9.

Step two: Convert the wage to 1981 dollars:

wage in 1981 = $15 × (90.9/82.4) = $16.55.

Table 14.1

Year or month	All items	Food and beverages: Total	Food and beverages: Food	Housing: Total	Housing: Shelter	Housing: Fuel and other utilities	Housing: Household furnishings and operation	Apparel and upkeep	Transportation	Medical care	Entertainment	Other goods and services	Energy
1954	26.9		28.2		22.5	22.6		43.1	26.1	17.8			
1955	26.8		27.8		22.7	23.0		42.9	25.8	18.2			
1956	27.2		28.0		23.1	23.6		43.7	26.2	18.9			
1957	28.1		28.9		24.0	24.3		44.5	27.7	19.7			21.5
1958	28.9		30.2		24.5	24.8		44.6	28.6	20.6			21.5
1959	29.1		29.7		24.7	25.4		45.0	29.8	21.5			21.9
1960	29.6		30.0		25.2	26.0		45.7	29.8	22.3			22.4
1961	29.9		30.4		25.4	26.3		46.1	30.1	22.9			22.5
1962	30.2		30.6		25.8	26.3		46.3	30.8	23.5			22.6
1963	30.6		31.1		26.1	26.6		46.9	30.9	24.1			22.6
1964	31.0		31.5		26.5	26.6		47.3	31.4	24.6			22.5
1965	31.5		32.2		27.0	26.6		47.8	31.9	25.2			22.9
1966	32.4		33.8		27.8	26.7		49.0	32.3	25.3			23.3
1967	33.4	35.0	34.1	30.8	28.8	27.1	42.0	51.0	33.3	28.2	40.7	35.1	23.8
1968	34.8	36.2	35.3	32.0	30.1	27.4	43.6	53.7	34.3	29.9	43.0	36.9	24.2
1969	36.7	38.1	37.1	34.0	32.6	28.0	45.2	56.8	35.7	31.9	45.2	38.7	24.8
1970	38.8	40.1	39.2	36.4	35.5	29.1	46.8	59.2	37.5	34.0	47.5	40.9	25.5
1971	40.5	41.4	40.4	38.0	37.0	31.1	48.6	61.1	39.5	36.1	50.0	42.9	26.5
1972	41.8	43.1	42.1	39.4	38.7	32.5	49.7	62.3	39.9	37.3	51.5	44.7	27.2
1973	44.4	48.8	48.2	41.2	40.5	34.3	51.1	64.6	41.2	38.8	52.9	46.4	29.4
1974	49.3	55.5	55.1	45.8	44.4	40.7	56.8	69.4	45.8	42.4	56.9	49.8	38.1
1975	53.8	60.2	59.8	50.7	48.8	45.4	63.4	72.5	50.1	47.5	62.0	53.9	42.1
1976	56.9	62.1	61.6	53.8	51.5	49.4	67.3	75.2	55.1	52.0	65.1	57.0	45.1
1977	60.6	65.8	65.5	57.4	54.9	54.7	70.4	78.6	59.0	57.0	68.3	60.4	49.4
1978	65.2	72.2	72.0	62.4	60.5	58.5	74.7	81.4	61.7	61.8	71.9	64.3	52.5
1979	72.6	79.9	79.9	70.1	68.9	64.8	79.9	84.9	70.5	67.5	76.5	68.9	65.7
1980	82.4	86.7	86.8	81.1	81.0	75.4	86.3	90.9	83.1	74.9	83.6	75.2	86.0
1981	90.9	93.5	93.6	90.4	90.5	86.4	93.0	95.3	93.2	82.9	90.1	82.6	97.7
1982	96.5	97.3	97.4	96.9	96.9	94.9	98.0	97.8	97.0	92.5	96.0	91.1	99.2
1983	99.6	99.5	99.4	99.5	99.1	100.2	100.2	100.2	99.3	100.6	100.1	101.1	99.9
1984	103.9	103.2	103.2	103.6	104.0	104.8	101.9	102.1	103.7	106.8	103.8	107.9	100.9
1985	107.6	105.6	105.6	107.7	109.8	106.5	103.8	105.0	106.4	113.5	107.9	114.5	101.6
1986	109.6	109.1	109.0	110.9	115.8	104.1	105.2	105.9	102.3	120.0	111.6	121.4	88.2
1987	113.6	113.5	113.5	114.2	121.3	103.0	107.1	110.6	105.4	130.1	115.3	128.5	88.6
1988	118.3	118.2	118.2	118.5	127.1	104.4	109.4	115.4	108.7	138.6	120.3	137.0	89.3
1989	124.0	124.9	125.1	123.0	132.8	107.8	111.2	118.6	114.1	149.3	126.5	147.7	94.3
1990	130.7	132.1	132.4	128.5	140.0	111.6	113.3	124.1	120.5	162.8	132.4	159.0	102.1
1991	136.2	136.8	136.3	133.6	146.3	115.3	116.0	128.7	123.8	177.0	138.4	171.6	102.5
1992	140.3	138.7	137.9	137.5	151.2	117.8	118.0	131.9	126.5	190.1	142.3	183.3	103.0
1993	144.5	141.6	140.9	141.2	155.7	121.3	119.3	133.7	130.4	201.4	145.8	192.9	104.2
1994	148.2	144.9	144.3	144.8	160.5	122.8	121.0	133.4	134.3	211.0	150.1	198.5	104.6
1995	152.4	148.9	148.4	148.5	165.7	123.7	123.0	132.0	139.1	220.5	153.9	206.9	105.2
1994: Jan	146.2	144.3	143.7	142.9	158.1	121.6	120.5	130.4	131.6	206.4	148.5	195.1	101.3
Feb	146.7	143.6	142.9	143.7	159.1	122.4	120.4	132.4	131.9	207.7	149.1	195.2	102.0
Mar	147.2	143.9	143.2	144.1	159.8	122.4	120.6	136.1	132.2	208.3	149.6	195.5	101.9
Apr	147.4	144.0	143.4	143.9	159.6	121.6	120.6	136.4	132.6	209.2	149.7	196.4	102.0
May	147.5	144.1	143.5	144.1	159.6	122.2	121.1	135.6	132.8	209.7	149.9	197.1	102.9
June	148.0	144.2	143.5	144.9	160.1	124.2	121.4	133.8	133.8	210.4	149.8	197.6	105.7
July	148.4	144.8	144.2	145.4	160.8	124.3	121.5	130.9	134.6	211.5	150.2	198.0	106.8
Aug	149.0	145.3	144.8	145.9	161.7	124.3	121.4	131.1	135.9	212.2	150.2	199.4	108.5
Sept	149.4	145.6	145.0	145.8	161.6	124.2	121.4	134.2	135.9	212.8	150.7	201.4	108.2
Oct	149.5	145.6	145.0	145.7	162.0	122.4	121.4	135.2	136.1	214.0	151.0	201.9	105.8
Nov	149.7	145.9	145.3	145.5	162.1	121.8	121.1	134.2	137.1	214.7	151.6	202.3	105.7
Dec	149.7	147.2	146.8	145.4	161.8	122.0	120.8	130.5	137.1	215.3	151.2	202.4	104.7
1995: Jan	150.3	147.9	147.5	146.4	162.9	122.9	121.8	129.4	137.3	216.6	152.1	203.0	104.2
Feb	150.9	147.8	147.4	147.0	163.8	122.6	122.4	131.1	137.5	217.9	152.5	204.1	103.7
Mar	151.4	147.9	147.4	147.4	164.5	122.3	122.6	134.4	138.0	218.4	152.6	204.0	103.2
Apr	151.9	148.9	148.4	147.4	164.7	122.1	122.6	134.8	139.1	218.9	153.3	204.3	103.9
May	152.2	148.7	148.3	147.6	164.8	122.5	122.7	133.4	140.3	219.3	153.6	204.9	106.3
June	152.5	148.4	147.9	148.5	165.5	125.0	122.5	130.5	141.1	219.8	153.2	205.3	109.3
July	152.5	148.6	148.1	149.2	166.4	125.1	123.0	128.3	140.1	220.8	153.6	205.7	108.1
Aug	152.9	148.9	148.4	149.6	166.8	125.7	123.4	130.1	139.2	221.6	154.1	207.7	107.4
Sept	153.2	149.4	148.9	149.5	166.8	124.9	123.8	132.7	138.8	222.1	154.9	210.2	106.2
Oct	153.7	149.8	149.4	149.7	167.3	123.9	123.9	134.5	139.4	222.9	155.2	210.7	104.5
Nov	153.6	149.8	149.4	149.4	167.3	123.1	123.6	133.7	139.4	223.5	156.0	211.2	102.8
Dec	153.5	150.3	149.9	149.7	167.4	123.7	123.8	130.6	139.1	223.8	156.2	211.1	103.3

Source: Department of Labor, Bureau of Labor Statistics

The wage in 1982 is \$15 × (96.5/82.4) = \$17.57. Proceeding similarly, we derive the information in Table 14.2.

Table 14.2

Year	Wage
1980	\$15.00
1981	\$16.55
1982	\$17.57
1983	\$18.13
1984	\$18.91
1985	\$19.59
1986	\$19.95
1987	\$20.68
1988	\$21.54
1989	\$22.57
1990	\$23.79
1991	\$24.79
1992	\$25.54
1993	\$26.30
1994	\$26.98
1995	\$27.74

2 (Practice problem: cost-of-living provisions) The Social Security tax is applied to earnings up to a statutory maximum. Any earnings above this limit are taxed. Table 14.3 gives the maximum earnings for selected years.

Table 14.3

Year	Maximum taxable annual earnings
1950	\$ 3,000
1960	\$ 4,800
1970	\$ 7,800
1980	\$25,900
1990	\$51,300

The maximum was \$3,000 in 1950. Adjust this number for inflation for 1960, 1970, 1980, and 1990, and compare the result with the actual numbers in Table 14.1. Has the maximum taxable earning limit kept up with or outpaced inflation?

3 (Practice problem: cost-of-living provisions) The Tax Reform Act of 1986 set the rates at 15 percent for the first \$17,850 of income for single persons and 28 percent for any income above that amount. To avoid "bracket creep," the income level at which the rates change is supposed to be indexed for inflation. Use the consumer price index numbers in Table 14.1 to adjust for inflation.

Answers to Problems

2 Adjusted limit in 1960 = \$3,000 × (29.6/24.1) = \$3,684.65; adjusted limit in 1970 = \$3,000 × (38.8/24.1) = \$4,829.88; adjusted limit in 1980 = \$3,000 × (82.4/24.1) = \$10,257.26; adjusted limit in 1990 = \$3,000 × (130.7/24.1) = \$16,269.71.

3 Adjusted level in 1987 = \$17,850 × (113.6/109.6) = \$18,501; adjusted level in 1988 = \$17,850 × (118.3/109.6) = \$19,267; adjusted level in 1989 = \$17,850 × (124.0/109.6) = \$20,195; adjusted level in 1990 = \$17,850 × (130.7/109.6) = \$21,286; adjusted level in 1991 = \$17,850 × (136.2\109.6) = \$22,182; adjusted level in 1992 = \$17,850 × (140.3/109.6) = \$22,850; adjusted level in 1993 = \$17,850 × (144.5/109.6) = \$23,534; adjusted level in 1994 = \$17,850 × (148.2/109.6) = \$24,137; adjusted level in 1995 = \$17,850 × (152.4/109.6) = \$24,821.

Chapter 15

UNEMPLOYMENT: UNDERSTANDING WAGE RIGIDITIES

Chapter Review

The last chapter focused on inflation. This chapter zeroes in on the labor market to examine the causes of unemployment more closely. The key issue is why wages fail to adjust to clear the market and bring about full employment. In recent years economists have put forward several new ideas about this problem, and these ideas are discussed and evaluated here. The next chapter completes Part Four on dynamics with some analysis of the policy issues involved in the unemployment–inflation trade-off.

ESSENTIAL CONCEPTS

1 While unemployment fluctuates substantially in the United States, there is little variation in real wages. Why not? We know that changes in product demand cause the labor demand to shift. Unless supply shifts to match the shifts in demand or supply is perfectly elastic (two propositions that are surely wrong), the explanation must lie in a microeconomic analysis of sticky real wages.

2 Wages may not adjust to bring about full employment for several reasons.

a **Union contracts** may specify wages above the market-clearing level. If the demand for labor falls, the union may not agree to accept lower wages.

b Firms may have informal agreements, or **implicit contracts**, with their risk-averse workers to provide fixed wages as a kind of insurance against economic downturns.

c **Insider-outsider theory** observes that because existing workers must train new hires, the current work force may not be willing to provide training to newly hired workers unless they are paid the same wage.

d **Minimum wage laws** mandate a price floor in the labor market.

e **Efficiency wage theory** shows how firms may make higher profits by paying wages that are above the market-clearing level, because workers have incentives to work harder and be more productive.

3 There are three reasons why firms can increase the productivity of their workers by paying the higher efficiency wage rather than the market wage.

a When a firm cuts its wage, some workers leave. These workers are likely to be the firm's most productive workers who will have good alternatives elsewhere. The pool of the firm's new hires will be of lower quality when the wage offer is less. Thus, the overall quality of the work force is poorer at lower wages. This phenomenon is called adverse selection.

b Workers may put forth greater effort on a job that pays more than alternative jobs. In effect, the higher wage makes the job more valuable to the worker and motivates her to work harder for fear of losing the high-paying job.

c By paying higher wages, firms can reduce the rate at which workers quit—the labor turnover rate. Because it is costly to hire and train new workers, a firm's profits may be higher than they would if it paid lower wages.

4 **Okun's law** says that a 2 percent increase in output is needed to bring about a 1 percent decrease in unemployment. One explanation for this is **labor hoarding,** where firms retain workers during downturns in order to have them available when demand returns. This is a form of disguised unemployment.

5 One policy option is to attempt to increase wage flexibility through profit sharing or substituting bonuses for some percentage of the wage bill. Another recommends reducing the costs of unemployment with a more generous unemployment insurance system. Both proposals run into the risk-incentive trade-off, which shows that when workers are protected from risk, they lose incentives to put forth effort.

a If workers receive more of their wages in the form of profit sharing, their earnings become more flexible, rising in booms and falling in recessions. Such a policy reduces the risk of unemployment, yet increases the risk of income loss during economic downturns.

b Unemployment insurance protects workers against income loss if they are laid off, yet it reduces their incentives to find and accept new jobs.

BEHIND THE ESSENTIAL CONCEPTS

1 While each of the reasons for wage rigidity listed above has some validity, the efficiency wage theory is the most satisfactory explanation. Economists favor efficiency wage theory because it explains three important facts about the labor market: the failure of wages to adjust to market-clearing levels, the fact that firms lay off excess workers during downturns rather than share the available work equally among the firm's total labor demand, and the fact that wages adjust slowly when economic conditions change.

2 The efficiency wage theory explains rigid wages in the following way. Suppose you are an employer. You need quality workers who put forth a lot of effort and remain loyal to your firm. Your problem is how to keep and motivate your good workers. If you pay the market-clearing wage, jobs with your firm will be worth no more than those of other firms. Your workers will know that they can quickly find work elsewhere at the going wage. The efficiency wage solves the problem in a very clever way. It is part carrot and part stick. You offer the carrot of higher wages, and gain influence over your workers with the stick, which is the threat to take away the job. Your workers have good incentives to stay, because the job is now worth more than their alternatives.

3 Once you understand why one firm gains by paying its workers wages above market-clearing levels, you can then see that other firms will do the same. It might seem to you that if all firms pay higher wages, then no firm offers anything special. But because all wages are higher than the market-clearing level, there remains a surplus of unemployed workers and not enough jobs to go around. Losing a valuable job represents a substantial cost to your workers, not because other jobs pay less, but because workers without jobs face a considerable time of unemployment.

4 Unemployment is a surplus of labor, or workers. You might ask, "Why don't the unemployed offer to work for less?" After all, the usual explanation for why the price of anything adjusts down to the market-clearing level is that the suppliers who cannot find buyers offer to sell at lower prices. In the efficiency wage world, however, if the unemployed offer to work at lower wages, the manager of the firm will conclude that they are either low-quality workers who will not make the required effort or that they will soon look for other employment. Remember that the efficiency wage is just high enough to attract, motivate, and keep quality workers. Any offer to do quality work for less is simply not credible.

5 When the demand for labor falls during economic downturns, firms use layoffs to reduce the size of the work force rather than share the available work among their workers. Why? According to the efficiency wage view, sharing work lowers average earnings in the same way that cutting wages does. If you let your employees share the work, you will lose your high-quality workers and have difficulty motivating those who stay. It is better to use layoffs.

6 A final implication of the efficiency wage theory is that wages adjust slowly. Put yourself again in the shoes of an employer. If business falls off, you may want to cut wages, but first you must see whether your competitors will reduce *their* wages. If you move too soon, you may lose your best workers. Efficiency wage theory counsels waiting, perhaps spending a few dollars more in labor costs.

SELF-TEST

True or False

1 The real wage is the nominal wage adjusted for inflation.

2 If supply is perfectly elastic, then when demand shifts, real wages will not change.

3 Whether they actually cause an increase in wages for

their members, unions slow the pace of wage adjustment.

4 Employment levels fluctuate quite dramatically; nevertheless, real wages are rather stable.

5 Most union contracts contain provisions for adjusting wages downward when the firm's demand for labor shifts.

6 Cost of living adjustment provisions (COLAs) allow real wages to remain stable even though inflation increases.

7 An implicit contract is an informal arrangement between workers and firms, often involving the firm's paying constant wages even as the wages its workers could receive elsewhere change.

8 Implicit contract theory also explains why real wages of job seekers do not decline significantly during recessions.

9 According to insider-outsider theory, a firm's current workers refuse to train new hires unless the new hires receive similar wages.

10 The minimum wage is a price ceiling in the market for unskilled labor.

11 According to efficiency wage theory, the firm can make more profits by paying higher wages.

12 One reason firms may not wish to pay lower wages is the adverse selection effect, whereby the average quality of the pool of workers willing to accept a job with a firm depends upon the wage offered.

13 As a general rule, the efficiency wage is less than the market-clearing wage.

14 Efficiency wage theory implies that wages will adjust slowly because firms are reluctant to change wages before their competitors do.

15 Unemployment affects most demographic groups equally.

Multiple Choice

1 The demand curve for labor studied in this chapter

a shows the total amount of labor demanded by all firms in the economy at each wage;
b is drawn assuming that product prices are fixed;
c may shift to the right but never shifts to the left;
d is upward sloping, according to efficiency wage theory;
e a and b.

2 The real wage

a equals the efficiency wage;
b equals the nominal wage when expectations have adjusted to the actual rate of inflation;
c equals the nominal wage adjusted for errors in forming expectations;
d equals the nominal wage adjusted for inflation;
e equals the wage negotiated in the union contract and modified by the COLA.

3 Which of the following is not a possible explanation for wage rigidity?

a The supply curve of labor is horizontal (perfectly elastic).
b The labor supply curve shifts along with the demand curve for labor.
c The demand curve for labor is perfectly inelastic.
d Union contracts restrict wage adjustment.
e Some firms have implicit contracts with their risk-averse workers to provide insurance by paying the same wage even as the market wage varies.

4 Unemployment results if

a the demand for labor shifts to the left, and wages fail to adjust;
b the supply of labor shifts to the left, and wages fail to adjust;
c the demand for labor shifts to the right, and wages fail to adjust;
d the supply of labor shifts to the right, and wages fail to adjust;
e a and d.

5 If the supply of labor is upward sloping and demand shifts to the right, then

a if wages adjust to the market-clearing level, anyone willing to work at the going wage can eventually find a job;
b if wages adjust to the market-clearing level, any unemployment will be involuntary;
c if wages adjust to the market-clearing level, employment will decrease;
d if wages do not adjust to the market-clearing level, any unemployment will be involuntary;
e if wages do not adjust to the market-clearing level, the supply of labor will shift to the right.

6 In modern economies, when the demand for labor falls,

a the real wage always falls to clear the market;
b the real wage does not change, but workers share the available jobs by each working fewer hours;
c the real wage does not change, but workers share the available jobs by rotating between full time and unemployment;
d the real wage does not change, and some workers are laid off while others retain employment;
e b and c.

7 Which of the following is an explanation of the failure of real wages to adjust to changes in the demand and supply of labor?

a union contracts;
b implicit contracts;
c insider-outsider theory;
d efficiency wage theory;
e all of the above.

8 The minimum wage is a

a price floor in the labor market, causing the quantity of workers demanded to exceed the quantity supplied;
b price floor in the labor market, causing the quanti-

ty of workers demanded to be less than the quantity supplied;

c price ceiling in the labor market, causing the quantity of workers demanded to exceed the quantity supplied;

d price ceiling in the labor market, causing the quantity of workers demanded to be less than the quantity supplied;

e a and d.

9 The theory that argues that firms have an informal agreement to protect risk-averse workers from variations in their incomes by paying the same wage even though their alternative wage changes is called

a efficiency wage theory;
b implicit contract theory;
c insider-outsider theory;
d minimum wage theory;
e none of the above.

10 The theory that points out that it is not in the interests of the firm's workers to train newcomers if the new hires receive lower wages is

a efficiency wage theory;
b implicit contract theory;
c insider-outsider theory;
d minimum wage theory;
e none of the above.

11 The theory that says that wages above market-clearing wages motivate workers to put forth effort and remain with the high-paying firm is

a efficiency wage theory;
b implicit contract theory;
c insider-outsider theory;
d minimum wage theory;
e none of the above.

12 Typically, when the firm's demand for labor falls, it

a immediately cuts wages for all workers;
b shares the available work among all its workers;
c reduces the size of its labor force through layoffs;
d idles some of its capital stock in order to keep its workers busy;
e retains its entire work force at current wages, hoping that business will return.

13 Efficiency wage theory emphasizes that higher wages are important to

a motivate workers;
b retain high-quality workers;
c attract high-quality job applicants;
d reduce turnover;
e all of the above.

14 Unemployment typically

a affects different groups in the economy equally;
b affects high-skilled, high-wage workers more because employers can save more in labor costs by laying them off;
c affects lower-skilled and part-time workers more;
d affects only those paid on a piece-work basis;
e none of the above.

15 The system under which workers are paid on the basis of what they produce is called

a efficiency wages;
b implicit contracts;
c the insider-outsider system;
d minimum wages;
e piece work.

16 If wages and prices fall in the same proportion, then real wages

a increase;
b decrease;
c stay the same;
d may increase or decrease depending on the absolute level of the real wage;
e may increase or decrease depending on the absolute level of the nominal wage.

17 Firms that keep their best workers on the payroll hoping that business will pick up are engaging in

a piece work;
b labor hoarding;
c profit sharing;
d layoffs;
e union busting.

18 Okun's law asserts that

a for every 1 percent decrease in output, unemployment increases by 1 percent;
b for every 1 percent decrease in unemployment, output increases by 2 percent;
c for every 1 percent decrease in unemployment, output increases by less than 1 percent;
d for every 1 percent decrease in output, unemployment increases 2 percent;
e for every 1 percent decrease in output, unemployment increases by less than 1 percent.

19 If workers received some of their compensation in the form of bonuses tied to the profit level, then

a wages would be more flexible;
b unemployment would fall;
c workers would be exposed to a greater risk of income fluctuations;
d all of the above;
e none of the above.

20 Unemployment compensation

a increases the risk of income fluctuations for workers;
b reduces unemployment;
c gives unemployed workers more incentive to look for and accept job offers;
d increases both risk and incentives to look for work;
e decreases both risk and incentives to look for work.

Completion

1 Wage __________ refers to the failure of wages to adjust sufficiently to changes in the demand or supply curve of labor.

2 An understanding between a firm and its workers that

requires the payment of constant wages is called an __________.

3 According to __________ theory, the current employees of a firm refuse to train new hires unless their wages are comparable.

4 The minimum wage is a government-mandated price __________ in the labor market.

5 Paying higher wages can increase __________ by attracting more qualified workers, increasing effort, and reducing turnover.

6 The wage that minimizes total labor costs is called the __________ wage.

7 Because it is expensive to hire and fire workers, firms may __________ employees during recessions.

8 __________ says that if output increases by 2 percent, unemployment falls by 1 percent.

9 Making wages more flexible by substituting some form of profit sharing may be unattractive to workers who are relatively __________.

10 Unemployment insurance reduces the risk associated with unemployment, but it also reduces the __________ of the unemployed to search for work.

Answers to Self-Test

True or False

1	t	6	t	11	t
2	t	7	t	12	t
3	t	8	f	13	f
4	t	9	t	14	t
5	f	10	f	15	f

Multiple Choice

1	e	6	d	11	a	16	c
2	d	7	e	12	c	17	b
3	c	8	b	13	e	18	b
4	e	9	b	14	c	19	d
5	a	10	c	15	e	20	e

Completion

1 rigidity
2 implicit contract
3 insider-outsider
4 floor
5 productivity
6 efficiency
7 hoard
8 Okun's law
9 risk averse
10 incentives

Doing Economics: Tools and Practice Problems

Involuntary unemployment results when the wage does not adjust to clear the market. Efficiency wage theory explains the failure of wages to bring about full employment. It also implies that firms will use layoffs (rather than job sharing)

Tool Kit 15.1: Determining the Efficiency Wage

Firms perceive that the productivity of their workers depends upon the wage. Higher wages motivate workers to put forth effort, attract a high-quality pool of applicants, and reduce turnover. When productivity depends on the wage, the profit-maximizing strategy for the firm is to set the wage at the level that attains the highest output per dollar. This level is achieved when the ratio of productivity (output per hour) to the wage rate is maximized.

Step one: Identify and graph the productivity-wage relationship.

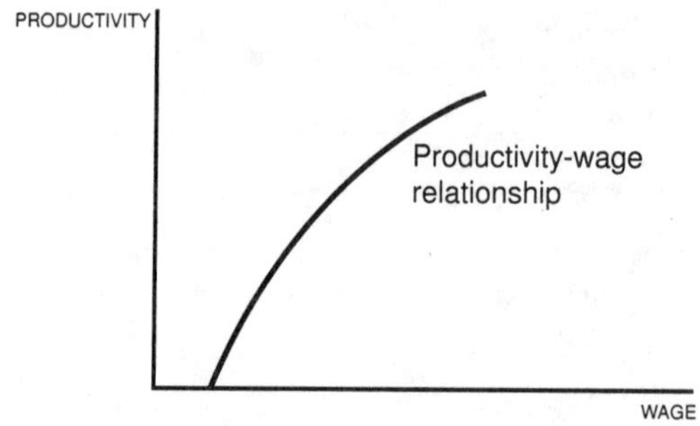

Step two: Calculate the ratio of productivity to the wage for each wage level. This ratio gives output per dollar spent on labor:

output per dollar = productivity/wage.

Step three: Choose the wage for which the corresponding productivity-wage ratio is the highest. Label this point *A* on the graph of the productivity-wage relationship.

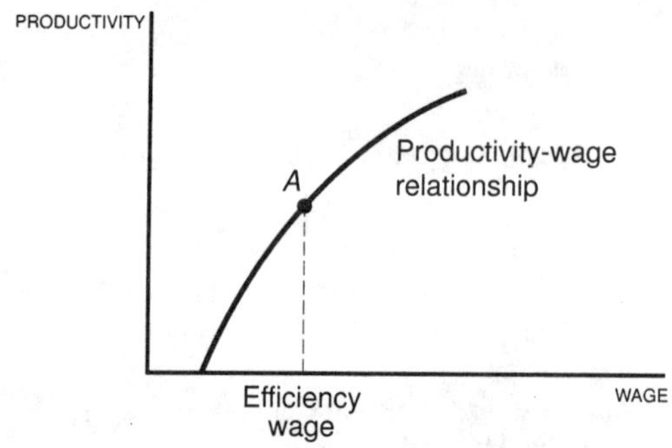

Step four: Draw a line from the origin to *A*. The slope of this line is the productivity-wage ratio. The line should be tangent, and so indicates that output per dollar is maximized.

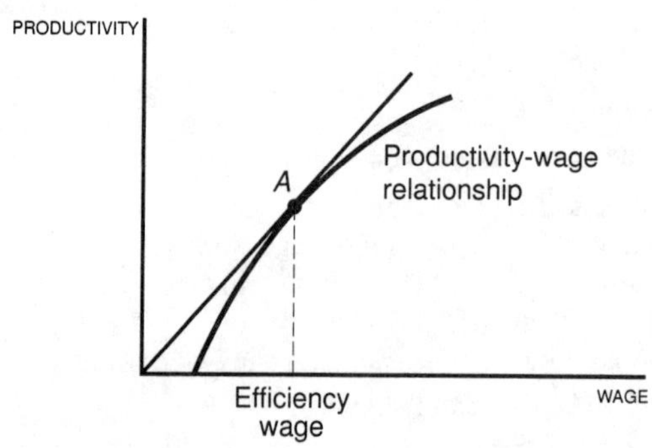

to reduce the work force when the demand for labor is low, and wages will adjust slowly as conditions change. In this section, we learn how to determine the efficiency wage.

1 (Worked problem: efficiency wage) Murray's Auto Parts has had trouble with labor turnover. Once its workers are trained, they leave. A consultant points out that productivity would be higher if the firm could keep its workers and that one way to discourage quitting is to pay higher wages. The consultant estimates that the relationship between productivity and wages is as shown in Table 15.1.

Table 15.1

Wage (per hour)	*Productivity ($ sales per hour)*
$4	8.00
$5	12.50
$6	18.00
$7	24.50
$8	26.00
$9	27.00

Determine the efficiency wage for Murray's.

Step-by-step solution

Step one: Identify and graph the productivity-wage relation-

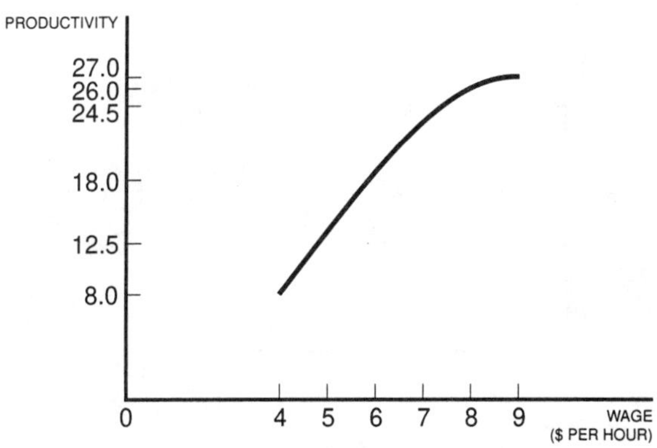

ship.

Step two: Calculate the ratio of productivity to the wage for each wage level. This ratio is shown in Table 15.2.

Table 15.2

Wage ($ per hour)	*Productivity ($ sales per hour)*	*Productivity/wage*
$4	8.00	2.00
$5	12.50	2.50
$6	18.00	3.00
$7	24.50	3.50
$8	26.00	3.25
$9	27.00	3.00

Step three: Choose the wage for which the corresponding productivity-wage ratio is the highest. The efficiency wage is $7 per hour and is shown as point *A*.

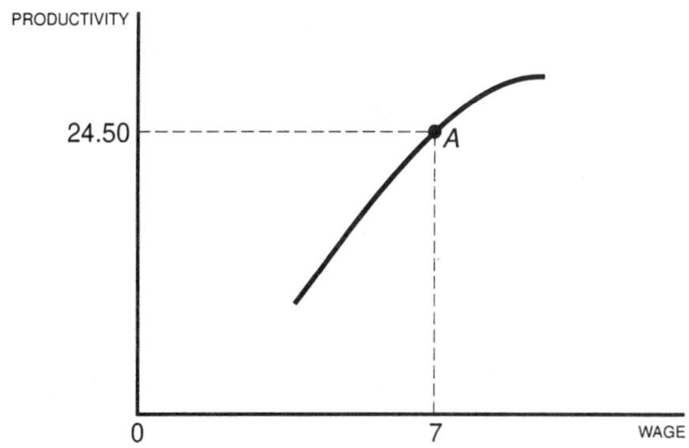

Step four: Draw a line from the origin to *A*. The slope of this line is the productivity-wage ratio, which is 3.5. The line is tangent, indicating that output per dollar is maximized.

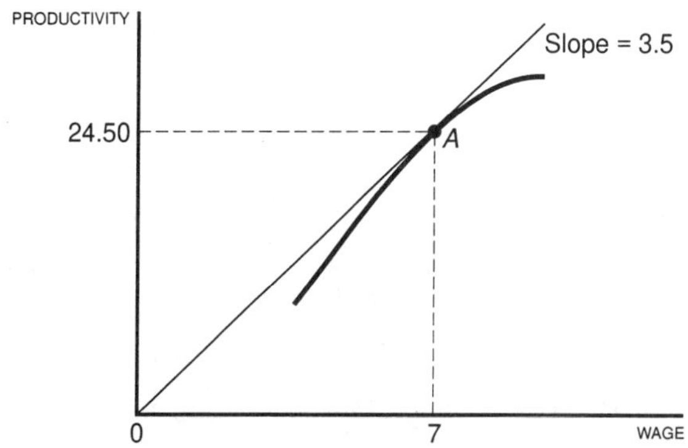

2 (Practice problem: efficiency wage) Moe's Lawn Care has plenty of customers, but Moe is having difficulty getting his mowers to work hard. He cannot monitor each worker all the time and suspects that there is considerable shirking on the job. His brother-in-law, always ready with helpful advice, suggests that if wages were higher, his workers would put forth more effort for fear of losing a well-paying job. Moe considers this and estimates that the relationship between wages and productivity is as appears in Table 15.3.

Table 15.3

Wage (per month)	*Productivity (acres mowed per month)*
$ 900	800
$1,000	1,000
$1,100	1,320
$1,200	1,680
$1,300	1,950
$1,400	1,960

Determine the efficiency wage for Moe's business.

3 (Practice problem: efficiency wage) Luke's Warm and Now food delivery business needs good drivers. He thinks that he may get a better pool of applicants if he offers higher wages. Table 15.4 shows the relationship between the wage and productivity.

Table 15.4

Wage (per hour)	*Productivity (deliveries per week)*
$200	110
$220	114
$240	130
$260	146
$280	160
$300	168

Determine the efficiency wage.

Answers to Problems

2 Table 15.5 shows the productivity-wage ratio. The efficiency wage is $1,300 per month, as shown in the diagram.

Table 15.5

Wage	*Productivity*	*Productivity/wage*
$ 900	800	0.89
$1,000	1,000	1.00
$1,000	1,320	1.20
$1,200	1,680	1.40
$1,300	1,950	1.50
$1,400	1,960	1.40

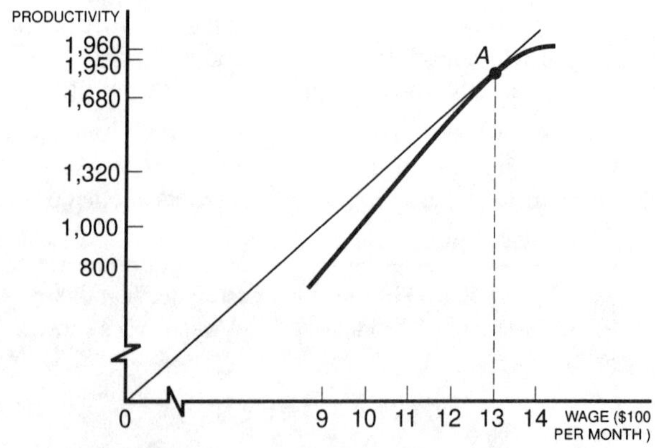

3 Table 15.6 shows the productivity-wage ratio.

Table 15.6

Wage	*Productivity*	*Productivity/wage*
$200	100	0.50
$220	114	0.52
$240	130	0.54
$260	146	0.56
$280	160	0.57
$300	168	0.56

The efficiency wage is $280 per week, as shown in the diagram.

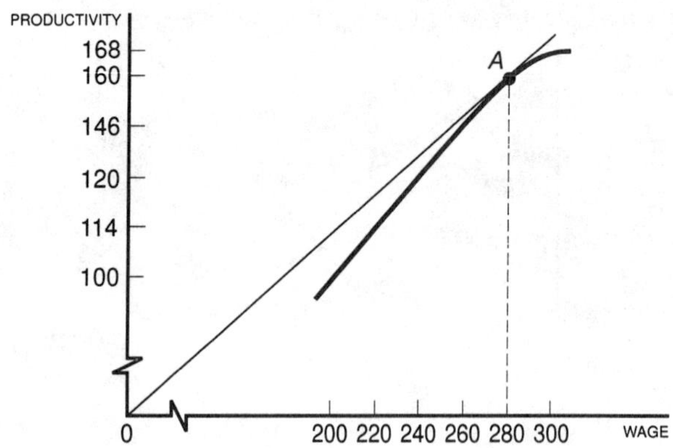

Chapter 16

INFLATION VS. UNEMPLOYMENT: APPROACHES TO POLICY

CHAPTER REVIEW

In closing the discussion of dynamics this chapter brings together the insights of Chapter 14, on the trade-off between inflation and unemployment, and Chapter 15, on the reasons for slow adjustment of real wages. Here the emphasis is on policy alternatives: what can be done to stabilize the economy, control inflation, and reduce the rate of unemployment. The book returns to the other major macroeconomic goal—growth—in the next chapter.

ESSENTIAL CONCEPTS

1 Attempting to push the unemployment rate below the NAIRU only results in increased inflation. There is always some uncertainty about the exact level of the NAIRU, however, and thus there is some room for disagreement. The main policy question is how aggressive should the government be in lowering unemployment or fighting inflation. The answer depends on how one values the relative costs of inflation and unemployment.

2 Facing the problem of the business cycle with its varying levels of output and occasional episodes of high unemployment, economists split into two camps. **Interventionists** believe that government has an important role to play in fostering a more stable economy. **Noninterventionists** see little prospect that government can succeed and much risk that government actions will exacerbate the economy's fluctuations.

3 Among the alternative schools of thought, there are the following.

   a **Real business cycle theory** places the blame for fluctuations on exogenous shocks, such as the oil price increases of the 1970s. They recommend that government leave hands off, letting the money supply increase at the rate of growth of real GDP.

   b **New classical macroeconomics** stresses the concept of rational expectations, whereby households and firms recognize and offset the effects of government actions. For example, current deficits motivate households to rationally anticipate future tax increases. They save more and that counteracts the fiscal stimulus of the deficit.

   c **Monetarism** stresses the inability of government to effectively carry out an interventionist program. Monetarists emphasize the lags in determining the need for and completing the interventionist policies and also the perverse incentives that the political environment gives to governments.

4 Non-interventionists recommend tying the hands of government with **fixed rules,** such as balanced budgets and stable monetary growth. They stress that this policy would remove one source of instability, namely uncertainty surrounding future government policy. Fixing government policy mitigates the problem of **dynamic consistency** by giving households and firms confidence that government will not reverse direction when conditions change.

5 Interventionists counter with arguments that downturns can persist for a long time and that government can reduce their duration both with automatic and discretionary policies. The leading school, new Keynesianism, emphasizes the endogenous forces in the economy that amplify shocks and cause their effects to persist. These include the **multiplier-accelerator,** according to which as firms try to keep a constant inventory to sales ratio, output varies much more than sales. These variations are further amplified by the multiplier process. The economy expands rapidly, only to bump against capacity constraints at full employment, and then it slumps into recession.

6 Interventionists call for policies, such as automatic stabilizers, that alter the structure of the economy and strengthen its ability to dampen shocks. They also support the use of discretionary fiscal and monetary policy. In recessions, government should increase the budget deficit to stimulate the economy. Also, the Fed should use active monetary policy to counteract economic fluctuations. Finally, interventionists advocate labor market policies that lower the NAIRU, including promoting labor mobility, reducing some types of business regulation, and opening the economy to free trade.

7 Recent macroeconomic history illustrates the ideas of this chapter. In the early 1960s a tax cut forestalled an impending recession and brought about an extended period of growth with stable prices. Late in the decade expenditures on the Vietnam War and Great Society programs overheated the economy. The increasing inflation was magnified by oil price increases in the 1970s. In the early 1980s the Fed tightened money growth to reduce inflation at the cost of a long and deep recession. With fiscal policy constrained by a decade of large budget deficits, debate in the early 1990s centered around the aggressiveness of monetary policy.

BEHIND THE ESSENTIAL CONCEPTS

1 Economists use the term business cycle to refer to the ups and downs of the economy. Although there are certain regularities (in recessions output falls, unemployment rises, the work week shortens, and inflation slows), the length of the cycle is quite unpredictable. For example, expansions can persist from 12 to more than 100 months, but their post World War II average is 50. The end of an expansion is difficult to predict, because the probability of its continuing hardly falls as it ages. All of this makes predicting the path of the economy a hazardous and uncertain endeavor.

2 When the economy is hit with a shock, such as an increase in oil prices, households and firms take actions. Some of these actions offset the impact of the shock and dampen its effects. For example, while you would reduce your demand for gasoline, you and others might buy high-mileage cars. Similarly, firms invest in energy-saving equipment, leading to increased production and employment in that sector. All of these responses to changes in relative prices keep aggregate demand, output, and employment high. On the other hand, there are mechanisms in the economy that amplify the shock. High energy use industries contract, firms go out of business, and their workers are laid off. Income and consumption fall and the multiplier process worsens the decline. Sometimes the dampening activities dominate; for example, when the stock market crashed in 1987, the economy continued its expansion. Other times the shock is amplified and the economy is thrown into recession.

3 If inflation is undesirable, why not simply outlaw it with **wage and price controls**? Although they have been used in wartime and were tried during the Nixon administration in the early 1970s, wage and price controls do not have much support among economists. The analysis of Chapter 3 shows why. Suppose that the government mandated that no price rise more than 1 percent per year. In some markets where relative prices were stable or falling, this regulation would make no difference. But in others where relative prices were rising, market prices would bump against the ceiling and shortages would appear. An alternative policy with a lighter touch is **moral suasion**, where the government tries to persuade firms to keep prices in check.

4 The discussion of this chapter draws a clear distinction in order to emphasize the differences among economists and explore the logic of their arguments. For example, the non-interventionists forswear discretionary policy and argue for fixed rules, such as a steady growth rate for the money supply. Interventionists point out that some discretion must be used in the choice of **monetary aggregate** and in the timing of open market operations. Once room for some discretion is admitted, they recommend a more active use of monetary policy.

SELF-TEST

True or False

1 If the government attempts to keep the inflation rate below the NAIRU, unemployment will accelerate.

2 Bondholders generally advocate an aggressive anti-inflation program.

3 Interventionists favor fixed policy rules such as balanced budgets and steady money growth.

4 There is little variation in the length of expansions in the United States since World War II.

5 The probability that an expansion will end rises rapidly with the length of the expansion.

6 The probability that a contraction will end rises rapidly with the length of the contraction.

7 A 1 percent reduction in the unemployment rate requires a 2 percent reduction in the economy's output.

8 Real business cycle theory attributes the variability of output to exogenous shocks.

9 The dynamic consistency problem refers to the difficulty of maintaining full employment when wages and prices change.

10 New classical economists such as Robert Lucas have emphasized the importance of rational expectations.

11 New Keynesians differ from older Keynesian economists in their emphasis on microeconomics.

12 The effectiveness of fiscal policy may be undermined by the lags in the time it takes government to make decisions.

13 If the economy slips slightly below the NAIRU, rapid inflation results.

14 The multiplier accelerator is an example of an endogenous cause of economic downturns.

15 The NAIRU is probably around 8 percent.

Multiple Choice

1 Lowering the unemployment rate by 1 percent increases output by

a 1 percent;
b 2 percent;
c 3 percent;
d 4 percent;
e 5 percent.

2 The probability that an expansion will end in the next month

a rises rapidly as the expansion ages;
b is constant;
c falls rapidly as the expansion ages;
d rises only slightly as the expansion ages;
e falls slightly as the expansion ages.

3 The probability that a contraction will end in the next month

a rises rapidly as the contraction ages;
b is constant;
c falls rapidly as the contraction ages;
d rises only slightly as the contraction ages;
e falls slightly as the contraction ages.

4 The idea variations in output are due to exogenous shocks to which the market reacts quickly to restore full employment is a tenet of

a real business cycle theory;
b new classical macroeconomics;
c monetarism;
d New Keynesianism;
e supply-side economics.

5 The idea that actions of rational individuals offset the impact of government actions is associated with

a real business cycle theory;
b new classical macroeconomics;
c monetarism;
d New Keynesianism;
e supply-side economics.

6 Doubts about the government's ability to carry out discretionary fiscal and monetary policy are stressed by believers in

a real business cycle theory;
b new classical macroeconomics;
c monetarism;
d New Keynesianism;
e supply-side economics.

7 The belief that government can be effective with discretionary fiscal and monetary policy is part of

a real business cycle theory;
b new classical macroeconomics;
b monetarism;
d New Keynesianism;
e supply-side economics.

8 Non-interventionist economists view government as a source of instability and advocate

a binding fiscal and monetary policy with fixed policy rules;
b using fiscal and monetary policies with discretion;
c returning oversight of the money supply to the private sector;
d dynamic inconsistency;
e repealing the accelerator.

9 Which of the following is not an example of a policy rule advocated by non-interventionists?

a The money supply should increase at a fixed rate each year.
b The money supply should be adjusted to stimulate aggregate demand in recessions and constrain aggregate demand in inflationary times.
c The budget deficit should be zero.
d Government expenditures should be a fixed percentage of GDP.
e The money supply should increase with the rate of output.

10 Dynamic consistency refers to

a the fact that most business cycles follow the same pattern;
b the recommendation that government policy follow certain fixed rules;
c the issue of whether the government will carry out its promises;
d the political business-cycle explanation for economic fluctuations;
e the need to harmonize fiscal and monetary policy.

11 The New Keynesian view is that economic fluctuations are

a due to endogenous forces and predictable;

b due to random, exogenous shocks and unpredictable;
c chiefly due to misguided monetary and fiscal policy;
d due to exogenous shocks but are amplified and made persistent by the economic system;
e none of the above.

12 The accelerator model of the economy assumes that firms want to keep the

a ratio of output to labor constant;
b ratio of investment to sales constant;
c level of unemployment constant;
d rate of growth in the money supply constant;
e level of full-employment GDP constant.

13 New Keynesians advocate

a policies to lower the NAIRU, such as reducing business regulation;
b discretionary monetary policy;
c discretionary fiscal policy;
d automatic stabilizers;
e all of the above.

14 Most economists agree that in the long run the Phillips curve is

a vertical;
b horizontal;
c upward sloping;
d downward sloping;
e inelastic.

15 The idea that the economy expands rapidly until it hits capacity constraints and then plunges in recessions argues that the causes of fluctuations are

a exogenous shocks;
b endogenous;
c uncertainty over government policy;
d rational expectations;
e dynamic consistency.

16 Which of the following represents a mechanism that amplifies shock to the economy?

a The multiplier.
b Changes in relative prices lead household and firms to change their consumption and production patterns.
c Changes in interest rates affect the demand for investment.
d Households and firms with rational expectations anticipate the effects of shocks.
e Government uses discretionary monetary and fiscal policy.

17 Which of the following might reduce the NAIRU by shifting aggregate supply to the right?

a moral suasion;
b wage and price controls;
c a fixed rule mandating steady money growth;
d unemployment insurance;
e policies that promote labor mobility.

18 Which policy likely promotes labor mobility?

a training programs for displaced workers;
b moral suasion;
c regulations requiring notification in anticipation of layoffs;
d reducing business regulation;
e automatic stabilizers.

19 A period of high inflation occurred during the

a 1950s;
b 1960s;
c 1970s;
d 1980s;
e 1990s.

20 The high deficits of the 1980s precluded the use of

a discretionary monetary policy;
b discretionary fiscal policy;
c automatic stabilizers;
d fixed rules for steady money growth;
e policies to reduce the NAIRU.

Completion

1 __________ shocks such as wars or monetary restrictions start outside the economy.

2 __________ holds that prices and wages are quite flexible and recommends that the government not try to smooth economic fluctuations.

3 Households and firms that understand the structure of the economy are said to have __________.

4 The __________ refers to the inability of government to credibly promise not to change policy.

5 __________ advocate discretionary fiscal and monetary policy, automatic stabilizers, and policies to reduce the NAIRU.

6 New Keynesians stress that although externally generated shocks may hit the economy, the system can __________ them and cause the effects to __________.

7 Regulations that prohibit rapid increases in wages and prices are called __________.

8 When the government attempts to persuade firms to keep prices and wages low, it uses __________.

9 Targets, such as M1 and M2, are called __________.

10 Unemployment insurance and income taxes are examples of __________.

Answers to Self-Test

True or False

1	t	6	t	11	t
2	t	7	f	12	t
3	f	8	t	13	f
4	f	9	f	14	t
5	f	10	t	15	f

Multiple Choice

1	b	6	c	11	c	16	a
2	b	7	d	12	b	17	e
3	a	8	c	13	e	18	a
4	a	9	b	14	a	19	c
5	b	10	d	15	b	20	b

Completion

1 Exogenous
2 Real business cycle theory
3 rational expectations
4 dynamic consistency problem
5 New Keynesian economists
6 amplify, persist
7 wage and price controls
8 moral suasion
9 monetary aggregates
10 automatic stabilizers

Doing Economics: Tools and Practice Problems

The economy is continually buffeted by shocks. Consumer tastes change, new technologies are discovered, bad weather appears, or import prices surge. There are mechanisms within the economy that dampen the impact of shocks. These include flexible prices, rational expectations, labor mobility, and government policies, such as automatic stabilizers. On the other hand, there are factors such as the multiplier and accelerator that amplify shocks. Tool Kit 16.1 illustrates how these mechanisms can exacerbate instability.

Tool Kit 16.1: The Multiplier-Accelerator Process

The accelerator is the capital-output ratio. Firms in many industries try to keep this constant. The multiplier determines how much aggregate demand shifts when there is a change in spending, such as an increase in investment. These mechanisms can combine to amplify shocks. Follow these steps.

Step one: Identify the accelerator, the multiplier, and the change in spending.

Step two: Multiply the change in spending by the accelerator. This gives the extra investment needed to keep the capital-output ratio constant.

Required investment = change in spending × accelerator.

Step three: Multiply the product in step two by the multiplier. This gives the change in output resulting from the extra investment.

Change in output = new investment × multiplier.

Step four: Multiply the product in step three by the accelerator. This gives the second round of additional investment needed to keep the capital-output ratio constant.

Required investment = change in output × accelerator.

1 (Worked problem: multiplier-accelerator) Output is \$5 trillion and the capital stock equals \$15 trillion. The multiplier is 2. Suppose that a new investment project of \$10 billion is undertaken.

a Trace through the impact of this using the multiplier-accelerator.
b Do you think the process can continue unabated? Why or why not?

Step-by-step solution

Step one: Identify the accelerator, the multiplier, and the change in spending. The accelerator is 15/5 = 3 and the multiplier is 2. The initial change in spending is \$10 billion.

Step two: Multiply the change in spending by the accelerator. This gives the extra investment needed to keep the capital-output ratio constant.

Required investment = change in spending × accelerator
= \$10 billion × 3 = \$30 billion.

Step three: Multiply the product in step two by the multiplier. This gives the change in output resulting from the extra investment.

Change in output = new investment × multiplier
= \$30 billion × 2 = \$60 billion.

Step four: Multiply the product in step three by the accelerator. This gives the second round of additional investment needed to keep the capital-output ratio constant.

Required investment = change in output × accelerator
= \$60 billion × 3 = \$180 billion.

Of course, the process cannot continue too long, because the economy has capacity constraints.

2 (Practice problem: multiplier-accelerator) Output is \$2 trillion and the capital stock equals \$4 trillion. The multiplier is 2.5. Suppose that a new investment project of \$30 billion is undertaken.

a Trace through the impact of this using the multiplier-accelerator.
b Do you think the process can continue unabated? Why or why not?

3 (Practice problem: multiplier-accelerator) Output is \$7 trillion and the capital stock equals \$14 trillion. The multiplier is 1.5. Suppose that a new investment project of \$15 billion is undertaken.

a Trace through the impact of this using the multiplier-accelerator.
b Do you think the process can continue unabated? Why or why not?

Answers to Problems

2 *a* Required investment = \$30 billion × 4/2 = \$60 billion; change in output = \$60 billion × 2.5 = \$150 billion; additional investment = \$150 billion × 2 = \$300 billion.

b No. The economy will eventually run into capacity constraints.

3 *a* Required investment = \$15 billion × 14/7 = \$30 billion; change in output = \$30 billion × 1.5 = \$45 billion; additional investment = \$45 billion × 2 = \$90 billion.

b No. The economy will eventually run into capacity constraints.

Part Five

Issues in Macroeconomic Policy

Chapter 17

GROWTH AND PRODUCTIVITY

Chapter Review

This chapter of the text begins Part Five, which builds on the lessons of the previous four parts and takes a detailed look at some major macroeconomic problems. The chapter focuses on the causes of growth and the potential for continued expansion. The key concept is productivity, defined as output per worker. The next two chapters turn to problems associated with recent U.S. history: budget deficits and trade policy.

ESSENTIAL CONCEPTS

1 Although the U.S. economy has grown enormously in this century, the rate of growth in **productivity** (output per hour worked) has slowed in the past two decades. This slowdown has led to a loss of confidence in U.S. technological leadership, caused real wages (although not family incomes) to decline, and exacerbated inequality in living standards.

2 The four causes of growth in productivity are the accumulation of capital goods, an improvement in the quality of the labor force, an increase in the efficiency of resource allocation, and technological advance. Concerns about productivity slowdown have led economists to propose policies designed to restore rapid growth.

3 Figure 17.1 represents the production function, which shows the relationship between inputs and outputs. It il-

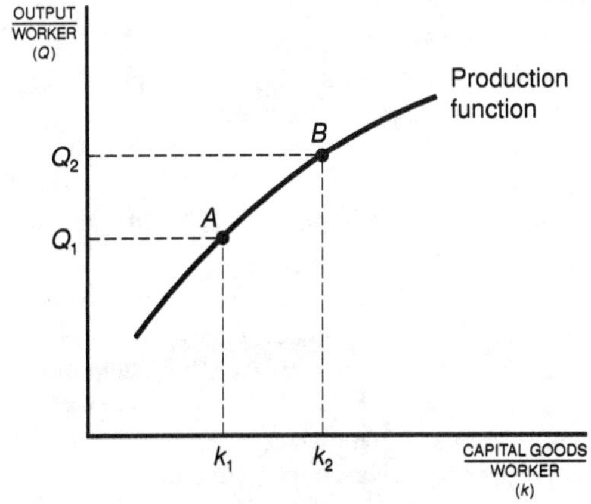

Figure 17.1

lustrates that the accumulation of capital goods per worker brings about an increase in output per worker; however, the increase is subject to the **law of diminishing returns.** Economists call the increase in captial per worker **capital deepening**.

4 Although today's world capital market allows international borrowing, **capital accumulation** clearly requires more domestic savings and investment. U.S. savings rates have fallen because more generous Social Security benefits have reduced incentives to save for retirement, while improved capital markets have made borrowing easier. In addition, savings rates have suffered because the fraction of the population in the prime savings years (45–65) has declined. Promoting savings through tax policy is likely to be ineffective because savings are relatively unresponsive to changes in after-tax returns, and investment is subject to diminishing returns. U.S. investment has fallen because of high real interest rates, an uncertain investment climate, and some unwise government regulations.

5 Investment in skills and education improves the quality of the labor force. Economists call this **human capital.** Although the U.S. educational system has considerable strengths, especially in higher education, there is concern about the level of funding, quality of teachers, and other problems.

6 The economy expanded during this century as resources moved from traditional agriculture to higher productivity employment in manufacturing. Presently, the movement is toward the service sector, where some economists think the potential for productivity gains is more limited.

7 **Technological change** shifts the production function up and can outstrip diminishing returns. Although not everyone benefits from every innovation, technological change increases productivity, employment, and living standards overall. **Learning by doing** and **research and development** are important sources of technological progress. Sound macroeconomic policies that encourage full employment, R & D funding and tax subsidies, more science and technology education, and better government regulation all promote technological advance.

8 Total factor productivity analysis helps quantify the role of different factors in increasing productivity. After accounting for the increase due to more physical and human capital, economists attribute the residual increase to improvements in technology. This analysis shows that most productivity increases are due to technological change.

9 Economic growth both creates and destroys jobs. As new techniques of producing drive old ways from the market, displaced workers see declining standards of living. The difficulty involved in transition to new lines of employment may call for government programs to finance retraining and ease the transition.

BEHIND THE ESSENTIAL CONCEPTS

1 You should be clear about the distinction between factors that lead to movements along the production function and those that cause shifts. Capital accumulation moves the economy along its production function, as shown in Figure 17.1. An improvement in technology, on the other hand, shifts the production function. In Figure 17.2, the technological advance increases output without increasing the capital stock.

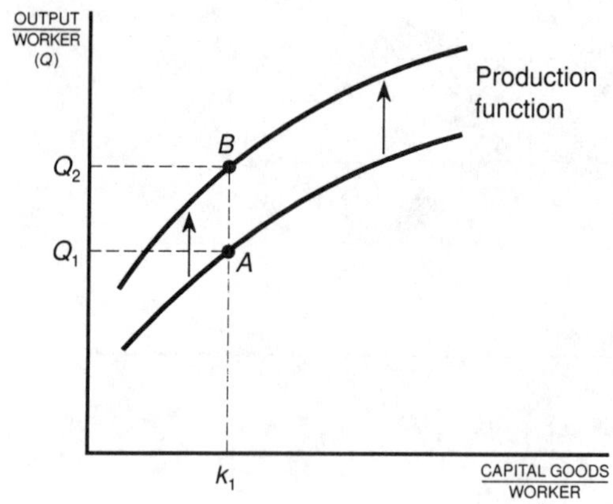

Figure 17.2

2 Productivity equals output per worker. As population grows, capital goods must be accumulated for the new workers to use. Because output per worker depends on how much capital each has to work with, this extra capital only keeps productivity constant. Additional capital goods must be accumulated to increase the amount of capital per worker, so that productivity can grow.

3 To see why U.S. savings rates are low, you need to understand the **life-cycle theory of savings.** According to this view, you save in order to consume in the future. Thus, the trade-off is current vs. future consumption. You will probably save during your working years to build up funds for retirement. Because the fraction of the population in the working years has declined, so has overall national savings. As Social Security and Medicare became more generous and individuals accumulated unexpected wealth through the increase in housing prices, the need to save for retirement declined. As private and public insurance improved, there has been less need to save for future emergencies. Many of these developments are good, but an unfortunate side effect is the accompanying disincentive to save.

4 Giving workers more capital to work with—capital deepening—accounts for only one-eighth of the growth in productivity. How do economists know this? One reason is that until recently productivity grew at a steady rate, a fact that cannot be explained by capital accumulation. If it were capital deepening, then the movement along the production function would run into diminish-

ing returns. Therefore it must be a shift in the production function, probably brought about by human capital accumulation or technological advance.

5 Some have argued that the available natural resources set up limits to growth. Certain natural resources, such as petroleum and agricultural land, are privately owned and traded in well-organized markets. These markets provide good incentives for conservation and preservation. If oil becomes scarce, for example, its price will rise, and world oil stocks will be conserved. This type of natural resource will probably not limit the world's growth. The ozone, oceans, and the genetic diversity in threatened natural habitats, on the other hand, are natural resources that are commonly owned and not traded in markets. The world's economy provides no incentive to conserve or preserve these resources. Their destruction is an external cost, not captured by prices. These global environmental problems may pose threats to increased living standards. Their solution requires cooperation among the world's governments.

SELF-TEST

True or False

1 Productivity measures output per unit of capital goods.

2 U.S. productivity growth slowed in the early 1980s.

3 Productivity in the United States is the highest among developed economies.

4 The law of diminishing returns says that technological advance must bring about slower growth in the future.

5 Capital deepening refers to increases in the number of workers per unit of capital.

6 During the 1980s taxes on capital income rose.

7 One reason for low U.S. savings rates during the 1980s is that the fraction of the population in the prime savings years declined.

8 A country's infrastructure includes its roads, bridges, sewer systems, and airports.

9 Investment in infrastructure has increased substantially during recent years.

10 Human capital refers to the plant and equipment that workers use on the job.

11 A great strength of the American educational system is its junior colleges and state universities.

12 Increased international trade raises U.S. productivity by shifting workers to export sectors where productivity is higher.

13 Everyone benefits from each technological advance through higher productivity and growth.

14 Total factor productivity analysis is used to distinguish between growth due to increases in labor and capital from that due to technological advance.

15 Market incentives ensure that such natural resources as rain forests and the global environment will be preserved.

Multiple Choice

1 Productivity is

a the extra output from the marginal worker;
b hours worked divided by output;
c output per hour worked;
d the number of workers required to produce the next unit of output;
e output divided by the total number of inputs.

2 The U.S. rate of growth in productivity

a sped up in the late 1960s and 1970s;
b has been nearly constant throughout the twentieth century;
c slowed significantly in the 1970s and early 1980s;
d increased steadily through the twentieth century;
e fell dramatically in the 1980s.

3 Over the business cycle productivity

a grows at approximately the same rate;
b falls as the economy enters a downturn, but rises faster than output as the economy commences recovery;
c rises as the economy enters a downturn, but falls as the economy recovers;
d grows faster during recessions because output falls less than employment;
e may grow at a faster or slower rate, depending upon monetary and fiscal policy.

4 The causes of growth include

a the accumulation of capital goods;
b improvement in the quality of the labor force;
c more efficient allocation of resources;
d technological advance;
e all of the above.

5 Capital deepening refers to

a increased numbers of workers per unit of capital;
b increases in capital per worker;
c decreases in capital per worker;
d reallocation of capital from less productive to more productive sectors;
e government investment in infrastructure.

6 According to the law of diminishing returns, as the economy accumulates more capital, output increases

a at the same rate as capital grows;
b at a slower rate than capital grows;
c at a faster rate than capital grows;
d only if new workers enter the labor force;
e only if the new capital equipment takes advantage of new and better technologies.

7 Savings accumulated for retirement are called

a life-cycle savings;
b target savings;
c precautionary savings;

d bequest savings;
e permanent income savings;

8 Savings accumulated for use in emergencies are called

a life-cycle savings;
b target savings;
c precautionary savings;
d bequest savings;
e permanent income savings.

9 According to the life-cycle theory, savings in the United States were low in the 1980s because

a the fraction of the population that is retired decreased;
b the fraction of the population in the prime savings years (45–65) increased;
c the fraction of the population in the prime savings years (45–65) decreased;
d the population as a whole increased;
e the fraction of the population in the prime savings years (21–44) decreased.

10 During the 1980s, tax changes

a encouraged savings by increasing the real after-tax rate of return to savings;
b encouraged savings by decreasing the real after-tax rate of return to savings;
c discouraged savings by increasing the real after-tax rate of return to savings;
d discouraged savings by decreasing the real after-tax rate of return to savings;
e had no impact on savings.

11 When the economy is at full employment, which of the following will not increase investment?

a reducing the fiscal deficit;
b shifting government spending toward infrastructure investment;
c subsidizing investment;
d using tax policies such as IRAs;
e All of the above increase investment.

12 The production function shows the relationship between

a the levels of inputs and the level of output;
b technology and growth;
c productivity and real wages;
d learning and experience;
e productivity and output.

13 During the 1980s, investment in infrastructure

a was adequate, but the level of business investment was low;
b was inadequate but was offset by a high level of business investment;
c was inadequate and exacerbated the effects of the low level of business investment;
d was low because tax changes made it more expensive;
e was adequate, as was the level of business investment.

14 Human capital refers to

a the capital goods that individuals own;
b education and skills that increase the productivity of individuals;
c fertility;
d output per hour worked;
e the capital goods that workers use on the job.

15 Which of the following is not a strength of the U.S. educational system?

a the absence of early tracking of students in lower grades;
b the relatively open system of junior colleges and state universitites;
c the research universities;
d the high percentage of students choosing majors in science and technology;
e All of the above are strengths.

16 Telecommunications deregulation and expanded international trade will

a raise overall productivity because productivity is higher than average in these sectors;
b raise overall productivity because productivity is lower than average in these sectors;
c reduce overall productivity because productivity is higher than average in these sectors;
d reduce overall productivity because productivity is lower than average in these sectors;
e leave overall productivity unchanged.

17 Technological change

a shifts the production function so that the same number of inputs produce more output;
b shifts the production function so that more output is produced but only if additional capital goods are used;
c shifts the production function so that more output is produced but only if additional workers are hired;
d increases productivity for capital but not for workers;
e increases productivity but does not shift the production function.

18 The method that attributes that part of the growth in productivity that cannot be explained by increases in labor and capital to technological advance is called

a total factor productivity analysis;
b partial productivity analysis;
c capital deepening;
d capital widening;
e sustainable development.

19 The economy's growth in output is equal to

a its growth in productivity;
b the sum of its growth in the labor force and its capital accumulation;
c the sum of its growth in hours worked and its growth in productivity;
d the marginal product of labor times the number of

hours worked plus the marginal product of capital times the capital stock;
e the sum of private savings, government savings, and net inflows of capital from abroad.

20 Sustainable development refers to growth without
a excessive technological advance;
b excessive population increase;
c excessive capital investment;
d excessive natural resource exploitation;
e all of the above.

Completion

1 __________ is defined as output per hour worked.

2 The __________ relates the levels of inputs to the level of output.

3 A country's roads, airports, bridges, sewer lines, and railroads make up its __________.

4 Economists refer to education and skills as __________.

5 Increases in capital per worker are called __________.

6 Savings for a specific purpose, such as college tuition, are called __________.

7 According to the __________, successive increments in capital lead to smaller increases in output per worker.

8 The savings that a household sets aside in case of emergency or illness are called __________.

9 Economists use __________ to discover the magnitude of technological advance.

10 Advocates of __________ seek policies to preserve the environment and natural resources while increasing living standards.

Answers to Self-Test

True or False

1 f
2 f
3 t
4 f
5 f
6 f
7 t
8 t
9 f
10 f
11 t
12 t
13 f
14 t
15 f

Multiple Choice

1 c
2 c
3 b
4 e
5 b
6 b
7 a
8 c
9 c
10 a
11 c
12 a
13 c
14 b
15 d
16 a
17 a
18 a
19 c
20 d

Completion

1 Productivity
2 production function
3 infrastructure
4 human capital
5 capital deepening
6 target savings
7 law of diminishing returns
8 precautionary savings
9 total factor productivity analysis
10 sustainable growth

Doing Economics: Tools and Practice Problems

Two important factors in the U.S. productivity slowdown are low savings and misallocated investment. In this section, we study some reasons for low savings rates: demographic changes, improved opportunities for consumer borrowing, and more generous Social Security benefits. Also, we see how favorable tax treatment of certain types of projects misallocates investment.

REASONS FOR LOW SAVINGS RATES: DEMOGRAPHIC CHANGES

One important fact about the current population of the United States is that generations, or cohorts, are of different sizes. The so-called baby boom generation, now around 35 to 50, is significantly larger than its parents' generation and also its children's generation. This fact has important implications for national savings because, as the life-cycle model predicts, individuals save at different rates during their lifetimes. Generally, people will save little in their early years, a great deal in middle age, and less when retired. When generations are of different sizes, then the national savings rate will fluctuate as the relatively large generation moves through the high-savings years.

1 (Worked problem: low savings rates) There was zero population growth in the state of Steady for centuries until now. People in Steady behave exactly as the life-cycle model predicts, saving at different rates during the successive periods of their lives. The savings supply curves for three age classes of equal size are given in Table 17.1.

Table 17.1

	Savings		
Interest rate	*Young*	*Middle*	*Old*
4%	$1,000	$20,000	$5,000
6%	$1,100	$25,000	$5,000
8%	$1,200	$30,000	$5,000
10%	$1,200	$35,000	$5,000

a Suppose the generation that is now young is twice as large as the other generations, which are of equal size. Calculate the supply of savings for the economy.

b Twenty years from now, the large generation will be middle-aged. The currently old will die and be replaced by the cohort that is now middle-aged. Calculate the supply of savings for the economy in 20 years.

c Forty years from now, the large generation will be old. The young and middle generations will be half the size of the large generation. Calculate the supply of savings in 40 years.

d Plot the three savings supplies, and notice the fluctuations in savings supply caused by the demographic transition.

Step-by-step solution

Step one (a): We find the market supply of savings by summing the total amount of savings at each interest rate. If the interest rate is 4 percent, then total savings will be

$$(2 \times \$1{,}000) + (1 \times \$20{,}000) + (1 \times \$5{,}000) = \$27{,}000.$$

We multiply the $1,000, which is the savings of the young, by 2 because there are twice as many young people.

Step two: At a 6 percent interest rate, the supply of savings is

$$(2 \times \$1{,}100) + \$25{,}000 + \$5{,}000 = \$32{,}200.$$

Continuing the process derives the entire supply of savings, which is as follows.

Interest rate	Savings
4%	$27,000
6%	$32,200
8%	$37,400
10%	$42,400

Step three (b): To find the total supply of savings 20 years from now when the large generation will be middle-aged, multiply the supply of savings in the middle-aged generation by 2 and add it to the others. For example, at a 4 percent interest rate, total savings are

$$\$1{,}000 + (2 \times \$20{,}000) + \$5{,}000 = \$46{,}000.$$

Continuing gives the supply of savings in 20 years.

Interest rate	Savings
4%	$46,000
6%	$56,100
8%	$66,200
10%	$76,200

Step four (c): Total savings 40 years from now are found by multiplying the savings of the old by 2 and adding them to the savings of the others. The supply curve is

Interest rate	Savings
4%	$31,000
6%	$36,100
8%	$41,200
10%	$46,200

Step five (d): Plot the curves. Clearly, supply shifts to the right as the large generation moves into the high-savings years and shifts to the left when they retire.

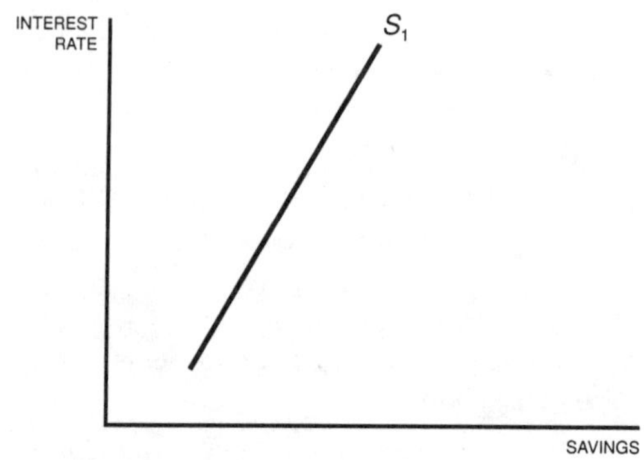

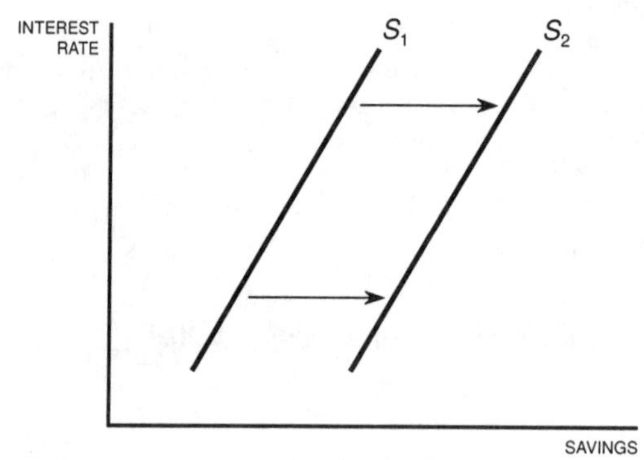

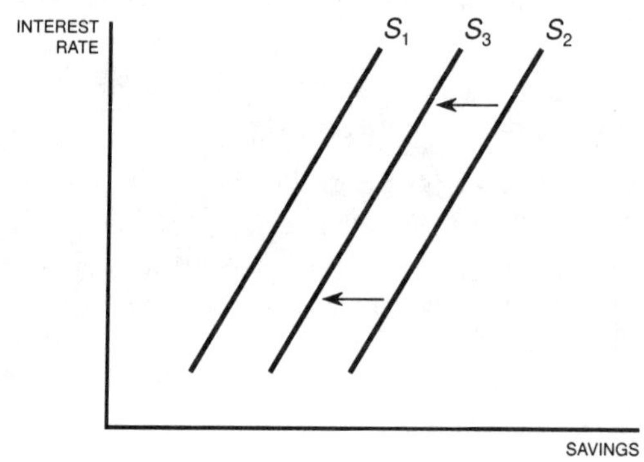

2 (Practice problem: low savings rates) Using the same data as in problem 1, suppose that a baby boomlet generation follows 40 years behind the large generation. In other words, every other generation will be twice as large as the generations were in Steady for centuries. Derive the supply of savings for the economy for 20-year intervals. Begin with a small young generation.

REASONS FOR LOW SAVINGS RATES: LOWER INTEREST RATES FOR BORROWING

One of the great strengths of the U.S. economy is its efficient capital market. Recently a combination of factors, for example credit cards, home equity loans, and bank deregulation, have increased access for borrowers. Lower interest rates for borrowers rotate part of the budget constraint out, giving the household more opportunities to consume more today. This is an application of the opportunity set with multiple constraints introduced in Chapter 2.

3 (Worked problem: low savings rates) Harold and Myla take home \$60,000 each year. They can earn 4 percent on any savings, but they must borrow at 14 percent.

a Plot their two-period budget constraint.

b A preapproved application for a new credit card arrives. The interest rate on the unpaid balance will be 8 percent. Plot their new two-period budget constraint, and compare it with the answer to part a.

Step-by-step solution

Step one (a): Plot the budget constraint with the 4 percent interest rate. The slope is 1.04, and it passes through the point \$60,000 now and \$60,000 next year.

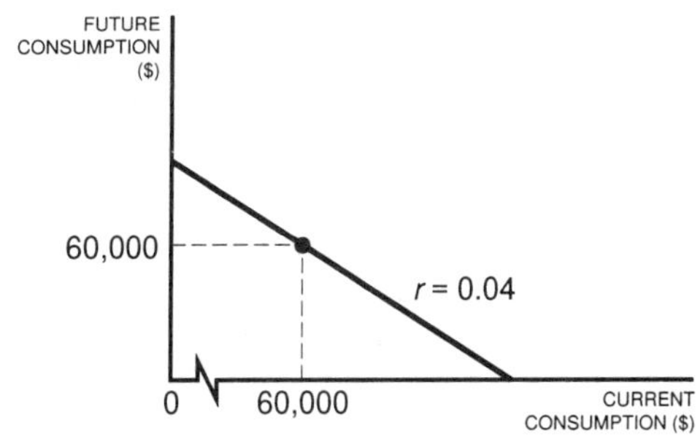

Step two: Plot the budget constraint with the 14 percent interest rate. The slope is 1.14, and it passes through the point \$60,000 now and \$60,000 next year.

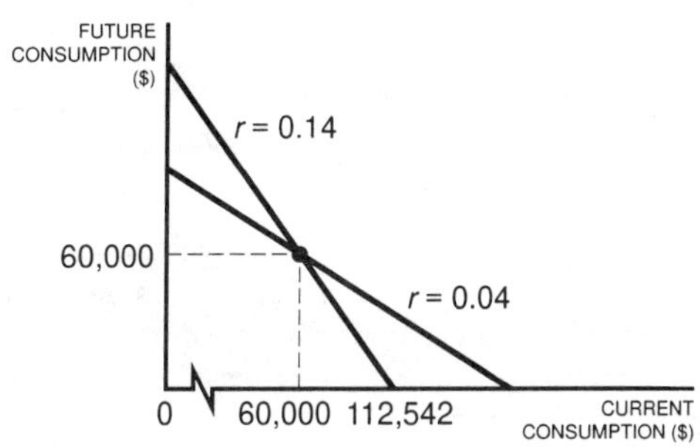

Step three: Darken the portion of each budget constraint that lies under the other constraint. This is the answer to part a.

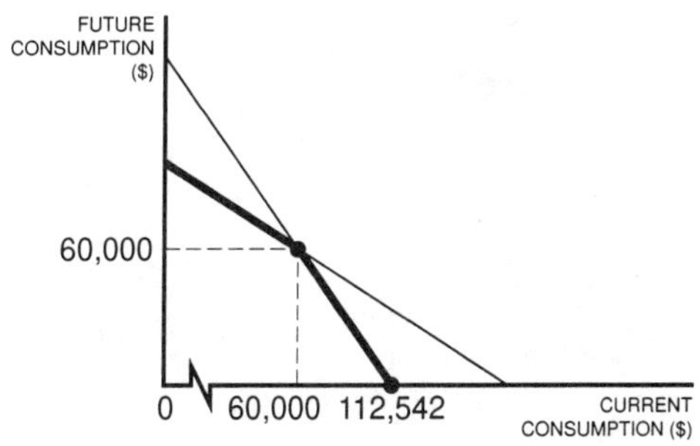

Step four (b): Again, plot the budget constraint with the 4 percent interest rate as in step one.

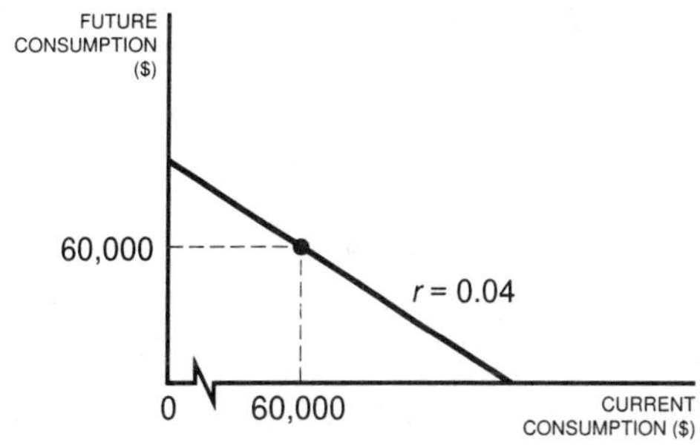

Step five: Plot the budget constraint with the 8 percent interest rate. The slope is 1.08, and it passes through the point \$60,000 now and \$60,000 next year.

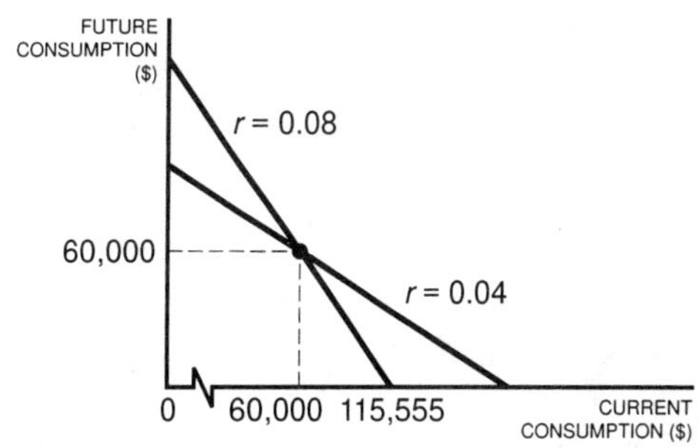

Step six: Darken the portion of each budget constraint that lies under the other constraint. This is the answer to part b.

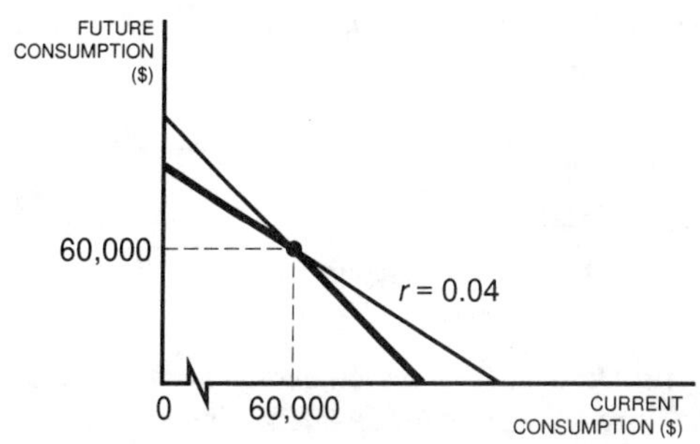

Step seven: Compare the two budget constraints. The lower interest rate gives Harold and Myla more opportunities, but the extra opportunities all involve borrowing.

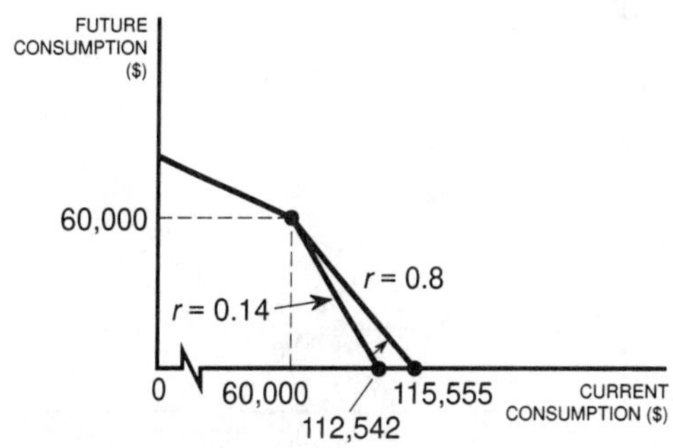

4 (Practice problem: low savings rates) Bill takes home \$10,000 this year, but he anticipates taking home \$30,000 next year. He can earn 8 percent on savings, but he has a poor credit rating and must pay 19 percent to borrow.

a Plot his two-period budget constraint.

b Through his credit union at his new job, Bill can obtain loans for 10 percent. Plot his new two-period budget constraint, and compare.

REASONS FOR LOW SAVINGS RATES: INCREASED SOCIAL SECURITY BENEFITS

Social Security certainly reduce people's incentives to save for retirement, and because it is financed on a pay-as-you-go basis, it reduces national savings. Increases in Social Security benefits during the 1970s further reduced savings incentives. The next two problems use the two-period budget constraint to illustrate this idea.

5 (Worked problem: low savings rates) Juwan has 10 years until retirement. He earns \$40,000 after taxes and expects to receive \$20,000 in Social Security benefits when he retires. He expects that over the 10-year interval until retirement he can earn a 100 percent rate of return, and he currently saves \$5,000 per year.

a Calculate the present discounted value of his Social Security benefits.

b Draw his two-period budget constraint, and plot his chosen point.

c Suppose that his Social Security benefits are increased to \$30,000. His Social Security taxes are also increased by \$5,000, which reduces his current net income to \$35,000. Draw his two-period budget constraint.

d How much does Juwan now save?

Step-by-step solution

Step one (a): The present discounted value of his benefit payment is \$20,000/(1 + *r*) = \$20,000/(1 + 1) = \$10,000.

Step two (b): Draw his two-period budget constraint. Label the axes "Current consumption" and "Retirement consumption." The slope is 1 + *r*, and the interest rate for the 10-year period is 100 percent. The horizontal intercept is the present discounted value of all income, which is \$40,000 + \$10,000 = \$50,000.

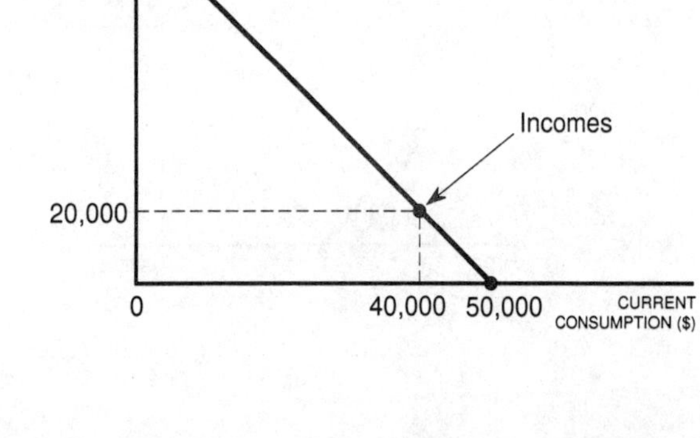

Step three: Plot his chosen point. Juwan chooses to save \$5,000; thus, he consumes \$40,000 – \$5,000 = \$35,000 now. The \$5,000 grows to \$10,000 in 10 years, which enables consumption of \$20,000 + \$10,000 = \$30,000.

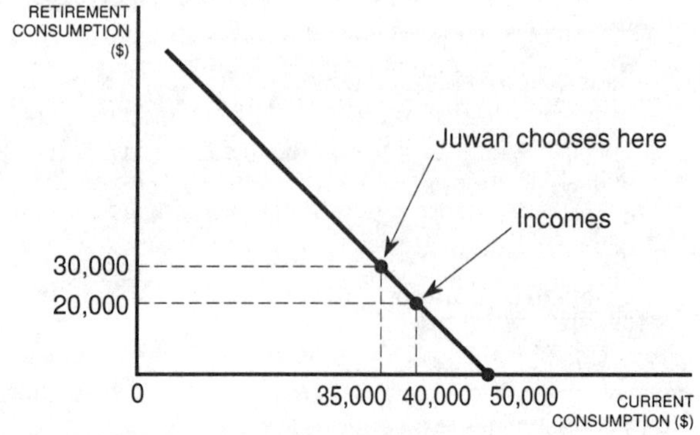

Step four (c): Plot his new budget constraint. The present discounted value of his benefits is now \$30,000/2 = \$15,000. The horizontal intercept is \$15,000 + \$35,000 = \$50,000, which is unchanged. Because neither the present discounted value of his two-period income nor the interest rate changes, the budget constraint remains the same.

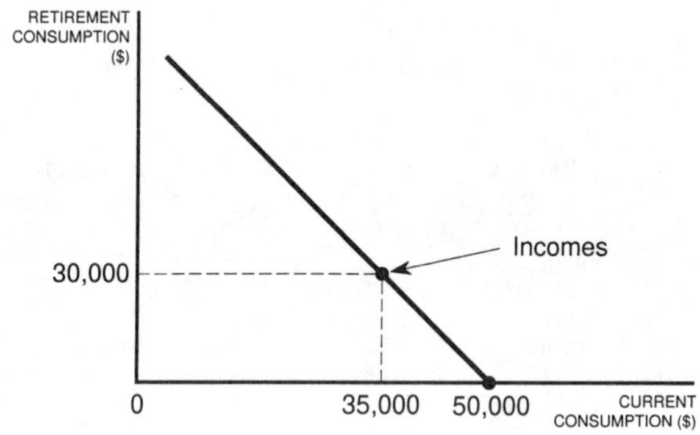

Step five (d): Because he has the same budget constraint, he chooses the same point. But he achieves this combination of current and retirement consumption by reducing his savings to zero. The increase in Social Security benefits has reduced Juwan's savings by exactly \$5,000.

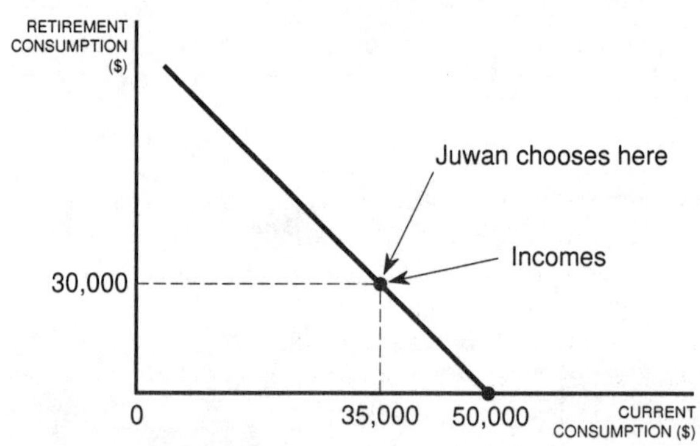

6 (Practice problem: low savings rates) Mai Lin is only 10 years from retirement. She can expect to receive $2 in interest for every $1 saved for retirement. She takes home $60,000 annually, saves $10,000 each year, and expects Social Security benefits of $30,000 when she retires.

a Plot her two-period budget constraint.
b Suppose the American Association of Retired Persons has a banner year lobbying Congress and wins a 50 percent increase in benefits. Taxes also rise so that the budget constraint does not change. How will Mai Lin's consumption now and during retirement change? How will her savings change?

Subsidies and the Allocation of Investment

Preferential tax treatment of certain types of investment can reallocate an economy's capital stock. A subsidy to a particular type of investment will raise its return, and since investors always seek the highest rate of return, they will reallocate their portfolio to take advantage of the subsidy. Tool Kit 17.1 shows the link between subsidies and reallocation.

Tool Kit 17.1: Showing How Subsidies Can Reallocate Investment

Subsidies shift up the demand for investment in the subsidized sector. This reallocates investment. These steps outline the procedure for analyzing the impact of a subsidy in one sector.

Step one: Add up the demands of each sector for capital.

Step two: Find the market-clearing rate of interest.

Step three: Substitute the market-clearing rate of interest into each demand to determine the allocation of investment that occurs without subsidy.

Step four: Add the subsidy to the demand for capital in the subsidized sector.

Step five: Repeat steps one through three.

Step six: Compare the allocation found in step five with that found in step three.

7 (Worked problem: allocation of investment) The 1986 Tax Reform Act eliminated certain provisions that gave preferential tax treatment to real estate. To see the effect that these tax subsidies have, consider Table 17.2, which gives the demands for capital by the real estate and manufacturing sectors in billions of U.S. dollars. The supply of financial capital for the two sectors is $3,900 billion.

Table 17.2

Interest rate	*Demand in the real estate sector (billions)*	*Demand in the manufacturing sector (billions)*
10%	$1,000	$2,000
9%	$1,100	$2,200
8%	$1,200	$2,400
7%	$1,300	$2,600
6%	$1,400	$2,800
5%	$1,500	$3,000
4%	$1,600	$3,200

a Find the market allocation.
b Suppose the tax subsidy amounts to an extra 3 percent annual earnings for a real estate investment. Find the allocation.
c How does the tax subsidy alter the equilibrium allocation of capital?

Step-by-step solution

Step one (a): Add the demands of each sector for capital. We choose an interest rate, and sum the quantity demanded in each sector. When the interest rate is 10 percent, the total quantity demanded is $1,000 + $2,000 = $3,000 billion. Continuing, we derive Table 17.3.

Table 17.3

Interest rate	*Real estate*	*Manufacturing*	*Total*
10%	$1,000	$2,000	$3,000
9%	$1,100	$2,200	$3,300
8%	$1,200	$2,400	$3,600
7%	$1,300	$2,600	$3,900
6%	$1,400	$2,800	$4,200
5%	$1,500	$3,000	$4,500
4%	$1,600	$3,200	$4,800

Step two: Find the market-clearing rate of interest. Quantity supplied, which is $3,900 billion, equals quantity demanded when the interest rate is 7 percent.

Step three: Substitute the market-clearing rate of interest into each demand to determine the allocation of investment. The 7 percent rate of interest brings about an allocation of $1,300 billion in real estate and $2,600 billion in manufacturing.

Step four (b): Add the subsidy to the demand for capital in the subsidized sector. Simply add 3 percent to the interest rate column for the real estate sector. Table 17.4 gives the result.

Table 17.4

Interest rate	*Real estate*
13%	$1,000
12%	$1,100
11%	$1,200
10%	$1,300
9%	$1,400
8%	$1,500
7%	$1,600

Step five: Repeat steps one through three. Table 17.5 gives the new total demand.

Table 17.5

Interest rate	*Real estate*	*Manufacturing*	*Total*
13%	$1,000	$2,000	$3,000
12%	$1,100	$2,000	$3,100
11%	$1,200	$2,000	$3,200
10%	$1,300	$2,000	$3,300
9%	$1,400	$2,200	$3,600
8%	$1,500	$2,400	$3,900
7%	$1,600	$2,600	$4,200
6%	$1,600	$2,800	$4,400
5%	$1,700	$3,000	$4,700
4%	$1,800	$3,200	$5,000

The market clears at an 8 percent interest rate with an allocation of $1,500 billion to real estate and $2,400 billion to manufacturing.

Step six (c): Compare the allocation found in step five with that found in step three. The tax subsidy increases the real estate sector's allocation from $1,300 to $1,500 billion, reducing the manufacturing sector's allocation from $2,600 billion to $2,400. In effect, $200 billion is reallocated from manufacturing to real estate.

8 (Practice problem: allocation of investment) Table 17.6 gives the demands for financial capital in the sector that produces goods for export and the sector that produces goods that compete with imports. The available supply of capital is $200 billion.

Table 17.6

Interest rate	*Demand in the import-competing sector (billions)*	*Demand in the export sector (billions)*
12%	$ 30	$ 40
11%	$ 50	$ 50
10%	$ 60	$ 60
9%	$ 70	$ 80
8%	$ 80	$ 90
7%	$100	$100
6%	$120	$110
5%	$140	$120

a Find the market allocation.
b Worried about lost market share to imports, a protectionist Congress passes a series of tax subsidies and trade barriers. Suppose that the tax subsidies and import controls amount to an extra 5 percent annual earnings for import-competing investment. Find the new allocation.
c How does the tax policy alter the equilibrium allocation of capital?

9 (Practice problem: allocation of investment) Preferential tax treatment can reallocate investment capital across regions. The enterprise zone idea offers tax breaks to firms that locate in specified areas such as impoverished inner cities. To see how this policy might work, consider Table 17.7, which gives demands for capital in enterprise zones and elsewhere. Assume that the tax breaks are worth 6 percent and the total quantity supplied equals $10 billion.

Table 17.7

Interest rate	*Demand in the the enterprise zones (billions)*	*Demand elsewhere (billions)*
9%	$0.6	$ 8.2
8%	$0.8	$ 8.6
7%	$1.0	$ 9.0
6%	$1.2	$ 9.8
5%	$1.4	$10.8
4%	$1.6	$12.0
3%	$1.8	$15.0
2%	$2.0	$20.0

a Find the market allocation without the tax breaks and the corresponding interest rate.
b Find the demand curves with the tax breaks.
c Find the new allocation brought about by the tax breaks. How does the tax policy alter the equilibrium allocation of capital?

Answers to Problems

2 With a small young generation, a large middle-aged generation, and a small old generation, the supply of savings is as follows.

Interest rate	Savings
4%	$46,000
6%	$56,100
8%	$66,200
10%	$76,200

When the young generation is large, the middle-aged generation small, and the old generation large, the supply of savings is as follows.

Interest rate	Savings
4%	$46,000
6%	$56,100
8%	$66,200
10%	$76,200

4 *a*

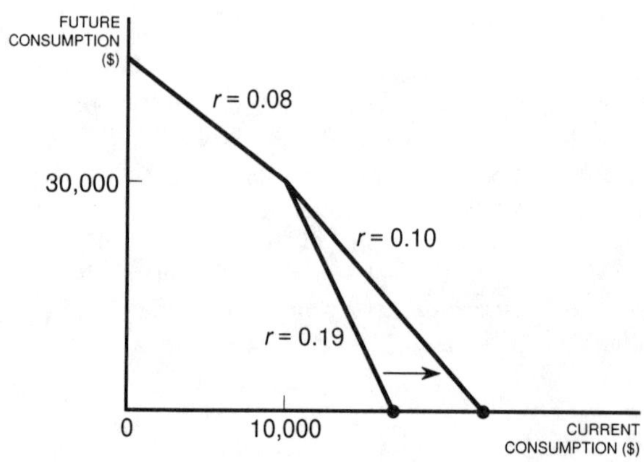

b With the lower interest rate for borrowing, Bill's budget constraint rotates out, giving him new opportunities, all of which involve borrowing more.

6 *a*

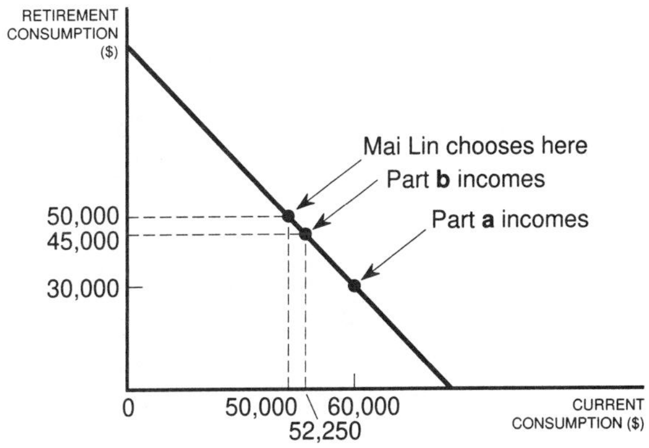

b The budget constraint does not change, so neither do her current and retirement consumptions. The increase in Social Security benefits reduces her savings by $7,500.

8 *a* The equilibrium interest rate is 7 percent, and the allocation is $100 billion to each sector.

b Table 17.8 gives the demands with the tax subsidy and trade protection policies.

Table 17.8

Interest rate	*Imports*	*Exports*	*Total*
17%	$ 30	$40	$ 70
16%	$ 50	$40	$ 90
15%	$ 60	$40	$100
14%	$ 70	$40	$110
13%	$ 80	$40	$120
12%	$100	$40	$140
11%	$120	$50	$170
10%	$140	$60	$200
9%	$140	$80	$220
8%	$140	$90	$220

c The market clears at an interest rate of 10 percent with an allocation of $140 billion to the import-competing sector and $60 billion to the export sector. The policies shift $40 billion from the export to the import-competing sector.

9 *a* The market allocation without the enterprise zone tax breaks is $1 billion in the zones and $9 billion elsewhere and the interest rate is 7 percent.

b Table 17.9 gives the demands with the tax breaks.

Table 17.9

Interest rate	*Demand in the enterprise zones*	*Demand elsewhere*	*Total*
15%	$0.6	$ 8.2	$ 8.8
14%	$0.8	$ 8.2	$ 9.0
13%	$1.0	$ 8.2	$ 9.2
12%	$1.2	$ 8.2	$ 9.4
11%	$1.4	$ 8.2	$ 9.6
10%	$1.6	$ 8.2	$ 9.8
9%	$1.8	$ 8.2	$10.0
8%	$2.0	$ 8.6	$10.6
7%	$2.0	$ 9.0	$11.0
6%	$2.0	$ 9.8	$11.8
5%	$2.0	$10.8	$12.8

c The new equilibrium allocation is $1.8 billion to the enterprise zones and $8.2 billion elsewhere at an equilibrium interest rate of 9 percent. The tax breaks shift $0.8 billion to the zones from elsewhere in the economy.

Chapter 18

DEFICITS AND DEFICIT REDUCTION

Chapter Review

The U.S. budget deficit exploded during the 1980s. This chapter discusses some of the causes and consequences and also looks into proposals to solve the deficit problem. How the deficit affects the economy, especially its future, is a key topic. There is also discussion of the long-term fiscal problems facing the United States.

ESSENTIAL CONCEPTS

1 **Federal budget deficits** rose dramatically during the 1980s, increasing the nation's debt to record levels, even though the 1980s were a time of peace and relative prosperity. The high deficits can be linked to five causes. Taxes were reduced, defense spending increased, Social Security and Medicare payments grew, more was spent on health care, and the accumulated debt required higher interest payments.

2 Government borrowing can affect future generations in three ways. First, the burden can be shifted directly to the future generation by increasing taxes after the current generation has retired. Second, borrowing drives up interest rates and crowds out private investment. Finally, since much of the borrowing comes from abroad and foreign investors are attracted by higher U.S. interest rates, current borrowing increases foreign indebtedness. Repayment of foreign debt then requires reduced future living standards. The Barro-Ricardo argument that private savings will offset the future effects of current deficits has not proven true.

3 Reducing the budget deficit requires either cutting expenditures or increasing taxes. Federal government expenditures fall into two categories. **Discretionary spending** is authorized on an annual basis and it includes defense, education, training, and the funds necessary to run the government. **Nondiscretionary spending** comprises interest on the debt and **entitlements,** which are automatic payments to individuals who meet certain legal requirements. These programs include Social Security, Medicare, Medicaid, food stamps, and unemployment insurance.

4 Another approach is to deal with the budgetary process itself. The Budget Enforcement Act mandates that the Congressional Budget Office calculate the cost of each new program. The line item veto gives the President the power to veto any particular line item of the budget. Finally, many advocate keeping a capital budget for the

government. Parallel with business accounting practices, this reform would distinguish between government investments and government consumption expenditures.

5 The long-term budgetary problem in the United States is entitlement spending for Social Security and Medicare, because of anticipated increases in both the size of the elderly population and health care costs. Proposed reforms in Social Security include reducing benefits by increasing the retirement age, means testing for benefits, and investing Social Security Trust Fund assets in equities. On the Medicare issue one set of reforms, including Medical Savings Accounts, focuses on patient incentives. Managed care moves in another direction, seeking to give doctors incentives to reduce the use and expense of medical care. Ultimately, the problem rests on the question of how much of society's resources should be allocated to health care for the elderly, especially for expensive technological innovations.

BEHIND THE ESSENTIAL CONCEPTS

1 If you are the age of the typical college student, say 19 or 20, you will pay for some of the current federal budget deficit. Government borrowing is sopping up private savings and crowding out private investment. Currently capital goods are not purchased, research and development is not undertaken, and businesses are not started. Furthermore, the trade deficit caused by the budget deficits is financed by selling off U.S. assets. Reduced investment and the sale of assets will result in lower living standards in the future.

2 The distinction between stocks and flows is important in this chapter. The annual federal buget deficit is a flow, and the corresponding stock is the federal debt, which is the sum of past accumulated deficits. The trade deficit is also a flow variable. It is the difference between what U.S. households and firms import and export. The basic trade identity makes it clear that the trade deficit is financed by capital flows. Now capital flows into the United States when foreign nationals buy U.S. assets and when U.S. firms borrow from abroad. Both of these activities affect the credit position of the United States. The relationship between these trade deficits and the U.S. status as a debtor nation is that the accumulated trade deficits have led to a stock of foreign indebtedness.

3 The Barro-Ricardo argument claims that current budget deficits have no impact. Specifically, whether government expenditures are financed by taxes or borrowing makes no difference in either the present or the future. If the spending is paid for with taxes, then current disposable income and consumption fall. If the government borrows, then rational individuals anticipate future taxes and put aside the money now. This increase in savings is just enough to pay for the future tax liability. In either case, the impact on the economy is the same.

4 There is an important distinction between solving the current budget deficit problem and setting up incentives to ensure that future deficit problems will not arise. Our current deficit problem came about, in part, because of unrealistic tax and entitlement decisions. Social Security and Medicare increases and tax cuts were made without adequate consideration of their budgetary consequences. The Budget Enforcement Act addresses this problem by forcing Congress to face the costs of any new program. Congress can choose to go ahead with the programs, but at least there is a scoring of the costs.

5 The main worry about budget deficits is how they affect the future standard of living. Of course, we want the current Congress to have incentives to recognize this. According to current procedures, however, there is little reason to recognize the future benefits of current government investments, because a dollar of current spending counts the same whether it is for investment or consumption. This is why many economists advocate capital budgeting. It would require computing the change in the value of government assets, giving incentives to create and maintain the infrastructure.

SELF-TEST

True or False

1 During the 1980s the U.S. budget deficit was high, but there have been other episodes of equally high peacetime deficits.

2 Early in the Reagan administration, taxes were cut well below their 1970s levels.

3 As a fraction of GDP, defense spending is higher today than it was during the Vietnam War.

4 Government borrowing does not matter because the bonds sold to finance the deficit are purchased by Americans.

5 Government borrowing drives up the interest rate and crowds out private investment.

6 The largest single component of government spending is national defense.

7 Welfare payments other than Medicaid account for slightly more than 25 percent of federal government expenditures.

8 The Barro-Ricardo argument claims that when the government runs a deficit, private savings increase to offset the government dissaving.

9 Defense spending is an example of a nondiscretionary expenditure.

10 The Budget Enforcement Act effectively outlaws budget deficits.

11 The United States government computes and publishes a capital budget each year.

12 Over the next few decades the proportion of the population that is elderly will remain about what it is today.

13 While health care costs have been rising, the rate of increase is no faster than the rate of inflation.

14 The Social Security Trust Fund currently is not invested in equities.

15 Managed care refers to reforms designed to give health care providers incentives to economize on health care.

Multiple Choice

1 During the 1980s, the United States ran

a very high federal budget deficits;
b very high federal budget surpluses;
c typical peacetime federal budget surpluses;
d typical peacetime federal budget deficits;
e balanced federal budgets.

2 The tax cuts enacted early in the Reagan presidency reduced the percentage of GDP taken in taxes

a to historically low levels;
b well below the levels taken in the 1970s;
c to about the level of the 1970s;
d to levels somewhat higher than in the 1970s;
e none of the above.

3 Which federal expenditures increased during the 1980s?

a defense;
b Social Security;
c Medicare;
d interest on the debt;
e all of the above.

4 Federal budget deficits

a increase private investment by reducing the interest rate;
b crowd out private investment by increasing the interest rate;
c may not reduce future output if the borrowing finances government investments such as roads or research and development;
d always reduce future consumption because future generations must pay taxes to repay the debt;
e b and c.

5 Government borrowing to finance the deficit

a crowds out both foreign and U.S. private investment;
b crowds out U.S. private investment by raising the interest rate but causes increased foreign investment;
c crowds out foreign investment by increasing the exchange rate but has no effect on U.S. private investment;
d attracts foreign investment, and the extra competition leads to increased U.S. private investment;
e causes the exchange rate to depreciate.

6 Which of the following is not true?

a The burden of current government deficits necessarily falls on the current generation.
b The burden of current government deficits may be shifted to future generations if taxes are increased after the current generation retires.
c The burden of current government deficits may be shifted to future generations if current borrowing replaces private investment.
d The burden of current government deficits may be shifted to future generations if current borrowing increases foreign indebtedness.
e All of the above are true.

7 The largest single component of government expenditure is

a defense;
b interest on the debt;
c Social Security;
d education;
e welfare.

8 The Barro-Ricardo argument states that

a government deficits crowd out private investment and consumption;
b the burden of government deficits falls on future generations;
c private savings increase to offset government deficits;
d increases in interest rates crowd out private investment;
e the deficit does not matter because we owe it to ourselves.

9 Which of the following is an example of discretionary spending?

a Medicare;
b Medicaid;
c Social Security;
d interest on the national debt;
e none of the above.

10 Which of the following is an example of nondiscretionary spending?

a defense expenditures;
b most education and training expenditures;
c money for roads and bridges;
d Medicare;
e money to run the government.

11 Which of the following is an example of an entitlement?

a Medicare;
b Medicaid;
c Social Security;
d Aid to Families with Dependent Children (welfare);
e all of the above.

12 The Budget Enforcement Act requires that

a the federal government budget is balanced each year;
b the federal government budget is balanced on average over each business cycle;

c the Congressional Budget Office calculate the cost of any new government program;
d the federal government must compute and balance its capital budget;
e the President be given the line item veto.

13 A capital budget

a keeps track of government investment expenditures;
b does not distinguish between government investments and government consumption expenditures;
c must equal the trade deficit, according to the basic trade identity;
d must always balance, according to the Budget Enforcement Act;
e gives the President the line item veto.

14 The line item veto

a keeps track of government investment expenditures;
b gives the President power to veto appropriations bills;
c repeals Congress's authority to override presidential vetoes;
d gives the Congressional Budget Office the power to veto new programs;
e gives the President the power to veto particular spending items in large appropriations bills.

15 Because of the increase in life expectancy,

a the proportion of elderly in the population will increase;
b the number of workers per retired person will decrease;
c Medicare payments will increase;
d Social Security payments will increase;
e all of the above.

16 The fraction of the Social Security Trust Fund currently invested in equities is about

a 0;
b one-fourth;
c one-half;
d three-fourths;
e 1.

17 During the 1980s and 1990s health care costs

a have increased on a pace with inflation;
b have increased less rapidly than inflation;
c have increased more rapidly than inflation;
d have fallen;
e have remained constant.

18 Means testing of Social Security and Medicare benefits refers to

a requiring all recipients to produce documents verifying their eligibility;
b charging beneficiaries a copayment for medical tests;
c ensuring that the trust funds have sufficient means to pay all current bills;
d limiting payments to doctors and hospitals;
e requiring higher payments from those with more income.

19 Programs that give health care providers greater incentive to economize on costs are called

a means testing;
b entitlements;
c managed care;
d capital budgeting;
e fee-for-service.

20 The proposal for Medical Savings Accounts would

a reduce payments to health care providers;
b limit payments for costly new technologies;
c give greater incentives to health care providers;
d allow individuals to set aside money in a tax-exempt account to meet medical expenses;
e invest the Social Security Trust Fund money in equities.

Completion

1 The difference between government expenditures and revenues is the __________.

2 The total accumulated sum of past deficits is the __________.

3 The __________ equals what the budget deficit would be if the economy were at full employment.

4 The __________ subtracts interest payments from the budget deficit.

5 The program that pays health costs for the elderly is called __________.

6 The __________ says that private savings rise to offset government deficits.

7 Interest on the government debt is an example of __________.

8 __________ gives incentives to health care providers to economize on health care.

9 __________ allow households to put aside money in tax-free accounts to pay for medical expenses.

10 __________ refers to requiring upper income recipients to pay more for Medicare.

Answers to Self-Test

True or False

1	f	6	f	11	f
2	f	7	f	12	f
3	f	8	t	13	f
4	f	9	f	14	t
5	t	10	f	15	t

Multiple Choice

1	a	6	a	11	e	16	a
2	c	7	c	12	c	17	c
3	e	8	c	13	a	18	e
4	e	9	e	14	e	19	c
5	b	10	d	15	e	20	d

Completion

1 budget deficit
2 government debt

3 structural deficit
4 primary deficit
5 Medicare
6 Barro-Ricardo argument
7 nondiscretionary spending
8 Managed care
9 Medical Savings Accounts
10 Means testing

Doing Economics: Tools and Practice Problems

The budget deficit may seem like a simple calculation: government spending minus government revenues. For different purposes, however, economists argue for different measures. We know that automatic stabilizers, such as unemployment insurance, bring about an increase in the budget deficit during recessions, even though there is no change in law. The structural deficit corrects for the effects of economic downturns by calculating what the budget deficit would be if the economy were at full employment. Another measure, the inflation-adjusted deficit, looks at the change in the real value of the outstanding government debt. Finally, the primary deficit ignores interest on the current debt. Tool Kit 18.1 shows how to keep all of this straight.

Tool Kit 18.1: Calculating the Deficits

The various deficit measures are explained. Follow the steps.

Step one: Identify the average tax rate, national income, full-employment national income, government expenditures, the outstanding debt, the nominal interest rate, and the inflation rate.

Step two: Calculate the budget deficit. This is just government revenues less its expenditures.

Budget deficit = government expenditures
– average tax rate × national income.

Step three: Calculate the structural deficit. Here we use what revenues would be if the economy were at full employment.

Structural deficit = government expenditures
– average tax rate × full employment income.

Step four: Calculate the inflation-adjusted deficit. This measure takes into account the change in the real value of the outstanding debt.

Inflation-adjusted deficit = government expenditures
– average tax rate × national income
– inflation rate × outstanding debt.

Step five: Calculate the primary deficit. This measure ignores interest on the debt.

Primary deficit = government expenditures
– average tax rate × national income
– nominal interest rate × outstanding debt.

1 (Worked problem: deficits) The Costa Guanoan Economic Report of the Dictator gives the following information.

Table 18.1

National income	\$60 million
Average tax rate	20 percent
Full-employment national income	\$80 million
Government expenditures	\$25 million
Outstanding debt	\$80 million
Inflation rate	10 percent
Nominal interest rate	15 percent

a Calculate the budget deficit.
b Calculate the structural deficit.
c Calculate the inflation-adjusted deficit.
d Calculate the primary deficit.

Step-by-step solution

Step one: Identify the average tax rate, national income, full-employment national income, government expenditures, the outstanding debt, the nominal interest rate, and the inflation rate. All are given in Table 18.1.

Step two: Calculate the budget deficit.

Budget deficit = government expenditures
– average tax rate × national income
= 25 – 0.20 × 60 = \$13 million.

Step three: Calculate the structural deficit.

Structural deficit = government expenditures
– average tax rate × full employment income
= 25 – 0.20 × 80 = \$9 million.

Step four: Calculate the inflation-adjusted deficit.

Inflation-adjusted deficit = government expenditures
– average tax rate × national income
– inflation rate × outstanding debt
= 25 – 0.20 × 60 – 0.10 × 80 = \$5 million.

Step five: Calculate the primary deficit.

Primary deficit = government expenditures
– average tax rate × national income
– nominal interest rate × outstanding debt
= 25 – 0.20 × 60 – 0.15 × 80 = \$1 million.

2 (Practice problem: deficits) The El Dorado Economic Report of the Government gives the following information.

Table 18.2

National income	\$8 billion
Average tax rate	25 percent
Full-employment national income	\$8 billion
Government expenditures	\$4 billion
Outstanding debt	\$6 billion
Inflation rate	20 percent
Nominal interest rate	30 percent

a Calculate the budget deficit.
b Calculate the structural deficit.
c Calculate the inflation-adjusted deficit.
d Calculate the primary deficit.

3 (Practice problem: deficits) The Erehwemos Economic Report of the Oligarchy gives the following information.

Table 18.3

National income	\$80 billion
Average tax rate	40 percent
Full-employment national income	\$100 billion
Government expenditures	\$50 billion
Outstanding debt	\$500 billion
Inflation rate	5 percent
Nominal interest rate	10 percent

a Calculate the budget deficit.
b Calculate the structural deficit.
c Calculate the inflation-adjusted deficit.
d Calculate the primary deficit.

Answers to Problems

2 *a* Budget deficit = 4 – 0.25 × 8 = \$2 billion.
b Structural deficit = 4 – 0.25 × 8 = \$2 billion.
c Inflation-adjusted deficit = 4 – 0.25 × 8 – 0.20 × 6 = \$0.8 billion.
d Primary deficit = 4 – 0.25 × 8 – 0.30 × 6 = \$0.2 billion.

3 *a* Budget deficit = 50 – 0.40 × 80 = \$18 billion.
b Structural deficit = 50 – 0.40 × 100 = \$10 billion.
c Inflation-adjusted deficit = 50 – 0.40 × 80 – 0.05 × 500 = \$7 billion surplus.
d Primary deficit = 50 – 0.40 × 80 – 0.10 × 500 = \$32 billion surplus.

Chapter 19

TRADE POLICY

Chapter Review

Governments affect the flows of traded goods through tariffs, quotas, other nontariff barriers, and a series of fair trade laws. This chapter discusses how these measures affect markets, who wins, who loses, and their political rationale. There is also discussion of the major international institutions governing trade.

ESSENTIAL CONCEPTS

1 Countries practicing protection use commercial policies to restrict imports. These trade barriers include tariffs, quotas, other nontariff barriers, and fair trade laws. Tariffs, which are taxes on imported goods, raise domestic prices, injuring consumers while providing some benefit to producers. Overall the economy suffers, losing consumer surplus and wasting resources producing goods that could be imported more cheaply.

2 Quotas are limits on the quantity of imports. By restricting supply they force up prices and lead to the same types of deadweight burdens as do tariffs. Rather than collecting tariff revenues, the government confers on certain firms extra profits from importing, called quota rents. Other nontariff barriers, such as voluntary export restraints (VERs), have similar effects. In the case of VERs the quota rent accrues to foreign exporters.

3 While ostensibly designed to promote competition, fair trade laws are protectionist. These include anti-dumping laws that prohibit the sale of imports below the cost of production and subsidies to domestic producers, usually justified to offset the impact of foreign subsidies.

4 The political rationale for trade lies in the fact that certain groups lose from trade. Competition from imports may lead firms to close plants or even cease operations. Their displaced workers suffer large losses. Also, foreign competition may drive down wages in certain sectors or erode market power. Lost profits and laid-off unionized workers create a demand for protectionist relief.

5 Other arguments for protection may have some limited validity. The **infant industry argument** claims that import barriers may allow a young industry time to acquire the experience necessary to be competitive on the world market. Usually, however, direct assistance is a better policy. There is also the strategic trade argument,

whereby protected domestic firms exploit economies of scale to undercut their foreign competitors.

6 After World War II the **General Agreement on Tariffs and Trade (GATT)** was founded to reduce trade barriers. Its three basic principles were reciprocity, nondiscrimination, and transparency, and it succeeded in greatly reducing tariffs. In 1995 it was replaced by the **World Trade Organization (WTO)** as attention turned to nontariff barriers and intellectual property. The WTO has procedures for adjudicating trade disputes.

7 Regional trading blocs, such as the **European Union** and the **North American Free Trade Agreement (NAFTA),** remove trading barriers for member countries, and this brings about the benefits of trade creation, expanded trade within the bloc. On the other hand, the discrimination against those outside the bloc causes trade diversion. Goods that may be less costly from outsiders are produced within the bloc.

BEHIND THE ESSENTIAL CONCEPTS

1 A tariff is just a tax on imports, and we analyze its effects in the same way that we analyze a tax on a domestic good. As you recall from Chapter 3, if the suppliers must pay the tax, it shifts the supply curve up by the amount of the tax and the price rises to the intersection of the demand and the new supply. In the case of a tariff the price is set on the world market. This price simply shifts up by the amount of the tariff, and the new equilibrium is read off the demand and supply curves. There is more on how to do this in Tool Kit 19.1.

2 Tariffs, quotas, and voluntary export restraints are equivalent in one sense. Each raises prices to consumers, reduces the quantity demanded, reduces imports, and increases domestic supply. In another way, however, they are quite different. Tariff revenue is collected by the government. In the case of quotas there is an equivalent amount of money collected by importers. They can earn excess profits because the quota protects them from competition. In the case of voluntary export restraints, the two governments force the foreign suppliers to restrict output. But we know from monopoly theory that this results in higher prices and monopoly profits. In each case there are extra revenues collected: tariff revenue to the government, quota rents to the licensed importer, and VER excess profits to foreign firms.

3 When a country enters a regional trading bloc, it eliminates trade barriers with the other members, while keeping barriers up against nonmembers. This discrimination favors production within the bloc. Trade that otherwise would have occurred with nonmember countries is diverted to member countries. Since this likely goes against the principle of comparative advantage, there is a waste. Balanced against this inefficiency are the benefits of expanded trade among member countries. When trade agreements are global, however, there is no downside. It is all trade creation.

4 Why do we care about dumping? After all, if foreign producers want to sell us goods below cost, then should we not just accept their generosity? One fear is that after driving domestic producers from the market, the foreign firms will take advantage of their monopoly position and raise prices. This practice is called predatory pricing and it is illegal in the United States. In theory, anti-dumping laws make the practice illegal for foreign firms. In practice, however, these laws are used to protect domestic firms from low-cost foreign competition.

5 The infant industry argument claims that temporary protection may allow firms to grow more efficient and ultimately to prosper. The policy is like an investment, sacrificing the current gains from importing cheaper goods for long-run profitability. Of course, it should only be applied if the present value of the future profits exceeds the current costs. But in that case firms in the industry should be able to raise capital to stay in business while they are gaining experience. Governments are in no better position to evaluate the prospects of infant industries than the capital market.

SELF-TEST

True or False

1 Policies that restrict the import of foreign goods are examples of protection.

2 Tariffs are taxes on exports.

3 Tariffs reduce the quantity supplied domestically.

4 Although they also result in higher prices, quotas differ from tariffs in that firms licensed to import earn quota rents.

5 Voluntary export restraints allow foreign firms to collude and raise prices.

6 Anti-dumping laws make it illegal to sell goods abroad below the cost of production.

7 Predatory pricing refers to selling below cost in order to drive rivals from the markets.

8 Strategic trade theory points out the possibility of protecting domestic firms so that they can exploit economies of scale to undercut their foreign rivals.

9 When there is free trade between two countries, the net benefits are positive in each country.

10 When there is free trade between two countries, all individuals gain.

11 Most of the recent decline in wages in the United States is due to international trade.

12 Regional trading blocs can divert trade from nonmember to member countries.

13 Regional trading blocs expand trade both among member and nonmember countries.

14 The GATT successfully reduced tariffs among most of the world's countries.

15 The WTO adjudicates trade disputes among the United States, Canada, and Mexico.

Multiple Choice

1 Which of the following are trade barriers?

a tariffs;
b quotas;
c voluntary export restraints;
d fair trade laws;
e all of the above.

2 Policies that affect imports or exports are called

a commercial policies;
b protection;
c free trade;
d nontariff barriers;
e fair trade laws.

3 Tariffs are

a taxes on exports;
b subsidies on exports;
c taxes on imports;
d subsidies on imports;
e voluntary export restraints.

4 When a small country imposes a tariff, the domestic price

a rises by more than the amount of the tariff;
b rises by an amount equal to the tariff;
c rises by less than the amount of the tariff;
d stays the same because only imported goods pay the tariff;
e falls.

5 Tariffs, quotas, and voluntary exports restraints are similar in that each

a raises domestic prices;
b reduces domestic prices;
c reduces domestic consumption;
d increases domestic output;
e a, c, and d.

6 When a tariff is imposed the net loss to the United States includes

a tariff revenues;
b lost consumer surplus due to less consumption of the good;
c higher costs of producing the good domestically;
d b and c;
e all of the above.

7 When a quota is imposed, the net loss to the United States includes

a quota rents;
b lost consumer surplus due to less consumption of the good;
c higher costs of producing the good domestically;
d b and c;
e all of the above.

8 When a voluntary exports restraint is imposed, the net loss to the United States includes

a excess profits;
b lost consumer surplus due to less consumption of the good;
c higher costs of producing the good domestically;
d b and c;
e all of the above.

9 Dumping refers to

a selling goods abroad for less than the going price;
b selling goods abroad without paying tariffs;
c selling goods abroad below the cost of production;
d selling goods abroad above the cost of production;
e selling excess inventories abroad.

10 Predatory pricing refers to

a pricing above cost to reap excess profits;
b pricing below cost to drive rivals from the market;
c bribing politicians to receive licenses to import;
d not reducing price when the firm is subsidized;
e using intellectual property without paying for it.

11 Which of the following groups generally favors free trade?

a exporters;
b unions;
c firms earning monopoly profits;
d workers in import industries;
e low-wage workers.

12 Economists estimate that the percentage of the recent fall in wages that is due to trade is

a 10;
b 20;
c 30;
d 50;
e 100.

13 Beggar-thy-neighbor policies attempt to

a increase national consumption by reducing exports;
b increase national savings by reducing foreign aid;
c increase national output by reducing imports;
d decrease national savings by reducing imports;
e decrease the budget deficit by exporting taxes.

14 During the Great Depression, the Hawley-Smoot tariffs

a raised tariffs on imported goods;
b drastically reduced imports;
c led to foreign retaliation;
d contributed to the economic downturn;
e all of the above.

15 During the first years of the Great Depression

a U.S. imports fell;
b U.S. exports fell;
c U.S. GDP fell;
d all of the above;
e none of the above.

16 Which of the following is not a result of international trade in the United States?

a lower wages for skilled workers;

b lower wages for unskilled workers;
c lower profits in industries where competition is limited;
d lower wages in industries where competition is limited;
e none of the above.

17 The infant industry argument advocates

a temporary protection while firms gain experience needed to compete with foreign rivals;
b lowering prices to drive foreign rivals out of business;
c protection so that domestic firms can take advantage of economies of scale;
d subsidizing firms that face competition from foreign firms subsidized by their governments;
e quotas rather than tariffs.

18 Strategic trade theory can be used to argue for

a temporary protection while firms gain experience needed to compete with foreign rivals;
b lowering prices to drive foreign rivals out of business;
c protection so that domestic firms can take advantage of economies of scale;
d subsidizing firms that face competition from foreign firms subsidized by their governments;
e quotas rather than tariffs.

19 The organization established after World War II for the purpose of reducing trade barriers is called

a WTO;
b GATT;
c NAFTA;
d European Union;
e OECD.

20 Regional trading blocs can lead to

a the diversion of trade from member to nonmember countries;
b the diversion of trade from nonmember to member countries;
c the creation of trade among member countries;
d the creation of trade between member and nonmember countries;
e b and c.

Completion

1 __________ involves restricting the import of foreign goods.

2 Policies that affect imports or exports are called __________.

3 Taxes on imports are called __________.

4 When the government imposes quotas, firms licensed to import may earn extra profits, called __________.

5 An agreement whereby foreign firms limit sales of their good in domestic markets is called a __________.

6 Selling products abroad at prices below the cost of production is called __________.

7 The __________ proposes temporary protection while firms gain experience to become competitive.

8 Formed after World War II, the __________ promoted free trade among most of the world's countries.

9 The global trading organization that directed attention toward nontariff barriers, agricultural subsidies, and intellectual property is called __________.

10 Regional trading blocs, such as NAFTA or the European Union, expand trade within the bloc but the net benefits may not be positive if there is too much __________.

Answers to Self-Test

True or False

1	t	6	t	11	f
2	f	7	t	12	t
3	f	8	t	13	f
4	t	9	t	14	t
5	t	10	f	15	f

Multiple Choice

1	e	6	d	11	a	16	a
2	a	7	d	12	b	17	a
3	c	8	e	13	c	18	c
4	b	9	c	14	e	19	b
5	e	10	b	15	d	20	e

Completion

1 Protection
2 commercial policies
3 tariffs
4 quota rents
5 voluntary export restraint
6 dumping
7 infant industry argument
8 General Agreement on Tariffs and Trade
9 World Trade Organization
10 trade diversion

Doing Economics: Tools and Practice Problems

We use the small open economy model introduced in Chapter 7 to study the effects of three commercial policies: tariffs, quotas, and voluntary export restraints. This model starts with the idea that price is determined on world markets and that relative to that world market the country's output is too small to affect price. The country, in other words, is a price taker. For each of the policies we will determine the effects upon the market equilibrium and also the deadweight burdens. Tool Kit 19.1 shows how to get started.

Tool Kit 19.1: Finding the Free Trade Equilibrium in a Small Open Economy

In a small open economy the quantity demanded is what consumers demand at the fixed world price, and the quantity supplied is what producers offer for sale at that price. These quantities need not be equal. The difference is the level of imports or exports. Follow these steps.

Step one: Identify the world price, the demand curve, and the supply curve.

Step two: Find the quantity demanded. This is read off the demand curve at the world price.

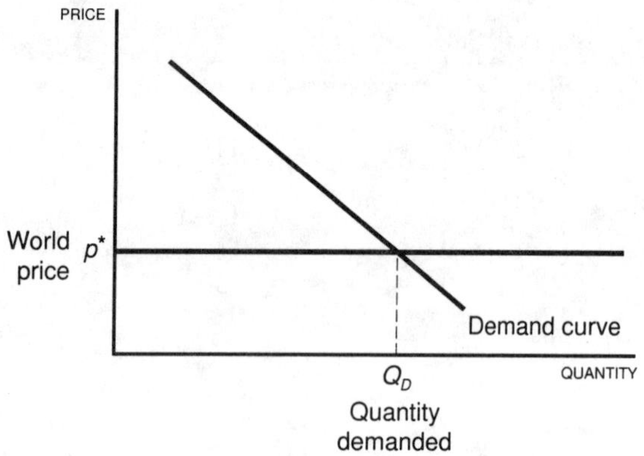

Step three: Find the quantity supplied. This is read off the supply curve at the world price.

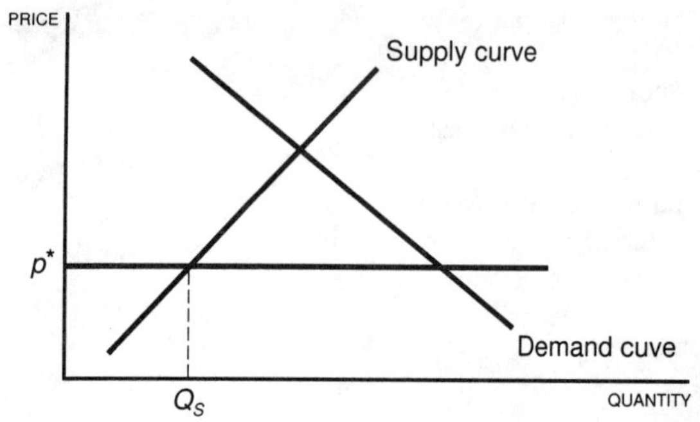

Step four: Find the level of imports or exports. If the quantity demanded exceeds the quantity supplied, then the country imports the goods. Otherwise the good is exported.

Imports = quantity demanded – quantity supplied (if positive).

Exports = quantity supplied – quantity demanded (if positive).

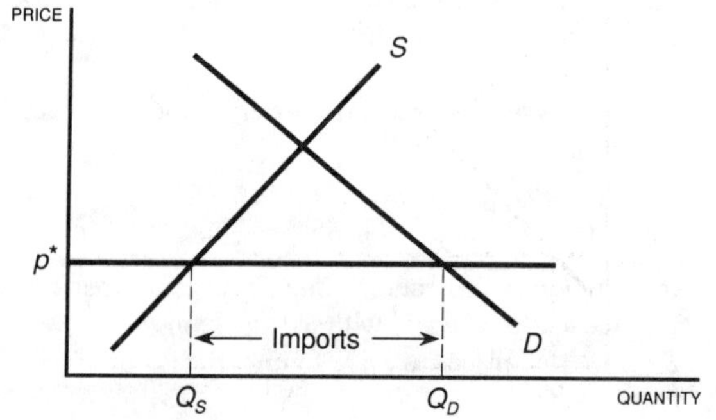

1 (Worked problem: small open economy) The world price of high-grade aluminum is $1,200 per metric ton. The United States demands and supplies are given below in Table 19.1.

a Find the quantity demanded and the quantity supplied.

b Is high-grade aluminum exported or imported? What is the amount?

Table 19.1

Demand		*Supply*	
Price	*Quantity (metric tons)*	*Price*	*Quantity (metric tons)*
$2,000	100,000	$2,000	400,000
$1,800	150,000	$1,800	300,000
$1,600	200,000	$1,600	200,000
$1,400	250,000	$1,400	100,000
$1,200	300,000	$1,200	50,000
$1,000	350,000	$1,000	25,000

Step-by-step solution

Step one: Identify the world price, the demand curve, and the supply curve. The world price is $1,400 and the demand and supply curves are given in Table 19.1.

Step two: Find the quantity demanded. When the price is $1,200, the quantity demanded is 300,000 metric tons.

Step three: Find the quantity supplied. When the price is $1,400, the quantity supplied is 50,000 metric tons.

Step four: Find the level of imports or exports. The quantity demanded exceeds the quantity supplied, so the country imports the good.

Imports = quantity demanded – quantity supplied
= 300,000 – 50,000 = 250,000.

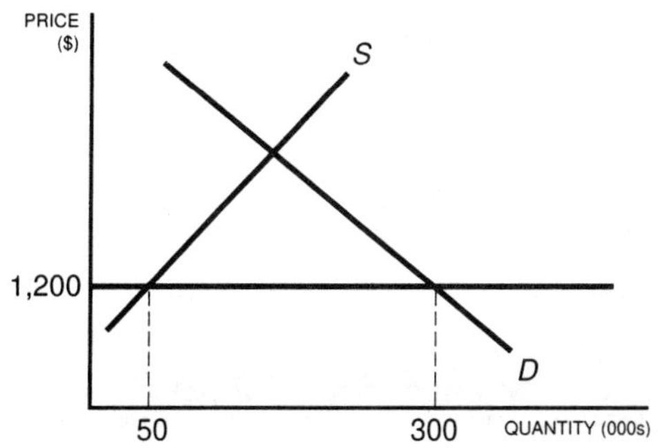

2 (Practice problem: small open economy) The world price of coffee is 4 cents per pound. The United States demands and supplies are given in Table 19.2.

a Find the quantity demanded and the quantity supplied.
b Is coffee exported or imported? What is the amount?

Table 19.2

Demand		*Supply*	
Price (cents per pound)	*Quantity (million pounds)*	*Price (cents per pound*	*Quantity (million pounds)*
8	14,000	8	20,000
7	16,000	7	18,000
6	18,000	6	16,000
5	20,000	5	14,000
4	22,000	4	12,000
3	24,000	3	10,000
2	26,000	2	8,000
1	28,000	1	6,000

3 (Practice problem: small open economy) The world price of sugar is 1 cent per pound. The United States demand and supply curves are given in Table 19.3.

a Find the quantity demanded and the quantity supplied.
b Is sugar exported or imported? What is the amount?

Table 19.3

Demand		*Supply*	
Price (cents per pound)	*Quantity (million pounds)*	*Price (cents per pound)*	*Quantity (million pounds)*
4.0	1,000	4.0	900
3.5	1,100	3.5	850
3.0	1,200	3.0	800
2.5	1,300	2.5	750
2.0	1,400	2.0	700
1.5	1,500	1.5	650
1.0	1,600	1.0	600

Tariffs

Tariffs are taxes on imported goods. Economists analyze their impact by looking at how markets adjust. Like other taxes, they change market outcomes and bring about deadweight burdens. Fewer goods are sold and consumers lose surplus. Also, the economy wastes resources by producing goods that are more cheaply obtained abroad. We follow the usual procedure of starting with an equilibrium, shifting curves, finding the new equilibrium, and comparing. Tool Kit 19.2 shows how to find the deadweight burden of tariffs.

Tool Kit 19.2: Determining the Effects of Tariffs

Tariffs raise domestic prices above world price. This increase reduces consumption and increases production and creates deadweight burdens. These steps show how to analyze tariffs.

Step one: Identify the world price, the demand curve, the supply curve, and the tariff.

Step two: Find the new world price. The new world price increases by exactly the amount of the tariff.

New world price = old world price + tariff.

Step three: Find the new equilibrium quantity demanded, quantity supplied, and level of imports. Follow the steps of Tool Kit 19.1.

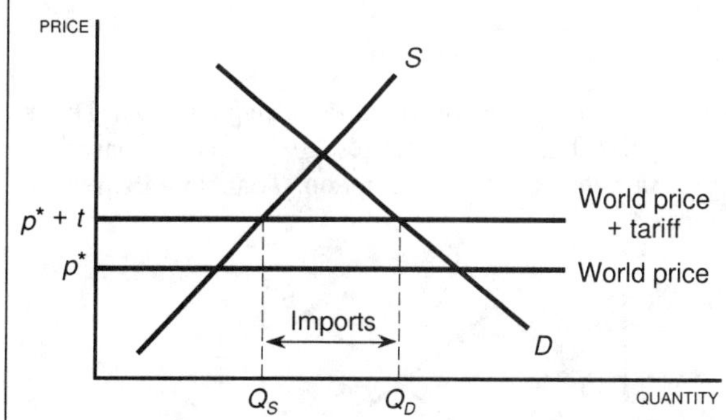

Step four: Calculate tariff revenue.

Tariff revenue = tariff × imports.

Step five: Show the area of the deadweight burden. There are two parts. Triangle DEF represents the loss in consumer surplus due to reduced consumption. Triangle ABC represents the waste of resources brought about by producing domestically when it is less expensive to import.

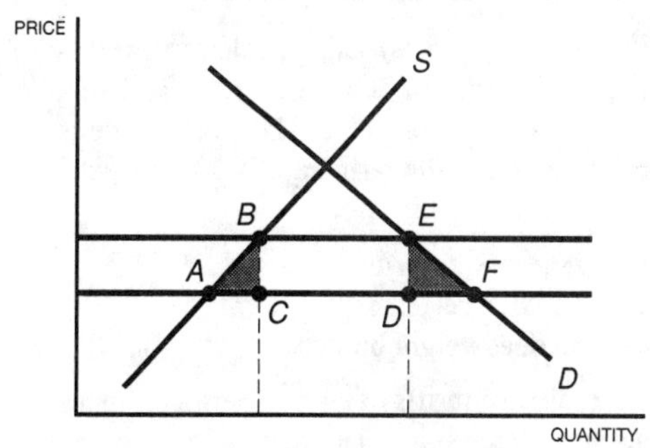

4 (Worked problem: tariffs) This problem continues with the market for high-grade aluminum. The demand and supply data are given in Table 19.1. The world price is $1,400 and the tariff rate is $200 per metric ton.

a Find the new equilibrium.
b Calculate tariff revenue.
c Show the deadweight burden.

Step-by-step solution

Step one: Identify the world price, the demand curve, the supply curve, and the tariff. The world price is $1,200, the demand and supply curves are in Table 19.1, and the tariff rate is $200 per metric ton.

Step two: Find the new world price. The new world price increases by exactly the amount of the tariff.

New world price = old world price + tariff
= $1,200 + $200 = $1,400.

Step three (a): Find the new equilibrium quantity demanded, quantity supplied, and level of imports. When the price is $1,400, the quantity demanded is 250,000, the quantity supplied is 100,000, and the level of imports is 250,000 – 100,000 = 150,000.

Step four (b): Calculate tariff revenue.

Tariff revenue = tariff × imports
= $200 × 150,000
= $30,000,000.

Step five (c): Show the area of the deadweight burden. There are two parts. Triangle DEF represents the loss in consumer surplus due to reduced consumption. Triangle ABC repre-

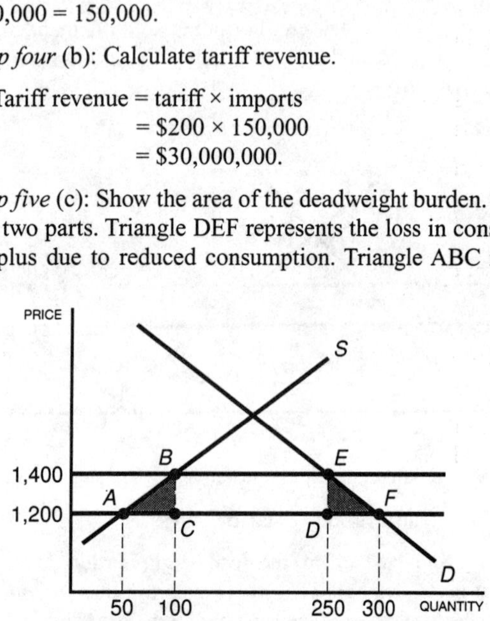

sents the waste of resources brought about by producing domestically when it is less expensive to import.

5 (Practice problem: tariffs) This problem continues with the market for coffee. The demand and supply curves are given in Table 19.2. The world price is 6 cents per pound and the tariff rate is 2 cents per pound.

a Find the new equilibrium.
b Calculate tariff revenue.
c Show the deadweight burden.

6 (Practice problem: tariffs) This problem continues with the market for sugar. The demand and supply curves are given in Table 19.3. The world price is 1 cent per pound and the tariff rate is 1/2 cent per pound.

a Find the new equilibrium.
b Calculate tariff revenue.
c Show the deadweight burden.

Quotas and Voluntary Export Restraints

Both quotas and VERs reduce imports. Quotas are imposed by the importing country, and VERs are "voluntarily" agreed to by the exporting country. Both raise prices, reduce consumption, and increase domestic production. Accordingly, both lead to deadweight burdens of exactly the same type as do tariffs. Follow along with Tool Kit 19.3.

Tool Kit 19.3: Quotas

Quotas, whether imposed or voluntary, raise prices, reduce consumption, increase production, and cause deadweight burdens. Follow these steps.

Step one: Identify the world price, the demand curve, the supply curve, and the quota.

Step two: Find the total supply curve. This is just the domestic supply curve added to the quota.

Total supply = domestic supply + quota.

Step three: Find the equilibrium price. Simply equate the total supply with the demand.

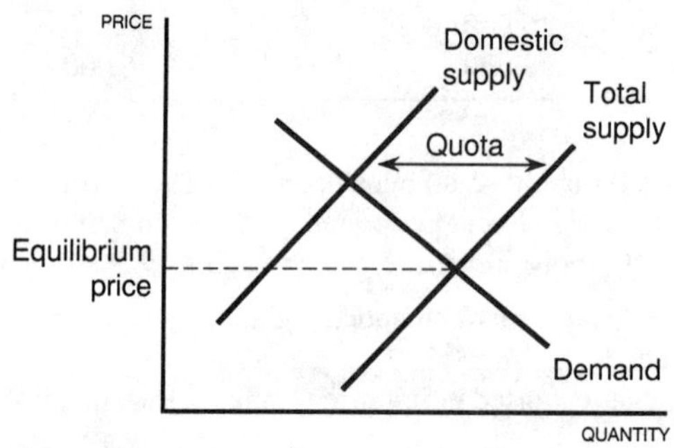

Step four: Find the domestic quantity supplied. This is read off the domestic supply curve.

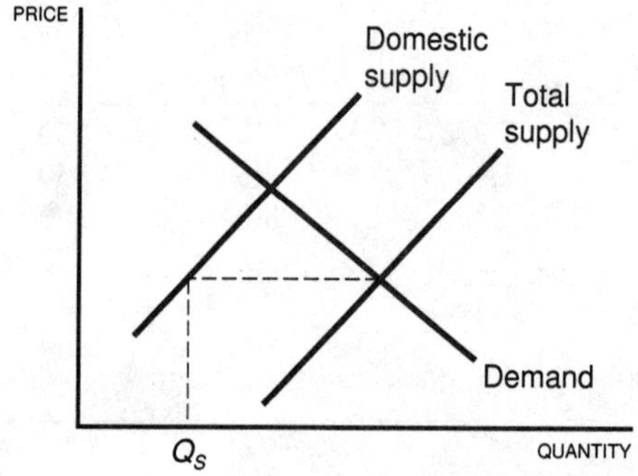

Step five: Calculate the quota rents. This is the extra money earned by licensed importers.

Quota rents = (new price – world price) × imports.

Step six: Show the area of the deadweight burden. There are two parts. Triangle DEF represents the loss in consumer surplus due to reduced consumption. Triangle ABC represents the waste of resources brought about by producing domestically when it is less expensive to import.

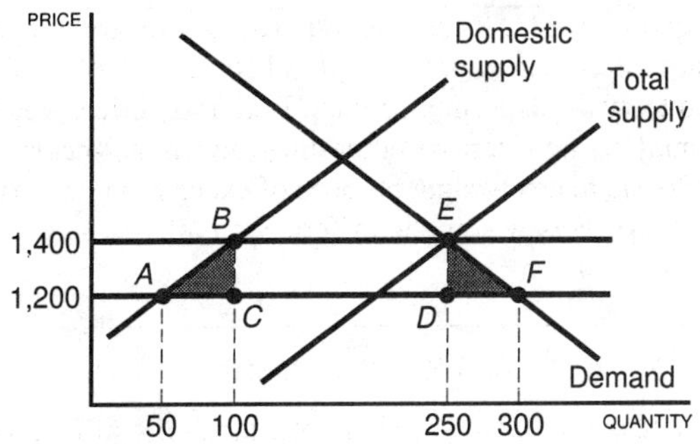

7 (Worked problem: tariffs) This problem continues with the market for high-grade aluminum. The demand and supply curves are given in Table 19.1. The world price is $1,200 and the import quota is 150,000 metric tons.

a Find the new equilibrium.
b Calculate quota rents.
c Show the deadweight burden.

Step-by-step solution

Step one: Identify the world price, the demand curve, the supply curve, and the quota. The world price is $1,200, demand and supply are given in Table 19.1, and the quota is 150,000.

Step two: Find the total supply curve. This is just the domestic supply curve added to the quota.

Total supply = domestic supply + quota.

Supply

Price	*Quantity (metric tons)*
$2,000	400,000 + 150,000 = 550,000
$1,800	300,000 + 150,000 = 450,000
$1,600	200,000 + 150,000 = 350,000
$1,400	100,000 + 150,000 = 250,000
$1,200	50,000 + 150,000 = 200,000
$1,000	25,000 + 150,000 = 175,000

Step three: Find the equilibrium price. Total supply equals demand when the price is $1,400. The equilibrium quantity is 250,000.

Step four: Find the domestic quantity supplied. When the price is $1,400, domestic supply equals 100,000.

Step five: Calculate the quota rents. This is the extra money earned by licensed importers.

Quota rents = (new price – world price) × imports
= ($1,400 – $1,200) × 150,000.

Step six: Show the area of the deadweight burden. There are two parts. Triangle DEF represents the loss in consumer surplus due to reduced consumption. Triangle ABC represents the waste of resources brought about by producing domestically when it is less expensive to import.

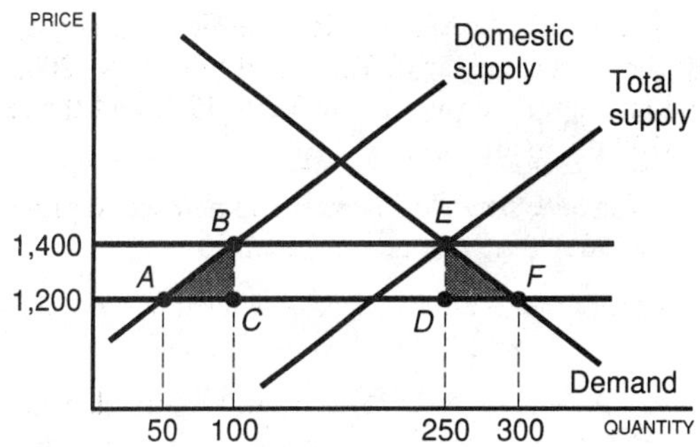

8 (Practice problem: quotas) This problem continues with the market for coffee. The demand and supply curves are given in Table 19.2. The world price is 6 cents and the import quota is 10,000 million pounds.

a Find the new equilibrium.
b Calculate quota rents.
c Show the deadweight burden.

9 (Practice problem: quotas) This problem continues with the market for sugar. The demand and supply curves are given in Table 19.3. The world price is 1 cent and the import quota is 1,000 million pounds.

a Find the new equilibrium.
b Calculate quota rents.
c Show the deadweight burden.

Answers to Problems

2 *a* Quantity demanded = 22,000; quantity supplied = 12,000.
b Imports = 22,000 – 12,000 = 10,000.

3 *a* Quantity demanded = 1,600; quantity supplied = 600.
b Imports = 1,600 – 600 = 1,000.

5 *a* Quantity demanded = 18,000; quantity supplied = 16,000; imports = 18,000 – 16,000 = 2,000.
b Tariff revenue = 2 × 2,000 = 4,000 million cents = $40,000,000.

c

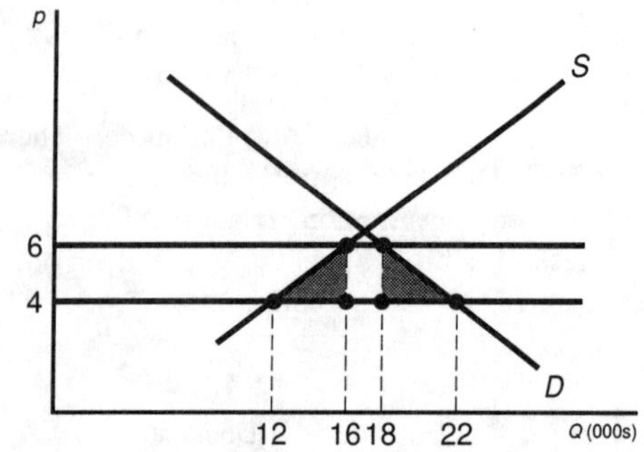

6 *a* Quantity demanded = 1,500; quantity supplied = 650; imports = 1,500 – 650 = 850.

b Tariff revenue = 0.5 × 850 = 425 million cents = $4,250,000.

c

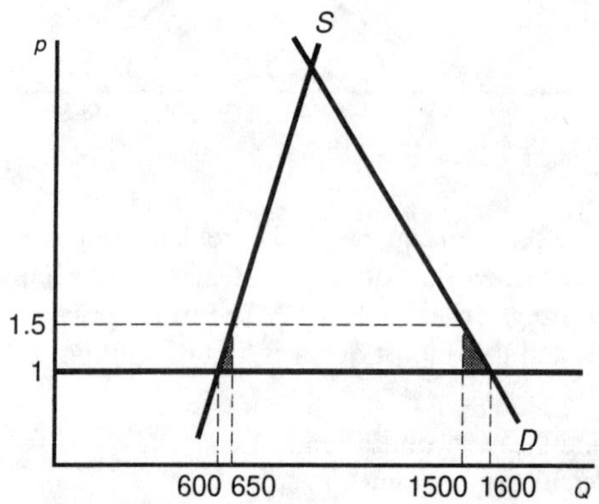

8 *a* New price = 6 cents per pound; quantity demanded = 18,000; quantity supplied = 16,000; imports = 18,000 – 16,000 = 2,000.

b Quota rents = 2 × 2,000 = 4,000 million cents = $40,000,000.

c

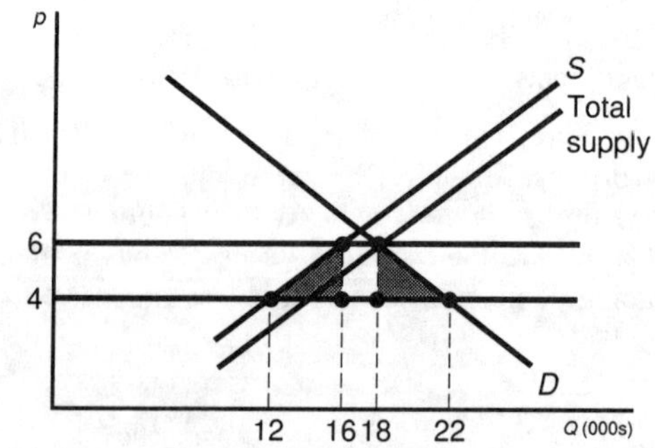

9 *a* New price = 1.5 cents per pound; quantity demanded = 1,500; quantity supplied = 650; imports = 1,500 – 650 = 850.

b Quota rents = 0.5 × 850 = 425 million cents = $4,250,000.

c

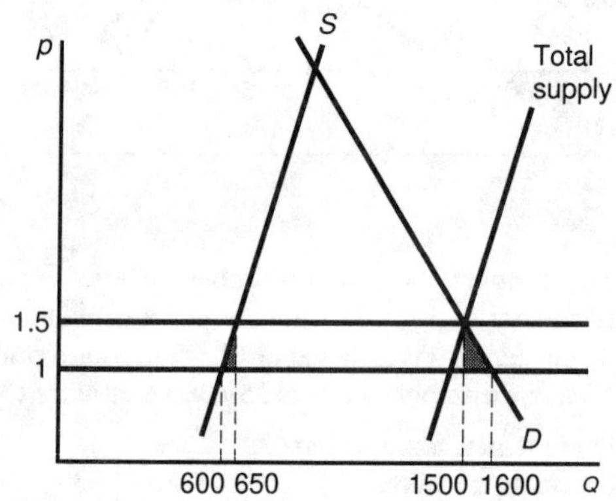

Chapter 20

ALTERNATIVE ECONOMIC SYSTEMS

Chapter Review

This chapter compares the nature and performance of the system we have studied throughout this book, the mixed economy, with some alternatives, namely the economic systems that evolved in the former Soviet Union and Eastern Europe in this century. The chapter includes some discussion of the worker-managed firms found in what used to be Yugoslavia as well as the incorporation of markets into the socialist economies of Hungary and Communist China. The book concludes in the next chapter with the topic of developing economies.

ESSENTIAL CONCEPTS

1 In **socialist** economies, the government owns the means of production; in **Communist** countries, it owns all property. Both systems have a high degree of government control of economic decisions, or **central planning,** which stands in contrast to the market system prevalent in the **market economies** (also called capitalist because of the prominent role played by private capital). The economies of Western Europe, Japan, and the United States rely on private property and markets for most economic decisions.

2 Appalled by the extreme economic inequality that accompanied the industrial revolution, Karl Marx predicted the downfall of capitalism and its replacement by a communist state. His ideas were implemented to some extent by Vladmir Lenin and Joseph Stalin in the Soviet Union from 1917 until recently.

3 **Soviet-style socialism** coordinated economic activity through a series of centrally administered plans that answered the basic economic questions of what is to be produced, how it is to be produced, and for whom. A system of political controls and rewards backed up by force replaced market incentives. In the labor market, this system assigned workers to jobs and limited labor mobility. The capital market was replaced by central directions that pursued a low-consumption, high-investment strategy emphasizing heavy industry. Goods were produced according to the plan and sold at prices controlled below market-clearing levels, leading to shortages and long lines at stores. Despite the ideology of "to each according to his needs," much inequality remained.

4 Soviet-style socialism failed for at least two reasons. It provided no *incentives* to managers; they could not keep

any profits, nor were they responsible for losses. Furthermore, the planning mechanism was unable to gather the needed *information* to allocate resources efficiently or to monitor workers and firms in order to ensure that the plan was carried through effectively. Prices, which were set arbitrarily, did not convey information about relative scarcity and value, as do market prices.

5 Under **market socialism** as in Hungary, the central planners set prices and order managers to maximize profits. This revision of the system performs only a little better than Soviet-style socialism; prices are set without good information, and managers, still without property rights, have no incentives to pursue profits. Some success was achieved with the "responsibility system" in China, where farmers were allowed to sell their produce and keep some of the proceeds. Yugoslavia instituted worker-managed firms as a partial step towards markets.

6 The transition from Soviet-style socialism to market economies is difficult and fraught with problems. The transition begins with a period of disruption, falling living standards, and high unemployment as old, inefficient factories are closed and resources are reallocated. Inflation rises as price controls are relaxed. Limiting budget deficits, controlling credit, and privatization of government-owned assets, including land, are difficult in countries making the transition. Finally, it will take a long time for all of the various institutions that support market economies to evolve. Nearly all of the former communist countries are moving toward the market economy, although the pace of transition varies widely.

BEHIND THE ESSENTIAL CONCEPTS

1 The main disadvantages of central government control are gathering the information needed to determine the optimal decisions, and giving incentives to managers and workers. Every organization, whether it operates within a market or a socialist economy, faces these problems. The difficulty with the socialist system is that the economy is simply too large an organization to control from the center.

2 The experiment with worker-managed firms in Yugoslavia showed interesting results. Since workers shared the profits, their goal was not to maximize total profits but rather to maximize profits per worker. This reduced the incentive to hire additional workers, because any new worker would cause the profit pie to be sliced more thinly. Further, the incentives to invest and increase the value of the enterprise were limited because it could not be sold.

3 The Soviet-style socialist economies bottled up inflation by controlling prices below the market-clearing levels and by providing fewer goods than people wanted to buy. Because there were so few goods to spend money on, savings rates were especially high, a phenomenon known as monetary overhang. As prices are freed from government control, they rise to market-clearing levels, but inflation grows even more as people spend their monetary overhang.

4 Despite claims of eliminating unemployment, the Soviet-style socialist economies did have disguised unemployment. Workers were assigned to firms, and layoffs were banned. Plants with excess workers simply kept them on the payroll. Because they were subject to the **soft budget constraint**, any losses resulting from the excess payroll were covered by the central government.

SELF-TEST

True or False

1 Under socialism, the state owns the means of production.

2 In mixed economies, there is a reliance on markets for most decisions, but government also plays a substantial role.

3 Karl Marx led the Russian revolution of 1917, establishing a Marxist state.

4 Under central planning, important decisions are made at the plant level.

5 In Soviet-style economies, incentives were provided by force.

6 In Soviet-style economies, there was little job mobility but some disguised unemployment.

7 The Soviet Union pursued a high-investment, low-consumption economic plan.

8 Soviet-style socialist economies nearly eliminated economic inequality.

9 Although socialist economies lost the competition for efficient production, they were able to protect their environment.

10 Most economists believe that the experiment in Soviet-style socialism was a failure.

11 Bureaucrats lacked the information to make efficient decisions under Soviet-style socialism.

12 Under market socialism, prices replace planning in determining investment decisions.

13 Worker-managed firms have little incentive to hire more workers.

14 The movement from socialism to a more market-oriented economy has caused prices to increase.

15 Privatization refers to the process of eliminating price controls and returning the function of setting prices to private firms.

Multiple Choice

1 Socialism is the system under which

a the state owns all property, including the means of production and all land;

b the state owns the means of production;
c there is a heavy reliance on firms and households interacting in markets;
d there is a heavy reliance on markets and a considerable role for government;
e workers own and manage the firms.

2 Under communism,

a the state owns all property, including the means of production and all land;
b the state owns the means of production;
c there is a heavy reliance on firms and households interacting in markets;
d there is a heavy reliance on markets and a considerable role for government;
e workers own and manage the firms.

3 In a mixed economy,

a the state owns all property, including the means of production and all land;
b the state owns the means of production;
c there is a heavy reliance on firms and households interacting in markets;
d there is a heavy reliance on markets and a considerable role for government;
e workers own and manage the firms.

4 The Russian revolution of 1917, which installed communism, was led by

a Marx;
b Oscar Lange;
c Lenin;
d Stalin;
e Mises.

5 The forced collectivization of agriculture was ordered by

a Marx;
b Oscar Lange;
c Lenin;
d Stalin;
e Mises.

6 Under Stalin the Soviet Union increased investment by

a maintaining high rates of return for savings;
b keeping wages low;
c limiting the supply of consumer goods;
d attracting foreign investment;
e b and c.

7 Under central planning,

a the government makes all significant economic decisions;
b government-owned property is sold or given to individuals;
c workers own and manage their firms;
d prices are set by the interplay of supply and demand;
e land is redistributed to those who have worked it.

8 Under socialism, in the labor market,

a wages adjust to clear the market;
b firms pay above market-clearing efficiency wages to keep and motivate their best workers;
c workers are assigned jobs, and there is very little labor mobility;
d unions set wages through collective bargaining;
e workers own and manage their own firms.

9 In Soviet-style socialist economies, the allocation of investment capital is determined by

a workers who own and manage their own firms;
b the capital market;
c the government;
d majority vote;
e none of the above.

10 In Soviet-style socialist economies, prices

a were outlawed;
b were set equal to market-clearing levels;
c were set above market-clearing levels;
d were set below market-clearing levels;
e were determined by the forces of supply and demand.

11 The Soviet Union pursued a policy of

a high investment and low consumption;
b high consumption and low investment;
c high investment and high consumption;
d low investment and low consumption;
e none of the above.

12 Socialist enterprises often face soft budget constraints, which means that

a workers share the profits equally;
b firms that continue to make losses are absorbed by larger firms;
c the government makes up any losses;
d workers do not have to work unless the firm makes a profit;
e workers are assigned jobs and thus are never unemployed.

13 Amomg the problems of central planning are

a the lack of incentives that managers have to operate firms efficiently;
b the lack of information needed to make efficient decisions;
c the fact that prices, not determined by markets, could not provide informative signals;
d the difficulty in monitoring the performance of managers and workers;
e all of the above.

14 Under market socialism,

a government makes the investment decisions;
b firms maximize profits at the prices they face;
c workers own and manage their own firms;
d all of the above;
e a and b.

15 In China, farmers were allowed to sell most of what they produced and keep the profits under

a collectivized agriculture;

b farmer cooperatives;
c the responsibility system;
d land reform;
e privatization.

16 Worker-managed farms were instituted in

a China;
b the USSR;
c Poland;
d Hungary;
e Yugoslavia.

17 Which of the following was not a problem with worker-owned cooperatives?

a Workers had little incentive to undertake investments that paid off after they left the firm.
b Keeping a share of the profits motivated workers to work hard in smaller firms.
c Cooperatives had little incentive to hire new workers.
d The aging work force diminished investment incentives.
e The reluctance to hire workers contributed to the unemployment problem.

18 Environment policy in the Soviet Union was characterized by

a low energy prices;
b lack of anti-pollution measures;
c intensive farming with high pesticide use and much soil erosion;
d lack of nuclear safety equipment;
e all of the above.

19 Privatization refers to

a the transfer to individuals of property formerly owned by the state;
b the fact that managers under Soviet-style socialism kept information private;
c the consolidation of agriculture into large firms;
d the policy that allowed private farmers in China to sell much of what they produced;
e the attempt to combine the best features of socialism and private enterprise.

20 Which of the following are problems involved in the transition from socialism to market economies?

a inflation;
b unemployment;
c the lack of a safety net;
d falling living standards;
e All of the above are problems.

Completion

1 The government owns and operates the means of production under __________.

2 Under __________, the government owns all property.

3 The system of __________ gives the government and its ministries control over economic decisions.

4 Economies with a heavy reliance on markets but also a considerable role for government are referred to as __________.

5 __________ believed that the capitalist system would eventually collapse and evolve into communism.

6 __________ forced the collectivization of farms, causing a famine in which millions died.

7 According to __________, economies can combine the advantages of market mechanisms with public ownership of the means of production.

8 Worker-owned __________, in which workers hired managers and received the profits, were countenanced in Yugoslavia.

9 Transferring businesses and property from public ownership to individuals is called __________.

10 Among the formerly Communist countries __________ proceeded most quickly in the macroeconomic aspects of the transition to a market economy.

Answers to Self-Test

True or False

1	t	6	t	11	t
2	t	7	t	12	f
3	f	8	f	13	t
4	f	9	f	14	t
5	t	10	t	15	f

Multiple Choice

1	b	6	e	11	a	16	e
2	a	7	a	12	c	17	b
3	d	8	c	13	e	18	e
4	c	9	c	14	e	19	a
5	d	10	d	15	c	20	e

Completion

1 socialism
2 communism
3 central planning
4 mixed economies
5 Karl Marx
6 Stalin
7 market socialism
8 cooperatives
9 privatization
10 Poland

Doing Economics: Tools and Practice Problems

In a planned economy, such as Soviet-style socialism, the state owns and must allocate the means of production. To gain some understanding of the allocation problem the state must solve, we first look at some relatively simple problems involving how to allocate a resource between different plants or regions that produce the same good. The next topic involves a Yugoslavian experiment with firms owned and managed by the workers. We explore the problem of how many workers to hire.

Efficient Resource Allocation

Compared to market economies, socialism allocated resources poorly. This means that resources were not assigned to task efficiently and that the economy produced inside its production possibilities. While markets use prices to guide allocations, socialist managers must gather a great deal of information about productivity in alternative uses, form a coherent plan, direct the allocation, and monitor performance to see that the plan is carried out. The combined information and incentive problems overwhelmed the capacity of planners. Tool Kit 20.1 shows how to solve allocation problems when the information is available.

Tool Kit 20.1: Finding the Efficient Allocation of a Resource

When new productive resources become available, state bureaucrats must decide how to use them. The solution to this problem requires information about production functions. Tool Kit 20.1 looks at how to allocate resources efficiently. Follow the steps.

Step one: Identify the production functions for each possible use.

Step two: Compute the marginal product for each quantity of the resource:

marginal product = change in output/change in input.

Step three: Allocate the first unit of the resource to the activity with the highest marginal product.

Step four: Allocate the second unit of the resource to the activity with the next highest marginal product.

Step five: Continue until the available supply of the resource is exhausted.

1 (Worked problem: planning and efficient allocation) The Commissar of Fishing has received eight new trawlers for cod. She must decide how to allocate the new vessels between the Black Sea and Caspian Sea fleets. The production functions for each fleet are given in Table 20.1.

Table 20.1

Number of trawlers	*Harvest of Black Sea cod (tons per week)*	*Harvest of Caspian Sea cod (tons per week)*
1	9	20
2	17	36
3	24	50
4	30	62
5	35	72
6	39	80
7	42	86
8	44	90

a Find the efficient allocation of trawlers;

b Suppose the commissar does not know the production functions and simply allocates the trawlers equally between the fleets. How many fewer tons of cod will be harvested?

Step-by-step solution

Step one (a): Identify the production functions for each possible use. They are given in Table 20.1.

Step two: Compute the marginal product for each quantity of the resource. The first trawler in the Black Sea harvests 10 tons. The second one increases the harvest to 19, which is a marginal product of 19 – 10 = 9. Continuing, we derive Table 20.2.

Table 20.2

Number of trawlers	*Harvest of Black Sea cod*	*Marginal product*	*Harvest of Caspian Sea cod*	*Marginal product*
1	9	9	20	20
2	17	8	36	16
3	24	7	50	14
4	30	6	62	12
5	35	5	72	10
6	39	4	80	8
7	42	3	86	6
8	44	2	90	4

Step three: Allocate the first unit of the resource to the activity with the highest marginal product. The highest marginal product is 20 in the Caspian Sea.

Step four: Allocate the second unit of the resource to the activity with the next highest marginal product. The next highest marginal product is 16, again in the Caspian Sea.

Step five: Continue until the available supply of the resource is exhausted. If 6 trawlers are allocated to the Caspian, where the output is 80, and 2 to the Black Sea, where the output is 17, then the output of cod is 97. The allocation is efficient, and this is the answer to part a.

Step six (b): If 4 trawlers are sent to each region, total output is 30 + 62 = 92, which is 5 less than if the allocation were efficient.

2 (Practice problem: planning and efficient allocation) Nine new tractors roll off the assembly line at the huge state-owned tractor works in Braslov. Many cooperative farms have requested new tractors, and the minister in charge must allocate them. The production functions for three farms are given in Table 20.3. Output is measured as thousands of bushels of wheat.

a Find the efficient allocation of tractors;

b Compute the waste if the tractors are divided equally among the three farms.

Table 20.3

Tractors	*Output at farm #1*	*Output at farm #2*	*Output at farm #3*
0	30	100	50
1	40	150	90
2	49	180	120
3	57	200	140
4	64	210	150
5	70	215	155
6	75	218	160
7	79	220	164
8	82	220	166
9	82	220	167

3 (Practice problem: planning and efficient allocation) Six new locomotives are made available for either the north-south route or the east-west route. The production functions for each route are given in Table 20.4. Output is measured as numbers of standard containers per week.

Table 20.4

Locomotives	*East-west route output*	*North-south route output*
1	1,000	1,000
2	1,800	1,600
3	2,500	2,000
4	3,000	2,200
5	3,300	2,300
6	3,500	2,400

a Find the efficient allocation of locomotives.

b How much output is wasted if all are allocated to the east-west route?

Worker-Managed Firms

One experiment in market socialism occurred in the former Yugoslavia when the government sanctioned the creation of firms owned and managed by workers. The profits from each firm were shared equally among the workers. Worker-managed firms do seek profits, but they do not maximize total profits; rather, their goal is to make profits per worker as large as possible. Generally, this practice results in fewer workers hired than under a full-fledged market system. Tool Kit 20.2 demonstrates this.

Tool Kit 20.2: Finding the Level of Employment in a Worker-Managed Firm

Because it is run by workers who share in the profits, a worker-managed firm will seek to maximize profits per worker. This differs from the goal of firms in market economies, which maximize profits. Follow these steps to find the level of employment in worker-managed firms.

Step one: Identify the production function and the product price.

Step two: Compute the total revenue at each level of employment by multiplying the output by the product price:

$$\text{revenues} = \text{output} \times \text{product price}.$$

Step three: Compute profits by subtracting costs from revenue:

$$\text{profits} = \text{revenues} - \text{costs}.$$

Step four: Compute profits per worker by dividing profits by the corresponding number of workers. This is the share of profits going to each worker.

$$\text{profits per worker} = \text{profits/number of workers}.$$

Step five: Find the level of employment for which profits per worker is highest. This is the equilibrium level of employment in the worker-managed firm.

4 (Worked problem: worker-managed firms) The new branch of the Hair Cuttery is ready to open. It will be owned and managed by the stylists. The price of haircuts is $10, and the production function is given in Table 20.5. Fixed costs equal $50 per day. Find the equilibrium number of stylists.

Table 20.5

Stylists	*Haircuts per day*
1	6
2	16
3	30
4	42
5	50
6	56
7	60

Step-by-step solution

Step one: Identify the production function and the product price. The production function is given in Table 20.5, and the price is $10.

Step two: Compute the total revenue at each level of employment by multiplying the output by the product price. When the number of stylists is 1, output is 6 and revenues equal 6 × $10 = $60. Continuing, we complete the column as shown in Table 20.6.

Step three: Compute profits by subtracting costs from revenue. We subtract $50 from the revenue column. The completed information is given in Table 20.6.

Table 20.6

Stylists	*Haircuts per day*	*Revenues*	*Profits*
1	6	$ 60	$ 10
2	16	$160	$110
3	30	$300	$250
4	42	$420	$370
5	50	$500	$450
6	56	$560	$510
7	60	$600	$550

Step four: Compute profits per worker by dividing profits by the corresponding number of workers. This is the share of profits going to each worker. For example, profits per worker when there is one stylist equal $10/1 = $10. Continuing, we derive Table 20.7.

Table 20.7

Stylists	*Haircuts per day*	*Revenues*	*Profits*	*Profits per stylist*
1	6	$ 60	$ 10	$10.00
2	16	$160	$110	$55.00
3	30	$300	$250	$83.33
4	42	$420	$370	$92.50
5	50	$500	$450	$90.00
6	56	$560	$510	$85.00
7	60	$600	$550	$76.57

Step five: Find the level of employment for which profits per worker is highest. The equilibrium level of employment is 4, where profits per worker equal $92.50.

5 (Practice problem: worker-managed firms) Moe's Lite-Brite Charcoal Company soaks charcoal in lighter fluid for $1 per bag. Its production function is given in Table 20.8. Moe is selling his business and all of the equipment to the employees. Their fixed cost including the payment on the loan to finance the sale will be $500 per day. Find the equilibrium level of employment when Moe's becomes worker managed.

Table 20.8

Workers	*Output per day*
1	100
2	500
3	1,500
4	2,500
5	2,900
6	3,300

6 (Practice problem: worker-managed firms) The Thelonius Thimble Company is to become worker owned and managed next month when the likable Thelonius retires. He is giving the business to the workers, and they will have no fixed cost. Thimbles sell for $.10 each. The production function is given in Table 20.9. Find the equilibrium number of employees of the worker-managed thimble company.

Table 20.9

Workers	*Thimbles*
1	2,000
2	5,000
3	10,000
4	13,000
5	15,000
6	17,000

Answers to Problems

2 Table 20.10 gives the marginal product of tractors at each of the farms.

Table 20.10

	Farm #1		*Farm #2*		*Farm #3*	
Tractors	*Output*	*Marginal product*	*Output*	*Marginal product*	*Output*	*Marginal product*
0	30	30	100	100	50	50
1	40	10	150	50	90	40
2	49	9	180	30	120	30
3	57	8	200	20	140	20
4	64	7	210	10	150	10
5	70	6	215	5	155	5
6	75	5	218	3	160	5
7	79	4	220	2	164	4
8	82	3	220	0	166	2
9	82	0	220	0	167	1

a The efficient allocation is 1 tractor to farm #1, 4 tractors to farm #2, and 4 tractors to farm #3.

b The output of the tractors divided equally is 57 + 200 + 140 = 397. The output at the efficient allocation is 40 + 210 + 150 = 400. The waste is 400 – 397 = 3, and since output is measured in thousands of bushels, this represents 3,000 bushels.

3 Table 20.11 gives the marginal product along each route.

Table 20.11

	East-west route		*North-south route*	
Locomotives	*Output*	*Marginal product*	*Output*	*Marginal product*
1	1,000	1,000	1,000	1,000
2	1,800	800	1,600	600
3	2,500	700	2,000	400
4	3,000	500	2,200	200
5	3,300	300	2,300	100
6	3,500	200	2,400	100

a The efficient allocation is 4 to the east-west route and 2 to the north-south route.

b Output is 3,500 if all are allocated to the east-west route. Output is 3,000 + 1,600 = 4,600 at the efficient allocation. The waste is 4,600 – 3,500 = 1,100.

5 Table 20.12 gives profits per worker, which are maximized when the firm includes 4 workers.

Table 20.12

Workers	*Output per day*	*Revenues*	*Profits*	*Profits per worker*
1	100	$ 100	–$ 400	–$400
2	500	$ 500	$ 0	$ 0
3	1,500	$1,500	$1,000	$333
4	2,500	$2,500	$2,000	$500
5	2,900	$2,900	$2,400	$480
6	3,300	$3,300	$2,800	$466

6 Table 20.13 gives profits per worker, which are maximized when the number of workers is 3.

Table 20.13

Workers	*Output per day*	*Revenues*	*Profits*	*Profits per worker*
1	2,000	$ 200	$ 200	$200
2	5,000	$ 500	$ 500	$250
3	10,000	$1,000	$1,000	$333
4	13,000	$1,300	$1,300	$325
5	15,000	$1,500	$1,500	$300
6	17,000	$1,700	$1,700	$283

Chapter 21

DEVELOPMENT

Chapter Review

This chapter takes up less developed countries. It examines living standards in these countries as well as the causes of underdevelopment and the prospects for bringing the living standards up to those of the developed countries. The chapter closes with a look at the policies some countries have pursued, namely the relative advantages of the export-led and import-competing strategies.

ESSENTIAL CONCEPTS

1 In **less developed countries (LDCs)** GDP per capita was less than $675 in 1992. The per capita income gap among developed countries has narrowed over the past century, while it has widened between the developed and less developed world. Although a few countries have successfully raised their living standards, most of the LDCs remain in grinding poverty. Agricultural gains from the **green revolution**, improvements in health and life expectancy, and the emergence of the **newly industrialized countries** of East Asia are some examples of successful economic development.

2 Although there is considerable variation among LDCs, agriculture dominates the economy in most. In the rural sector, farming takes place on small, labor-intensive farms with poorer techniques and less fertilizer than in the developed world. **Sharecropping** remains a widespread arrangement. Redistribution of land ownership through **land reform** has at times been successful, but dramatic inequality remains. In the urban sector, wages are far higher, and many individuals have migrated to the cities. Such migration has caused massive unemployment and squalor. The term **dual economy** describes the vast difference between the rural and urban sectors.

3 The institutions and structure of the economy in LDCs do not facilitate growth. Although savings rates are high, there is a shortage of capital. The absence of efficient capital markets keeps the limited capital from its most productive use. An inadequate supply of skilled workers accompanies burgeoning population growth, which reduces the ratio of capital to workers and lowers productivity. Also, the lack of developed capital markets and ill-advised government interventions have kept the limited capital from its most productive use. All of this plus extreme inequality characterize LDCs.

4 The failure of markets in their countries has led most

LDCs to adopt *central planning*. Because planners do not have sufficient information to make correct decisions, central planning has not been successful. An overreliance on heavy industry, corruption, and widespread interference in trade and foreign exchange are common problems of actual LDC development efforts. A common policy, import substitution, emphasizes the development of domestic markets by substituting domestic production for imports. The pervasive role of government also motivates wasteful rent seeking. Another clear failure has been in providing needed **infrastructure**, especially a sound legal system.

5 The success of the East Asian economies points to several policy successes. These countries practiced the sound macroeconomic policies of low budget deficits and low inflation. Other policies encouraged high savings rates, literacy, college education, and the explicit promotion of certain export-oriented industries. This export-led strategy protects and encourages certain industries judged to be potentially successful against world competition. Dynamic comparative advantage, based on acquired education and skills, has guided the most successful of these policies, but there have been some failures. One final benefit is the high level of economic equality, suggesting that there is not necessarily a trade-off between growth and equality.

BEHIND THE ESSENTIAL CONCEPTS

1 The case for central planning in LDCs has always rested on the pervasive *market failures*. Clearly, markets do a poor job allocating resources in these countries. Yet the failure of planning provides a salient example of *government failure*. Although the potential for beneficial government intervention exists, governments have made matters worse.

2 Real world markets are complicated, and the institutions that help them work have taken time to evolve. Reputations, repeated business arrangements, implicit contracts, and other institutions help ease the information problems that trouble imperfectly competitive markets. In the LDCs, these institutions are not present, and in their absence, resource allocation is worse.

3 Observing varying levels of success and failure around the world, we can compile a list of good development policies. First, there must be sound macroeconomics, i.e., fiscal responsibility and a stable monetary system. Second, the economies must direct themselves toward the rest of the world by reducing trade barriers, encouraging foreign investment, and promoting exports. This approach helps to transfer more advanced technology from abroad and provides a natural test for success. Government can allocate more of its budget to investment and less to consumption, such as food subsidies. Finally, policies such as land reform and universal education (including women) not only contribute to development, but also promote equality.

4 The term "vicious circle" is often used with respect to LDCs. Poor households cannot afford education and must scratch out a living in labor-intensive activities, such as subsistence farming. They not only lack the education to practice birth control, but also have incentives to raise more children, who are economically useful. The population growth reduces capital per worker, keeping the economy in underdevelopment.

5 The education of women plays an especially important role in development. You can see this in terms of the costs and benefits of children. More educated women understand and practice birth control. Also, as education allows their earnings to increase, they realize that the opportunity cost of having children is high and limit family size. Lower population growth means more capital per worker and higher output.

SELF-TEST

True or False

1 Over the past century, the income gap between the industrialized and less developed economies has narrowed.

2 One success story in the less developed world has been the emergence of the newly industrialized countries, such as Singapore and Taiwan.

3 Increases in life expectancy and improvements in infant mortality have allowed rapid population growth in many LDCs.

4 In poor countries, agriculture plays a more prominent role, often accounting for 80 percent of GNP.

5 The LDCs have much less capital per person than the United States because their savings rates are very low.

6 The absence of capital markets in LDCs prevents the limited supply of capital from finding its most efficient use.

7 Land reform transfers agricultural land to those who work it.

8 Inequality can inhibit development by leading to political instability and a poor climate for foreign investment.

9 Sharecropping gives good incentives for the tenant farmer to work hard and maintain the productivity of the land.

10 Central planning enables developing countries to coordinate all the related activities in a single coherent development strategy.

11 An important element of a country's infrastructure is its legal system.

12 A difficulty with the export-led strategy is that it protects inefficient domestic producers from the competition of foreign firms.

13 One problem with import substitution is that it is difficult to remove trade barriers once they are imposed.

14 The successful East Asian economies have achieved high growth rates, but this has occurred at the cost of extreme inequality.

15 Educating women leads to lower birth rates because as their education brings higher wages, the opportunity cost of devoting time to raise children rises.

Multiple Choice

1 What fraction of the world's population lives in LDCs?

a one-fourth;
b one-half;
c three-fourths;
d one-third;
e one-sixth.

2 Over the past century, the income gap

a has widened among high-income countries;
b has narrowed among high-income countries;
c has grown wider between high- and low-income countries;
d has narrowed between high- and low-income countries;
e b anc c.

3 The green revolution refers to

a the spread of concern for the environment in the LDCs;
b the World Bank's largely successful efforts to aid development by lending money for infrastructure investment;
c the development and spread to LDCs of new agricultural technologies, which brought about huge increases in output;
d improvements in life expectancy and infant mortality statistics in the LDCs;
e none of the above.

4 Agriculture in the developed countries

a uses larger farms than in the LDCs;
b uses fewer workers per acre than in LDCs;
c uses more fertilizer per acre than in LDCs;
d is more mechanized than in LDCs;
e all of the above.

5 Sharecropping refers to

a the fact that much of the agricultural output in the LDCs is taken in taxes;
b the World Bank's policy of matching agricultural gains in LDCs with food shipments;
c the sharing of technological know-how between agricultural research centers in the developed world and the LDCs;
d the system in which the landlord takes a share of the output of a farm;
e the system in which farmers set aside a fraction of their output to support religious institutions.

6 The term dual economies refers to

a the disparity between the developed and underdeveloped economies;
b the disparity between men's and women's earnings in the LDCs;
c the disparity between upper and lower incomes in the LDCs;
d the disparity between rural and urban life in the LDCs;
e the disparity between the efficiency of the market sector and the inefficiency of governments in LDCs.

7 In LDCs, it is generally true that

a savings rates are low;
b because it is in short supply, capital is used very intensively;
c because the capital stock is so low, the marginal return to capital is much higher than in developed countries;
d the lack of effective capital markets keeps capital from its most productive uses;
e the stable political environments attract foreign investment.

8 The debt crises experienced by several LDCs in the 1980s were caused by

a high interest rates;
b the world recession in the early 1980s;
c lack of prudence in lending by banks;
d U.S. government deposit insurance;
e all of the above.

9 In LDCs, the population

a is large and well educated;
b is falling because of the poor medical care and meager diets;
c is growing too rapidly, causing an excess supply of trained workers;
d is growing too rapidly, but includes too few vocationally trained, skilled workers;
e none of the above.

10 The low returns to capital in the LDCs are the result of

a shortages of capital;
b low supplies of capital;
c lack of markets to allocate capital efficiently;
d b and c;
e all of the above.

11 In LDCs,

a both labor and capital markets work well;
b while labor markets work well, capital markets fail to allocate efficiently the scarce capital;
c while capital markets work well, ethnic divisions and language barriers hinder the labor market;
d neither capital nor labor markets work efficiently;
e there are no labor or capital markets.

12 Sir Arthur Lewis argued that the surplus of labor contributes to economic growth by

a supporting strong governments that can provide stability needed to attract foreign investment;
b keeping wages low, which leads to high profits and investment;

c discouraging population growth through high unemployment;
d emigrating and sending earnings home;
e attracting foreign investment with low wages.

13 Export-led growth strategies have promoted

a agriculture, where LDCs have had comparative advantage;
b substitution of domestic production for imported goods;
c land reform;
d export industries aligned with the principle of dynamic comparative advantage, which is based on acquired skills, education, and technology;
e government control of production in order to maximize exports.

14 What best describes the relationship between inequality and economic growth?

a The countries that have developed most rapidly have lower levels of inequality.
b The countries that have developed most rapidly have higher levels of inequality.
c There is no consistent relationship between inequality and the pace of development.
d Planned economies have developed rapidly with low inequality, but unplanned ones have only developed when inequality is high.
e Planned economies have developed rapidly with high inequality, but unplanned ones have only developed when inequality is low.

15 Inequality may inhibit development by

a leading to political instability and a poor investment climate;
b fostering the development of sharecropping;
c leading governments to impose high tax rates;
d forcing governments to spend on food subsidies rather than investment;
e all of the above.

16 Most economists

a favor central planning by LDCs because planners can better coordinate all the aspects of major projects;
b favor central planning by LDCs because planners have better information about whether projects will be successful;
c are skeptical about central planning because planners lack the needed information;
d see no need for planning of any kind;
e view planning as neither beneficial nor harmful because of the policy ineffectiveness proposition.

17 Rent seeking refers to

a the payments made by sharecroppers;
b activities by individuals to get special benefits from governments;
c campaigns to attract foreign investment;
d the failure of sharecroppers to maintain the land;
e none of the above.

18 Which of the following is not part of a country's infrastructure?

a roads;
b bridges;
c ports;
d legal system;
e All of the above are part of the infrastructure.

19 Encouraging the production and export of goods in which the country has a comparative advantage is the strategy called

a export-led growth;
b central planning;
c dynamic comparative advantage;
d import substitution;
e laissez-faire.

20 Encouraging the development of a domestic market by substituting domestically produced goods for imports is called

a export-led growth;
b central planning;
c dynamic comparative advantage;
d import substitution;
e laissez-faire.

Completion

1 Economists refer to the poorest nations of the world as __________.

2 Nations that have recently moved from being quite poor to being middle-income countries, including South Korea and Hong Kong, are called __________.

3 The development of new seeds, fertilizers, and agricultural practices that brought about increases in agricultural output in the LDCs during the 1960s and 1970s was called the __________.

4 In many LDCs, there is a __________, which includes a poor rural sector alongside a relatively more advanced urban sector.

5 A country's roads, ports, bridges, and legal system compose its __________.

6 __________ is a strategy according to which governments encourage exports to stimulate growth.

7 __________ is a strategy whereby the focus is on substituting domestic goods for imports to develop self-sufficiency.

8 Countries that have large numbers of unemployed or underemployed workers are said to have __________.

9 __________ refers to activities designed to secure government favors, such as import licenses or access to foreign exchange.

10 The __________ is the most important of the international agencies that lend funds to LDCs to aid in development.

Answers to Self-Test

True or False

1	f	6	t	11	t
2	t	7	t	12	f
3	t	8	t	13	t
4	t	9	f	14	f
5	f	10	f	15	t

Multiple Choice

1	c	6	d	11	d	16	c
2	e	7	d	12	b	17	b
3	c	8	e	13	d	18	e
4	e	9	d	14	a	19	a
5	d	10	e	15	e	20	d

Completion

1 less developed countries
2 newly industrialized countries
3 green revolution
4 dual economy
5 infrastructure
6 Export-led growth
7 Import substitution
8 labor surplus
9 Rent seeking
10 World Bank

Doing Economics: Tools and Practice Problems

Two important problems that impede growth in underdeveloped countries are the absence of markets to allocate resources efficiently, and the prevalence of institutions, such as sharecropping, that provide weak incentives. We study both of these problems in this section. Underdeveloped economies not only have limited supplies of capital and skilled labor, they also lack good markets to allocate what supplies they have. In this section, we consider the efficient allocation of resources, how markets achieve this allocation, and the losses that result from misallocation.

1 (Worked problem: absence of markets) The World Bank has made $10 million available for development projects in Costa Guano. Two possible uses for the money are building roads and building irrigation systems. The present discounted value of investments in each sector is given in Table 21.1.

Table 21.1

Investment (millions)	*Irrigation projects (millions)*	*Roads (millions)*
$ 1	$10	$ 25
$ 2	$18	$ 45
$ 3	$25	$ 60
$ 4	$31	$ 72
$ 5	$36	$ 83
$ 6	$40	$ 93
$ 7	$43	$102
$ 8	$45	$110
$ 9	$46	$116
$10	$46	$120

a Find the efficient allocation of the $10 million.
b How would competitive markets allocate the money?
c The party in power in Costa Guano draws much of its support from agriculture. If it used all of the money for irrigation, how much less would the benefits be?

Step-by-step solution

Step one (a): To find the efficient allocation, we adapt the procedure outlined in Tool Kit 20.1. Identify the production functions for each possible use. Here we are given the relationship between investment and the benefits of investment in Table 21.1.

Step two: Compute the marginal benefit for each quantity of the resource. We compute marginal benefit in the usual way. For example, the marginal benefit of the first $1 million in investment in irrigation is $10 million. Continuing, we derive Table 21.2.

Table 21.2

Investment (millions)	*Irrigation projects*	*Marginal benefit*	*Roads*	*Marginal benefit*
$ 1	$10	$10	$ 25	$25
$ 2	$18	$ 8	$ 45	$20
$ 3	$25	$ 7	$ 60	$15
$ 4	$31	$ 6	$ 72	$12
$ 5	$36	$ 5	$ 83	$11
$ 6	$40	$ 4	$ 93	$10
$ 7	$43	$ 3	$102	$ 9
$ 8	$45	$ 2	$110	$ 8
$ 9	$46	$ 1	$116	$ 6
$10	$46	$ 0	$120	$ 4

Step three: Allocate the first unit of the resource to the activity with the highest marginal benefit. The first $1 million is allocated to road building, where it has a marginal benefit of $25 million.

Step four: Allocate the second unit of the resource to the activity with the next highest marginal benefit. The second $1 million is allocated to road building, where it has a marginal benefit of $20 million.

Step five: Continue until the available supply of the resource is exhausted. We allocate $8 million to roads and $2 million to irrigation.

Step one (b): To find the competitive market allocation, simply interpret the marginal benefits as the demand for the investment money, and follow the procedure in the first three steps of Tool Kit 17.1. Add each sector's demand for capital. When the price is $25 million, the total quantity demanded is $1 million by the road-building industry. When the price falls to $20 million, the quantity demanded is $2 million. Continuing, we derive the demand in Table 21.3.

Table 21.3

Price (million/million)	*Quantity (millions of investment)*
$25	$ 1
$20	$ 2
$15	$ 3
$12	$ 4
$11	$ 5
$10	$ 7 ($1 each for roads and irrigation)
$ 9	$ 8
$ 8	$10
$ 7	$11 etc.

Step two: Find the market-clearing price. The market clears at a price of $8 million.

Step three: Substitute the market-clearing price into each demand to determine the allocation of investment. At a price of $8 million, road builders will purchase $8 million, and irrigation firms will purchase $2 million. This is exactly the efficient allocation.

Step four (c): If all the investment money is used in irrigation projects, then the total benefit will be $46 million. The efficient allocation gives benefits equal to $18 million (irrigation) + $110 million (roads) = $128 million. Thus the waste that is due to misallocation is $128 – $46 = $82 million.

2 (Practice problem: absence of markets) Eight engineers return to Zaire with their diplomas from MIT. They can work for the government building bridges or in the mining sector. The (U.S. dollar equivalent) value of output produced in each sector is given in Table 21.4.

Table 21.4

Engineers	*Roads*	*Mining*
1	$200,000	$100,000
2	$280,000	$190,000
3	$350,000	$270,000
4	$410,000	$330,000
5	$450,000	$360,000
6	$480,000	$380,000
7	$500,000	$400,000
8	$500,000	$400,000

a Find the efficient allocation of the 8 engineers.
b How would competitive markets allocate the engineers?
c The president for life likes roads. How much is wasted if all 8 engineers are sent to build roads?

3 (Practice problem: absence of markets) The Zambizi River can provide up to 100 million gallons annually for irrigation. Both the cotton and millet crops would benefit from irrigation, and the benefits are given in Table 21.5.

Table 21.5

Water (millions of gallons)	*Cotton (millions)*	*Millet (millions)*
1	$ 50	$ 25
2	$ 95	$ 50
3	$135	$ 75
4	$170	$100
5	$200	$125
6	$225	$150
7	$245	$175
8	$260	$190
9	$270	$200
10	$275	$200

a Find the efficient allocation of the water.
b How would competitive markets allocate the water?
c The president for life allocates 80 million to millet and the rest to cotton. How much value is wasted?

Sharecropping

In underdeveloped economies, much farming takes place under conditions of sharecropping, where the landlord receives a fixed percentage of the output of the farm. The landlord's share of output is an externality from the point of view of the tenant, and as in all similar situations, there are incentive problems. Tool Kit 21.1 shows how to analyze sharecropping.

Tool Kit 21.1: Analyzing Sharecropping

Under sharecropping the farmer pays a fraction of the output to the landlord. This creates poor incentives to work hard and maintain the land and equipment. Follow these steps.

Step one: Find the full marginal benefits and costs of the tenant's effort.

Step two: Find the efficient level of effort, which is the level at which marginal benefits equal marginal cost.

Step three: Calculate the tenant's marginal private benefits, multiplying the full marginal benefits by the tenant's share.

Step four: Find the equilibrium level of effort, which is the level at which marginal private benefits equal marginal cost.

Step five: Compare the equilibrium and efficient levels of the activity.

4 (Worked problem: analyzing sharecropping) Mahragh grows sorghum on 20 acres in Chad. He gives one-half of his output in rent to the landlord. The current price is $1 per bushel, and Table 21.6 gives the production function. Finally, Mahragh could devote time each day to his wife's bicycle manufacture business, where he could earn $30 for each daily hour.

Table 21.6

Effort (hours per day)	*Sorghum (bushels)*
1	120
2	210
3	270
4	300
5	315
6	321
7	324

a Find the efficient level of effort.
b Find the equilibrium level of effort.

Step-by-step solution

Step one (a): Find the full marginal benefits and costs of the tenant's effort. We first compute the marginal product in bushels of sorghum and then multiply by the price of sorghum to find the dollar value. The first 2 hours of daily effort increase output to 120 bushels, which sell for $120. Continuing, we derive Table 21.7.

Table 21.7

Effort (hours per day)	*Sorghum (bushels)*	*Marginal product (bushels per daily hour)*	*Marginal benefits (per daily hour)*
1	120	120	$120
2	210	90	$ 90
3	270	60	$ 60
4	300	30	$ 30
5	315	15	$ 15
6	321	6	$ 6
7	324	3	$ 3

Step two: Find the efficient level of effort, which is the level at which marginal benefits equal marginal cost. The marginal cost, which is $30, equals marginal benefits at 4 hours per day.

Step three (b): Calculate the marginal private benefits by multiplying the full marginal benefits by the tenant's share. Mahragh's share is one-half; so if he works 1 hour each day, his marginal private benefits equal $120 × 1/2 = $60. Continuing, we derive Table 21.8.

Table 21.8

Effort	*Marginal private benefits (per daily hour)*
1	$60.00
2	$45.00
3	$30.00
4	$15.00
5	$ 7.50
6	$ 3.00
7	$ 1.50

Step four: Find the equilibrium level of effort, which is the level at which marginal private benefits equal marginal cost. The marginal private benefits equal marginal cost at 3 hours per day.

Step five: Compare the equilibrium and efficient levels of the activity. Mahragh works 3 hours each day, which is 1 less than the efficient number of hours.

5 (Practice problem: analyzing sharecropping) Mr. Droulig is a sharecropper on a farm owned by the bank. He gives one-third of his revenues from farming 20 acres in rural Mali to the bank. Table 21.9 gives the relationship between his effort and the revenues from the farm.

Table 21.9

Time (hours)	*Total revenues*
1	$18
2	$33
3	$45
4	$54
5	$60
6	$63

Mr. Droulig, when not sharecropping, can work in town and make $6 per hour.

a If he owned the farm himself and did not share revenues with the bank, how much would he work on the farm?
b How much does Mr. Droulig choose to work on the farm?

6 (Practice problem: analyzing sharecropping) Protecting farms against soil erosion is vital in the Sahel region of sub-Saharan Africa. The benefits of effort (in U.S. dollar equivalent) for a typical farm are given in Table 21.10. Assume that the marginal cost of effort is $100 and that sharecroppers pay one-half their yield in rent.

a Find the level of effort for owners.
b Find the level of effort for sharecroppers.

Table 21.10

Effort (days)	*Benefits*
1	$ 500
2	$ 900
3	$1,200
4	$1,400
5	$1,500
6	$1,500

Answers to Problems

2 The marginal benefits of the engineers in each sector are given in Table 21.11.

Table 21.11

Engineers	Roads	*Marginal benefits*	Mining	*Marginal benefits*
1	$200,000	$200,000	$100,000	$100,000
2	$280,000	$ 90,000	$190,000	$ 90,000
3	$350,000	$ 80,000	$270,000	$ 80,000
4	$410,000	$ 60,000	$330,000	$ 60,000
5	$450,000	$ 40,000	$360,000	$ 30,000
6	$480,000	$ 30,000	$380,000	$ 20,000
7	$500,000	$ 20,000	$400,000	$ 20,000
8	$500,000	$ 0	$400,000	$ 0

a The efficient allocation is 4 engineers to each sector.

b The market would allocate 4 to each sector with a wage of $60,000.

c The total benefits if all are allocated to roads equal $500,000. At the efficient allocation, the total benefits equal $410,000 + $330,000 = $740,000. The waste is $740,000 – $500,000 = $240,000.

3 Table 21.12 gives the marginal benefits of irrigation water for each crop.

Table 21.12

Water	*Cotton*	*Marginal benefit*	*Millet*	*Marginal benefit*
1	$ 50	$50	$ 25	$25
2	$ 95	$45	$ 50	$25
3	$135	$40	$ 75	$25
4	$170	$35	$100	$25
5	$200	$30	$125	$25
6	$225	$25	$150	$25
7	$245	$20	$175	$25
8	$260	$15	$190	$15
9	$270	$10	$200	$10
10	$275	$ 5	$200	$ 0

a The efficient allocation is 6 million gallons to cotton and 4 million to millet.

b The market would allocate 6 million to cotton and 4 million to millet with a price equal to $25.

c Using 8 million for cotton and 2 million for millet gives benefits equal to $260 + $50 = $310. The efficient allocation gives benefits equal to $225 + $100 = $325 million. The waste is $325 – $310 = $15.

5 Table 21.13 gives the full marginal benefits and the private marginal benefits of time.

Table 21.13

Time	*Total revenues*	*Full marginal benefits*	*Private marginal benefits*
1	$18	$18	$12
2	$33	$15	$10
3	$45	$12	$ 8
4	$54	$ 9	$ 6
5	$60	$ 6	$ 4
6	$63	$ 3	$ 2

a The efficient amount of time is 5 hours.

b Mr. Droulig works 4 hours each day.

6 Table 21.14 gives the owner's and sharecropper's marginal benefits of efforts to reduce soil erosion.

Table 21.14

Effort	*Benefits*	*Owner's marginal benefits*	*Sharecropper's marginal benefits*
1	$ 500	$500	$250
2	$ 900	$400	$200
3	$1,200	$300	$150
4	$1,400	$200	$100
5	$1,500	$100	$ 50
6	$1,500	$ 0	$ 0

a The owner would devote 5 days.

b The sharecropper would devote 4 days.